Conflict in Africa

Conflict in Africa

edited by
OLIVER FURLEY

Tauris Academic Studies
I.B.Tauris Publishers · London · New York

Published in 1995 by
Tauris Academic Studies
An imprint of I.B.Tauris and Co Ltd
45 Bloomsbury Square
London WC1A 2HY

175 Fifth Avenue
New York
NY 10010

In the United States of America
and Canada distributed by
St Martin's Press
175 Fifth Avenue
New York
NY 10010

A full CIP record for this book is available from the British Library

A full CIP record for this book is available from the Library of Congress

Library of Congress Catalog card number: 93–60682

ISBN 1–85043–690–8

Typeset by Photoprint, Torquay, Devon
Printed and bound in Great Britain by
WBC Ltd, Bridgend, Mid Glamorgan

CONTENTS

CONTENTS

Conflict in Africa

INTRODUCTION: AFRICA: THE HABIT OF CONFLICT

Oliver Furley

The 1990s have so far seen no diminution in the number of conflicts in Africa, and most forecasts predict a further increase. If we take the term 'conflict' to include struggles which have produced over one thousand casualties, it is reckoned that 32 conflicts were in progress in the world in 1991, and if smaller armed conflicts are included the total is 150. These conflicts have generated forty million refugees, and that figure is likely to reach a hundred million by the year 2000.[1] The vast majority of these conflicts have occurred within developing nations, and the continent of Africa alone had some five million of the world's refugees in 1990. African minority communities defined as at risk are reckoned to total 72, making up 45 per cent of the population of sub-Saharan Africa.[2] While Africa has had its share of inter-state wars, the majority of its conflicts are internal, and these internal conflicts appear to be increasing, as elsewhere. A tragic factor in this is that the civilian populations bear the brunt of the casualties in such conflicts, estimated at some 80–90 per cent of total casualties. Africa has also suffered an alarming number of military coups: over half of all African countries since independence have had them, and even comparatively stable states have suffered attempted coups, as in Gambia in 1981 and Kenya in 1982. Others, especially in Francophone Africa, have avoided them only because of support of the existing regimes by the former colonial power.[3] These coups are often only the beginning of a long internal conflict, and lead to counter-coups or a succession of coups as in Nigeria. It is small wonder that the dominant trend in African politics has been towards the disintegration of states, as Neil MacFarlane comments: 'There is hardly a state in black Africa which appears more viable today than it did on the eve of independence.'[4] These conflicts cause not only casualties and refugees but contribute vastly to the spread of disease, malnutrition and starvation, social and economic decline and moral deterioration, as these chapters show. The Sudan provides perhaps the worst example: for 26 out of 36 years since independence the country has suffered internal conflicts, with consequences that everyone knows. Are these African conflicts the product of an overreaching rush towards an ill-thought-out goal of modernity? Ali Mazrui asks this and many other reflective questions in the first chapter of this book.

The causes of conflict in Africa are many and they frequently recur. Common to many conflicts is the unsatisfactory nature of inter-state borders. Nearly all these borders were inherited from colonial times, and were the product of negotiations and treaties between the colonial powers, decided in Europe with the aid of poor maps and with scant attention to African peoples. At independence the new African governments shied away from making adjustments, and in any case this was difficult as they did not all reach independence at the same time. The Organization of African Unity (OAU), recognizing that to open the question of borders would foment discord and strife when the urgent need was to promote unity, declined to tackle the question, and indeed the OAU Charter is very specific about the permanence and sanctity of the existing borders. 'Respect for existing borders is practically fetishized by the OAU' complains Kwesi Prah, and he calls for borders to be redefined in their role and significance, involving negotiations by groups in adjacent areas and not just by the dominant classes in existing states: 'the existing state structures do not satisfy variously the aspiration for cultural identity, autonomy, economic democracy and self-determination of different nationalities co-existing within the contemporary states'. In the consequent splitting up of tribes, colonialism had split the Kakwa between three borders, the Somalis between five, and the Beja between three.[5] Atieno Odhiambo echoes this when he writes of the marginalized peoples of East Africa, living in the borderlands of Kenya with Uganda, Sudan, Ethiopia and Somalia. These nomad groups like the Turkana, Pokot and Karimojong are neglected as 'peoples' or 'identities'. Instead they suffer permanent occupation by state armies or by cattle rustlers (sometimes hard to distinguish) and bandits roam their land. If some new resource like oil is found, then war threatens, arms are distributed to these marginalized peoples and this promotes regional conflict.[6] The existence of such peoples has the effect of prolonging guerrilla conflicts also, as guerrillas can easily cross into 'friendly' territory and hide among peoples either the same as or related to themselves, as Uganda, Kenya, Zambia and Zaire know to their cost. The ease with which dissidents are harboured in neighbouring countries, and guerrillas armed and trained there, is itself a cause of both internal and inter-state conflict.

Ethnicity in fact has often been a major cause of African conflicts and it continues to be so. The creation of new nation-states at the time of independence was accompanied by urgent calls for 'nation-building' by the new African leaders, who were well aware of the difficulty in transcending African ethnic and regional loyalties. The European concept of a nation was exported to Africa. If we take Stephen McCarthy's definition of a nation as 'a complex web of common cultural, social and economic interests among people, leading to a sense that what they share in common is greater than their regional, tribal or other differences',[7] then many new African states did not have these features. There have been a number of separatist movements causing attempts at secession such as Katanga in Zaire, Biafra in Nigeria, and others in Sudan, Ethiopia and Somalia. Military coups have also often been caused by ethnic rivalry, as well as personal rivalry such as Idi Amin's coup in Uganda in 1971, caused by inter-ethnic rivalry among leading army officers as well as by ethnic resentments against the civil head of state. Idi Amin was easily able to recruit soldiers loyal to him from across the northern border, from the Sudan, for his own Kakwa tribe had been split in two by the colonial border. Thus it came about that it was Sudanese troops who played a large part in the coup, and Sudanese officers commanded key positions in the subsequent military regime. Use of 'foreign' troops in such cases tends to exacerbate the cruelties and abuse of human rights inflicted on the civilian population, for these troops feel little affinity with the populations they are sent to control.

In 1992 Timour Dmitrichev listed 29 major causes of potential tensions and conflicts,[8] which could perhaps be summarized and classified as follows:

1. Military: inter-state aggression, annexation, intervention, or hostility, for example support for the rebels of other states, or for separatist movements.

2. Political/International: ideological or political campaigns, territorial claims, religious expansionism against other states, regional rivalries, terrorism, coercion or discrimination respecting the trade or economies of other states.
3. Political/Domestic: power struggles, hostile groups, overpopulation, economic or religious disparities, oppression, demands for democracy, communal or ethnic violence related to economic, social, religious, cultural or ethnic issues.
4. Persecution: violations of human rights, mass movements of refugees, poverty or instability caused by the mismanagement or ineptitude of the government. (One could add here: evident and perceived levels of corruption by the government beyond any acceptable limits of traditional toleration.)

A more basic and long-term cause of conflict has been the catastrophic economic performance of many African countries. The World Bank noted that in the 1970s output per person grew more slowly in Africa than in any other region. Seven countries in Africa had negative growth in their GNP, and eight more had negative per capita rates of growth. In sub-Saharan Africa the per capita growth rate in food production dropped by 1 per cent per annum, while the population rose by 2.7 per cent per annum. Coupled with the debt problem, poor flows of private capital into these countries, and foreign aid programmes often inefficient, as Neil MacFarlane points out, economic discomfort can boil up into conflict. In 1992 Boutros Boutros Ghali, Secretary-General of the UN, stated as the deepest causes of conflict: 'economic despair, social injustice and political oppression'.[9] In the midst of poverty African ruling classes, or the elite groups who happen to hold power at a particular time, have enriched themselves and become the targets of envy, or more particularly, of rivalry by other elite groups. Ted Gurr writes that conflict in Africa is often a fight for shares of a shrinking pie of economic resources, protecting patterns of distribution and control: 'the extraordinary privileges of most African rulers and bureaucrats and their use of state power for private gain would be regarded as prima facie evidence of illegitimacy and a potent incentive for political changes'. In practice, he notes, resentment seems confined largely to the less-advantaged members of the elite. The well-educated and vocal segments of the elite become impatient when denied greater political access.[10] This is echoed by Paul Richards in his chapter when he writes that in Liberia both warring factions continue because they have evolved into business ventures. The rewards of power have been so great in proportion to any other form of activity in Africa that coups and conflicts often arise out of desperation to achieve power when no other means seem available. Politics is 'a commercial adventure in its own right', as Roger Tangri puts it; conflicts arise not so much out of clashes of ideologies or programmes, but for profit – often for just an elite few, for the masses take little part in this type of conflict: 'nearly all "tribal" or ethnic conflicts are rooted in competition between individuals', for the scarce resources of wealth, state and power. He quotes Amilcar Cabral's dictum: 'There are no real conflicts between the peoples of Africa. There are only conflicts between their elites.'[11] Ali Mazrui quotes Nigeria as an example of the tendency. In the African state there is a pull towards privatization of the state and towards militarization. The resources of Nigeria under civilian rule from 1979 were the private hunting-ground of those in power and their supporters. Rampant privatization caused the military to act, in the coup of 1983.[12]

There have been several attempts recently to produce a typology of conflicts in Africa.[13] It has been suggested there are five main types of domestic political conflict. First, elite conflicts can be between old guard politicians and younger technocrats; between ideologies and bureaucrats; between party functionaries and civil servants. The object is to alter the uses of state power. Second, factional conflicts can be organized by elites but reach down to a variety of social groups, involving regional and ethnic inequalities, where mobilization in the conflict may be based on appeals to ethnicity or class. Third, communal conflicts involve a threat to the state by a sub-group, such as a secessionist movement or civil war, often involving external support, or it may transform itself into a guerrilla struggle. It may also alternate between periods of violence and political negotiations, as in Sudan, Eritrea and Chad. Fourth, there are mass conflicts where political movements call for a complete revolution and change in the power structure, which have only rarely occurred so far in Africa, as in the Ethiopian revolution of 1974. Last, there are conflicts where popular political protest is made against existing patronage networks that exclude large numbers among whom resentment results in combining together to confront the regime, often with outbreaks of violence.[14] To these Zartman would add decolonization power struggles that preceded or accompany independence, as in Angola,

Zimbabwe, Namibia and Western Sahara; struggles to consolidate new independence as in Ogaden, Chad and Angola; left-over liberation movements such as the Union for the Total Independence of Angola (UNITA) or the Front de Libération Nationale du Tchad (FROLINAT) in Chad; conflicts arising out of ill-defined territory, for example between Chad and Libya, or Ghana and Togo; structural rivalries like Algeria and Morocco or Ethiopia and its neighbours; and those conflicts fuelled by runaway means such as Soviet aid to Somalia and later to Ethiopia.[15]

Kumar Rupesinghe bases his typology more on fundamental rivalries at issue: conflicts based on ideological rivalries; or on rivalry for scarce or new resources; or for governance and authority, or on assertions of identity. (These can also be questions of self-determination.)[16] Not included so far in this list are the military coups and the conflicts either coterminous with them or arising out of them. Huntington has classified three types of coup: the breakthrough coup, to replace an outmoded and traditional elite, as Nasser did in Egypt or Mengistu in Ethiopia; the guardian coup, where a new urban middle-class elite already enjoys unchallenged control but is dislodged (as Clapham puts it, 'It may simply be the army's turn to find a seat in the game of musical chairs.'[17]); or it may be one group of army officers ousting another group. It does not necessarily mean a change in ideology or political structure, though often the army steps in ostensibly to clear away corruption, and to pose as a more 'puritanical' regime by contrast, as Mazrui says. In Nigeria the post-coup government called itself the 'corrective government'. In Ghana it was 'National Redemption Council'.[18] David Throup in his chapter stresses that the 'colonial legacy' had much to do with these military coups. Finally one must add to the list of conflicts the case of military intervention by one state against another, such as Tanzania's invasion of Uganda in order to 'liberate' Uganda from a tyrant, Idi Amin, in 1978–9;[19] or the combined forces of West African states, ECOMOG, in efforts to establish peace and stabilize it in the internal conflicts of Liberia and Sierra Leone. The most recent example is the intervention of military forces of the United States in Somalia as part of the UN peace-keeping operations, in an effort to 'rescue' the country from anarchy and so enable food supplies to be brought to starving people. Africa has also had a number of army mutinies, again leading to foreign intervention. In 1964 there were simultaneously mutinies in the armies of Uganda, Kenya and Tanzania, and at the invitation of the governments concerned British troops were flown in to assist in quelling them. In January 1993 the army in Zaire mutinied when it was paid in new bank notes which proved useless. Looting and anarchy followed, leading to threatened intervention by the French and actual intervention by Belgian troops to protect their nationals resident in the country and evacuate them. The French in fact have a record of fairly frequent intervention in Francophone African states, often to bolster failing regimes which may have the effect of merely postponing conflict to emerge with greater force later on.

The ending of the Cold War between the Western powers and the Eastern Communist bloc must feature in any discussion of conflict in Africa, as indeed it does in Peter Lyon's chapter. In a sense, it ended one era of conflict in Africa and ushered in a contrasting era. During the Cold War, the new African states were courted by both East and West, and there was competition for spheres of influence in a new scramble for Africa. Many African states benefited from aid, technology, personnel (and arms) in return for ideological support for East or West and of course import/export markets. Many African regimes were bolstered by this support for many years. The founding fathers of the new states profited either from retaining friendship with the former colonial power or switching their allegiance to the East, playing off one side against the other. Africa was seen by the big powers as an arena to be won, for strategic, ideological and economic purposes. For stable states, this was something of a golden era, but where conflicts arose, both internal and inter-state, the Cold War often had the effect of exacerbating these through interference of the big powers. Thus uprisings which might have been put down quickly often lasted for years, and inter-state wars grew lengthier and more severe through outside support. In the Horn of Africa, as Christopher Clapham and Peter Woodward detail in their chapters, in Mozambique and Angola, such interference has been most prominent, but the list is a long one and is referred to many times in this book.

With the ending of the Cold War, Africans felt the shock waves of a major change, whether conflict was in progress or not. They perceived that with the collapse of the Russian empire and the Eastern European states, together with the economically disruptive reunification of Germany, the 'new frontier' for Western capital and technology would now be eastern Europe and the Commonwealth of Independent States (ex-USSR). Africa would no longer get much of a share of these resources. Furthermore, as Olajide Aluko put it, 'The western powers have become disenchanted with Africa, largely because of misrule, mismanagement and an unparalleled level of corruption in public life. Their honeymoon with the continent has ended.'[20] 'Africa's Patrons Depart' was a heading in *The Times* of 24 January 1992: Zaire had been abandoned by its patrons, so had Ethiopia and Somalia. The oil-rich Arab states no longer felt the need to buy African votes at the United Nations to secure the passing of anti-Israeli resolutions. Almost simultaneously, the reforms announced by the South African government appeared to mark 'the beginning of the end' of apartheid in that country. While this may have removed the threat of a conflict between South Africa and the so-called 'front-line' or 'frontier' states bordering on that country, and pledged to oppose apartheid by force if necessary, it may have removed a vital sense of purpose among these states and removed sources of international support for them. South Africa may see less need to conduct destabilizing campaigns in these countries, but in Angola at least, civil war has continued to flourish with its own internal enemies. The former goal of 'destroying apartheid' has been removed, and the southern states will have to look for other goals to win support, both national and international.

One type of support has never been lacking for African countries, and is of the utmost concern for those seeking to transform or to end conflict, namely the arms trade. On the one hand, some African governments have budgeted for plentiful supplies of heavy arms – aeroplanes, tanks, artillery, rocket launchers etc, while on the other, the clandestine small arms trade to guerrillas and dissident groups continues unabated. The Stockholm World Watch Reports (SIPRI) have recorded much of this trade, and the UN University is publishing a report on it also. At independence, many African states made arrangements with their former colonial power giving them military protection from both external and internal aggression. France and Britain were pre-eminent in this, and often secured the right to maintain military or naval bases in the new states, or the provision of training facilities. The new states in return received weapons and logistic support, and many of their officers received training in Britain and France. On the whole this had the effect of preserving and stabilizing governments in power, and when there was danger of conflict threatening or breaking out Britain and France would intervene to assist the government, providing always that it was a friendly government with good relations with the mother country.

Thus for example British troops intervened to quell the mutinies in 1964 in Uganda, Tanzania and Kenya; France has intervened quite frequently in Chad, Cameroon, the Central African Republic, Congo-Brazzaville, Gabon, Mauritania and Niger.[21] In some cases former colonial powers have sent in troops to protect their own nationals in times of civil disorder, as Belgium and France did in Zaire 1992–3. This has often had the effect of bolstering the existing governments. In cases of civil war on a large scale, however, the opposite has often been true, for Cold War opponents took different sides. In the Nigerian civil war, there was indirect intervention by Britain, France and the USSR; in Angola, Cuba and South Africa these countries actually deployed troops there, while USA and the USSR were indirectly involved. Kathryn O'Neill's and Barry Munslow's chapter on Mozambique shows how deeply various external powers were involved. Zaire's civil wars have been supported by France, Morocco and others. In Uganda, Britain and Israel had supported President Idi Amin militarily, and when Tanzania invaded in 1978, Amin got troops from Libya. The effect of foreign intervention has usually been to deepen the crisis and escalate the seriousness of the civil war. With the ending of the Cold War, however, the western and eastern powers no longer use surrogate African conflicts to fight out their own rivalries. The Cuban troops have departed from Angola and Mozambique: USSR and China no longer figure as major providers of weaponry to African governments, while the western powers no longer have the concern to counterbalance eastern military influence on the continent.

Instead, Africa's conflicts are becoming more indigenous to Africa whether inter-state or internal. Naturally the industrialized countries supply African governments with arms, and they get these from a wide variety of states, whether ex-colonial powers or not. Ali Mazrui has pointed out that this very supply underlines the inequalities between the industrialized north and the developing south. In the west, militarization often meant industrialization, with new technology, etc, but not in Africa, for Africa buys all its weapons outside, including the ammunition and even the uniforms.[22] It is a new type of dependency, especially with the increased sophistication of weaponry. The great difficulty in defending the ex-colonial boundaries, so strongly upheld by the OAU's rules, illustrates this dependency as Christopher Clapham points out: 'These rules, in turn, can only be policed by the industrial states, either through arms supplies to indigenous governments or in extreme cases through direct military intervention'.[23] The prospect for conflict in Africa is greatly worsened by the ease with which arms can be smuggled in to guerrillas and dissident groups. Private arms dealers from all parts of the world are involved in this trade. The ready supply of Kalashnikovs, grenade launchers, heavy machine guns etc seems never likely to dry up, and Kalashnikovs are so numerous that they are cheap to buy. No guerrilla force, however small, seems to be short of guns or ammunition. And to create a conflict and destabilize a government it needs only quite a small force of guerrillas to attack strategic points periodically and then melt into the bush. Uganda is such a country, where Museveni's government has been severely harassed for several years by what are probably very few armed men, in the north and north-west regions. If a guerrilla campaign fails, their arms can be hidden away, and used again: the huge volume of arms in Africa can last a long time. The 1983 war in Sudan was begun with hidden stockpiled weapons from the previous war.[24] In Somalia, American force tried to impose peace, when the concern was whether the warring clans can ever be genuinely disarmed: they can simply hide their weapons. In Angola the ceasefire at the end of 1992 was supposed to include demobilizing the warring factions, but UN observers watched the process with deep cynicism, since none of the specialized weapons, such as Stinger Sam missiles or the new American semi-automatic M79 grenade launchers were handed in. 'They turned up with rusty old blunderbusses and useless Sterling sub-machine guns but none of their sexy kit', one observer said.[25] Conflict soon broke out again, and with the great volume of arms so readily available in all parts of Africa, the potential for conflict is ever present. The same is true for the national armies, many of them equipped to very high levels, while others have been left behind. The result is great regional disparities in military power, with some states far outstripping others, as was the case for example in the 1980s in Libya, Algeria, Morocco, Ethiopia, Nigeria and South Africa. The temptation has been to intervene in other conflicts: Algeria in Morocco's conflict with the Polisario, Nigeria in Chad, South Africa in Angola and Mozambique. This has sometimes brought counter-intervention by others and consequent escalation of the conflict.[26]

Several chapters in this book deal with the appalling consequences of Africa's conflicts. Douglas Rimmer writes of the great economic costs – the great losses in GNP through war, destabilization, the costs of the military, and the heavy burden imposed on neighbouring countries by the influx of refugees. High mortality and casualty rates, along with destruction of infrastructures, have chaotic economic effects. Outside intervention often makes the destruction worse. Economically, Europe has recovered and even profited by war. Not so in Africa, he writes: 'only the killing arts have been refined'. Conflict causes the flight of capital and a brain drain: the development of enterprise is deterred. It also causes famine, notably in Somalia, Ethiopia, Sudan, Angola, Mozambique, Liberia and Burkina Faso, threatening the lives of at least 30 million people south of the Sahara. Drought is a factor but civil wars play a big part in this: countries such as Zimbabwe with severe drought but no war have been able to cope. In Somalia it has been clearly demonstrated that even the utmost efforts of the UN and the charitable agencies have been unable to check or ameliorate famine while warring parties were roaming at large; it needed massive intervention by U.S. forces to impose a degree of peace in rural areas before matters could be improved, while in Mogadishu it has raised other problems.

Similarly African conflicts are extremely destructive of human rights. The world has seen bold declarations of human rights – by the UN Universal Declaration of Human Rights, the International Covenants on Civil and Potential Rights and on Economic, Social and Cultural Rights, the Declaration of Commonwealth Principles signed at Harare in 1991, and various others. In 1985 Charles Humana drew up a 'Human Freedom Index' based on UN conventions using 40 different criteria, called the *World Human Rights Guide*. A number of African countries scored badly. The UN Development Programme (UNDP) Report of 1991 contained this index but it warned that an updated index is long overdue (it was omitted in the 1992 report). Louise Pirouet's chapter gives further details of human rights documents. Conflicts in Africa have caused immense damage to the human rights of the inhabitants: they face massacres, the burning of villages, mass deportation, forced recruitment – often of children – torture, imprisonment, loss of livelihood etc. Amii Omara Otunnu refers in his chapter to 'the human debris of tragic and disastrous proportions' left by conflicts. In Uganda, the people faced conflict and tyranny for so many years that their moral fibre was undermined, and Museveni's restoration of security in most parts of Uganda is merely the start of a long rebuilding process. It is notable however that Uganda is unique in establishing a human rights commission to look into the crimes of the past. Museveni's troops are also severely punished for breaches of human rights. An element of accountability is beginning to emerge in Africa, partly due to the forthright reports of such groups as Amnesty International, and also to the increasing pressure for democracy and freedom of expression. Togo, Benin and Congo have held national conferences on human rights. Awareness is increasing. A Kenyan lawyer expressed it thus: 'Whether these leaders like it or not, Africa is at the threshold of a new chapter in our history. They cannot separate Africa from ideals guiding the rest of the world. We want the rule of law, we want accountable government and respect for human rights.'[27] Yet conflict causes the opposite to occur: many Africans lament the fact that African western-style bureau-cracies, armies and police forces have not brought law and order but 'dis-modernization' – a reversal of westernization.[28] The protection of rights, lives and property is so often missing: 'the non-delivering state is here', claimed Atieno Odhiambo.[29] As early as 1987 Richard Dowden noted this when he wrote that parts of Africa were almost entirely run by aid agencies[30] – a view that could be applied more widely by 1993. As David Throup writes in his chapter, the African state is an overdeveloped device for extracting resources (for the fortunate few) but underdeveloped for providing security and services.

The destructiveness of conflicts in Africa has caused increasingly intensive efforts to be made for peace-making, for 'conflict trans-formation'. This is attempted by international bodies, by powerful states attempting intervention, and by non-government groups trying to facilitate mediation processes. Intervention by powerful states has not always been successful in bringing peace. On the contrary, as Douglas Rimmer points out in his chapter, this may greatly *increase* the destruction wrought by the warring factions. It can increase the economic damage: for instance South African intervention in Angola led to the mining of roads and the destruction of bridges, while the increased fire power and more advanced weaponry made available may not end conflict but prolong it. Sometimes it causes a cycle of intervention by other competing powers: Angola was one case, but Chad provides an extraordinary example with intervention by Libya, Egypt, the Sudan, France and the USA,[31] also by Nigeria in 1979 and OAU forces from the Congo in 1980 and from Zaire, Nigeria and Senegal in 1981–2. Such interventions have seldom brought an end to conflict nearer. Even where this has been successful, as in the intervention of British troops to quell the mutinies in Uganda, Kenya and Tanzania, it may damage the existing patterns of authority and may have only a temporary effect.

The UN has a more impressive record in mediation and peace-keeping activities. But Kumar Rupesinghe argues that its mandate is limiting its effectiveness. It can deal with inter-state conflicts but its mandate regarding internal conflicts needs revising to give it more scope: 'The UN has a clear mandate to deal with international conflicts but its mandate to deal with internal wars, the norms for intervention, are still in the process of evolution. The clearest manifestation of this is the absence of any global institution which could decide on claims for self-determination, particularly after decolonisation.'[32] Considering the wide variation of types of conflict in Africa, it is plain that the UN does need to update its role in this respect. The hesitations of the UN over a possible intervention and mediation in Somalia, where the state has dissolved itself and anarchy prevails, is a case in point. Suggestions are being made that the UN should set up a 'UN protectorate' to establish peace. No-one has marked out ground rules for this, but a beginning has been made. In his chapter on Morocco's conflict with the Polisario in Western Sahara, George Joffe writes that attempts have been made to end it with a UN-sponsored ceasefire and a UN force to keep the peace, in 'legally the most ambitious of the UN peace-keeping projects to date', but he observes that it cannot cope with the task, and the issue is not finally solved, in spite of support by the OAU and the North African states as well as the UN. Reginald Green in his chapter on Namibia says that although a UN Contact Group started negotiations for a settlement early on, it was a group of big powers – South Africa, USA and USSR (by now with improved relations) plus Angola that procured the end of the conflict. Later the UN did play an important role, with its Transitional Assistance Group from 36 countries, in supervising and monitoring the transition to independence and ensuring the election results were accepted as legitimate by the internal parties and the international community. This was of course part of a larger scenario, with the departure of Cuban and South African forces from Angola, as described in Kathryn O'Neill and Barry Munslow's chapter. Although it was the UN Security Council Resolution 435 of 1978 that provided the platform for a settlement, it was again the same big powers that negotiated the 1988–9 peace. The UN monitored the subsequent elections and pronounced them 'free and fair', but by October 1992 Dr Savimbi and his party, UNITA, had rejected the election results and started large-scale civil war again. In spite of the attempts by the UN Secretary-General, Boutros Boutros Ghali, to organize a ceasefire, fierce fighting continued, and Angola provides a severe object lesson in showing that although conflict can be transformed with internationally supervised elections to follow, it is another thing to secure the acceptance of the results by the contending parties. The UN has no answer to this problem as yet.

The OAU also has a mixed record of some success and some failure by default, in efforts at conflict transformation. It has been called a conservative body not easily open to change in its procedures, which are slow. The Secretary-General and the Secretariat do not have wide executive powers. A commission for Mediation, Conciliation and Arbitration has never been 'empanelled' or used. The principles of non-interference, and of territorial integrity are rigidly adhered to. The OAU has stayed out of most of Africa's civil wars – Biafra, Eritrea, Sudan. Instead, troubled states have called in other African states to help them on a bilateral basis without reference to the OAU. On the occasions when the OAU has intervened in a conflict, as it did in Chad in 1980 and in 1981–2, its peace-keeping force was criticized as linked to French and American 'neo-colonialist' efforts there and caused disillusionment. Nigeria's suggestion that there should be an OAU Pan-African military force was not taken up.[33] An interesting side-shoot has grown from this, however, in the combined forces of the Economic Community of West African States (ECOWAS) which set up their Monitoring Group (ECO-MOG) to try to enforce peace-keeping in the civil war in Liberia. Nigeria, Ghana, Guinea, Gambia and Sierra Leone sent troops to Liberia, and as Francophone states also joined in the peace negotiations, Senegal sent troops also. These troops were involved in heavy fighting, but a peace plan was produced and a ceasefire procured for a while. Presidential and general elections were to be prepared, but in 1992, as Paul Richards relates in his chapter, the rebel leader Charles Taylor refused to abide by the ceasefire and heavy fighting broke out again. Thus, although it looked as if concerted action by the force of regional states might be the answer in conflict transformation in Liberia, sadly it does not appear so.[34] In May 1993 the OAU did mandate President Zenawi of Ethiopia to mediate in Somalia – with little apparent success.

Meanwhile a new type of pressure on African states has built up which may remove the root causes of many conflicts but may in itself cause other types of conflict. The western powers, who are the main aid donors to Africa, are applying certain political standards and norms, making aid conditional on 'good government' and progress towards multi-party democracy and the better observance of human rights. The 1990 World Bank Report gave much impetus to this movement when it spoke with unprecedented bluntness that the root cause of poverty in Africa was bad, despotic government. The UN Development Programme Report, referred to above, followed this with similar denunciations of corruption and misgovernment. Africans themselves were not slow to take this cue, and spoke of Africa's 'Second Liberation' in which the old generation of leaders was being removed. The transformation and liberation of East Europe gave them encouragement in speaking out and demanding change. Ali Mazrui spoke of a 'crusade for African democracy'. The struggle against apartheid in South Africa took new heart and began the breakthrough, as Alexander Johnston describes in his chapter. In a ten-month period, up to August 1991, nine African presidents were removed, three by elections, and six by violence.[35] Some of the other old 'big-man'-style dictators like Mobutu of Zaire are in a shaky position, without their former international support. The donor countries are applying pressure to several countries to improve their record, and using aid as a weapon. 'Western money can buy good government,' claimed Lynda Chalker, British Minister for Overseas Development, in 1991. The most prominent recent example of this pressure has been on Kenya, when President Moi had aid withdrawn by the main donors until he made more progress in democracy and human rights. He protested that multi-party democracy in Kenya would promote more conflict, not less. He went ahead with presidential and general elections, but these were preceded by considerable conflict and loss of life. This situation continued afterwards in some areas. Much of this may have been deliberately stirred up by Kenya African National Union (KANU), the ruling party, to prove that the former one-party rule was the right solution for Kenya. This has promoted a widespread debate on the morality of pressing western ideals on countries where multi-party democracy, for instance, may not be either feasible or suitable. It has been criticized as a new form of 'cultural imperialism'. Nevertheless, the wave of pro-democracy movements is sweeping through Africa and appears bound to continue. The question is whether conflict, as a direct or indirect consequence of this, can be contained and limited.

Some ideas are being advanced which may help to solve this problem. One is the concept of an 'early warning' system. Academics have for some time been proposing types of information that could be fed into databases to provide early warning of possible future conflicts. This has been taken up by various bodies such as International Alert in Britain, the Carter Centre in USA, by personnel in the UN High Commission for Refugees (UNHCR), Amnesty International, the International Press Service and several other non-government organizations. Kumar Rupesinghe, head of International Alert, says that the international system is built on reaction – to conflicts, emergencies etc. It needs to change to a system of prevention. There is a growing awareness that preventive diplomacy is needed, whereby information-gathering, monitoring and the provision of databases can be utilized by governments, international agencies, humanitarian organizations, the media etc, for action to prevent the breaking-out and escalation of conflicts. The UN itself perceives this and 'is moving rapidly towards accepting preventive diplomacy as a key element in its long-term strategic goals'. Codes of conduct are needed which assist training in the arts of mediation, the healing processes, ceasefires, zones of peace, disarming the military and so on.[36] Training is in fact a key need, for often such processes as mediation or peace-keeping require attitudinal changes in the actors involved. A 'climate of peace' has to be created in the potential conflict area, and a 'culture of negotiation' has to be developed with all parties. If direct violence and retaliation have already occurred, it is too late a stage for early warning: John Galtung says that the warning should come when political, economic or cultural exploitation – 'top-dog versus under-dog' – is perceived, and it should be made very public, with recommendations for solution.[37] Boutros Boutros Ghali is prominent in this whole movement, and has proposed a 'peace enforcement' mission under UN command in Somalia, consisting of up to 25,000 men to replace the US-led force. In his UN report, *Agenda for Peace*, June 1992, he proposes 'preventive deployment' of peace-keepers, for the creation of 'peace enforcement units' and the setting-up of a UN reserve army. Mozambique is to receive 7500 UN peace-keepers. The report of course is not just relating to Africa but for the world, and it represents an important phase in this new movement to anticipate, limit and end conflict. It is hoped that this book, with its chapters analysing case studies of conflict, and others concentrating on general causes and effects of conflict, will contribute to this movement.[38]

Sadly a new and terrible conflict and consequent refugee crisis has arisen in Rwanda during 1994 which is still ongoing. This must await a detailed analysis which cannot be given in this volume.

Notes

1 *The SIPRI Yearbook: World Armaments and Disarmaments*, OUP, 1991; K. Rupesinghe, 'Conflict Transformation in Multi-Ethnic Societies', International Peace Research Association (IPRA) Conference, Kyoto, July 1992.

2 Ted Gurr, 'Theories of Political Violence and Revolution in the Third World', in F. M. Deng and I. W. Zartman (eds), *Conflict Resolution in Africa*, Brookings Institution, Washington, DC, 1991, p. 154.

3 C. Clapham, *Third World Politics*, Croom Helm, London, 1985, pp. 137–8.

4 S. Neil MacFarlane, 'Africa's Decaying Security System and the Rise of Intervention', *International Security*, 8 (4) Spring 1984, p. 131.

5 Kwesi Prah, 'Regional and Comparative Perspectives of Armed Conflict in the Horn and Eastern Regions of Contemporary Africa', International Seminar on Internal Conflict, Makerere University, Kampala, September 1987.

6 Atieno Odhiambo, 'The Economics of Conflict among Marginalized Peoples of Eastern Africa', in Deng and Zartman, op. cit., pp. 292–6.

7 S. McCarthy, 'Development Stalled: the Crisis in Africa: a Personal View', *European Investment Bank Papers*, December 1990, p. 19.

8 Dr Timour Dmitrichev, paper for round table discussion on 'Early Warning and Conflict Prevention', IPRA Conference, Kyoto, July 1992.

9 MacFarlane, op. cit.; Boutros Boutros Ghali, 'An Agenda for Peace: Preventive Diplomacy, Peace-making and Peace-keeping', Report to the UN, 17.6.92.

10 Gurr, op. cit., pp. 158–61.

11 Roger Tangri, *Politics in Sub-Saharan Africa*, James Currey, London, 1985, pp. 29 and 35.

12 Ali Mazrui, 'Is Africa Decaying? The View from Uganda', conference on Uganda, Universities of London and Copenhagen, Roskilde, 1985.

13 See in particular I. W. Zartman, *Ripe for Resolution: Conflict and Intervention in Africa*, 1985; Gurr, op. cit.; and N. Chazan, R. Mortimer, J. Ravenhill and D. Rothchild, *Politics and Society in Contemporary Africa*, Macmillan, London, 1991.

14 Chazan *et al.*, op. cit., pp. 183–201.

15 Zartman, op. cit., *passim*.

16 K. Rupesinghe, 'Early Warning and Conflict Resolution', International Alert Conference, London, 1992.

17 Clapham, op. cit., p. 145.

18 Ibid., p. 146.

19 Oliver Furley and Roy May, 'Tanzania's Military Intervention in Uganda', conference on Uganda, Universities of London and Copenhagen, Roskilde, 1985.

20 Olajide Aluko, 'The Foreign Policies of African States in the 1990s', *Round Table*, no. 317, January 1991, p. 36.
21 C. O. Chikeka, *Britain, France and the New African States*, Edwin Mellen Press, 1990, Lampeter, *passim*.
22 Mazrui, op. cit.
23 Clapham, op. cit., p. 185.
24 Deng and Zartman, op. cit., p. 38.
25 *The Times*, 2.11.92.
26 MacFarlane, op. cit.
27 Makau Wa Mutua, Director of the Harvard University Law School Human Rights Programme, in the *Guardian Weekly*, 22.9.91.
28 Mazrui, op. cit.
29 Atieno Odhiambo, 'Kenya in the 1990s', Canadian African Studies Association Conference, York University, Toronto, May 1991.
30 *The Independent*, 15.10.87.
31 MacFarlane, op. cit.
32 K. Rupesinghe, 'The Role of International Alert: the Role of NGO's in Early Warning and Conflict Resolution', International Alert Conference, London, 1992.
33 W. J. Foltz, 'The Organisation of African Unity and the Resolution of Africa's Conflicts', in Deng and Zartman, op. cit.
34 D. E. Spencer and W. J. Spencer, 'War, Politics, Peace and Process: Lessons Learned from Mistakes made in Sudan, Ethiopia and Liberia', IPRA Conference, Kyoto, July 1992.
35 *The Times*, 4.6.91 and 7.8.91; Ali Mazrui, 'Raised Voices', *Leadership*, 10 (5), October/November 1991.
36 Kumar Rupesinghe, addresses to the IPRA Conference, Kyoto, 1992 and the International Alert Conference, London, 1992.
37 Ibid.; see also John Galtung, 'Early Warning: an Early Warning to the Early Warners', IPRA Conference, Kyoto, 1992.
38 I am grateful for the helpful comments of my colleague Roy May. A short version of some of this material is published in the Autumn 1993 issue of the *Oxford International Review*.

1· CONFLICT AS A RETREAT FROM MODERNITY: A COMPARATIVE OVERVIEW

Ali A. Mazrui

This book addresses issues of conflict in Africa in all its varied forms – social contradictions which may differ in method, motive, purpose and causality. But is this also a book about development and Africa's retreat from modernity? Are Africa's conflicts caused by failures in development? Is Africa's development *dependent* upon at least a partial retreat from modernity?

Development is a process which seeks to combine the expansion of relevant skills with the realization of human well-being. Modernization is a process which seeks to maximize, or at least optimize, social and technological efficiency. There are occasions when development and modernization are mutually reinforcing. There may be other occasions when modernization (the quest for efficiency) and development (the quest for relevant skill and human well-being) pull in divergent directions. Both processes carry the risk of conflict, especially in post-colonial societies.

Such issues cannot be studied without some degree of social comparison, implicit or explicit. A student of development in Africa is inevitably using a comparative yardstick of some kind which goes beyond Africa's borders. A student of conflict in Africa is similarly inevitably drawn to a vision of other societies elsewhere – whether that vision is made explicit or not.

Let us make the comparative approach more explicit. Let us look at conflict and development in Africa partly in relation to experience outside Africa.

   This introductory essay attempts a comparative overview of the African condition in relation to conflict. Are African conflicts symptoms of a retreat from modernity? The conflicts are bad news – but is the *dis-modernization* to be celebrated? Is the retreat from modernity good news?

   For the colonial state one of the earlier stages of political modernization and development must include *decolonization*. But how early a stage in development should decolonization be? Could decolonization come *too* early?

   Kwame Nkrumah, the founder president of Ghana, was quite emphatic about the sequence: 'Seek ye *first* the political kingdom and all else will be added unto it.' The beginning of political development was political independence, according to Nkrumah. Conflict would be reduced and prosperity increased.

   But the history of Ghana and much of Africa has shown that while political independence may be a necessary condition for political development, it is by no means a sufficient condition. Ghana did not develop further as a result of gaining political independence except in the sense of accumulating experience of what does *not* work. Some of the other ingredients necessary for development were missing. Nkrumah himself was overthrown in the first of recurrent military coups in Ghana.

   Would Nkrumah have been closer to the truth about development had he said 'Seek ye first the *economic* kingdom and all else will be added unto it'? Are economic modernization and development the real foundations of political development and the lessening of conflict?

   Certainly in the 1990s the debate has warmed up as to whether economic liberalization should precede political liberalization. Mikhail Gorbachev is perceived as having attempted *the technique of simultaneity* – the pursuit of both political liberalization (*glasnost*) and economic liberalization (*perestroika*) at the same time. The result was catastrophe for the Soviet Union – the country disintegrated into different unstable republics and economic decay. Ancient forms of tribalism have been reactivated from Belarus to Bosnia.

   The People's Republic of China, on the other hand, is seen as having rejected the technique of simultaneity in liberalization – having decided to pursue only economic liberalization without its political equivalent. The result has been one of the most spectacular growth rates of the last years of the 20th century, in spite of the violence at Tienanmen Square in 1989.

Did Hong Kong, Taiwan and South East Asia also first avoid the technique of simultaneity – and pursue economic liberalism before experimenting with political liberalism? Have they all fared much better politically and economically than either Kwame Nkrumah's Ghana or Mikhail Gorbachev's Soviet Union?

Kwame Nkrumah's more recent successor in Ghana, Flt Lt Jerry Rawlings, did in effect shift to a policy of 'Seek ye first the *economic* kingdom and all else will be added unto it.' Certainly a lot was added unto it from an approving World Bank, International Monetary Fund and the Western Donor community. While Ghana in the early 1980s was economically in shambles, Ghana in the 1990s is beginning to be regarded as an African show-case once again. Has Ghana's electoral experiment of the 1990s avoided the political tensions of the Busia and Limann years?

But is there not a third route to modernization and development in any case – not 'seek ye first the political kingdom', but 'seek ye first the *cultural* kingdom and all else will be added unto you'? Can this lessen the danger of conflict and increase prospects for prosperity?

One major test is how to hold the cultural balance in the face of economic modernization. The Japanese asked themselves in 1868 after the Meiji Restoration: 'Can we economically modernize without culturally Westernizing?' The Japanese said 'Yes, it can be done – Western technique, Japanese spirit!' Indeed, that became the slogan of their modernization drive. In the first Japanese miracle they seemed to maintain the cultural balance while rapidly pursuing economic modernization. Did Japan avoid internal convulsion in the period between 1868 and 1945?

In the years between the two World Wars the Turks asked themselves the same question: 'Can we economically modernize without culturally westernizing?' Turkey under Mustapha Kemal Ataturk said 'No, we must culturally westernize if we are to modernize economically.' And so Turkey westernized even those aspects of culture which were not self-evidently relevant to economic development – such as abolishing the *tarbush* (headgear), or adopting the Latin alphabet instead of the Arabic orthography for the Turkish language. The returns in terms of economic development were much more modest than those in Japan, though the difference in performance had many other causes as well. The returns in terms of political conflict have fluctuated.

Our third cultural model is colonized Africa: 'Can we economically modernize without culturally westernizing?' Unfortunately most African countries have been culturally westernizing without economically modernizing – perhaps getting the worst of both worlds. They have been adopting those aspects of Western culture which are not productive or developmental – and are seldom relevant for conflict resolution. Western tastes without western skills, secularization without scientification, Western consumption patterns without Western production techniques, urbanization without industrialization, capitalist greed without capitalist discipline. African cultures are being eroded without the compensating returns of either economic prosperity or political development. Has this been a pre-eminent setting for tension and conflict?

Indeed, a more fundamental question has arisen in the 1990s. Were we too hasty in equating decolonization with liberation from the 1950s into the 1980s? Can decolonization mean something very different from liberation? We used to think that decolonization for most colonies meant the transfer of power from the governor or governor-general to a local incumbent, the changing of flags, the singing of a new national anthem, a seat at the United Nations.

In the 1990s in Africa we have been witnessing the *collapse* of the colonial state in such countries as Rwanda, Somalia and (in a special sense) Liberia. The flag is there, the national anthem is there. Sometimes so is the seat at the United Nations. Nevertheless is the collapse of the colonial state a deeper version of decolonization? In places such as Rwanda are we witnessing the colonial slate being washed clean with buckets of blood? Are these death pangs of a dying colonial order? Or are they birth pangs of a new African political order trying to be born? Is this a retreat from modernization or an advance towards post-modernity?

If decolonization is not merely a transfer of power but the death or displacement of colonial structures, we can sometimes have a paradox in former colonies. In some African countries political development begins with political decay. Some degree of dis-modernization gets under way. It may not be a matter of regret. On the contrary, political development begins with the painful decomposition of the old colonial structures. From Lusaka to Lagos, from KwaZulu to the Casbah, all is not well. The new clashes with the old, tradition battles with modernity, the indigenous engages the alien, and nemesis catches up with colonial structures. The new plant germinates out of a decaying old seed; political development begins out of political decay. Is conflict the womb of creativity?

Africa had previously attempted to bridge the gap between too much government and too little government. One-party systems in the 1960s and 1970s led to too much government; multi-party systems in such countries as Nigeria, Ghana and Sudan even in the 1980s led to too little government. Too much government is the high road to tyranny; too little government leads to anarchy.

In the 1990s there is a new clarion call for democratization. Over twenty African countries have legalized political opposition parties since 1990. Sometimes military rulers have been forced to go to the polls (as in Ghana); one-party systems have had to go multi-party (as in Kenya, Tanzania and Côte d'Ivoire); founder presidents have been voted out of office (as in Malawi and earlier in Zambia). African people have served notice on their dictators. Even apartheid has collapsed.

But the tension between too much government and too little remains – between tyranny and anarchy. The Rwandan state collapsed when it was at long last trying to democratize.

It is partly these considerations and contradictions which have raised the issue of whether Africa should skip the modernization stage and proceed directly to post-modernism. There used to be debates about whether Russia could bypass the capitalist stage and proceed at once to socialism. There is now the question whether Africa can skip the modern stage of development and take a leap into post-modernity.

One aspect of political post-modernism would be democracy in a nation-state but without political parties. This would avoid the sanctification of either class interest or ethnic interest.

Uganda under Yoweri Museveni has been striving for such a post-modernist solution – a partiless polity. Elections held in Uganda in the last week of March 1994 for a Constituent Assembly were divided mainly by the issue of whether Uganda should proceed towards a democracy without parties. Candidates in favour of such an experiment for five years seemed to have won a majority of seats.

An alternative post-modernist system could be a *no-party presidency* combined with a *multi-party legislature*. The president (or governor-general) would definitely be forbidden from belonging to a political party in order to ensure his or her presiding over the nation as a whole impartially.

One cost of such an arrangement is that only very rich people would be able to compete for the presidency, as was the case with Ross Perot in the US presidential elections of 1992 or, in a different sense, Chief M. K. O. Abiola in the Nigerian presidential elections of 1993. Such people can financially afford to dispense with political parties and mobilize support in other ways.

Another post-modernist theme is a quest not for *secular* state but for the *ecumenical* state. In a secular state, the government maintains a distance from religion, as in the USA. In a country with an established church, church and state are interlocked constitutionally – as in the UK, where the monarch is both the Head of State and Head of the Church of England. But in an ecumenical state, the state is either an active referee among different religions or has worked out a social contract with religious institutions *de jure* or *de facto*. Senegal in West Africa – which is over 80 per cent Muslim – has often behaved like an ecumenical state. For 20 years this Muslim society had a Roman Catholic president (Leopold Senghor), a silent social compact between the state and the religious leaders (the Marabouts).

This is the more remarkable when we remember that 200 years after establishing a secular state, the USA has still not had a non-Christian president. It is worth remembering that Jewish Americans have been successful in all other fields of endeavour, and that there are now as many Muslims as Jews in the USA. But the possibility of a Muslim president in this secular state remains unimaginable.

Today Muslim Senegal has a Muslim president (Abdou Diouf). But Senegal's first lady is Roman Catholic. In American politics any presidential candidate who confesses to having a Shi'ite Muslim wife on the *Larry King Live* television show had better wind up his presidential campaign.

The post-modernist ecumenical state in Senegal is very fragile (like everything else in post-colonial Africa). But it is remarkable that it has survived the first quarter-century of Senegal's independence. Today Muslims protest against the Muslim president at a level of rage they never displayed against Leopold Senghor, their Roman Catholic president.

The case for political post-modernism arises because of the crisis of the modern state, not just in Africa but world-wide. While it is true that citizens in the *liberal* state have been getting safer and safer from their governments, they have been getting less and less safe from their own fellow citizens.

In almost every liberal country crime is escalating, violence sometimes quadrupling, street mugging is on the rise, and the culture of the fortress city is developing. Africa is therefore not alone in at least the escalation of violence.

20th-century history shows that what happens in the USA today may be happening in much of the rest of the world tomorrow. According to statistics supplied by the Federal Bureau of Investigation (FBI), slayings by teenagers rose by 124 per cent between 1986 and 1991. In 1992, according to the FBI, young Americans killed 3400 other Americans nation-wide.

It is true that part of the casualty rate is a shift in weaponry from the knives of yesteryear to the guns of today. But the Bureau of Statistics shows that in 1992 young Americans committed twice as many assaults *without* a weapon as in 1982 (143,368 up from 73,987).

It is true that race and racism are part of the picture in the USA. Young African Americans are arrested at five times the rate of young whites for violent crimes, making blacks judicially responsible for half such crimes.

Nevertheless from 1982 to 1992 FBI statistics indicate that the rate of arrests for violent crimes rose twice as fast among young whites as among young blacks. Crime is crossing racial boundaries even faster (Wilkerson).

The African family may be more intact than the American. Since 1960 in the USA children born out of wedlock have increased more than 400 per cent (Bennett, p. 46). And unlike in Africa, there is no extended family support for such children. In the USA in 1961 and 1991 approximately the same number of babies were born (about four million). But in 1991 five times as many of them were born out of wedlock – without Africa's extended family support (Bennett, p. 47).

In the USA, of the children born in 1950, 52 per cent of the black children and 81 per cent of white children lived with both parents until the age of 18. By comparison, of the children born in 1980 only 6 per cent of black children in the USA and 30 per cent of white children are likely to live with both parents until the age of 18 (Bennett, p. 51).

Marriages may be on the rise in Africa, but in the USA the rate at which people are getting married is more than 25 per cent lower in the 1990s than it was in 1960 in the USA (Bennett, p. 55). Married couples are more numerous in Africa but make up the smallest percentage of American households in two centuries – only little more than half of the nation's 92 million households (Bennett, p. 56).

The rate of births to unmarried American teenagers has increased almost 200 per cent since 1960. As the Children Defense Fund stated: 'Every 64 seconds . . . a baby is born to a teenage mother in this country [USA]. Five minutes later, a baby will have been born to a teenager who already has a child.' And as Alvin Roussain of Harvard pointed out: 'Teens who have children out of wedlock are more likely to end up at the bottom of the socio-economic ladder' (Bennett, pp. 72–4).

America does not have child marriages. It just has child impregnations. Children are having children without the support of the wider social system which such situations in Africa would provide.

William J. Bennett, former US Secretary of Education, has reminded us that since 1960 violent crime in the USA has increased by more than 550 per cent; total crimes have increased by more than 300 per cent; teen suicide has more than tripled. Suicide is now the second leading cause of death among American adolescents. The causes including decaying family values, economic injustice, racial degradation, and a more general national malaise. By comparison suicide is a rare form of violence in Africa.

The crisis of the liberal state is still one where citizens are safer from their governments than ever before – but less and less safe from fellow citizens. The quality of life is becoming increasingly violent in the West. It is less frightful than in Africa, but the direction of social change is towards increasing social conflict.

One solution elsewhere in the world is a return to *pre-modernism*, to indigenous disciplines and values as in the Islamic Republic of Iran. The other solution is the search for *post-modernism*.

Teheran, the capital of Iran, is a city of some ten million people. In 1993 I saw families picnicking with small children in public parks between 11 p.m. and midnight. In four different cities I saw people walking late at night with their children or womenfolk, seemingly unafraid of mugging or rapes or slaying. This is a society which has known large-scale purposeful political violence in war and revolution – but a society where petty inter-personal violence in the streets is much rarer than it is in Washington or New York.

Iranian citizens may be less safe from their *government* than US citizens are from theirs. But Iranian citizens are safer from each other than US citizens are. The Iranian solution is, in the moral sphere, *pre-modernism.*

Can ravaged Africa find *post-modernist* solutions to its own anguish? There are indeed two ways of escaping modernity – retreat to pre-modernism or the aspiration to transcend modernity. A close study of this book may provide evidence as to which scenario is more realistic for Africa. Alternatively, the study of conflict in Africa may discredit even further the older paradigms of either development or modernization for dealing with the African condition.

References

Bennett, William J., *The Index of Leading Cultural Indicators: Facts and Figures of the State of American Society* (New York and London: Simon and Schuster, 1994).

Hoffman, Mark (ed.), *The World Almanac and Book of Facts, 1993* (New York: Pharos Books, 1993).

Mazrui, Ali A., 'The African State as a Political Refugee: Institutional Collapse and Human Displacement', symposium in Addis Ababa on the theme 'African Refugee Issues and Problems', sponsored by the Organization of African Unity (OAU) and the United Nations High Commission for Refugees (UNHCR), 5–7 September 1994.

Mazrui, Ali A., 'The Anatomy of Violence in Contemporary Black Africa', in Helen Kitchen (ed.), *Africa: From Mystery to Maze* (Lexington, MA and Toronto: Lexington Books, 1977), pp. 45–7.

Nkrumah, Kwame, *Ghana: The Autobiography of Kwame Nkrumah* (New York: International Publishers, 1957).

Seregeldin, Ismail, and June Taboroff (eds), *Culture and Development in Africa*, proceedings of an international conference held at the World Bank, Washington, DC, 2–3 April 1992.

Wilkerson, Isabel, 'Young American Criminals: (A Game Right)', *International Herald Tribune*, 17 May 1994 (*New York Times Service*).

Wilson, James Q., and Richard Herrnstein, *Crime and Human Nature* (New York: Simon and Schuster, 1986).

2· CHILD SOLDIERS IN AFRICA*

Oliver Furley

It is fitting that a book on conflict in Africa and its effects should include a chapter on child soldiers, for in the last decade or so they have become a remarkable phenomenon that has caused surprise and concern. This investigation began as a study of child soldiers in Museveni's National Resistance Army (NRA) in Uganda, but it developed further with the realization that their use has been widespread in a number of African conflicts, mainly by the guerrilla forces involved. This has attracted sporadic and sometimes sensational attention in the press, but deserves more investigation. How and why were they recruited? Why did they stay? What effect may this have on their generation and what of their future? The reasons for their enlistment seem to fall into four main categories: first, in times of civil war the refugee camps and the displaced children and youths in devastated towns became an easy recruiting ground, as in Sudan and Somalia; second, some guerrilla forces specially targeted children for recruitment by coercion and for training as soldiers, as in Mozambique; third, Museveni's NRA had large numbers of orphans and unaccompanied children who simply 'tagged along' for food, protection and survival; and last, in situations of complete anarchy such as Liberia, social tensions between generations played a part.

Child soldiers have often taken some part in wars throughout history. In Europe, perceptions of the child as merely a small adult have been widely held until towards the end of the last century,

* This chapter was originally presented as a paper at the British International Studies Association Conference at Swansea University in December 1992.

witness the 'adult' clothes in which children were usually dressed. The heroic deeds of drummer boys etc are celebrated in poetry and song. There were boys of 12 and over in Napoleon's armies, Nelson's navy, and young naval cadets or midshipmen of 15 or over at the Battle of Jutland. Even today, protests were expressed that the British Army sent youths of 17 on active service in the Gulf War. What constitutes a child soldier in this context? In Britain, for example, the 13–18 age group can join naval, air or army cadet forces, and they can join the armed forces at 16. But a large number of international agreements define a child as such up to the age of 15, and the UN Geneva Convention of 1949 forbids recruitment into the armed forces of member states at under 15 years of age; children up to that age are not allowed to take part in hostilities. This is also laid down in the UN Convention on the Rights of the Child. The African Charter of the Rights of the Child defines a child as up to 18 years of age, and Article 22 paragraph 2 forbids their recruitment or participation in war.[1]

The child soldiers we are dealing with here are all in the guerrilla movements, and may be anything from six years old up to 16. In other words, we are dealing with children and 'young teenagers'. Guerrilla groups of course pay scant attention to international conventions in these matters. Yet in pre-colonial African societies it appears it was not common to employ child soldiers. The child went through various steps in status during his growth and adolescence, marked by solemn rites, and did not become a fully fledged 'warrior' until he was well past childhood. The Masai warrior, for example, with his heavy spear and throwing-stick, was certainly not a child. In Mozambique, 'elders who recall the tales of their fathers and grandfathers have no recollection of children being used in battle in the anti-colonial wars that took place around the turn of the century and afterwards' – nor was there a tradition of organized child violence.[2] Today the situation is very different, in guerrilla movements at least. 'There is a growing militarisation of children around the world,' reports Macpherson, and recently the UN Secretary-General, Boutros Boutros Ghali, and Vitit Muntarbhorn, as special reporter, have investigated the phenomenon of child soldiers for the UN.[3]

Equally in the Horn of Africa, there is plenty of evidence of the use of child soldiers. In Ethiopia, between 1987 and 1991 under Mengistu's regime, thousands of underaged boys were taken in sweeps of public places and forcibly recruited, trained as soldiers and then deployed directly on the fighting front.[4] In the Sudan, Khartoum government forces were reported to have kidnapped child soldiers for training, but far more prominent has been the recruitment of them by the Sudan People's Liberation Army (SPLA), and its splinter groups. John Garang, leader of the main group, was accused of forcibly enlisting them,[5] as Peter Woodward points out in chapter 5, by the group which split away in August 1991.[6] It is significant that the leaders of the coup should make this accusation against him, as an act which was considered as wrong, but it has to be said that the civil war caused large numbers of children to be displaced and to congregate in children's camps where they must have been an easy target for recruitment. In June 1991 a delegation of the International Committee of the Red Cross (ICRC) discussed with the Khartoum government the plight of 12,000 children in southern Sudan who had walked from the Ethiopian border at Pochalla to Narus under SPLA supervision. The government claimed they were forcibly abducted by the SPLA and even accused the ICRC of complicity, which they denied. These children were mostly of the Dinka tribe who had fled, along with tens of thousands of adults, to Ethiopia, then under the Mengistu government. A number of SPLA training camps were in that area. When Mengistu fell they were forced back into the Sudan. A correspondent in *The Independent* wrote: 'The relation between civilians in the southern Sudan and those fighting in the war is an intimate one. The children now in Narus belong to one of the ethnic groups that have taken the lead in fighting against the Khartoum government; they live in an area until recently under the military control of the rebel government. It is therefore quite likely that many of them support the SPLA and intend to join it.' They were however now coming under the care and protection of international agencies.[7] A little later, the civil war caused thousands of refugees to flee from southern Sudan into camps in northern Kenya. Some 20,000 Sudanese, most of them homeless children, were in a refugee camp at Lokichokio. The Kenya government found them to be a security problem, and joined UN officials in moving them to Kakuma, some 50 miles south. It was then discovered that up to 3000 of the boys were missing, and were believed to have crossed the border again to join the SPLA. Indeed the SPLA was suspected of kidnapping them or persuading them.[8] Whether force was used or not, abduction was used by both sides in the civil war. According to a report by the Commission on Human Rights for the UN Economic and Social

Council, a militia group of the Khartoum government abducted 5000 Nuba children aged between eight and 16, and held them in a camp where they were given military training and indoctrination by the National Islamic Front.[9] Reports as to whether under-age soldiers actually participate in fighting are absent.

In Somalia there is no such dearth of reports. The civil war there seemed to cause the nearest possible approach to complete anarchy, with a collapsed government and competing warlords destroying the whole structure of civil society. Weapons are readily available and are easily picked up and purloined by quite small children. It is not so much a question of whether gangs recruit child soldiers, it is rather that children bearing arms are to be seen everywhere, living as best they can. The BBC commentator Michael Buerk reported that Somalia was 'a nihilist nightmare', with groups of armed youths and children of eight and nine armed with Kalashnikovs. In the capital, Mogadishu, 'even eight-year-old boys have got guns'.[10] Arms have flowed there from Italy, Germany, France, Britain, the USA, India, Pakistan and China. For Buerk, this indicates 'a continent sliding backwards into darkness'. These children were not so much 'child soldiers' as looters and bandits, profiting from the chaos. At the 'green line' dividing the rival militias in Mogadishu, armed boys of 14–15 demanded money from journalists who wanted pictures. Aid was pouring in but reporters said armed young men and boys had stolen at least half the food and medicines shipped to Somalia, and the port and airport of Mogadishu were virtually shut down by May 1993.[11] American troops, sent in to help the UN to enforce peace, began handing over to other UN forces in June but the UN faced great difficulties because the warring factions were still armed: 'even children bear arms,' reported *The Times*, so the nightmare continues.[12] How will such children and youths ever be reintegrated into civil society?

Mozambique: children deliberately targeted

First of all, in the war of independence fought by the Marxist Frelimo movement to oust the Portuguese colonial government, children actually became involved on both sides. Portuguese soldiers based in Niassa province in the north attracted a number of school children to them, keen to earn a few escudos for doing odd jobs. However, they often accompanied the troops on journeys to towns, which involved dangers of ambush by Frelimo. The soldiers indeed regarded the children as an insurance against such attacks. On the other hand many families fled up into the hills, driven there by the excesses of the Portuguese *Fusileiros* (marine commandos) and sought refuge with Frelimo.[13] It does not seem however that either side actually employed child soldiers as such, in the long war of independence of 1964–74. But when Frelimo then took power, it was faced with a new guerrilla war, the Mozambique National Resistance (MNR) known usually as Renamo (backed by South Africa and Rhodesia), who were renowned for their recruitment of children to fight, usually kidnapping them and forcing them to train as soldiers. There were widespread reports that Renamo took children as young as 10 or 12, also that they took them from refugee camps in Malawi. The Frelimo government accused Malawi of aiding Renamo. In one instance it took 100 children from a school in the small town of Cambine in southern Mozambique.[14] It deliberately targeted children for kidnapping and training, with the most brutal methods, which earned it the name of the 'Khmer Rouge of Africa'.

'Among the most horrific aspects of the war in Mozambique was Renamo's use of children as slaves and soldiers, thousands of them under 16, some only 6 years old', reported the *New African*. UN sources in Maputo said seven to eight thousand children could be among the rebel ranks as soldiers, and many more as porters and slaves.[15] According to a report for the Centre on War and the Child, 1988, Renamo had a 'systematic preference' for child soldiers, because it was easier to keep them under control than adults, who had a tendency to escape.[16] As early as 1981 Renamo began capturing young men and killing them if they fled, according to Alex Vines:

> Renamo has more recently used children (some as young as 10) to fight. An increasingly large number of refugees tell of this phenomenon in southern Mozambique, something that was virtually unheard of until the late 1980's. Unlike children used by the NRA in Uganda during its guerrilla war against Milton Obote, Renamo's child combatants appear undisciplined and sometimes to be on drugs. They too seem to have been put through psychological trauma and deprivation, such as being hung upside down from trees until their individualism is broken, and encouraged and rewarded for killing. Some commentators believe that massacres in southern Mozambique are committed by these child combatants, who have been programmed to feel

little fear or revulsion for such actions, and thereby carry out these attacks with greater enthusiasm and brutality than adults would.[17]

By 1990 children as young as six were being captured and forced to train as soldiers. Child soldiers were ordered to 'sack villages, shoot townspeople and in some cases even burn their own homes and kill their own relatives'. The philosophy seemed to be that the more horrific the task set them, the more bonded to Renamo the child soldiers would become. One child who later escaped said he had been forced to set his home ablaze, saw his parents and five brothers and sisters executed as they fled, then he was forced to work for Renamo. Another had killed six people when he was 13, and at 14 he led a group of more than a dozen other Renamo soldiers, all younger than him.[18] It was a deliberate policy to dehumanize them with the maximum possible psychological trauma. They were first subdued by beating, torture and fear. Then they were trained for two or three weeks before being sent out to kill, often their own relatives, in their own villages. If they did not obey, they were killed. Their psychological burden was enough to prevent most of them trying to escape, for if they went home they would be either shunned or killed, or have no means of survival. Hilary Anderson wrote: 'Reports of attacks by Renamo where the "men" have been children of 8, 9, 10 or 12 years old, are frequent. From the reports it seems that the child attackers are almost more brutal than their masters. Wielding AK 47's and machetes these children made beasts are extremely vicious.'[19] A photo in *Die Zeit* of 4 March 1990 reveals that some Renamo fighting units were made up entirely of children. Stories abound of young boys like 12-year-old Manuel, forced to bayonet an old woman, then behead her, or another, ordered to execute disobedient peers, and then forced to kill members of his own family as they fled from home. As Dorothea Woods wrote, 'they are forced to commit acts which so brutalize them that they lose all sense of right and wrong'.[20] Youths who voluntarily joined Renamo often had the vaguest motives for taking up arms. One said he joined 'to fight the communists' but Carolyn Nordstrom, who has investigated their motives, found them markedly devoid of political or military ideology – they fought for personal ideas of violence, inter-personal loyalties and antipathies, individual gain, and in response to immediate threats. They did not fight for ideological reasons as their commanders and political leaders would like the world to believe. One village youth told her he fought 'because I wanted a pair of shoes'.[21] Violence and anarchy breeds the most casual motives for taking up arms. No doubt many children and youths joined rebel groups for protection, food, the possibilities of loot and a sense of power with a gun in their hands. The teenage soldier image has already spread to fiction: William Boyd's *Brazzaville Beach*, (London, 1990), supposedly set in the Congo Republic, has the heroine captured by a stray guerrilla leader who is supported only by a group of boys, whose identity is centred on the fact that they are remnants of a youth's basketball team called 'Atomique Boum'.

In Mozambique, as elsewhere, some deeper causes have been advanced for the phenomenon of child soldiers. Christian Geffray in *La Cause des Armes au Mozambique* (Paris, 1990) says Renamo's child soldiers were not merely the result of threats and fears. Youth in Mozambique was in crisis: after independence, youths had flocked to the towns, but by 1978–89 they were returning to the country, unable to find work. In the 1980s the Marxist government in fact sent them back as 'unproductive'; hundreds of them were sent to Niassa in the north. The state had closed its doors on them as parasites. Back in rural society, they no longer fitted in with local customs and mores. So the discontents now rebelled against the central government, and Renamo offered them a different purpose in life.[22] The element of social theory is echoed in Alex Vines' book: 'Other disenchanted social strata – the young in particular, who have been unable to obtain secondary school education or upward mobility in the village structure because it has fallen into the hands of the dominant lineage's elders – probably find life with Renamo offering the only alternative, providing some excitement and the potential of authority denied to them in their villages – albeit by the barrel of a gun.[23] An enormous social problem arises now that the war is officially over. Some say the number of child soldiers and young teenagers in Renamo number ten thousand. Many had been captured by government forces, or had finally escaped from Renamo. The first priority was to try to reunite them with their families, or with substitute families. Abubaker Sultan of Save the Children Federation has worked with hundreds of them, but they have great psychological problems. Festivals are held to welcome them back to 'normal' society, and UNICEF supports these programmes. But many children leave home again as they are used to a vagabond existence.[24] UNICEF has launched a programme for 40,000 ex-child soldiers, or 'children in particularly difficult circumstances'. It is interesting that they are at the same time turning to local knowledge regarding purification rites as well as using more modern methods of rehabilitation.[25]

Uganda: acquiring child soldiers as a rescue operation

Child soldiers were employed in many African countries, for instance by Mugabe's Zanla guerrillas in Rhodesia as it then was, and by Dr Savimbi's UNITA guerrilla army in Angola.[26] In Uganda, however, the recruitment of child soldiers by Museveni's National Resistance Army (NRA) became a much-discussed issue mainly because of the special nature of his force and the way in which he claimed to have 'rescued' these children. A precedent was created when the Tanzanian troops marched from their border up to Kampala, to 'liberate' Uganda from the tyranny of Idi Amin, and General Msuguri's men 'adopted' Ugandan orphans along the way.[27] Milton Obote was subsequently elected in 1980 (by a rigged election, it is alleged) and his Uganda National Liberation Army (UNLA) also had some child soldiers, or at least some boys bearing firearms.[28] It was the rigged election which made Museveni form a guerrilla group and take to the bush, and several other groups also contested Obote's regime. His response was to give an excuse for the UNLA to conduct a campaign of appalling repression, slaughter and destruction in those areas of Uganda thought to be disaffected. The area known as the Luwero Triangle, just to the north-west of Kampala, was the worst hit, in which farms, villages and towns were destroyed and hundreds of thousands of people lost their lives.

In August 1984 Elliott Abrams, then Under-Secretary for Human Rights in the USA, repeated the charge of the US ambassador to Uganda that Obote's regime had created a human rights situation which was 'horrendous'. At least 200,000 people had perished at the hands of the UNLA and 300,000 had become refugees.[29] A month later Britain belatedly agreed with the American version of the appalling casualties that the UNLA's counter-insurgency campaign was causing, and this had the effect of focussing the international press on the NRA. Museveni had his guerrilla headquarters in the Luwero Triangle, and from very small beginnings he had now recruited a force of 6000 men. The international press began seeking out Museveni and his men in the bush, when it began to appear that he might win the war. The child soldiers in his army were soon

noticed. The first reference appears to be in the *Daily Telegraph* of 16
August 1984, and the second was by Charles Harrison, *The Times*
correspondent, when he wrote 'The large numbers of young guerrillas
– some as young as 12 – should either be sent back to school or be
found jobs.' The *Sunday Times* reported soon after that 'some of the
soldiers are no more than 10 years old and many are orphans'.[30]

It should be noticed that the character of Museveni's guerrilla
movement was unusual, and this was partly an explanation for the
large number of child soldiers in his units. He always insisted that he
was leading not merely an uprising to oust Milton Obote, but a
'revolution' back to a liberal and humane type of rule and political
behaviour. He imposed strict discipline on the NRA and training in
behaviour towards the civilian population, enforcing respect for
human life and property. His men were to pay for food and anything
else they had taken on the march. They created something akin to a
'Robin Hood' legend: typically when they robbed the bank at Kabale,
they bought the townspeople a public lunch and bought them shoes,
before disappearing into the bush. The officers (who did not hold
ranks) were mostly from educated classes – teachers, lawyers, etc.
There was a leadership code for them and a code of conduct for all
members of the NRA. Museveni was concerned to show that after
over 15 years of anarchy, Ugandans could relearn through the
example of the NRA how to behave in a civilized manner. When he
came to power in 1986, it was said 'the triumph of the NRA signals a
return to sanity . . . for the survivors it was like being born again . . .
The NRA has introduced a political culture long forgotten in
Uganda.'[31] (Later when soldiers from other Ugandan groups joined
the NRA it did not always keep up this reputation.) It was perhaps
inevitable that a 'humane' guerrilla force, progressing slowly through
the south and west of Uganda towards Kampala, should attract in its
train the orphans, the displaced and unaccompanied children who
were the flotsam of war. Phares Mutibwa has written: 'It was the
orphaned children of those who had been butchered who in
desperation joined the freedom fighters in order to drive out men who
were totally alien to a civilised society, who represented backwardness
and death.'[32] Most had never known a life without violence and war.
Some had even fled to the forest and lived with monkeys. Museveni
said they came into his army to eat, and to take revenge on these who
killed their parents and relatives. He admitted that some were as
young as five, and the NRA had taken them in to protect them. The

NRA must be given some credit for the humanitarian effort in taking them in, even so young. In many cases of older children however, revenge was one motive, as well as seeking food and protection, a sense of identity and a purpose: Kabanda was a corporal at 11; his family had been killed by the UNLA, and he said 'the men who killed my mother made me angry. I decided to go into the army [NRA] to beat them. If I find them, I will kill them.' George Kakosi was a corporal at 14, and said his parents were killed – 'I heard that Museveni's people were collecting boys and girls so I joined them.'[33] Some expressed a hatred of the northern tribes who had killed their parents and a desire to kill them in turn. Cole Dodge, working for UNICEF in Uganda, and Magne Raundalen, chairman of the UNICEF committee in Norway, interviewed a number of the NRA's child soldiers, and found them disciplined, cheerful and confident. The book which they edited as a result of their studies, *War, Violence and Children in Uganda*, concerning the plight of all children affected by the war, is one of the very few publications on this subject and makes considerable reference to the child soldiers of the NRA.[34]

Estimates of their numbers vary greatly. The BBC television ran a special *Panorama* programme on them on 24 March 1986 and said there were 3000 of them. *African Concord* the following month said the NRA was 8000 strong, of whom up to 10 per cent were child soldiers of 15 or under. Dodge and Raundalen also gave that figure. Macpherson however puts the NRA total at 15,000, of whom 3000 were child soldiers.[35] The *Sunday Times* of 27 April 1986 went further, and claimed that of the NRA's 10,000 troops, almost a half were under 15. The rest were mostly under 20, and even commanders were in their early twenties. Many of these child soldiers merely cooked and cleaned and carried messages or served as personal aides to the officers.[36] But many others, even as young as eight, carried Kalashnikovs and fought as soldiers. Museveni was somewhat embarrassed by the many questions from reporters about his child soldiers, and tried to play down their role. He said they came into the army to eat. 'We gave them guns because they asked for them. We don't use them as soldiers.' But in fact they did participate in the war, and there was a well-known story that in the seige of Kampala, dressed as civilians, they mingled freely with the population and reported back on UNLA positions. They then threw grenades into the trucks of the fleeing UNLA troops. Further north, when the NRA took the town of Mbale – where there was fierce fighting leaving

300 dead in the streets – the inhabitants emerged from hiding after five days and 'seemed amazed that this army of boys had driven off the marauding troops'.[37]

By the time Museveni was installed as President of Uganda, the war was over except in parts of the extreme north and east. At the ceremony, a prominent place was given to 'the children's bush army', but after that their high profile rapidly diminished. Museveni said they were given jobs as watchmen, and had been withdrawn from the front line.[38] Indeed they were to be seen manning roadblocks, and in 1987 the author was stopped at several of these by heavily armed boys of 13 or 14, who impressed by their discipline and solemn politeness. They arrested a man near one of the roadblocks and behaved with firmness and authority but with absolute correctness. Many people of course were worried about how these child soldiers would be returned to civilian life. Uganda's much-publicized child soldiers, the Bakadogo – are going back to school, demobilized, and had received orders to hand back their guns and uniforms, reported *The Times*. As from January 1986 any Bakadogo found armed or in uniform without papers would be arrested. Two special military academies were to be set up for their schooling. In actual fact, many of them continued in the NRA, and *The Times* added 'their continued use on military duties, even maintaining law and order, has come in for widespread criticism'.[39] Foreign reporters focussed on this but Ugandans also feared that ex-child soldiers would be disruptive. The Rt Revd Misaeri Kauma, Anglican Bishop of Namirembe Diocese in Kampala, said the upbringing of young people was his major concern. 'Now we have this further element of the many young people who have held guns, fought and killed people. I have an eleven year old son – what type of boy is he going to be mixing with?' This concern partly explains why Museveni established some special military schools for them, where he said they could continue their military training along with the regular schools curriculum. He claimed that the NRA had 'partially educated' them.[40] It should be realized of course that although many of the child soldiers had had terrible experiences, they had not undergone the traumatic and dehumanizing initiation rites of child soldiers in Mozambique, for example. Gradually they disappeared from public view and from the reports of foreign journalists – to Museveni's relief. One simple reason for their 'disappearance' was of course that they were now older – a 'child soldier' recruited in the early days could now be an NRA soldier of 20 years old. Most of them went to school or 'faded into society', according to Cole Dodge, and UNICEF maintained an active working relationship with the NRA regarding efforts for their rehabilitation.[41] They form an extraordinary episode in Uganda's history, but Museveni surely deserves praise for his humanitarian and protective role towards them.

Liberia: drugs, bribes and disaffected youth

Civil war began in Liberia in December 1989 when Charles Taylor led his invasion force of the National Patriotic Front of Liberia (NPFL) from Côte d'Ivoire. A combined peace-keeping force of the West African states (ECOMOG) did succeed in reducing hostilities for a time but the NPLF renewed the war in October 1992 and it continued until the peace negotiations in the summer of 1993. The press and media soon noted the NPLF's use of child soldiers. 'In Liberia's war, children are forced into combat, drugged, shot, abandoned, tortured and maimed,' stated *The Observer*:

> Taylors' National Patriotic Front is notorious for making children fight its war. A rival revel group, the United Liberation Movement for Democracy for Liberia, and the country's armed forces also use children between the ages of 9 and 18 . . . Major-General Adetunji Olurin, field commander of the seven-nation West African force, said "It is disgusting to see children between the ages of 9 and 11 drugged, walking like robots and getting killed. That is the work of a madman."[42]

It appears true that several groups including the government used children; that force and terror was used to coerce them into joining the fighting ranks and that drugs, magic and psychological trauma were then utilized. In addition there were orphans and displaced children who attached themselves to the rebel armies. As elsewhere, these child soldiers were often seen to be the fiercest and most brutal fighters. They often painted their faces and bodies with magic paint believing it would protect them from bullets, or they drank traditional potions with the same belief.[43] Taylor was said to run a 'Small Boy Unit', with boys as young as nine. A Liberian businessman said 'They can be the best fighters, because they have no fear. They have nothing to lose; they have never slept with women and usually they are orphans. Their loyalty to Taylor is total.' An article in *The Independent* of 27 March 1993 was headed: 'Liberia's Boy Soldiers Leave a Swathe of Ruin . . . Some of the fiercest fighters in the civil war are children, hardly higher than an AK-47.' The combination of childlike tastes and habits with the role of fanatical soldiers led to some bizarre situations. One of the child soldiers, aged 13, rode a small pink bicycle, with a loaded AK-47 slung across his chest. On one occasion the ECOMOG troops tried to call a truce and to lure them into surrendering with sweets, chewing-gum and teddy bears as bait, and they brought along three journalists to observe. This was a much-photographed event, producing perhaps some of the strangest war pictures in Africa. After a long wait the child soldiers came out to receive their presents – 'some wearing wigs, frocks and make-up to enhance their ferocity'.[44] But they went back to their positions and did not surrender. Earlier, when Charles Taylor had his headquarters in Paynesville, a visitor observed:

a group of child soldiers awaiting his bidding nearby, in ragged, dirty clothes, a rifle in one hand and a bottle of spirits in the other. Manning road-blocks they jauntily display human skulls with sunglasses, but they themselves are now dull-eyed with hunger. Before they let a car pass through they ask for bread.[45]

Paul Richards, in his chapter on Liberia and Sierra Leone (see chapter 7 below), refers to the young teenagers rather than the child soldiers under 15, and he produces social and economic explanations for their widespread participation in guerrilla movements. These include the economic frustrations of the rural population in which young teenagers were denied both the completion of their education and chances of employment: many were young drop-outs, frustrated by blocked economic opportunities. Further, the 'youth culture of violence' was fuelled by modern 'drugs', by which he means not only such drugs as crack but also violent videos which the NPFL purposely showed non-stop at various centres. For the younger child soldiers, one has to add loss of parents, family, home and the resources for survival. Once lured into the guerrilla camps they were traumatized and drugged into audacious and brutal military action.

As peace returns to Liberia, the rehabilitation of these youths and children will be a major task. In November 1992 the ICRC requested UNICEF to intervene regarding child soldiers who had been detained, along with adult prisoners of war, by the forces of ECOMOG and the armed forces of Liberia. The Geneva Convention lays down that juveniles must be housed in a separate facility. So a beginning was made by UNICEF, setting up a War-Affected Children's Home where 42 child soldiers aged nine to 15 were released into UNICEF custody and cared for in a residential programme. They were to receive counselling, education, medical care and vocational training. Social workers were to assist in tracing their homes and in preparation for their future release. In anticipation of child soldiers' demobilization, UNICEF and the Children's Assistance Programme planned using a site previously owned by the US Peace Corps. Up to one hundred would be accommodated.[46] Other proposals followed but the scale of the task was forbidding. Father Glackin commented that the more ex-child soldiers felt they were contributing to society – after having committed atrocities themselves – the better chance they had of recovering and leading a normal life. 'But it is on such a huge scale, that's the scary thing. You're talking about thousands and thousands of children.' Not all child soldiers could make that colossal adjustment: when fighting erupted again in October 1992 a teenage former child soldier with whom Father Glackin had been working stole a bicycle and rode off to join the rebel leader Prince Johnson.[47] For many no doubt the pull of the excitement and dangers of life in the bush had its attractions.

Conclusion

Child soldiers will no doubt continue to be kidnapped, coerced or enticed to join guerrilla groups as they arise in Africa. But at least the world is becoming alerted to the evils of this practice, and is more prepared to assist with their rehabilitation and reintegration into civil society. Ressler and his fellow reporters for UNICEF wrote in 1993 that concern for the child soldiers 'is rooted in humanitarian respect for the vulnerability of youth and recognition of the life-threatening and life-altering consequences of participation in conflict. The consensus of people around the globe is that children, by merit of their youth, should be protected from participation in war.'[48] This consensus has been a long time building up, through the reports and debates of various agencies. In 1959 the UN Declaration of the Rights of the Child led the way. Twenty years later the Society of Friends (better known as the Quakers), through the Friends' World Committee for Consultation, took a stand more specifically against the use of children in armed conflict. Since then, the Quaker UN Office in Geneva has gathered information and distributed it, notably through Dorothea Woods' monthly bulletin *Children Bearing Military Arms*.

Other bodies focusing on this are the Red Cross Peace Conference, UNHCR, the UN Commission on Human Rights, Amnesty International, World Vision and many others. In 1988 there was the UNESCO/NGO Symposium on the Rights of the Child. In the symposium, held in Nairobi, Dorothea Woods asked, 'In Uganda, UNICEF has been the main spokesman for demilitarising child soldiers. Will such action become a regular responsibility of UNICEF?'[49] The answer has been yes to some extent, and the Executive Board of UNICEF has helped rehabilitation programmes in Africa, its 1988 session specifically including child victims of conflict and army recruits. In 1990 the African Charter of the Rights of the Child was drawn up, and the World Summit for Children was attended by 71 heads of state and government. It produced some bold new initiatives: the World Declaration on the Survival, Protection and Development of Children and the Plan of Action for implementing it in the 1990s. This mainly focussed on health, food and education but also on improved protection for 'children in difficult circumstances', which would include child soldiers.[50] More specifically, at a conference in Arusha, Tanzania, organized by the Economic Commission for Africa with the UN in 1990, basic strategies were agreed which included number H 4, that 'the advancement of youth participation in development also requires the protection of Africa's minors against forced military service, whether by national or insurgent/rebel groups'. There is thus no shortage of internationally agreed principles and declarations of humanitarian intent regarding child soldiers. Governments can be very clear about what is permissible. Guerrilla movements, on the other hand, can choose to ignore all these precepts. However, pressure against the use of child soldiers is gradually building up, exerted by the international agencies, NGOs, the churches, the press, books and other published material on the subject. Museveni in Uganda felt this pressure; the hope is that it may be effective elsewhere on the continent.

Notes

1 These conventions are all listed in Martin Macpherson (ed.), *Child Soldiers: The Recruitment of Children into the Armed Forces and their*

Participation in Hostilities, Report of the Quaker Peace and Service, Friends House, London, 1992, pp. 43–52.

2 E. M. Ressler *et al.*, *Children in War: A Guide to the Provision of Services*, A Study for UNICEF, New York, 1993, p. 144.

3 Macpherson, op. cit., p. 7.

4 Dorothea Woods, 'Children at War in Africa', *Bulletin of the UN Quaker Office*, Geneva, 1991.

5 *The Times*, 1.2.92.

6 *The Independent*, 3.9.91.

7 *The Independent*, 6.6.92; *Sudan Update*, 19.6.92. I am grateful to Peter Woodward for this reference.

8 *The Times* 17.8.92

9 Dorothea Woods, *Children Bearing Arms*, report of May 1993 for the UN Quaker Office, Geneva.

10 Michael Buerk, 'Deadline for the Dark Continent', BBC Radio 4, February 1992.

11 Dorothea Woods, *Children Bearing Arms*, reports of December 1992 and May 1993; *The Times* 2.12.92.

12 *The Times*, 5.5.93.

13 John Paul, *Mozambique: Memoirs of a Revolution*, Penguin, 1975, pp. 117 and 186.

14 Margarida Cuitunga, paper on Mozambique in conference on *Children in Situations of Armed Conflict in Africa*, Nairobi, July 1987, African Network on Prevention and Protection against Child Abuse and Neglect and UNICEF, Nairobi, 1988, pp. 56–7. Jack Wheeler, whose chapter on Mozambique is very favourable to RENAMO, omits any mention of child soldiers, in Michael Radu (ed.), *The New Insurgencies: Anti-Communist Guerrillas in the Third World*, Transaction Publishers, 1990, pp. 161–96.

15 *New African*, February 1993, p. 20.

16 Macpherson, op. cit., p. 24.

17 Alex Vines, *Renamo Terrorism in Mozambique*, James Currey, 1991, pp. 95–6.

18 Macpherson, op. cit., pp. 24–5. See also Derrick Knight, *Mozambique: Caught in the Trap*, Christian Aid, 1988, p. 11.

19 Hilary Anderson, *Mozambique: A War against the People*, Macmillan, 1992, pp. 59–60 and note 30, p. 177.

20 Dorothea Woods, *Children Bearing Arms*, report of April 1993, p. 3; Cole Dodge and M. Raundalen (eds), *Reaching Children in War: Sudan, Uganda and Mozambique*, Sigma Forlag, Bergen, and Scandinavian Instiute of African Studies, Uppsala, 1991, p. 53; *New African*, February 1993, p. 20; William Finnigan, *A Complicated War: The Harrowing of Mozambique*, University of California Press, Berkeley, 1992, p. 69.

21 *Africa Events*, May 1987; Carolyn Nordstrom, 'Contested Identities/ Essentially Contested Powers', IPRA Conference, Kyoto, July 1992.

22 Quoted in Dorothea Woods, *Children Bearing Arms*, report of May 1993. Tom Young also cites Geffray in referring to the 'profound crisis in youth', which may partly explain the habit of extreme destruction, apparently for its own sake, in RENAMO raids. He is referring to young

teenagers rather than child soldiers. Tom Young, 'The MNR/ RENAMO: External and Internal Dynamics', *African Affairs*, 89, October 1990, p. 506.
23 Alex Vines, op. cit., p. 116.
24 *New African*, February 1993, p. 20.
25 UNICEF Feature, *Young Mozambicans Battle War Trauma*, UNICEF House, New York, n.d.
26 Michael Nicholson describes his coming across these in his book, *Measure for Danger*, Fontana, 1992, pp. 185 and 206; see also *Africa Events*, March 1990, p. 7, and UNICEF, *Children on the Front Line*, New York, 3/1989, p. 23.
27 T. Avirgan and M. Honey, *War in Uganda: The Legacy of Idi Amin*, Tanzania Publishing House, 1982, p. x.
28 Jeff Crisp, 'Uganda Refugees in Sudan and Zaire', paper for UNHCR, April 1985.
29 *The Times*, 6.8.84, 8.8.84, 9.8.84, 5.9.84.
30 *The Times*, 11.11.85; *Sunday Times*, 2.2.86.
31 *Africa Report*, November–December 1985; *Africa Events*, March 1986.
32 Phares Mutibwa, *Uganda since Independence: A Story of Unfulfilled Hopes*, Hurst & Co., 1992, p. 157.
33 *Africa Now*, April 1986; Macpherson, op. cit., p. 30.
34 Cole Dodge and Magne Raundalen (eds), *War, Violence and Children in Uganda*, Norwegian University Press, Oslo, 1987, p. 7; see also their book of 1991 cited in note 20 above.
35 Macpherson, op. cit., p. 30.
36 Ressler, op. cit., p. 118.
37 *Africa Now*, April 1986; *Sunday Times*, 27.4.86. The British reporter Gavin Hewitt, however, thought that a 'mythology' had inevitably been built up regarding the actions of the child soldiers; 'these tales are more probably the product of an irrepressible hope that has seized Ugandans'. *The Listener*, 27.3.86.
38 *Daily Telegraph*, 29.1.87; *Africa Now*, April 1986.
39 *The Times*, 20.1.87.
40 *African Concord*, 5.2.87, p. 23, and 17.4.86.
41 Dodge and Raundalen, op. cit., 1991, p. 80.
42 *The Observer*, 29.11.92.
43 Dorothea Woods, *Children Bearing Arms*, report of April 1993; Nicholas Horne, *The Independent*, 3.12.92, magazine, p. 14.
44 Horne, op. cit., p. 14; Macpherson, op, cit., pp. 23–4.
45 Dorothea Woods, *Children Bearing Arms*, report of June 1993 quoting *Time*, 10.9.90.
46 UNICEF, 'Emergency Appeal – Liberia', April 1993 (typescript).
47 *The Observer*, 29.11.92. World Vision cared for a number of orphans, 25 of whom were captured by rebel forces, but they escaped back to Monrovia. 257 children at their orphanage could be accounted for, although 140 were still held at the rebel headquarters in Gbarnya. *World Vision Magazine*, no. 1, Spring 1993.
48 Ressler, op. cit., p. 119.

49 Dorothea Woods, 'Quaker Concern for Children Bearing Military Arms', in *Children in Situation of Armed Conflict*, UNICEF, 1988, p. 105.
50 *UN Chronicle*, 23 (4), August 1986, pp. 94–5, 25 (3), September 1988, p. 70, and 27 (4), December 1990, p. 64. See also Philip Weiss, 'The Geography of Child Survival in the Front Line', *Geography*, 74, 1989, pp. 151–5.

3· CONFLICT IN SOUTH AFRICA

Alexander Johnston

Political conflict in South Africa cost the lives of nearly 20,000 people between 1984, when the struggle against apartheid intensified, and April 1994, when the country's first non-racial election finally brought the apartheid years to an end.[1] This grim toll of casualties, which continued until literally the eve of the election, represented not only the high price of struggle but the even costlier convulsions of transition. The New South Africa came into being, then, with a twofold legacy of conflict, both from the apartheid years and from the first four uncertain years of transformation.

Conflict in South Africa and the legacy of apartheid

Until the beginning of the transition period, marked by the lifting of bans on the African National Congress (ANC) and other political movements in February 1990, conflict in South Africa was probably easier to simplify than anywhere else. The central theme of conflict in South Africa has been white minority rule, with all the exclusions and deprivations it has directly and indirectly created for the black majority. Colonial dispossession, racial ideology and the visible signs of privilege and affluence amidst poverty and oppression have provided a matrix in which the shape of South Africa's conflicts has been cast in universally recognizable form. Not only were the principal elements of this matrix mutually dependent and reinforcing, but they were codified in the policy of apartheid.

This unusually coherent system of authoritarian rule and violent social engineering greatly exaggerated, both for its adherents and its opponents, the incentives and opportunities for simplification. Analogous perhaps to the way in which thinking about the Cold War simplified interpretations of global conflict between 1945 and 1990, 'apartheid' provided an all-embracing explanation. It allowed its opponents to reduce all South Africa's conflicts to 'the struggle', and its defenders to coin the ideologies of 'total strategy/total onslaught'.[2] These constructs in turn reduced all conflicts to one, providing the test by which all friends and enemies were labelled, the legitimacy of all policies and institutions judged.

Apartheid has shaped the nature and form of conflict in South Africa in a number of other ways. First, because of its own violence and the comprehensive way it denied political space to opponents, apartheid forced dissidents into violent forms of resistance and armed struggle.[3] It is worth noting in this context that apartheid itself rested partly on a crude theory of conflict; this insisted that the 'groups', 'peoples' and 'nations' which make up the South African population (as the theory of apartheid had it) live in a situation which can be stabilized only if they are kept separate and organized in 'their own' states. By forcing opponents into armed struggle, apartheid gave this theory (to those already predisposed to it) a self-fulfilling quality and this was one of the reasons why apartheid continued to hold the allegiance of so many Afrikaners for so long. One of the crucial preconditions for political change came when a critical section of the Afrikaner elite came to recognize the apartheid system as a source of conflict and not a solution to it.

A second important effect of apartheid was to block the emergence of legitimate institutions to regulate and resolve conflict. This ensured that no culture of bargaining and compromise could develop among the groups and organizations in and through which people mobilized to advance their claims and interests. At the height of Verwoerdian apartheid, the Nationalists' aim was to allow for conflict management between South Africa's 'peoples' only through the governments of 'their' states – through diplomacy, not politics.

Reform- or neo-apartheid in the Botha years (1979–89) represented considerable movement away from this ideological goal. The conflicts which the Durban strikes (1973) and the Soweto uprising (1976) revealed could not be treated, as hitherto, with massive repression alone. As this became clear in the late 1970s, institutions were created to manage conflict rather than merely repress it. The Tricameral Constitution (1983) and the framework of industrial relations legislation which followed the report of the Wiehahn Commission (1979) represented attempts to open up space in which conflict could emerge and be dealt with in ways which would not threaten to destabilize an increasingly sophisticated industrial society.[4]

Repression did remain central to state policy however, as the states of emergency (1985–90) were to illustrate. It was in fact the very instrument which guaranteed the passage of the 'reforms' and their acceptability to the security-conscious majority of the white electorate. Partial, fragmentary, and flatly contradicted by massive reliance on repression as they were, the neo-apartheid reforms of the 1970s and 1980s did allow the beginnings of a culture of negotiation tentatively to emerge. This was particularly true of the labour field, but also to a lesser extent around the United Democratic Front (UDF) and the civic organizations which made it up. Through consumer and educational boycotts and similar tactics, these bodies began to force negotiations on the government, provincial authorities, white municipalities and organized business. This meant that as the emphasis of conflict management shifted dramatically towards negotiation after February 1990, there was at least something to build on.

The central question of the exclusion of the African majority from full political rights and the central political institutions was left unresolved by reform-apartheid however, and African political aspirations continued to be repressed. This led to intensified resistance which exposed the failure of reform-apartheid as a system of conflict management.

A third way in which apartheid has shaped conflict in South Africa has been in encouraging lines of division among blacks. This can be seen in two principal effects, the first of which relates to patterns of settlement. A central component of apartheid was the exclusion of blacks from urban areas in 'white' South Africa. One effect of this has been to create two marginalized classes of person – the migrant labourer hostel dweller, and the city-dwelling inhabitants of 'informal' shack settlements.[5] It is true that all industrializing Third World countries have problems of urbanization and informal settlement. But in South Africa the imperatives of racial dogma and the preservation of white privilege prevented adequate provision for orderly urbanization. This has made South Africa's problems of urbanization much worse than they might have been.

Conditions in hostels are often brutal and characterized by deprivation. In Cape Town (where 11 per cent of the African population live in hostels) a survey revealed that in the township of Langa, hostel dwellers lived 2.8 to a bed, 130 to a working lavatory and 117 to a tap.[6] The rigours of existence in hostels encourage organization along ethnic lines, and their institutionalized single-sex composition encourages paramilitary organization in the formation of armed, mobile and trained units for defence or raiding.[7] Conflicts between hostel dwellers on the one hand and township or informal settlement residents on the other have often been quick to acquire ethnic or political dimensions. Such conflicts have been among the principal flashpoints in the struggle between the Inkatha Freedom Party (IFP) and the ANC since 1990, although as early as 1976, in the Soweto uprising, clashes between residents and hostel dwellers were a feature of violent conflict.[8]

The large informal settlements which ring South Africa's cities are often in conflict with each other, or with more established townships over scarce resources such as land and water.[9] 'Warlords' who control shackland territories and raise funds through rents and taxes for both peaceful and warlike purposes, are an exacerbating factor in the conflicts between black political movements for the control of informal settlements and the allegiance of the people who live there.

The second way in which apartheid has encouraged lines of conflict among blacks is by using the homelands as surrogates in the struggle with anti-apartheid organizations. It is doubtful for instance whether the conflict between the UDF/ANC and Inkatha[10] would have become so widespread, or reached such intensity, if Inkatha, through the KwaZulu government,[11] had not had access to substantial resources from the South African state. Important in this context is the patronage dispensed by the KwaZulu government, and the coercive power available to it in the form of the KwaZulu Police.

Above all, apartheid ensured that all conflict in South Africa was related to white minority rule and the exclusion of blacks from effective political participation. Despite this, the anti-apartheid struggle was carried on substantially through campaigns on specific issues. Prominent among these were education, transport, rents and food prices. The ANC and the government were happy to portray each of these conflicts as a test of the legitimacy of the state. One of the major features of conflict in a post-apartheid South Africa will be that these areas of conflict will remain, but will have to be robbed of their destabilizing quality. This will be particularly difficult for an ANC government (or one with a substantial ANC component) faced with critical choices in dispensing scarce resources, and probably committed to encouraging foreign investment and international competitiveness. The crucial question will be whether such a government can persuade its constituents that inequalities and inadequacies which were intolerable under apartheid will be any more tolerable under conditions of political freedom and sharply rising expectations.

Conflict and transition
Since the unbanning of the liberation movements and the freeing of political activity in February 1990, conflict in South Africa has taken on a much more complex character than the artificial reductionism of 'the struggle', or the 'total onslaught'. In this transitional period, peaceful theatres of conflict (the most obvious being constitutional negotiations), which were impossible before, have opened. At the same time, violent conflicts have mushroomed. The situation was now one of a diffuse constellation of conflicts, rather than a single axis of conflict. This in turn has meant that neither the causal nor the moral dimension of discourse about the conflict is as apparently clear as before.

Conflict in contemporary South Africa
In the period since the reforms and unbannings of February 1990, conflict in South Africa has had three principal spotlights: the first is the group of conflicts associated with the rejectionist white right; the second is centred on conflict between rival black political groups;[12] and the third concerns the central relationship between the National Party and the ANC.

The White Right
The success of President De Klerk in achieving a clear mandate for the continuation of reform and negotiation in the whites-only referendum of March 1992[13] put the electoral strength of the white right in perspective and conclusively ended right-wing hopes of derailing progress towards an inclusive democracy through the existing, racially exclusive political system. Although the referendum was a heavy defeat for the right, a substantial constituency of dissatisfaction remained among whites and one of the principal questions during the latter stages of constitutional negotiation was

whether this dissidence could be given an organizational form sufficiently coherent to disrupt the process of transition.[14]

Support for the right wing has been based on social groups which had the most to gain from apartheid and the most to lose from a transformation which empowers blacks politically and economically. White workers,[15] public servants,[16] members of the security forces[17] and farmers[18] have all been prominent in the various right-wing groups. Another source of support has been Afrikaner nationalism. With the National Party gradually abandoning nationalist symbols and pieties, the white right has been able to appropriate their emotional appeal.

In the aftermath of the referendum, this support remained organized into political, cultural and paramilitary movements whose relationships were at best uncoordinated and at worst competitive and even hostile.[19] They ranged from the neo-Verwoerdian Conservative Party (CP) through other political parties (including a post-referendum offshoot from the CP[20]), research groups, paramilitary organizations and cultural fronts. In the aftermath of the referendum, right-wing energies became focussed on plans for a more radical partition than the Verwoerdian blueprint of the CP and the achievement of a Volkstaat for Afrikaners. This concept embraces the right's essential ideas: partition, ethnicity, territorial control and political self-determination.

The emergence in May 1993 of the Afrikaner Volksfront seemed to place organizational dynamism and the prospect of unity behind the varied demands for Afrikaner self-determination. Essentially, the Volksfront was an initiative of retired generals and organized agriculture, which traded heavily on the prestige of the former and the corporate grievances of the latter.[21] General Constand Viljoen, former chief of the South African Defence Force, emerged as the leader, but it was clear that even the almost mythical status which this 'soldiers' general' commanded could not overcome the serious differences between the neo-fascist paramilitaries and the respectable right, and between the proponents of resistance and negotiation. In the altered circumstances of post-1990 South Africa it was clear that the white right could not hope for success without black allies. The Afrikaner Volksfront helped form a coalition of the disaffected, the so-called Freedom Alliance, with black homelands interests.[22] What bound them together was alarm at the increasingly close negotiating partnership between the ANC and the government/National Party axis, which dominated the latter stages of the negotiations for an interim constitution. The weakness of the Alliance's rejectionist stance was exposed when Chief Lucas Mangope's Bophuthatswana government refused to cooperate with the transitional authorities[23] in preparing for election in the territory. A combination of popular uprising and pressure from the ANC/government alliance overthrew Mangope's rule and efforts by the paramilitary white right to keep him in power ended in ignominy and tragedy. It is likely that these developments were instrumental in persuading Viljoen and his followers to contest the election (as the Freedom Front), while the Conservative Party, by insisting on boycott, made sure that Afrikaner divisions opened wide again.

Rivalry in black politics

The costliest and most threatening axis of conflict during the transition period has been between the rival black political groups, the IFP and the ANC.[24] While this statement is adequate for the purposes of generalization, two qualifications are necessary. First, allegations of security-force and 'third-force' involvement, usually on the side of Inkatha, muddy the image of a straight fight between two black groups.[25]

Second, numerous studies of the violence have stressed that ideological rivalry and the competition for control of territory between the two main protagonists often overlay a variety of other conflicts.[26] It is useful to bear these conflicts in mind in order to keep the ANC/IFP rivalry in perspective.

Many of the tensions on which these conflicts feed are associated with urbanization. They have been greatly exacerbated by the artificial restrictions on movement and settlement demanded by the apartheid system, and then by their removal with the repeal of influx-control laws in the 1980s. There are movements of population from rural to urban areas, from overcrowded established townships to shack dwelling in peri-urban areas, and the long-established patterns of migrant labour which plant thousands of hostel dwellers in townships.[27] Competition for land and water, access to schools, taxi wars[28] and straightforward crime are all sources of conflict. This rapid social change undermines respect for traditional ways and statuses, leading to generational tensions between youth and elders. Tensions also arise between tribal and chiefly patterns of authority (which have often been manipulated by the state as a form of indirect control) and 'progressive' forms of mobilization like community associations, trade unions and liberation movements. Protagonists in these various forms of conflict often take on a patina of identity from either the ANC or the IFP, without necessarily being under the central control of one or other organization, or properly reflecting its values or ideologies. This lack of tight central control has bedevilled the various attempts at peace accords between the two rivals.[29]

The resurgence of black resistance in the early and mid-1980s, which crystallized around the rejection of the Tricameral Constitution and found institutional expression in the UDF's coalition of community, labour, youth and other organizations, was crucial in the development of conflict between Inkatha and the ANC in Natal.[30] This conflict first made itself felt in the townships and informal settlements around Durban, spreading in the late 1980s with particular intensity to townships in the Pietermaritzburg area and from there to rural areas of the Natal midlands and south coast. In all of these places, the rivalry became mixed with opportunistic conflicts of the kind described above.

The UDF's tactics of school, consumer and transport boycotts, work stay-aways and resistance to the incorporation of Durban townships into KwaZulu soon marked the collision course between the two. The fundamental point of conflict was Inkatha's determination to work within the homelands system, and (in its own view) to use the resources available to it as the government of KwaZulu to undermine the system. Inkatha also rejected the armed struggle, sanctions, and what it saw as the hegemonic leadership of an out-of-touch generation of ANC exiles. Inkatha became a focus for the fears and discontents of parents who wanted their children to go to school, workers who resented being intimidated into stay-aways, councillors in black local authorities who were threatened and sometimes killed if they did not resign, owners of businesses and 'warlords' whose status in the community was threatened. The resentments of these conservative forces were greatly exacerbated by the fact that their antagonists were principally youthful, the 'comrades' who provided the foot soldiers of township revolt. In this way a strong element of generational conflict was added to the other contentious issues.

For their part, the ANC and the UDF regarded Inkatha's claims to be opposing apartheid from within the system to be hollow, and classified it and the KwaZulu administration, which it ran effectively as a one-party state, as collaborators in the maintenance of the apartheid system. Hostile propaganda campaigns both locally and on the ANC's broadcasting station Radio Freedom particularly incensed Chief Mangosuthu Buthelezi, leader of Inkatha and Chief Minister of KwaZulu, who was invariably singled out for personal abuse.

Their diverse constituents notwithstanding, these conflicts resolved themselves into costly and brutal struggles for control of territory and people; these would reach a peak of contest and then stabilize as one group or another confirmed the upper hand in a given area. The violence would then spread, sometimes across newly realigned borders, sometimes carried by refugees from stricken areas to previously peaceful ones, sometimes grafting the UDF/Inkatha division onto some purely local or factional dispute.

The 'spread' of violence between black political organizations to the townships of the Witwatersrand which followed the unbanning of the ANC makes it necessary to consider the violence between the UDF and Inkatha in Natal in perspective. In fact, although the violence was more widespread, intense and costly in Natal, it was not unique to that region.[31] The same mixture of conflicts arising from rapid urbanization, generational differences and above all 'progressive' and 'conservative' orientations towards the state and the liberation struggle were present in many parts of the country, certainly in all major urban areas. Clashes between UDF aligned groups and groups of vigilantes (sometimes called 'fathers' or 'witdoeke'[32]) who often received support from regular or clandestine arms of the security forces under the states of emergency were commonplace.

Only in Natal, however, was there an organization capable of mobilizing people on a large scale, harbouring pretensions to national leadership and being recognized by the government as a force to be reckoned with. An important factor in Inkatha's and Buthelezi's ability to make such claims is the appeal to Zulu ethnicity and cultural chauvinism which the movement in part represents and on which it is partly (and increasingly) mobilized.

The nature of Inkatha's appeal to Zulus and the claim that the ANC is dominated by Xhosas has prompted commentators to refer to the violence in Witwatersrand townships which erupted in August 1990 as ethnic or tribal in nature.[33] This designation risks oversimplification in perceptions of black politics in the crucial period of transition and negotiation. Certainly the violence in the Reef townships has had an indisputably ethnic aspect. It is clear that tribal identities offer some shape to what are otherwise puzzlingly spontaneous and confusing spasms of violence and there are clearly documented reports of victims being singled out on the basis of peculiarities of dress and accent. But this shape cannot provide a plausible explanation for the major lines of mobilization and conflict in black politics.

The major theatre of conflict in black politics has been Natal and KwaZulu. As argued above, there are several lines of division: ANC/ Inkatha; shack dweller/township resident; youth/elder. All of these lines, however, divide people who are identifiably Zulu. The violence takes place in peri-urban and rural areas which are overwhelmingly Zulu, and not in the parts of Natal/KwaZulu where there is an interface between Zulus and Pondos, Swazis, or Xhosas.[34]

The hostels which house migrant workers are central to the violence on the Witwatersrand. Because hostel populations are often easily (if superficially) identifiable in ethnic terms, the pursuit of grievances and conflicts of interest or the avenging of slights take on the same quality. By contrast, the local residents are more concerned with struggles around rents, municipal facilities, wages and education than they are with ethnic identity, although hostel dwellers are categorized by them in ethnic terms for the purposes of self-defence or reprisal.

As for the townships themselves, 40 per cent of Soweto's residents might reasonably be described as Zulu, yet there is no organized ethnic conflict between township dwellers themselves, only between them and hostel dwellers.

Perhaps the most misleading application of ethnic explanations lies in categorizing the ANC as a 'Xhosa organization'. Only if two things are accepted as given would it be meaningful to say that the leadership of the ANC is disproportionately Xhosa. The first is that 'Xhosa' is a meaningful category in the political (as distinct from the linguistic and cultural) sense. The second is that, as the leadership of the IFP and conservative whites often claim, Zulus (8 million[35]) form the largest identifiable ethnic group in South Africa.

There is little or nothing to suggest that head-counting of 'Xhosas' in the ANC is of much analytical or interpretative significance. The ANC's ideology is explicity non-racial and non-ethnic, stressing at every opportunity its own inclusive nature and the inclusive nature of the South African citizenship it takes as its goal. There is no evidence to suggest that this is a smokescreen, obscuring an ethnic agenda aimed at favouring Xhosas. It is hard to believe that the many non-

Xhosas (including significant numbers of whites and Indians) in leadership positions have calculated on rising to power on the back of a 'Xhosa revolution' or are simply its dupes. In addition, the ANC has absolutely nothing to gain by overtly or covertly favouring one black ethnic group, or of basing its support on only a fraction of the black population. The ANC's most essential operating premise has always been that white power and control could not be confronted and transformed by a divided black opposition.

It is possible that 'Xhosa domination' in the ANC reflects a general feature of South African politics – the importance of regions. South Africa is a large country with widely separated centres of population. Regional conflicts in white politics reflect this, and in the history of Afrikaner nationalism the balance of power between the Cape and the Transvaal has always been important. The years of P. W. Botha's ascendancy for instance marked the ascendancy of the Cape, but this was not interpreted as a 'tribal' affair.

The regional dynamics of the ANC are not yet widely enough appreciated. To an important extent the ANC is composed of regional concentrations of strength, each with its own internal power structure and local preoccupations. 'Xhosa' domination may reflect the traditional ANC strength in the Eastern Cape, and the concentration of power usual in a revolutionary underground movement, which may give way to greater circulation now that the ANC can openly organize and operate.

There is no doubt that 'Zulu' is a category with important political significance, since so much of the IFP's appeal is bound up with Zulu ethnicity. But while there may indeed be 8 million Zulu speakers in South Africa, opinion polls and other data make clear that the number for whom 'Zuluness' shapes political orientation is very much smaller, and they are concentrated in KwaZulu and Natal. And it is equally clear that the ANC has substantial support in Natal, giving the violence there the quality of a 'Zulu civil war'.

In the light of these contradictions, to explain the township violence in ethnic terms, to extrapolate this division to the rest of black South Africa, and to understand the ANC as a 'Xhosa' organization, is to misinterpret the significance of ethnicity in the situation. Such ethnic divisions as there are in black South Africa are not symmetrical in the way that Greek/Turkish (in Cyprus), Protestant/Catholic (in Northern Ireland), Fleming/Walloon (in Belgium) or Christian/Muslim (in Lebanon) are. The pattern of two ethnic groups standing in opposition to each other, each with its political, social and (perhaps) paramilitary organizations, does not hold for Zulu and Xhosa.

What the intrusion of an ethnic dimension into the township violence does show is that the ANC's sophisticated message of non-racialism, nation-building and democratic grass-roots organization around community issues has only a patchy cover.[36] There is enough of a vacuum at the heart of African popular politics (which have been repressed so thoroughly and for so long) to allow for the exploitation of tribal identities which have been encouraged by apartheid structures, perpetuated and exaggerated by the local peculiarities of the migrant labour system and heightened by the blood-feud aspects of the continuing violence. In concrete terms, especially for some marginal groups like host dwellers and squatters, the certainties and securities of tribal identity have been preferable to the fragile abstractions of non-racialism and nation-building.[37]

The manipulation of ethnicity in black politics has largely been the preserve of Buthelezi and the IFP. Much of the movement's appeal is based on Zulu cultural chauvinism, expressed for instance in the practice of carrying 'traditional' weapons, in the central symbolic role the monarchy plays in the IFP, the part played by traditional chiefs in its structures, and the consciously fostered appeal to the heritage of the Zulu state's expansionism and resistance to British colonialism. Yet these emphatic ethnic overtones are diluted by another more secular and universal discourse which includes power-sharing, federalism, civil liberties, the free market and foreign investment and an inclusive identity embracing white, Indian and other non-Zulu inhabitants of Natal and KwaZulu.

The contradictions between the tribal nature of the IFP's support, and the 'modernized' nature of the values its leadership professes, indicate the ambivalent nature of the ethnic factor in South African conflicts. They also reflect the changing balance of forces in the transition period, and the fluid nature of the political processes at work. As Buthelezi's national ambitions receded in 1991–2, so the emphasis on the 'Zulu nation' in his rhetoric increased along with the prominence given to a strong role for regions in constitutional negotiations. As Buthelezi's disaffection heightened and the conflict between the IFP and the government/ANC axis sharpened after the date for the country's first non-racial election was agreed in June 1993,[38] the IFP's mobilizing and negotiating strategies became progressively more and more concerned with the position and the prerogatives of the Zulu monarchy. In the final weeks of tense negotiations (February to April 1994) on IFP participation in the election, it was the guarantee of the king's position under a new government which allowed Buthelezi the face-saving formula to agree to take part.

By extending political space to black political organizations and removing the long-term imperative of defeating the apartheid state, the new political conditions of 1990–94 turned the largely underground war between Inkatha and the ANC into an open and bitterly contested rivalry for territory and allegiance. Although the war was fought almost exclusively in black townships, peri-urban and rural areas, and largely by black paramilitary forces, it should not be seen in isolation from the larger political conflicts. Both sides related their conflicts to the white-controlled state and the transitional negotiations, each bitterly claiming that the government was favouring the other. The ANC pointed to 'third-force' activities and failure to curb the partial behaviour of the KwaZulu Police, while the IFP bitterly resented what it saw as the government's 'capitulation' to the ANC's negotiation demands in return for assurances on power-sharing, continuity in the bureaucracy and security forces and junior partner status in the new government.

If on the one hand it would be wrong to see the contest between the IFP and the ANC purely in terms of 'black politics', however, it is equally necessary to note that the conflicts of transition showed that conflict resolution, nation-building and reconciliation are not exclusively about accommodating the clash of black and white interests and identities.

The ANC and the National Party

Perhaps the most striking aspect of South African politics in transition has been the juxtaposition of parallel patterns of conflict. The conflicts involving the white right have been characterized by dogmatic rejectionism and preparations for violent confrontation. The conflicts of black politics have exhibited extremes of intolerance and cycles of retaliatory atrocities, subject to control by local and national peace initiatives that are only partially and temporarily effective. Right up to the eve of the election of April 1994, these patterns suggested that conflict in South Africa could not be contained within present or foreseeable institutions and that crude trials of strength would have to be endured.

At the same time, the opposite impression was given by the emergence of a structure of bargaining and compromise principally involving the ANC and the National Party government. This structure was hesitant and patchy in its development, but given the history of antagonism between them, the parties to it made remarkable progress, driven by the imperative that neither had a viable alternative to adversary partnership. In order to make this progress, both the National Party and the ANC had to transform their respective institutional natures and their understandings of conflict.

The National Party's official ideology has moved away from a vision of conflict in which ethnically composed nations clash by virtue of their warring cultures and have to be kept apart. The corresponding institutional stage to that was grand apartheid. An intermediate resting point was marked by the view that ethnically composed groups have to be accommodated separately within a single political system. This corresponded to the Tricameral Constitution, although the logic of the system was never extended to include Africans. Elements of the belief in the group basis of politics and conflict briefly remained in National Party thinking even after the reforms and unbannings of February 1990. But by 1991, the central component in the National Party's thinking on conflict was the need to protect minorities from possible excesses of power in the hands of a majoritarian government.

The ANC's acceptance of the desirability of a negotiated end to apartheid, rather than its destruction in the victory of a revolutionary struggle, forced it seriously to confront the issue of conflict. From a position in which its understanding of conflict was conditioned by struggle and victory, the ANC has had to evolve a philosophy which accepts that some form of conflict is an endemic and legitimate part of a political and social system's functioning. The tension between revolutionary aspirations and the recognition that there are other elements in society which have to be accommodated is apparent in ANC statements and policy documents. The ANC's 'Guidelines on Strategy and Tactics' (1991) vividly express revolutionary aspirations:

> The contradiction between the oppressed black majority and the white oppressor state is the most visible and dominant within South Africa. Conflict within our society derives from the system of oppression and exploitation ... The sense of national grievance against oppression and the fight against exploitation constitute the driving force of the national democratic revolution.

The liberation movement faces the challenge of harnessing these elements into a mighty force to sweep aside the apartheid state and create a united, non-racial and democratic society.[39]

In contrast to this view of the present, in which the only axes of conflict are those of 'exploitation and oppression' and a vision of the future composed of harmony and transcendence, ANC President Nelson Mandela has consistently drawn attention to 'national minorities' whose mistrust and fears the ANC has not done enough to allay:

We can ill-afford to be content with the relatively low level of success that we are making with regard to drawing whites, coloureds and Indians into the organisation. We must ask ourselves frankly why this is so. In this context, we should not be afraid to confront the real issue that these national minorities might have fears about the future which fears we should address.[40]

In addition, as it has approached the prospect of forming a government in a post-communist world which is not at all hospitable to the kind of revolutionary transformation it contemplated in exile, the ANC has had to moderate its expectations greatly. This development is most noticeable in economic policy, where an unthinking acceptance of nationalization has given way to sophisticated macro-economic strategies with the goal of fiscal stability in a mixed economy.

After the unbanning of the ANC and other liberation movements in February 1990, the principal tasks of conflict resolution between the ANC and the government were: removing obstacles to negotiation (notably the definition and release of political prisoners); the normalization of conditions of political competition (or, 'levelling the playing field'); securing agreement on basic constitutional principles, a transitional authority, and finally, a new constitution.

Each of these components of the final settlement was prey to differing interpretations of agreements reached and in all cases endemic political violence corrupted and enervated the will to agreement. As a result, progress was halting, costly and fragile. Twice, in May 1991 and between July and September 1992, the negotiation process was halted altogether, as the ANC withdrew from talks and lodged a list of demands for resumption with the government. A measure of the pace of conflict resolution is that some of the same demands (notably those relating to the release of political prisoners and specific measures to control the violence like the banning of carrying 'cultural weapons') were on both lists.

The second hiatus in the talks was followed by bilateral meetings between the ANC and government. These bore fruit in the Record of Understanding (September 1992) and the acceptance by the ANC of temporary power-sharing and 'sunset clauses' guaranteeing white positions in the bureaucracy and security forces to ease the transformation process (November 1992).[41] A multi-party negotiating forum reconvened in March 1993, and by December had completed agreement on constitutional issues and transitional structures. This remarkable achievement represented the completion of a process in which both the ANC and the government completely revised their respective understandings of the nature of conflict and its place in politics and society.

The verdict of the April 1994 election and the future of conflict in South Africa

During the five months between the finalizing of the interim constitution in December 1993 and the April 1994 election, a war of nerves and a trial of strength took place between, on one side, the fragile coalition of the white minority government and the ANC, and on the other, a disparate alliance of white and black conservative forces. This period was crucial for the future of conflict in South Africa. If the programme of phased and moderate transformation which the government/ANC coalition represented was prevented by rejectionist forces from achieving a popular mandate and/or failed to hold the allegiance of the major organs of state, then a chaotic descent into secession and anarchy was a possibility.

Not surprisingly, the electoral process became the theatre of this trial of strength. It was Mangope's refusal to cooperate with the Independent Electoral Commission (IEC) which fanned the civil uproar in his territory and stiffened the government's attitude towards him. And although the monthly death toll of 3–400 in KwaZulu/Natal was obviously central to the declaration of a State of Emergency there in late March, the rough treatment accord to IEC and Transitional Executive Council (TEC) members in Buthelezi's capital of Ulundi was certainly crucial too.

In both cases the security forces were loyal and the centre held. Mangope headed for political oblivion, while Viljoen and Buthelezi made their separate accommodations with what they now recognized to be the new legitimate state power.

The election confirmed this new status quo in spectacular fashion by giving the ANC a resounding victory, yet denying it the two-thirds majority which would have given it (according at least to the letter of the law) a free hand to alter and finalize the constitution. At the same time, the National Party kept a foothold in power at the centre thanks to the power-sharing arrangements, and in the important Western Cape region, where it won a majority in the provincial parliament. The IFP was rewarded for its participation by winning the KwaZulu/Natal region, although allegations of widespread electoral fraud cast some doubt on the legitimacy of this victory.

The most significant result for the future of conflict in South Africa, however, is that all major political forces had been drawn into legitimate constitutional politics. Only the extreme white right wing stubbornly persisted in boycotting. However, perhaps persuaded by the exposure in the election of their status as a very small minority, even these resisters began negotiations with President Mandela in the immediate aftermath of the election.

Despite the evolution, against all the odds, of a political system which is regarded as legitimate by the overwhelming majority of its citizens, the resolution of conflict in South Africa will not be easy.

South Africa remains a profoundly unequal society. Despite the repeal of the cornerstones of apartheid, the Land Acts and the Group Areas Act, land remains overwhelmingly in white hands. Access to medical care and education is grossly unequal.[42] Underlying all this is the differential distribution of wealth. In terms of the Gini coefficient (which measures inequality) South Africa has the highest measure of inequality of all 57 states for which data are available.[43] It is true that the income gap is narrowing, but it is still very considerable. In 1987, whites (16 per cent of the population) had 57 per cent of disposable income, while blacks (70 per cent) had 31.5 per cent. Asian (3 per cent) had 7.9 per cent of disposable income, and coloureds (11 per cent) had 3.6 per cent. In 1988, an estimated 60 per cent of disposable income accrued to the top 20 per cent of the population and 15 per cent to the bottom 40 per cent.[44]

A fuller picture of inequality is offered by the United Nations Human Development Index (HDI) which measures, in addition to income, a set of indicators such as life expectancy, access to safe water, infant mortality, adult literacy and mean years of schooling. What is most significant is not South Africa's overall position – about half-way among the 173 countries measured – but the disparity between blacks and whites. As has been calculated, 'If white South Africa were a separate country it would rank 24 in the world (just after Spain). Black South Africa would rank 123 in the world, just above Congo.'[45]

A further concern is revealed by the income gap between black people in different regions. In the Pretoria/Witwatersrand/ Vereeniging (PMV) region – the country's industrial heartland – average black incomes are two-and-a-half times the national average for blacks, while they are six times the average for blacks in the Northern Transvaal region.[46]

The effects of recession on the economy paint a grim picture too. More than 50,000 jobs were shed in the mining industry in 1990– 91;[47] and officials of the National Union of Mine Workers (NUM) estimate that 200,000 more workers could be retrenched by 1995.[48] Statistics compiled by the Development Bank of South Africa revealed in 1991 that fewer than 10 per cent of the annual entrants to the job market (over 300,000) find employment down from over 70 per cent in the early 1970s, and that unemployment affected 38 per cent of the economically active population.[49] One year later, figures produced by Stellenbosch University put the unemployment total at 43.68 per cent, while the Boland Bank calculated that only 3 per cent of newcomers to the job market could find employment, and according to the Central Statistical Service, there have been 250,000 retrenchments in the non-agricultural sector since September 1979.[50]

Population growth will make it difficult to address these high unemployment figures. The present total is 38 million[51] and the rate of increase is 2.3 per cent per year. Two-thirds of the black population (including the 'independent' states) is under the age of 27 and two-fifths under the age of 14. A recent projection offers the 'plausible guess' that the population will increase to 48 million by the turn of the century and to 60 million a decade later.[52]

In addition to this picture of inequality and material deprivation, South Africa is a very violent society. There were more than 20,000 murders in 1992. According to the South African Institute of Race Relations (SAIRR), 'In the ten years from 1983 to 1992 the murder rate in South Africa (excluding the ten homelands) increased by

135%, robbery by 109%, housebreaking by 71% and rape by 62%. Over the same period the population increased by 25%.' [53]There are more than 3 million legally held firearms in South Africa and estimates of illegal weapons run to hundreds of thousands.[54]

To set against this picture of potential conflict, the New South Africa has some tangible assets. The first is an inclusive political settlement with a negotiated constitution, power-sharing arrangements and a popularly elected government, all of which have been legitimized in free elections. The second is a spirit of national reconciliation symbolized in the election itself, the inauguration of President Mandela and his maiden speech in parliament. This spirit has a solid underpinning in the hard-headed realization that there is no alternative to reconciliation other than chaos and destruction.

The third asset is a strong culture of negotiation which has rapidly and extensively developed in South Africa since 1990. While attention has been focussed on the 'high politics' of constitutional negotiation, at the same time practically every sphere of public life has been the subject of comprehensive debate aimed at restructuring and development. Among the most important areas and issues in this regard have been local government, education and training, housing, health and the legal system. Each of these has its own negotiating forum, widely representative of statutory and non-statutory bodies, many of whom were, as recently as the late 1980s, implacable enemies.[55] Perhaps most important of all is the National Economic Forum (NEF), a tripartite body involving organized labour, business and the government. The NEF operates as a policy research group as well as a forum for debate and negotiation and has played an important role in stabilizing potential conflict over economic policy in the transitional period. It has the potential to become an important instrument for managing conflict in the period of reconstruction and development, though whether or not it will develop into full-blown corporatism remains open to question.

The fourth and last asset which will be available for the management of conflict in South Africa's future rests in a vigorous civil society. The struggle against apartheid involved not only the liberation movements but a host of church, civic and non-governmental organizations, while numerous new bodies were set up to promote democracy and voter education between 1990 and 1994. Not all of these will survive in the post-apartheid era, but many, especially those which were politically non-aligned, are determined to carry forward their work into the period of reconstruction. In addition, business, labour and the churches became heavily involved in peace and conflict resolution initiatives during the transition period. All three of these actors had important roles to play in brokering the Peace Accord of September 1991. In fact the peace process grew out of a church and business initiative, when the ANC and other opposition groups refused to attend a summit meeting on the violence, sponsored by the government.[56] The accord required intensive lobbying by business and church facilitators right up to the last moment, and its form owed much to the Congress of South African Trade Unions' (COSATU's) experience of industrial bargaining and to the climate of negotiation which its tripartite talks with employers and government had created.[57]

The shadow of apartheid lies long across the socio-economic structure of South Africa. Although the major political conflicts have been resolved, the distortions, deprivations and inequalities of apartheid carry with them the potential for future conflict. South Africans will have to deploy all the ingenuity and resolve which they showed in extricating themselves from an apparently hopeless, violent, historical cul-de-sac in order to deal with the challenges of reconstruction and development.

Notes

1 The South African Institute of Race Relations (SAIRR) *Annual Survey* for 1993–4 (p. 291) states that between 1 September 1984 and 30 September 1993 there were 17,636 deaths in political violence. The monthly reports of *South African Conflict Monitor* (Centre for Socio-Legal Studies, University of Natal, Durban) indicate a total of 983 for the last three months of 1993. The *Sunday Times* (24.4.94) quotes a running total for 1994 (based on SAIRR figures) of 1,226. This yields a grand total of 19,845. This is probably an accurate figure, although there is a measure of endemic disagreement between the numerous monitoring and collating groups as to the definition of incidents and the relative reliability of official (mainly the police) and unofficial sources.

2 On total onslaught and total strategy, see Geldenhuys, D., *The Diplomacy of Isolation*, Southern Book Publishers, Johannesburg, 1984; Frankel, P., *Pretoria's Praetorians*, Cambridge University Press, Cambridge, 1984; Grundy, K., *The Militarization of South African Politics*, Oxford University Press, Oxford, 1988.

3 For discussions of how and why the ANC took up armed struggle, see *Attack, Advance, Give the Enemy No Quarter!*, message of the National Executive Committee of the ANC, 8.1.86, ANC document, Lusaka, 1986. This source includes the manifesto (dated 16.12.61) of Umkhonto

We Sizwe (MK), the movement's armed wing. See also *Umkhonto We Sizwe: Born of the People*, ANC document, Lusaka, 1986; and Hani, C., 'The ANC and Armed Struggle', paper delivered at a conference on *The Future of Security and Defence in South Africa*, Harare, 24–7 May 1990.

4 On the crisis of the 1970s, see Saul, J., and Gelb, S., *The Crisis in South Africa*, Monthly Review Press, New York, revised edition, 1986. For general accounts of the new constitution and of the reformed industrial relations legislation, see Murray, M., *South Africa: Time of Agony, Time of Destiny*, Verso, London, 1987, pp. 116–18, 147–51.

5 According to the SAIRR (*Annual Survey 1993–4*, p. 319) there are 411 hostels and more than a million hostel residents throughout the country. 'Informal settlement' covers a wide range of situations, reflecting a hierarchy of statuses and relationships with the authorities. More than 7 million city-dwelling South Africans live in informal housing. It is estimated that there will be 12 million more 'new' people in cities by 2010. See *The Economist*, 29.2.92, p. 22.

6 See *Weekly Mail*, 7–13 June 1991, p. 13.

7 See 'An Insider's Account of the Hostel Regiments', 'Putting a Human Face on the Hostels' and 'The Men who Dream of Distant Homes' *Weekly Mail*, 30 August–5 September 1991, pp. 20–21. See also 'Scrap the Hostels' and 'Many will die on that day', *Weekly Mail*, 30 May–6 June 1991, p. 17. For a discussion of the role of hostels in violence, based on a case study, see Shaw, M., 'Hostels, Violence and the Possibility of Lasting Peace: A Case Study of Ratanda Township, Heidelberg', in Minaar, A., *Communities in Isolation: Perspectives on Hostels in South Africa*, Pretoria, Human Sciences Research Council (1993).

8 See Keto, C., 'Zonal Dynamics in Black Politics', in Keller, E.J., and Picard, L. (eds), *South Africa in Southern Africa*, Lynne Rienner, Boulder, 1989, pp. 69–103. Keto notes (p. 95) that before this vigilante role, hostel dwellers (in the 1950s and 1960s) 'supported protest and resistance to apartheid' and concludes of the change, 'Whether this was due to their isolation from township politics or because the organisers of protest looked upon them as unimportant or peripheral may be difficult to gauge with the insufficient information at hand.'

9 See 'The Toilets that Caused all the Trouble', *Weekly Mail*, 12–18 April 1991, p. 16. This report describes clashes between two squatter camps on the east Rand which left 15 people dead. The theft of portable toilets by one camp which has no facilities or water, and relies on the other, was central to the outbreak of violence between the two settlements, both of which are allied to the ANC.

10 Inkatha was formed (or, more strictly, revived) as a 'national cultural liberation movement' in 1975. In 1991 it was formally recast as a political party and renamed the Inkatha Freedom Party (IFP). In this chapter the pre- or post-1991 title is used according to context.

11 As the 'Inkathagate' revelations of August 1991 made clear, the resources openly available by virtue of Inkatha's control of KwaZulu were supplemented by covert subventions through the security police direct to Inkatha. Further revelations in late 1993 and early 1994 implicated police

generals in arming and training irregular paramilitary forces loyal to the IFP.

12 Neither the ANC nor the IFP is in any strict sense a 'black' political movement, but both draw the overwhelming bulk of their support from the African population, and it is in the context of competition for the allegiance of Africans that the conflict between them is carried on. The designation 'black political groups' is meant to be understood in these terms.

13 In an 85.5 per cent poll, 2.8 million voters cast their ballots on the question of whether De Klerk's policies of reform and negotiation should continue. 68.6 per cent of them voted 'yes', and 31.4 per cent 'no'.

14 For a discussion of the white right wing after the referendum, see Grobbelaar, J., 'The CP and Broedertwis: Restanters and Volkstaters', *Indicator SA*, 9 (3), Winter 1992, pp. 17–20.

15 See Jochelson, J., 'Unions and Right Wing Politics', *Work in Progress* [Johannesburg], 37, 1985, pp. 27–9. Later a memorandum leaked from Spoornet (the rail parastatal), which accepted that whites in management would be reduced from 100 to 75 per cent, caused anger in right-wing circles: 'It was now clearer than ever before that the National Party was the enemy of the white worker, and that white workers would have to act in a more unified way to protect their interests, the Conservative Party said' (*Natal Mercury*, 17.9.91).

16 About 60 per cent of employed Afrikaners work in the public sector, and nearly 40 per cent of all whites.

17 The *Weekly Mail*, 10–16 November 1990, quotes a senior police officer as saying that there is 'an alarming level of support for political parties and organizations of the right in the SAP, with the situation especially serious in the Transvaal'. In the same issue, a Human Rights Commission report asserts that frustration among police at new political conditions 'finds increasing expression in unauthorised activities, in addition to authorised but illegal security force activities'. The sources of frustration are discussed in 'SAP Blues', *Sunday Tribune*, 28.1.91, as part of an investigation into the then high resignation rate (11 per day) from the force. Allegations of security-force collusion with conservative black forces in their conflicts with the ANC are often linked to right-wing sympathies of individual police and soldiers. For a discussion, see Nathan, L., and Phillips, M., 'Security Reforms: The Pen and the Sword', *Indicator SA*, 8 (4), Spring 1991, pp. 7–10.

18 See Henning, H., 'Hard Times on the Platteland: The Erosion of White Farmers' Privilege', *Cross Times* [Cape Town], February 1991, pp. 18–19. See also 'Farmers Plan Self-defence Units to Fight for Survival', *Sunday Times*, 5.5.91.; 'Farmers on the Warpath', Daily News, 16.5.91.

19 On the ideology and organization of the white right wing, see Zille, H., 'The Right Wing in South African Politics', in Berger, P.L. and Godsell, B., *A Future South Africa*, Human and Rousseau, Cape Town, 1988, pp. 55–94; Bekker, S., Grobbelaar, J., and Evans, R., *Vir Volk en Vaderland: A Guide to the White Right*, Indicator SA, Durban, 1989.

20 The Afrikaner Volksunie, a group of five former Conservative Party MPs, favoured negotiation, a greatly reduced claim for territory to form an Afrikaner state, and an explicit renunciation of racism. See 'Master Plan for Survival', *Daily News*, 25.8.92.; ' "New right" pledges itself to negotiate at whatever forum it can', *Sunday Tribune*, 16.8.92.; 'Afrikaners should fly like an eagle', *Daily News*, 29.10.92.

21 Among these were debt, the maize price, crime and terrorist attacks on farmers.

22 Notably the Bophuthatswana and Ciskei governments and the IFP.

23 These were the Transitional Executive Council (TEC), set up by act of parliament in October 1993 as a multi-party organ to supervise the business of government in the run-up to the election, and the Independent Electoral Commission (IEC), whose task it was to administer the election.

24 There were occasional outbreaks of fighting between ANC supporters and members of the Pan Africanist Congress (PAC) and the Azanian People's Organization (AZAPO), but casualties were insignificant compared with the fighting between ANC and Inkatha. See *Weekly Mail*, 8–14 June 1990, p. 1.

25 See for instance the reports of monitoring groups; Human Rights Commission, Special Report 8, *A Study of Repression and the Links between Security, Vigilantes and Hit Squads*, Johannesburg (1990); Human Rights Commission, Special Report 12, *Checkmate for Apartheid: Special Report on Two Years of Destabilisation July 1990 to June 1992*, Johannesburg (1992); Amnesty International, *South Africa: State of Fear*, London (1992). See also Institute of Criminology, University of Cape Town, *Back to the Laager*, Cape Town (1991), especially pp. 103–21. Among the book-length accounts by investigative reporters are Laurence, P., *Death Squads: Apartheid's Secret Weapon*, Harmondsworth, Penguin Books (1990); Pauw, J., *In the Heart of the Whore: The Story of Apartheid's Death Squads*, Johannesburg, Southern Book Publishers (1991). By early 1994 the Goldstone Commission on violence was pronouncing with increasing confidence on 'third-force' involvement, notably the *Weekly Mail*, *Vrye Weekblad* and *New Nation*. For summaries of such allegations see 'Complaints that police "take sides" in fighting are now a key issue', *Southern Africa Report*, 8 (35), 31.8.90, pp. 1–3. See also 'The Bonfire of the Memos', *Weekly Mail*, 24–9 May 1991, p. 8. For an ANC view, see J. Nhlanhla (Director of ANC Intelligence and Security), 'Camouflaging State Violence', *Mayibuye*, May 1991, pp. 6–8.

26 A particularly useful example is D. Hindson's and M. Morris's 'Understanding the Conflict in Natal' in *Towards the New Natal*, supplement to the *Sunday Tribune*, 14.10.90, pp. 3, 5. See also Taylor, R. and Shaw, M. 'Interpreting the Conflict in Natal', *Africa Perspective*, 2 (1), December 1993, pp. 1–14.

27 On the role of hostels in political violence in the townships, see Seekings, J., 'Hostel Hostilities: Township Wars on the Reef', *Indicator SA*, 8 (3), Winter 1991, pp. 11–15.

28 There are an estimated 100,000 taxis serving the black population of South Africa, and this service industry is the biggest employer of black labour. See 'Taxi wars come easy when you earn R150 a week', *Weekly Mail*, 8–14 June 1990. Territorial competition between taxi owners frequently erupts into violence, especially in the townships and shack settlements around Cape Town. See for instance '13-year-old among Dead in Taxi Wars', *Natal Mercury*, 19.9.91. This report detailed five deaths, the destruction of 36 taxis and the burning of 62 dwellings within 24 hours in Cape Town.

29 For an account of how conflict developed in a Natal midlands community, see Minnaar, A., 'Mayhem in the Midlands: Battle for Bruntville', *Indicator SA*, 9 (3), Winter 1992, pp. 60–64. The conflict began with a divide between youth and parents, and went on to embrace social tensions between the community and hostel dwellers, before the antagonists turned to the ANC and Inkatha for support.

30 For the development of this conflict, see Booth, D., 'A Strategic Divide: Townships on Contested Terrain', and Hartley, W., 'The Aftermath: A Separate Civil War', both in *Political Conflict in South Africa: Data Trends 1985–88*, Indicator South Africa Project, Durban, 1988, pp. 73–80, 81–8. See also Stavrou, S., 'The Five Stages of Conflict in the Province', in *Towards the New Natal*, op. cit. (note 26), p. 3.

31 It was commonplace for media reports to refer to 'the Natal Violence'. The ANC rejected this nomenclature, and insisted on 'the violence in Natal', in order to avoid the impression that there was something unique about the province. I am grateful to my colleague Dr Ian Phillips for pointing this out to me.

32 'Witdoeke' were named for the pieces of white cloth worn by combatants to identify themselves. Perhaps the best example of large-scale vigilante activity by such groups was the destruction of squatter camps at Crossroads in Cape Town in 1986. See Cole, J., *Crossroads: The Politics of Reform and Repression 1976–86*, Ravan Press, Johannesburg, 1987.

33 See Johnson, R. W., 'Spears of the Nation', *Independent on Sunday*, 14.10.90. The article attracted critical comment from historians Shula Marks (*Independent on Sunday*, Letters, 21.10.90) and Jeff Guy ('The Role of Ethnicity in the Homelands and Towns of South Africa', Conference on South Africa, Copenhagen, 21–3 February 1991). R. W. Johnson replied to the first wave of criticism in the *Independent on Sunday*, 2.12.90.

34 But see 'Fears that South Coast violence might escalate into Zulu/Xhosa conflict', *Natal Witness*, 16.8.91. This report chronicles a conflict which began as a succession dispute within a tribal authority, broadened into an ANC/Inkatha dispute, and threatened to take on an ethnic character.

35 The 1991 population census counted 8,354,470 people as having Zulu as their home language in South Africa. The corresponding figure for Xhosa was only 2,513,411. But if the populations of Transkei and Ciskei are added to that of 'South Africa', the figure for Xhosa rises to 6.7 million.

See Harber, A. and Ludman, B., *The Weekly Mail and Guardian A-Z of South African Politics*, Harmondsworth, Penguin (1994), pp. 285–6.

36 The ANC's difficulties are made plain in this account of ANC supporters at a peace rally addressed by Umkhonto We Sizwe chief Chris Hani (assassinated 1993), after there had been fighting in an east Rand squatter settlement: 'They arrived bearing an ANC flag and singing Xhosa songs: "My home is in Umtata, my home is in Pondoland". Doubtless perturbed by this display of Xhosa nationalism, Hani took pains to tell the crowd that the ANC was a home for all tribes and races. He laid specific emphasis on the role played by Zulu leaders in the building of the ANC' (*Weekly Mail*, 12–18 April 1991).

37 For theoretical discussions of ethnicity in contemporary South African politics, see Bekker, S., *Ethnicity in Focus: The South African Case*, Indicator SA, Durban (1993); Mare, G., *Brothers Born of Warrior Blood: Politics and Ethnicity in South Africa*, Ravan Press, Johannesburg, 1992. See also de Haas, M., 'How the Conflict Began . . .', *Towards the New Natal*, op. cit. (note 26), p. 1.; Rickard, C., 'The Power and the Danger Behind the Ethnic Wave', *Weekly Mail*, 30 May–6 June 1991, pp. 16–17.

38 Buthelezi's principal complaint was that the government and the ANC used the formula 'sufficient consensus' to steamroller decisions in the multi-party negotiating forum, whose brief was to decide on transitional structures and an interim constitution.

39 'Advance to National Democracy: Guidelines on Strategy and Tactics of the African National Congress', ANC document, February 1991.

40 Nelson Mandela's opening address at the ANC National Conference, Durban, 2–7 July 1991, mimeo, p. 10.

41 For an excellent summary of the negotiating process, see Welsh, D., 'Negotiating a Democratic Constitution', in Spence, J. E. (ed.), *Change in South Africa*, London, Frances Pinter/Royal Institute of International Affairs (1994), pp. 22–49.

42 For concise, informative summaries see Gerwel, J., 'Education in South Africa: Means and Ends', and Savage, M. and Shisana, O., 'Health Provision in a Future South Africa', both in Spence, J. E., op. cit.

43 For discussion and basis of calculation, see Wilson, F. and Ramphele, M., *Uprooting Poverty: The South African Challenge*, David Philip, Cape Town, 1989, pp. 4, 18.

44 *South Africa: An Inter-Regional Survey*, Development Bank of South Africa, October 1991. See also *Natal Mercury*, 3.10.91.

45 Quoted in 'Disparity in SA's Human Development', *Natal Mercury*, 1.6.94.

46 Statistics compiled by the Bureau for Market Research, University of Stellenbosch; reported in the *Daily News*, [Durban], 18.5.94.

47 'Pioneer Talks in the Mining Industry', *Weekly Mail*, 26 April–2 May 1991.

48 'NUM and Chamber Hit Problems in Talks', *Weekly Mail*, 27 September–3 October 1991, p. 13.

49 *Natal Mercury*, 18.9.91.

50 *Sunday Tribune*, 8.11.92.

51 One side-effect of the election in April 1994 was to make clear how unreliable all existing population statistics are; all such figures should be treated with caution.
52 *The Economist*, 29.2.92, p. 19.
53 SAIRR, *Annual Survey 1993–94*, p. 292.
54 *Weekly Mail*, 26 April–2 May 1991.
55 A most useful summary of these negotiating forums can be found in Harber and Ludman, op. cit. (note 35), pp. 236–52.
56 See for instance 'Church Offer to Save Peace Talks', *Natal Mercury*, 27.5.91.
57 See 'The trip that saved the peace talks' and 'Labour provided the blueprint', *Weekly Mail*, 20–26 September 1991, p. 5.

4· THE HORN OF AFRICA: A CONFLICT ZONE

Christopher Clapham

No part of Africa, not even the 'front line' bordering South Africa, has been so riven with conflicts as the Horn. Secessionist, irredentist, regional, ethnic and ideological conflicts combine with straight-forward power struggles and the disorder resulting with the prolifera-tion of imported weaponry to form a bewildering variety of interrelated acts of violence which give the region, already the poorest in the world, one of the globe's highest concentrations of refugees. Such a range of conflicts, obviously enough, can be ascribed to no single cause; nor do they lend themselves to any ready-made solution. Yet the moment of writing in early 1994 provides at least a relatively favourable vantage point from which to survey the sources and course of recent conflicts, and the bases on which attempts are currently being made to resolve them.

The bases of conflict

Looking at the broadest configuration of conflict in the Horn, what is most immediately striking is how little the region owes to European colonialism. Certainly colonialism had its impact on the Horn, and left its inevitable legacy of artificial boundaries, but the colonies established in the great partition – Italian Eritrea and Somalia, British Somaliland, French Djibouti[1] – were among the smallest and weakest in the whole continent. All were overshadowed by the giant of the region, independent Ethiopia. Nor did the end of colonialism follow the normal pattern by which European colonies were transformed within their existing boundaries into independent African states. On the contrary, they followed a logic of indigenous rather than colonial statehood, such as might well have been recommended by an advocate of a truly African process of state formation. In the Somali Republic, a people separated by colonialism democratically united to form what could plausibly be regarded (despite internal clan divisions) as Africa's sole indigenous nation-state. Eritrea was a typically artificial colonial creation, encompassing diverse ethnic and religious groups, but its core population had historically formed part of the Ethiopian empire, and its federation with Ethiopia in 1952 (following a process of consultation with the local population, however flawed and controversial, conducted under the auspices of the United Nations) might likewise be regarded as continuing a process of African state consolidation which, as in Zululand and the Sahel, had been interrupted by colonialism.

The first conflicts to arise in the post-colonial era could indeed be seen as following from the artificiality of the inherited colonial boundaries, and from the anomalies which consequently arose when colonial dispositions were rectified in the interests of indigenous statehood. The union of Somali peoples in former British Somaliland and Italian Somalia left out of the national fold the substantial Somali populations in south-eastern Ethiopia, north-eastern Kenya, and Djibouti (where Somalis and Afars each accounted for about half of the population). The Ethio-Somali conflict, which briefly flared into armed confrontation in 1964 and led to a full-scale war in 1977–8, could thus be seen as an irredentist one, along with corresponding claims for the incorporation into the Republic of Somalis in Kenya and Djibouti. Similarly, the federation of Eritrea with Ethiopia, though broadly supported at the outset by Christian highland Eritreans who had strong historical and ethnic links with Ethiopia, had been opposed by most of the Muslim peoples of the Eritrean lowlands, and especially those in the western part of the territory bordering Sudan. The outbreak of a guerrilla insurgency in this area in the early 1960s, orchestrated by a movement, the Eritrean Liberation Front (ELF), which had links with radical Arab states, could thus also be regarded as an adjustment problem resulting from the lack of fit between indigenous peoples and colonial boundaries.[2]

Even this signalled an important distinction between the Horn and other parts of Africa. In colonial Africa, the incongruence of territorial boundaries and indigenous peoples was often taken to extremes, but rarely raised immediate political conflicts because there was no indigenous basis of statehood to clash with the colonial territorial demarcation. The state was as artificial as its frontiers, and no-one was inherently excluded from the state because no-one was represented by it. Once the Somali state was regarded as the embodiment of the Somali people, however, this justified claims on the allegiance of Somalis living outside the national territory: Kenya's frontier with the Somali Republic was thus a source of conflict, in a way that its equally artificial frontiers with Uganda and Tanzania were not. Still more dangerously, the Ethiopian state had a profound identity of its own, which was discriminatory as between different peoples and regions within its territory. The Ethiopian empire historically 'belonged' to the Orthodox Christian peoples of the northern plateau, who have sometimes been conveniently lumped together as 'Abyssinians'. It was not, as is often claimed, merely an Amhara state, since it was from the start multi-ethnic and had some capacity to incorporate peoples from different groups into the ruling structure.[3] From the distant past, however, it had arrogated to itself the right to rule any of the neighbouring peoples whom it was able to bring under its control, and it frontiers had historically fluctuated in keeping with the strength of its central government and the balance of military and demographic advantage. The empire's ability to resist European conquest, achieve recognition of its independent statehood, and thus gain access to external armaments, decisively shifted the military advantage in its favour in the later 19th century, and enabled it to incorporate large areas to the south and west of the historic heartland into a greatly expanded state. This state, which from 1889 onwards was dominated by the central province of Shoa, thus had built into it an inherent inequality between the original Abyssinians and newly incorporated peoples who included a large number of Muslims. The ELF rebellion in western Eritrea could thus be regarded as a local manifestation of a more deep-seated structural weakness.

This weakness, however, can no longer plausibly be regarded as the basic source of the intense level of conflict that has occurred within the region. It postulates the existence of relatively stable and coherent political units, firmly rooted in an indigenous concept of nationhood, which arouse conflict at their peripheries through their attempts to incorporate further people and territory in the Somali case, or to maintain their control over those that they have already incorporated in the Ethiopian one. It provides no explanation for the escalation of regional violence that led to the overthrow in the first half of 1991 of the governments both of Mohammed Siyad Barre in Somalia, and of Mengistu Haile-Mariam in Ethiopia, and to the collapse – at least in the Somali case – of the whole machinery of statehood itself. In each case, the state was overthrown by the very people who, according to the scenario just outlined, should have been expected to sustain it. The Somali state collapsed as the result of vicious internecine fighting among Somalis that belied the mythology of any uniting Somali nationhood. Still more remarkably, the Mengistu government fell to an insurgent coalition, the Ethiopian People's Revolutionary Democratic Front (EPRDF), which was overwhelmingly drawn from regions of the country which had historically formed part of the 'Abyssinian' state, aided by the Eritrean People's Liberation Front (EPLF), in which the 'Abyssinian' elements in the population of Eritrea were prominently represented. To understand the underlying problems, it is evidently necessary to take a broader view.

Paradoxically, the sources of conflict may be traced back to the very ideal of 'nation-building' which has been the leitmotif of post-independence Africa. In the Horn, the fact that the 'nation' had a base in indigenous culture and tradition raised expectations – at least on the part of ambitious elites associated with the state – which the governments of the 1960s were unable to realize. This was not entirely their fault. For one thing, the Horn of Africa is probably the poorest region of the world,[4] and any structure of government rests on a precarious economic base. Furthermore, the same factors that gave the two principal countries of the region an enhanced sense of nationhood simultaneously gave them a weakened state structure. The Somali Republic was created by amalgamating two different colonial territories, each of which – and especially the former British Somaliland – had been very lightly governed. Even in former Italian Somalia, the larger and politically dominant territory, Italian rule had been interrupted by nine years of British occupation between 1941 and 1950. The new political parties formed during the 1950s mirrored clan divisions, and – in a political structure marked by considerable openness and the absence of any dominant leader – led to the progressive degradation of Somali politics into a petty clan-based factionalism which undermined the ideal of unity. In Ethiopia, Haile-Selassie's imperial regime certainly had a dominant leader, but the state machinery was weak, lacking the ability either to establish an effective tax base or to build a viable bureaucracy outside the capital; regional government rested heavily on local bosses who dealt directly with the emperor, who by the later 1960s increasingly appeared to a new generation of educated Ethiopians to be ineffectual and anachronistic.

The emergence of radical militarism

In retrospect, the 1960s look like a golden age, compared with what was to follow. Both Ethiopian and Somali societies have historically been marked by a strong undercurrent of violence, and this did not disappear, but it was kept within manageable bounds. In the Somali Republic, there were occasional eruptions of inter-clan fighting, especially at election times, but not until the assassination of President Ali Shermarke in 1969 did this seriously threaten national political stability; the assassination, however, swiftly prompted Siyad Barre's *coup d'état*. In Ethiopia, Haile-Selassie's major failure was in Eritrea, where his subversion of the federal system created in 1952 helped to prompt a reaction first from the Muslim elements and then increasingly from the population as a whole, including Christians whose support for federation had been eroded by economic decay and the high-handed actions of the central government. The emperor, highly adept at the traditional politics of factional manipulation, lacked the ability to manage a region which, alone in Ethiopia, had been mobilized into party politics. Elsewhere, there were scattered outbreaks of dissent, including a rebellion in northern Bale in the later 1960s, and protests in the Amhara region of Gojjam against a projected agricultural income tax.[5] But taken as a whole, at few times in its turbulent history can Ethiopia have been as widely at peace as during the final two decades of Haile-Selassie's empire.

From 1969 in the Somali Republic, and from 1974 in Ethiopia, these apparently ineffectual governements were overthrown by military regimes with much more ambitious ideals of national unity and state consolidation. The Somali takeover was a straightforward *coup d'état*, even though it was soon glorified (from the month in which it occurred) with the title of the October Revolution. The Ethiopian one *was* a revolution, and involved the overthrow of the whole imperial structure of government and the economic and social base that sustained it, and a bloody and bitter fight for the succession that eventually resulted in the victory of Mengistu Haile-Mariam. Both military regimes espoused a Marxist–Leninist ideology in alliance with the Soviet Union, a combination to which John Markakis has given the striking title of 'garrison socialism'.[6] My own view is that the enormous differences in the level of social transformation sought and achieved by the two regimes make it harzardous to fit them too neatly into a single phrase, but both sought in socialism a doctrine that would help to further state power, national unity, economic development and superpower support.

Since it was under Siyad Barre and Mengistu respectively that the Somali Republic and Ethiopia collapsed into appalling bloodshed and civil war, and since both were overthown with the capture of their capitals by the opposition in the first half of 1991, it is obviously tempting to look for parallels between them. It is not enough, however, to ascribe the violence of the Horn simply to the seizure of power by two ruthless dictators. Certainly the level of state-imposed violence escalated dramatically under both leaders, in a way that reflected their own lack of moral scruples and a determination to impose control regardless of cost; Mengistu in particular is associated with numerous claims, most of them impossible to verify, of personal brutality. But these were not mere personal tyrants, such as Idi Amin in Uganda and Samuel Doe in Liberia. They were rulers who sought to impose, by whatever level of force was needed, a concept of centralized statehood – and even, in a sense, of nationality – that was more widely shared. Both were, as rulers, anonymous, reclusive and dull. And although both countries suffered dreadfully as a result of their rule, each regime carried to its self-destructive conclusion an ambition that was implicit in its foundation, and that followed from the perceived deficiencies of the previous forms of governments.

The role of external powers

If personalist explanations of violence are inadequate, so are globalist ones. The Horn has often been regarded as the classic African example of conflicts caused, or at least greatly exacerbated, by rivalries between the superpowers. Yet this too is a highly simplistic view. The level of state repression in the Horn, and subsequently of civil war, has unquestionably been made possible by the quantities of armaments pumped into the region by the major powers, and especially in the two decades after 1969 by the Soviet Union. Since the region's capacity to produce its own weapons is minimal, the scale of warfare experienced over that period would have been unsustainable without an arms inflow measurable in millions of small arms, thousands of tanks and other heavy weapons, and hundreds of sophisticated aircraft.[7] Originally provided in order to strengthen the states of the region, these weapons found their way into the hands of insurgent movements – either by capture, or as the result of governments' effort to destabilize their regional rivals – and ultimately weakened and in the end virtually destroyed the very states that they had been intended to support.

Yet the Horn has not seen an arms race so much as a succession of regional hegemonies. Before the early 1970s, this hegemony was maintained by the United States of America, which had a long-standing client in Haile-Selassie's Ethiopia. Even though, from the mid-1960s onwards, the Somali armed forces were armed and trained by the Soviet Union, they were not maintained on a scale which enabled them to pose a serious challenge to Ethiopia, until after the US commitment to Ethiopia declined. The change-over started to occur during the final years of Haile-Selassie's reign, when the USA's reluctance to become involved in further regional conflicts during the Vietnam War period coincided with a substantial increase in Soviet arms supplies to Somalia after Siyad Barre's take-over in 1969. Although US arms supplies to Ethiopia continued on an irregular basis for the first two or three years of the revolution, they did not match the dramatic increase in Soviet shipments to Somalia which took off after 1974, reaching their peak in 1976–7 when the danger of American retaliation had virtually disappeared. The Ogaden war of 1977–8, when the Somalis invaded Ethiopia and the USSR switched to the Ethiopian side, was fought between two states that were both overwhelmingly armed by the Soviet Union.[8] Nor did the USSR's continued high level of military support for Ethiopia lead, even under the Reagan administration, to any substantial retaliatory US supplies either for the Somalis or for the Mengistu regime's domestic opponents. Instead, the USA waited – whether as a result of far-sighted restraint, policy paralysis or the lack of any viable alternative – until the collapse of Soviet power in the region enabled it once again to take a leading role, a shift aptly indicated by the US-brokered talks that coincided with the fall of the Mengistu regime, and by the US intervention in Somalia in December 1992.

The Somali catastrophe
In both the Somali Republic and Ethiopia, the quest for a centralized and socialist state achieved initial apparent successes, before collaps-ing in disaster. The Siyad regime could call on a sense of Somali identity which had been subverted by the bickering of the civilian

parties, and in its early years it notched up some worthwhile achievements. It resolved the vexed problem of a script for writing the Somali language, launched a moderately successful literacy campaign, and responded energetically to the drought of the early 1970s that helped prompt the fall of Haile-Selassie. Even though it was probably always at least popular in the former British Somaliland, home of the ousted Prime Minister Mohammed Haji Ibrahim Egal, its quest for national unity was not entirely fraudulent. Ultimately, however, the pursuit of Somali nationhood was inseparable from the aspiration for the unification of all the Somali peoples, and hence from conflict with Ethiopia. There is room for dispute over whether Siyad deliberately provoked the war by rejecting a Soviet-brokered peace plan, or whether he was pushed into it by an overwhelming tide of nationalist sentiment. At all events, the revolutionary upheavals in Ethiopia appeared to offer a once-in-a-lifetime opportunity, which he took and which disastrously failed.

The most remarkable thing about Siyad's subsequent fall is that it should have taken so long. Nearly 13 years elapsed between the defeat in the Ogaden and Siyad's flight from Mogadishu in January 1991, during which time his regime was bent on little more than survival. One important reason for this longevity was that the disintegration of the Somali political order into its constituent clan fragments, while it deprived the regime of any plausible claim to national legitimacy, did exactly the same for its opponents. Each opposition movement was little more than a cover for a disaffected clan grouping, every bit as wary of other such movements as it was of the government in Mogadishu. The government, based on a coalition of clans with blood ties to the president, was favourably placed to manipulate the divisions between its opponents. It helped, too, that the main opposition derived from the northern Isaq clans, under the banner of the Somali National Movement (SNM), who were too far away from the capital to pose any direct threat to the regime.[9] The Ethiopians encouraged the opposition, but were unable either to get them to unite, or to set in train the hoped-for bandwagon that would topple Siyad Barre.

The turning-point that led to the escalation of the Somali civil war, and ultimately to Siyad's fall, was paradoxically the EPLF's capture of Afabet in northern Eritrea in March 1988. The Mengistu government, desperate to move troops northwards to stabilize the Eritrean front, needed to make its peace with Siyad Barre, and accordingly agreed to expel SNM fighters from their sanctuaries in Ethiopia. Forced back over the frontier, these launched attacks on government-held towns in the northern region, and were only ejected from the northern capital, Hargeisa, after massive casualties caused by government bombing. From then on, the government's position steadily deteriorated, as even members of previously loyal clans defected, leaving Siyad shuffling military commands among members of his family. The formation of a new opposition group, the United Somali Congress (USC), among the clans immediately around Mogadishu delivered the *coup de grâce*. But since all of these movements were clan-based, there was little foundation for the formation of a viable successor regime between the SNM, which controlled the northern region and had borne the brunt of opposition, the Somali Patriotic Movement (SPM), which was drawn from the largest group of clans and was essential to any national equilibrium, and the USC, which after overthrowing Siyad and seizing the capital regarded itself as entitled to take the leading role in the new regime. The USC fragmented, the SNM declared a secession of the northern region (as the Republic of Somaliland) which has largely been ignored by the international community, and the country collapsed into the fiefdoms of rivals warlords, leading to a humanitarian disaster which in turn prompted US and eventually UN intervention. The story of that intervention, and its own entanglement in Somali politics, falls beyond the scope of this chapter, while at the time of writing the prospects of rebuilding a Somali state (or even two states, if the Somaliland secession survives) remain unclear. It is however clear that any viable Somali political order would have to take a form far more in keeping with the decentralized nature of pre-colonial Somali politics than with the disastrous quest for centralized statehood.

The failure of Ethiopian centralism

The Ethiopian case is more complex. The 1974 revolution brought into the open a series of conflicts which had previously been masked by the imperial regime, and in seeking to settle them often succeeded only in making them worse. Some issues were quite straightforwardly resolved. The representatives of the old regime, for example, put up only a limited resistance. Some landlords and noblemen took to the hills with their retainers, and a 'white' opposition, the Ethiopian Democratic Union (EDU), was launched in Tigray and Gonder under the leadership of two local aristocrats; it was brutally but effectively suppressed, and its leaders took refuge abroad. The rural land reform, by far the most drastic measure of revolutionary transformation instituted by the new regime, was implemented with remarkably little violence, given the scale of the operation and the centrality of land holding to the Ethiopian economy and social structure. It also did much to defuse the deep-seated tensions in southern Ethiopia that had resulted from central conquest and land alienation, and goes far to explain why, despite the brutality of the Mengistu government and the opposition that it aroused, most of agricultural southern Ethiopia remained quiescent right up to the overthrow of the regime in 1991.

The conflicts that attracted most attention in the early years of the revolution arose between rival groups in Addis Ababa over the control of central government: between 'moderates' lead by the Eritrean General Aman Andom and 'hardliners' in the military council (or *derg*) led by Mengistu Haile-Mariam; between other rival groups within the *derg*; and between civilian revolutionary factions, some of which were at times allied with the military regime and others opposed to it.[10] These conflicts were conducted with a brutality which is not easily explained either by the ostensible differences between the contestants, which were often expressed in stupefying Marxist jargon, or by the composition of the factions themselves, which often derived from personal contacts established at officer training establishments, or in student organizations in Europe or North America. The losers were usually killed. But insofar as these conflicts reflected genuine policy differences, the main dividing line lay between those who sought to use the revolution to sweep away obstacles to a united and centralized state, and those who sought to recognize ethnic and regional differences within the country. This division, which was itself often obscured by internal conflicts and shifts of allegiance, did not correspond to any simple distinction between Amharas (or 'Abyssin- ians') and other peoples. The leader of the centralists, Mengistu Haile-Mariam, was in all probability a Wollayta from Sidamo in the south; the movement that eventually overthrew him, the EPRDF, was almost entirely derived from the northern 'Abyssinian' regions, and notably from Tigray. Members of Ethiopia's largest ethnic group, the Oromo, could be found in every camp. But once Mengistu had, by 1977–8, succeeded in imposing his domination over the towns, the remaining opposition was forced into rural insurgency, and the battle lines became more clearly drawn.

Once the initial upheavals of the revolution had given way to Mengistu's undisputed dominance by the end of the 1970s, it seemed that the centralist drive would succeed. The Somalis launched their attack and were decisively defeated. Shortly afterwards, the central government transferred much of its army to the north, and – with the aid of Soviet weapons – rolled back the Eritrean insurgent movements which by early 1978 had controlled almost the whole territory. The original Muslim-centred opposition, the ELF, was destroyed as an effective fighting force; its local rival the EPLF, which proclaimed a composite and secular Eritrean nationalism guided by Marxism–Leninism, proved much harder to defeat. Possessing a formidable discipline and organization, it succeeded in clinging on to its base area around Nacfa in the extreme north, and beating off a series of bloody central assaults. By far the greater part of Eritrea was however brought under central control. In Gonder, the EDU was removed from contention, and although the Tigray People's Liberation Front (TPLF) in Tigray continued to maintain a guerrilla struggle, this was largely restricted to small-scale operations in inaccessible areas, which threatened neither the central government nor any zone of economic importance.

Central control was consolidated through an institutional apparatus which rested on the peasants' associations in the countryside, and the urban dwellers' associations in the towns.[11] These divided land and people into small units which were controlled by government supporters and bound into a national hierarchy. The autonomy and local democracy which had sometimes characterized the associations in their early years were severely restricted. Their effectiveness was demonstrated by their capacity to allocate rural land, collect urban rents, implement agricultural production quotas in the countryside and food rationing in the towns, enforce military conscription, and carry out a multitude of other tasks. From 1965 onwards, the peasants' associations managed the villagization campaign, under which peasants were obliged to abandon their scattered homesteads and concentrate in centralized locations, generally close to roads where it was much easier for the central authorities to supervise them. The Workers' Party of Ethiopia (WPE), a Leninist vanguard party constructed on the Soviet model, was formally established in 1984, and its control was extended down through the administrative hierarchy over the following few years.

The spectacular collapse of communist parties throughout the world, notably in the Soviet Union itself, has demonstrated that the Leninist technology of organizational control is actually much less powerful than it once seemed, and it should cause no surprise that the same proved true in Ethiopia. The process by which the apparent central triumph of the early 1980s was transformed into the defeat of 1991 nonetheless needs to be explored. At its base was a dual political and economic failure. Politically, the regime had nothing much to offer once land reform had been achieved. There was some expansion of central services, notably in literacy and education, but this was more than made up for by the central exactions, both financial and human, imposed especially in order to meet the demands of war. Political representation was negligible. An initial willingness to appoint administrators to their native regions, especially in the south, was abandoned after the group to which many of them belonged split from the Mengistu regime in 1977. Elections to the national *shengo*, the parliament or supreme soviet created under the 1987 constitution, were no more than a rubber-stamping exercise. Especially in the key northern regions of Gonder and Tigray, people were driven into the opposition by the brutality of centrally appointed military administrators, and the experience of military reprisals.

Economically, the regime suffered from the familiar defects of socialist management, and notably the priority given to extraction and control over the encouragement of production. The restriction of private trade, the imposition of punitive prices and labour practices, the villagization campaign, the waste of available resources on uneconomic state and collective farms, the pursuit of socialist gigantism in industry, all demonstrated the counter-productive effects of the belief that economic development can be created by a military style of top-down organization. In May 1990 the Mengistu government reversed its previous economic policies, abandoning villagization, collectivization, and restrictions on agricultural marketing. But as the experience of Eastern Europe has shown, for such a regime to reform itself is all but impossible. The reforms simply reflected government weakness, and hastened the collapse of local organs of central control. All this fed through into the military sphere. An attempted *coup d'état* in May 1989 indicated the disaffection of the senior officer corps, while at the crisis of the regime in 1989–91 its armies progressively refused to fight for it.

The new regimes

The Mengistu regime fought for all those objectives that make, or made, Marxism–Leninism so alluring an ideology for Third World leaders and intellectuals: a heady combination of national unity, economic development and social transformation, all created through state power. The insurgent movements which in May 1991 emerged as the new rulers of Ethiopia and a separated Eritrea had been Marxist–Leninist, too, until they abandoned the claim as a result of their search for allies against a Soviet-backed central government and the declining utility of Marxism as a means of generating domestic support. Their attempts to construct a new political order provide the latest twist in the politics of the Horn.

The EPLF in Eritrea is the more straightforward of the two. It consistently fought for the independence of Eritrea as a sovereign state within the Italian colonial boundaries, which was formally attained in May 1993. Though much of the *raison d'être* for the EPLF's existence can be traced to the growing alienation of highland Eritreans from the central Ethiopian regime, as the result of economic decay and the absence of any meaningful structure of political representation, any mobilization of ethnicity in opposition to the central power could only have been counter-productive. In terms of such criteria as language and religion, highland Eritreans were almost indistinguishable from their compatriots in Tigray to the south, from whom they had been separated by Italian colonialism. These criteria simultaneously divided them from the Muslims who constituted about half of the Eritrean population, and who occupied the greater part of the territory. Such communal appeals had fragmented the Eritrean response to the opportunity presented in the late 1940s and early 1950s, when the disposal of the former Italian colonies by the United Nations had given them at least some chance to express their aspirations. They continued to dog the ELF which, based in the western lowlands and supported by radical Arab regimes, proclaimed an 'Arab Eritrea' which necessarily alienated the highlanders. Some Christians joined the ELF out of disaffection from the Ethiopian government, but they could scarcely feel at home in it. For the EPLF, therefore, Marxism served much the same function as for the Mengistu regime, as a non-sectarian doctrine of centralized power and multi-ethnic nationalism, but within the boundaries of Eritrea rather than Ethiopia. The EPLF clung every bit as rigidly to the artificial frontiers of Eritrea as the Mengistu regime did to the somewhat less artificial frontiers of Ethiopia. They required a nation-building ideology which would provide a strong centre and mask ethnic and religious differences, while formally recognizing the rights of individual 'nationalities'. And while Mengistu could use Marxism as a means of maintaining his alliance with the Soviet Union, the EPLF could deploy it as an ideology of insurgent warfare.

About the military capacity of the EPLF there can be no question. That has been attested by its success in holding off and ultimately defeating an Ethiopian army greatly superior in numbers and weaponry. Nor is there any reason to dispute the accounts by admittedly sympathetic observers of the efficiency of its organization in the field, including its maintenance of an impressive infrastructure of workshops, hospitals, communications and other facilities, in the face of continuous aerial attack.[12] The question that remains is whether these capacities can be converted into the successful government of an independent Eritrea. This is turn rests essentially on two issues. The first is whether a level of Eritrean identity has actually been created in the course of the conflict against the Ethiopian state which is capable of surviving the different conditions of peacetime. The second is whether the leadership attitudes and structures of control engendered by a long and bitter war can be transformed into a politically and economically effective peacetime government. On the affirmative side, the long struggle against a common enemy may well provide an ideal basis for creating a national identity, while the EPLF's abandonment of Marxism after its 1986 congress indicates a measure of flexibility. On the other hand, the examples of the former Yugoslavia and Soviet Union demonstrate how fragile the apparent national unity of a multi-ethnic state may turn out to be, and Eritrean nationhood may be strained by regional rivalries which pull its own diverse population in different directions; the Islamic fundamentalism espoused by the Beshir regime in Sudan, for example, presents a serious potential threat to a multi-confessional state. Equally, the experience of successful insurgency, culminating in the triumphant achievement of independence, is likely to foster attitudes of centralization and control more suited to warfare than to effective political and economic management. The promised intro-duction of a multi-party political system, postponed for two years after the EPLF's capture of Asmara in May 1991, was delayed for a further four years after the attainment of independence.

The TPLF, which forms the core of the movement that developed into the EPRDF, and at the time of writing in early 1994 dominates the provisional government in Addis Ababa, developed under rather different circumstances. Like virtually all the movements which emerged from the 1974 revolution, its intellectual origins lay in the student opposition to the Haile-Selassie regime, which found in Marxism the almost automatic ideology of liberation, both internally against a deeply antipathetic imperial regime, and internationally against the Western powers and notably the USA. Several of its most articulate leaders had been absorbed into the TPLF after their flight from the terror in Addis Ababa. Unlike either the central government or the EPLF, they were not concerned to create an ideology of state consolidation, since there was no plausible basis under which Tigray might become independent. Nor, since Tigray was ethnically fairly homogeneous, did they have any need for Marxism as an ideology of supra-ethnic nation-building. Their immediate goal was regional autonomy, and thus a weak state rather than a strong one, and they incongruously sought a basis for it in the Stalinist doctrine of the national question. They were strongly opposed to the Soviet Union, which was heavily committed to the Mengistu regime against which they were fighting, and which they dismissed as 'state capitalist', looking instead (again rather bizarrely) to Albania as a possible model for a state which was both socialist and autonomous.[13]

This combination of Stalinism and isolation, allied to a pedantic Marxist rhetoric, gave some external observers (this writer included) the impression of a movement with some affinity with the Khmer Rouge. In retrospect, this appears to have been mistaken. The TPLF lacked the organizational capacity to control its base areas in the same way as the EPLF and was much more pragmatic on the ground than its formal ideology suggested. This pragmatism contained unresolved contradictions: it took a *laissez faire* approach to economic management, for example, while regarding private entrepreneurs as class enemies who must ultimately be extirpated. But the collapse of the Mengistu regime occurred in circumstances which encouraged a pragmatic rather than a doctrinaire approach. Domestically, as it advanced with unexpected speed from its base in Tigray, it became aware of the deep disaffection created by the *dirigisme* of the ousted government, and gained instant popularity by encouraging people to do what they liked. Internationally, its emergence from isolation coincided with the collapse of socialism in Eastern Europe and elsewhere; and it also, it seems, received some tacit help and guidance from the USA. The immediate aftermath of its seizure of Addis Ababa was thus much less disruptive than many had feared. In striking contrast to the breakdown of order that followed the fall of Siyad Barre in Mogadishu, this took place with minimal casualties and received widespread acceptance, if not approval, from the population of the capital.

It left, nonetheless, important issues to be faced. The old centralized government had failed, and in its place the new regime sought to erect an ethnic confederation in which each 'nationality' would control its domestic affairs, while retaining a central government with limited powers in Addis Ababa. In the Council of Representatives established in mid-1991 as an unelected transitional legislature, membership was almost exclusively reserved for movements claiming to represent the different nationalities, on a basis roughly corresponding to their share of the population. Provincial boundaries were redrawn to correspond with ethnicity, and embryonic administrations were established (after badly flawed elections) in 1992.

On the face of it, this initiative offered an original and imaginative solution to the problems, not merely of centralized statehood in Ethiopia, but of artificial African states as a whole. Ethnicity, the regime argued, was a reality which could not be suppressed, and which should be recognized and incorporated within the structure of government. But however attractive in principle, this scheme faced considerable problems in implementation. First, the claim of the new ethnic movements to be authentic representatives of their own peoples was soon contested. The TPLF had, in the two or three years before May 1991, sought to broaden its political base by forming a set of satellite organizations which were linked under TPLF leadership into the EPRDF. One of these, the Ethiopian People's Democratic Movement (EPDM), had effectively served for several years as the TPLF's surrogate in parts of Wollo and Gonder regions. Another, the Oromo People's Democratic Organization (OPDO), had been formed from Oromo prisoners captured from the central army. Another claimed to represent the peoples of the Gambela salient. But it was far from clear whether any of these movements possessed either effective organizations or popular support among the people whom they claimed to represent. The OPDO, in particular, was implicitly at odds with the Oromo Liberation Front (OLF), which sought (at least as a maximum goal) to create an independent Oromo state, and had established some military presence in two widely separated Oromo areas, Hararge in the south-east and western Welega along the Sudanese border. When the Council of Representatives was established, both OPDO and OLF received an allocation of seats, but relations between OLF and the regime remained uneasy, and broke down altogether when the OLF withdrew from the Council shortly before the regional elections in mid-1992. The claims of the EPDM to represent the Amhara were likewise contested; an opposition movement, the All Amhara People's Organization (AAPO), was established, and subsequently subjected to harassment by the regime. Though in some areas, like the Afar region in the east, it was possible to set up organizations which enjoyed some legitimacy through their association with traditional authority structures, in others the new 'people's democratic organizations' were led by ambitious individuals who had been based in Addis Ababa or even abroad, and had few evident links with their regions of origin.

Nor could Ethiopia be neatly parcelled up between the territories of the different nationalities. Few areas enjoyed the ethnic homogeneity of Tigray. Considerable population movement has taken place in Ethiopia, especially from north to south, in response to land degradation, the economic opportunities created by incorporation into the global market, and the uneven distribution of political power. In the new structure, people who found themselves in 'their own' nationality region were favoured over non-nationals, and there have been plausible reports of what we have come to know as 'ethnic cleansing', especially from Arsi. In a country where economic opportunities are very unevenly distributed, and some areas are quite unable even to produce the means of their own subsistence, the ethnicization of government creates considerable dangers. One of the most threatened groups, paradoxically, are the Tigrinya speakers who form the core of the EPRDF regime; their desperately impoverished homeland is unable to feed itself and produces virtually no marketable surplus, with the result that Tigrayans have emigrated either southwards or north into Eritrea in search of work. The new political dispensation threatens to close both options, and the TPLF's evident concern to retain control over the structure which it has created is eminently understandable.

Nor can the legacy of Ethiopian centralism be ignored. Ethiopia has a tradition of statehood which is more than simply a cover for Amhara domination, and which has been strengthened by a century of common government and the creation of a national bureaucracy, economy and communications network. The Mengistu government's attempts to impose a rigid central control fomented the level of opposition that eventually broke it, but did not destroy all basis for a wider Ethiopian identity. Ethiopian history has over many centuries fluctuated between periods of fragmentation and consolidation, and though the current trend is towards fragmentation, an eventual reversal cannot be ruled out.

Conclusion

In concentrating on the major conflicts in an exceptionally violent region, it is easy to overlook both the interrelationships between apparently different conflicts, and the general degradation of social life produced especially by the spread of armaments, and the progressive breakdown of effective controls over their use. The micro-state of Djibouti, often regarded as an oasis of peace, collapsed in 1992 into civil war between its two main communities, the Afars and the Issa Somalis, as a result partly of failures of internal government, but equally of the accessibility of weapons.[14] With people who move freely across the artificial frontiers into Eritrea, Ethiopia and northern Somalia, the war in Djibouti necessarily affects all of the neighbouring states. There are intimate connections likewise between conflicts in the Horn and the ongoing war in Sudan: the fall of the Mengistu regime, which had aided the SPLA against the government in Khartoum, changed the balance of power not only in Sudan but also in neighbouring parts of south-west Ethiopia, where some groups had supported the SPLA while others had opposed it. The proliferation of modern automatic weapons has led to a massive escalation of violence in what were previously minor local conflicts[15] and prompted a return to the banditry that has long been endemic in the region.

The dismal record of the Horn has much to tell us about the nature of conflicts in Africa, and may possibly also offer some indication of how these may be resolved. On the one hand, the imposition of powerful centralized states on deeply impoverished societies has in the Horn been a recipe for disaster, especially when the pretensions of the state are enhanced by an ideology of revolutionary socialism. The attempt to maintain states through the import of armaments, a tempting solution both for African governments and for their external patrons, ultimately proved to be entirely counter-productive, since by giving those governments a false impression of absolute power, it fostered dictatorship without even creating the order which might have rendered it partially tolerable. On the other hand, there can be no doubt either that states are needed, since no alternative mechanism is available to provide a framework of order, to lay down the underlying conditions for economic development and to mediate the relations between the domestic society and the outside world. The contrast between Ethiopia and the Somali Republic, in the immediate aftermath of the overthrow of their respective dictators in the first half of 1991, makes the point all too clearly. What is at issue, then, is how to reconcile statehood with a basic level of popular acceptance, and how to control the abuses of state power which have aroused opposition not only in the Horn but in many other parts of the continent.

But while the question is clear enough, the answer is not. One important element, illustrated by the contrast between Ethiopia and the Somali Republic, is the importance of a tradition of government. Ethiopia did not dissolve into anarchy when the old regime fell, in the way that the Somali Republic did, because of a shared recognition both by the insurgent forces and by those who had at least tolerated the old regime that government was a necessity which must be maintained. This in turn reflected a level of discipline, notably in the EPRDF, that was missing in the Somali case, and which ultimately may have rested on the structure and values of an agrarian society with a long tradition of statehood. A tradition of government, however, can only apply to those who are prepared to accept it, and in both countries civil war has jeopardized the viability of the frontiers of the existing state. The most remarkable paradox here, given the artificiality of the colonial borders and the readiness with which these were dissolved in 1952 and 1960, is that in each case they have been revived through the secession of Eritrea on the one hand, and the former British Somaliland on the other. The putative northern Somali state is actually the less artificial of the two, since it broadly corresponds to the territory of the Isaq clans which suffered most heavily under Siyad Barre, though the chaos in the Somali Republic at the time of writing is such that it is difficult to discern its chances of success. Eritrea is now independent, and the major outstanding question is whether the EPLF will seek to govern it through a formula which has failed elsewhere in the region, or try to find an alternative.

In the remainder of Ethiopia, the need for such an alternative is recognized, but the search for it is still in progress. Until or unless it can be found, the peace which has for the moment descended on that war-weary country can only be regarded as precarious.

Notes

1 It is most convenient to refer to the territory as Djibouti, even for the period when it was called the Côte Française des Somalis, or the Territoire Française des Afars et des Issas; for regions within Ethiopia, I have used the names and boundaries in operation before the regional government changes of 1988, let alone those of 1992, since these provide the most widely recognized way of referring to the areas concerned.

2 The best available account of the origins of the Eritrean insurgency is in John Markakis, *National and Class Conflict in the Horn of Africa* (Cambridge University Press, 1987), chapter 5.

3 This issue is explored in C. Clapham, *Transformation and Continuity in Revolutionary Ethiopia* (Cambridge University Press, 1988), chapter 7.

4 See World Bank, *World Development Report 1991*, Table 1.

5 See Gebru Tareke, *Ethiopia: Power and Protest* (Cambridge University Press, 1991) for an account of these insurgencies.

6 Markakis, op. cit.

7 See Paul B. Henze, *The Horn of Africa: From War to Peace* (Macmillan, 1991), chapter 4.

8 See, for example, Robert G. Patman, *The Soviet Union in the Horn of Africa* (Cambridge University Press, 1990), pp. 573–9.

9 See I. M. Lewis, 'The Ogaden and the Fragility of Somali Segmentary Nationalism', *African Affairs*, 88, 1989.

10 The best account of these events is Andargachew Tiruneh, *The Ethiopian Revolution 1974–1987* (Cambridge University Press, 1993).

11 See Clapham, op. cit.

12 See Markakis, op. cit., pp. 245–8; for examples of the polemical literature, see R. Pateman, *Eritrea: Even the Stones are Burning* (Trenton: Red Sea Press, 1990); and A. Wilson, *The Challenge Road: Women and the Eritrean Revolution* (London: Earthscan, 1991).

13 There is very little material on the TPLF, but see Markakis, op. cit., pp. 248–58; and J. Firebrace and G. Smith, *The Hidden Revolution* (War on Want, 1982).

14 See P. J. Schraeder, 'Ethnic Politics in Djibouti: From "Eye of the Hurricane" to "Boiling Cauldron" ', *African Affairs*, 92, 1993, pp. 203–21.

15 See, for example, D. Turton, 'Warfare, Vulnerability and Survival: A Case from Southwestern Ethiopia', *Cambridge Anthropologist*, 13 (2), 1988–9.

5. SUDAN: WAR WITHOUT END

Peter Woodward

Sudan was one of the first countries in Africa to become independent. The Anglo-Egyptian condominium – in effect British rule – was forced to an end after complex political manoeuvring on 1 January 1956. Even in the independence settlement itself there were signs of trouble to come. Members of parliament from the southern Sudan had already voiced their concern at the speed of the changes fearing a new internal 'colonization' by northern Sudanese, and consented to vote for independence only after being promised future consideration of federation. As a warning of trouble to come a mutiny of southern troops in Equatoria and pogrom of northern traders in the area had already taken place in August 1955. This political uncertainty and demonstration of violence was an ill omen for a country which has since spent most of its years of independence involved in two periods of civil war, broken only by an uneasy decade of peace from 1972 to 1983.

The most simple characterization of the conflict in Sudan depicts it as the Arab and Muslim majority in the north fighting against the African and often Christian minority in the south. But such a simple depiction distorts the lengthy and complex relations that reflect not only developments within Sudan, but in the wider world as well.

Indeed William Y. Adams has argued that in time and breadth the division between north and south in Sudan is truly immense. Following a softer interpretation than Immanuel Wallerstein, Adams broadly accepts a world-systems view arguing that 'the Sudan since the dawn of history has been linked to a succession of world-systems, within which it was always at the periphery rather than at the core'.

He proceeds to sketch these briefly, including the Pharaonic, Greek, Roman, Byzantine, Islamic, and Modern world-systems, and concludes:

> Almost throughout history there has always been a part of the Sudan – the North – that was encompassed within a world-system, and another part – the South – that was not. The role of the northerners within the system was to supply exotic African goods that were mostly obtained from the hinterlands beyond the frontier; that is, from the South. The northerners were collectors: the southerners were a part of the collected. They were fair game for capture and sale on the same basis as were other indigenous resources.

Adams goes on to argue that this was a typical 'frontier' situation and that those exploited by successive world-systems 'often developed an implacable hatred for their oppressors and for the institution of civilisation that they represented . . . I believe that the typical attitude of northern and southern Sudanese today are carryovers from the deeply-rooted historical relationship'.[1]

While some historians might dispute this in detail, pointing for instance to the believed Shilluk, or 'southern' origin of the Kings of the Funj Kingdom based on Sennar, with most Adams' analysis would strike some kind of chord. Historians of the modern period frequently point to the 19th century when there was the first attempt to establish a state in an area roughly corresponding to contemporary Sudan. That Turco-Egyptian enterprise, which started in 1820, was the first step of the 'modern world-system' into the Upper Nile, as Mohamad Ali sought to exploit new resources in his attempt to pull Egypt into the new expanding Euro-centric world. But it was not only that it involved exploitation of the south, initially for ivory, but the nature of the penetration which some believe left a bitter legacy in the south. As a leading work on that era remarks:

> through the southern Sudan. . .a new ruling caste of traders established itself during the 1860's. . .the deadlock between traders and tribes was broken by a violence which cumulatively created a class of destruction. The search for ivory brought not legitimate commerce but robbery and in some areas the slave trade was following in its train.[2]

There is argument as to the extent of the legacy of this 19th-century confrontation between north and south in the oral history of the south. While some would say that its memory is part of the culture of at least some southerners, northern Sudanese prefer to lay the blame on British rule for emphasizing the differences between north and south. Whatever the factors that created southern consciousness, there is little doubt that it exists, or that British policy at least contributed to it. Northern Sudanese writers were swift to spot the British attempt to isolate the south, seeing in it an attempt at least to contain Arabic and Islam by promoting English and Christianity, and at worst an attempt to divide Sudan and hive off the south to East Africa. Subsequent historical research in British archives has revealed that there was little more than brief speculation on the latter, while the former goal, though true, was not just a matter of cultural division, but of ways to try and check the spread of nationalism after World War I. Egyptian nationalism had dealt Britain a sharp shock, and had spread southwards it was believed to inspire the events of Sudan's 1924 'revolt'. While isolating Sudan from Egypt, it was also necessary to check the spread of nationalism within Sudan. It was primarily for this reason that the Sudan government introduced the secret and divisive 'southern policy' in 1930. In addition to emphasizing Christianity and English at the expense of Islam and Arabic, it also checked any economic integration ensuring that while some development was under way in the north, mainly centred on the giant cotton-growing Gezira scheme, little was done in the south, which even some British critics of the period referred to as a 'human zoo'.

The consequences of this isolation of the south were not to become apparent until after World War II. The war and its aftermath in the Middle East, particularly in Palestine, weakened Britain's position: at the same time Britain and its Western allies sought new security arrangements. The price of Egyptian agreement to a new defence pact was concession on Sudan (still nominally a condominium); and the only legitimate counter to that was the encouragement of rapid constitutional development towards self-government (and choice of independence or unity with Egypt) for the Sudanese. That process in turn was to reverse rapidly the isolation of the southern Sudan as northern Sudanese politicians sought to undo what they saw (correctly) as a deliberate attempt to create an obstacle to Sudanese nationalism.

The impact on the south was disastrous. Education had been held back in the south when compared with the north, and the few educated southerners on whom responsibility for representing the south rapidly devolved were in danger of being overwhelmed by their more numerous and worldly northern counterparts. Furthermore the lack of economic and social development in the region meant that they had few resources or communities on which to build a southern political movement; this was in contrast to the northerners who had both money and the existence of Islamic orders, most notably the Mahdists and Khatmiyya, on which to build political parties. In addition the greater educational opportunities available to northerners ensured that as the British were hurriedly ejected from Sudan by 1956, their replacements in the administration of all areas, including the south, would be overwhelmingly from the north; and that many of the new northern officials and traders who went south would be seen as new colonialists.

First civil war
The feeling that the south had been largely omitted from the processes that led to Sudan's independence was to grow in the years from 1956. Left with a simple Westminster-style parliamentary government in a unitary state, the promise that there would be subsequent constitutional discussion, including federalism and redress for the grievances of the south, soon proved to be false. There was consideration of federation, but with no serious interest on the part of northern politicians; and with the committee involved packed against the south. Instead 'assimilationist' tendencies on the part of northern politicians were revealed by the decision of the government in 1957 to nationalize the Christian mission schools operating in the south. In response, by 1958 some southern politicians had abandoned the old quarrelsome Liberal party to establish a new Federal Bloc; a leading proponent of which announced in parliament, 'The south claims to federate with the North. . .the South will at any moment separate from the North if and when the North so decides, directly or indirectly, through political, social and economic subjection of the South.'[3]

The marginalization of southern politicians was made greater by the intervention of the army in 1958 and the elevation to the presidency of General Ibrahim Abbud. Often seen as reflecting the frustration with unstable northern-dominated party politics, the southern-led federal challenge, which was receiving support from representatives of other outlying regions, has been suggested as a major motive for Abbud's intervention. Whatever the truth of this allegation it was certainly the case that Abbud's new military regime embarked on a robust programme to bring the south more into line with the north. The public holiday was changed from Sunday to Friday, to make the south the same as the north; and Arabic and Islam were vigorously promoted. A particular target were the secondary schools for young southerners in Rumbek and Juba. The attempts at discipline and the growing reaction of the young educated southerners were a harbinger of an alienated generation.

However, the first reaction to Abbud's military regime came from the existing generation of southern politicians, now deprived of any dreams of extracting a federal system. Some, like some of their northern counterparts, found themselves detained at different times, and began to escape from the country, both to East Africa, and especially to the Congo, which was independent from the 1960s and where the chaotic conditions meant little concern for the new self-exiles. Then, in 1962, a new organization was established, the Sudan African Closed Districts National Union (SACDNU), which a year later became the more manageable Sudan African National Union (SANU). SANU sought international recognition and support, especially from Christian groups. But SANU made little headway within Sudan where among the educated groups of southerners in the towns, particularly in Khartoum, a rival organization,, the Southern Front, emerged.

The alienation of educated southerners was understandable, but not in itself a guarantee that civil war would develop in the south. It has been common to state that civil war began in Sudan in August 1955 with the mutiny in Equatoria, but in reality sustained guerrilla warfare did not break out until 1963, though the intervening period had contributed to the build-up. It was true that a hard core of mutineers from 1955 had never surrendered but taken to the bush and survived in remote corners of the south, but these did not mount sustained resistance. A greater impetus came from miscalculations by the regime: while the military was generally taking an increasingly tough stance in the south, causing growing unpopularity, in 1961 hundreds of those imprisoned after the mutiny of 1955 were released. These men had been soldiers, policemen and prison warders, and on release into the increasingly repressed south, many fled into the bush or the neighbouring states, where they linked up with those who had remained free. Then in mid-1963 it was announced that a guerrilla army called the Anya-nya had been established.

It was a portentous announcement, but initially the guerrilla attacks were uncoordinated. The southern rebels were ill-armed and consisted largely of autonomous groups who staged sporadic hit and run attacks, few of which caused serious damage to the Sudan army. But once more government action was designed to worsen the situation. The military engaged in reprisal patrols which did more damage to the innocent civilians on whom they were inflicted than on the Anya-nya, and as a result contributed to the growing alienation of the civilian population in rural areas, which in turn assisted in recruitment to the new guerrilla movement.

The knowledge that sustained guerrilla warfare had broken out in the south, however fragmented, contributed to the pressure mounting on the Abbud regime in Khartoum. Many elements were discontented with military rule, including the old northern politicians who had contributed to the initial alienation of the south, but it was the prevention of a meeting called in the University of Khartoum to discuss the south that provided the initial spark for the 'October revolution' of 1964. Faced with public protests, a general strike, and threatened defection by junior army officers, Abbud and his senior colleagues decided to agree to abdication (and the enjoyment of a comfortable retirement). Abbud was replaced by a civilian transitional government led by Sirr al-Khatim al-Khalifa, one of whose first tasks was to seek to convene a conference to end the civil war.

It took several months to convene the conference which was held finally in March 1965. Known as the Round Table Conference, not everyone – most notably the Anya-nya groups, who ignored the ceasefire – was around it; while the shape indicated the range of views expressed, taking in just about 360 degrees. As a result the ten-day conference was unable to arrive at a solution, and broke up in considerable confusion and acrimony on all sides, not just between north and south. A 12-man committee was established to continue the negotiations, and made proposals that were eventually to be built on, but not until several more years of bloodshed in the south had elapsed.

The fighting after 1965 grew in scale as a result of changes in both north and south. A new government under Mohamed Ahmed

Mahjoub was formed following the elections of 1965, and Mahjoub believed that after the failure of the Round Table Conference, and faced with apparent intransigence by the Anya-nya a new wave of repression was justified. The army was therefore given its head once more and now encouraged to go farther than it had under Abbud in an unavailing attempt to crush the Anya-nya groups. Meanwhile, among the Anya-nya changes were also under way. Sudan had permitted the movement of arms across her territory from Algeria to the Simba rebels in the northern Congo (now Zaire), but in 1965 the revolt collapsed and many of its participants fled into Sudan where they readily traded their arms to the Anya-nya. This sudden influx of arms allowed the Anya-nya to escalate their attacks at the same time as the army was increasing repression. In the following years there were also greater attempts to unify both the military and political fronts in the south; and while not successful, for factionalism was still rampant, the efforts showed that at least the need was recognized in principle.

In fact it took until 1969 for a unified command to emerge in the south, and when it did, it owed something to outside involvement. The conflict in the south had hitherto attracted relatively little international attention (when compared, for instance, with the earlier civil war in the Congo or the simultaneous one in Biafra), though there is evidence that Egypt had had a hand in encouraging the mutiny in 1955. Now, however, the interest came from Israel, prepared to fish in the murky waters of Africa with a view to isolating Arab North Africa from the sub-Saharan continent. Initially via Ethiopia, where it had long ties, and later via Uganda, Israel sought to supply the Anya-nya and looked for a suitable conduit. The Israelis eventually directed their munitions through an energetic young leader from Equatoria, Joseph Lagu, and with the help of this steady flow of support Lagu was in time able to establish overall command of the Anya-nya (now known as the Southern Sudan Liberation Movement, SSLM). Militarily, however, Anya-nya was predominantly confined to the border regions of the south, and never appeared likely to drive the national army out of the region as a whole. Politically, too, the fragmentation survived and relations between the southern politicians outside Sudan or in the cities and the Anya-nya were less than clear.

The expansion of the war in the late 1960s had another political effect, however. The failure of suppression and the growing political and financial cost of the war contributed to the undermining of

Sudan's second period of liberal-democratic politics, and the decision of the Free Officers led by Ga'afar Nimeiri to stage a coup in May 1969. Ending the war in the south was one of the top priorities of the new regime, but its method smacked of ideological fiat. From 1969 until a violent coup and counter-coup in July 1971 Nimeiri's regime was backed by the Sudan Communist Party which had its own distinctive view of the south enunciated by the minister appointed to the new Ministry for Southern Affairs, Joseph Garang. Though a southerner himself, Garang viewed most of the other politicians from the south as *petit bourgeois* figures, and the Anya-nya as Israeli (i.e. imperialist) controlled. The southern problem was the product of economic imperialism in the south, and the solution lay in the creation of a broad socialist movement in the region through the new Sudan Socialist Union (SSU).[4] Garang's position did little to inspire confidence among either southern politicians or the Anya-nya and his failure to deliver any cessation of conflict, in spite of energetic efforts, contributed to the growing tension between the Communist Party and Nimeiri's followers in the region which resulted in the bloody showdown of 1971.

Peace 1972–83

While Sudan was just one of a number of countries in Africa to experience the pains of civil war, it was singularly unusual in achieving a negotiated peace in 1972, finally agreed at Addis Ababa. From the years of warfare in the south and heightened instability in the north from May 1969 to July 1971, it seemed extraordinary that Sudan could suddenly turn round and embark on a path of peace. Yet it was precisely that violence and uncertainty that served to promote peace.

There were those in both north and south who perceived the gains of peace. President Nimeiri was looking dangerously exposed after his bloody break with the Communist Party and his hostility to the old sectarian establishment, and placed his hopes on a new deal with the south to be made by able ambitious non-party politicians such as Ga'afar Bakheit and Mansour Khalid. On the other side southern politicians led by Abel Alier sought to recapture ground from the SSLM in the bush and were prepared to talk once the ideologist Joseph Garang was gone (executed after the abortive coup of July 1971). At the same time the perception of the military situation on both sides was comparable. The government was not facing defeat, but war was costly both financially and politically since the southern problem appeared related to the instability of 1958, 1964 and 1969. And while the SSLM was not in danger of defeat, changes were taking place that put pressure on the need to negotiate. In particular there was a rapprochement between Sudan and Ethiopia by which Sudan would be less 'accommodating' to the Eritreans in return for Ethiopian pressure on the SSLM. At the same time events in Uganda were forcing a change with the aftermath of Idi Amin's coup of 1971 leading to the ejection of the SSLM's Israeli suppliers.

While the climate was thus changing to accommodate peace, there were facilitators at hand. The World Council of Churches and the All-African Council of Churches had been patiently building credentials with both sides and were able to facilitate meetings both before the first negotiations and at Addis Ababa. In addition the Organization of African Unity gave its blessing; and behind the scenes there were hints of Western aid to a regime that had just broken not only with the Communist Party but the Soviet Union as well.

The Addis Ababa agreement did bring an end to civil war in the southern Sudan for ten years, but there were to be growing political, economic and social question marks as time passed. From the outset the agreement had been a series of compromises that would be sufficient to appease the south, while ensuring that it remained bound into Sudan as a whole. In granting Regional Autonomy to the Southern Region – a status unmatched by any other region of the country – the south was being established as a kind of semi-detached edifice, the bricks and mortar of which looked increasingly vulnerable to erosion.

The Regional Autonomy promulgated for the south was further incorporated into the country's first Permanent Constitution in 1973. But institutional intention was rapidly overtaken by the increasing personalization of politics at both national and regional level. At the top the pattern was set by President Nimeiri as he appeared ever more skilled a political manipulator. His 'machiavellian' manoeuvres were to move him to return to the support of the sectarian groups he had overthrown in 1969, and to move from his initial alliance with the Communist Party to embracing the Muslim Brotherhood and introducing Islamic law (*sharia*) in 1983.[5] With regard to the south, Nimeiri involved himself in manipulation from the outset. Abel Alier was declared the SSU candidate to head the new High Executive Council (HEC) to avoid a contested election; later in the ·1970s

Nimeiri was to come to back those (e.g. Lagu) supporting the redivision of the south into three regions which would be on a par with the other new regional governments being created in the north. It was hardly surprising that within the south personalities also seemed more important than institutions. In particular the HEC and the elected parliament were often at loggerheads with mutual accusations of unconstitutional behaviour. Divisions reflected intense personal and factional rivalry, as well as wider differentiation between those who had been outside the country during the civil war and those inside; in addition there were later accusations that the region's largest ethnic group, the Dinka, was seeking to dominate.

Economically there were also hopes that gave way to bitter disillusionment. Fuelled by foreign funds there was initially a flood of new jobs and plans for the development of one of Africa's remotest areas; but it was when prospects really did seem to improve that trouble became most intense. It began with the project to build the long-proposed canal at Jonglei in southern Sudan to improve the flow of the Nile by bypassing the vast Sudd swamp. It was a joint Sudanese–Egyptian project and it appeared that vast sums were suddenly available for a scheme that promised most for the agriculture of northern Sudan and Egypt, and which some environmentalists argued might even damage the regional ecology in the south. The criticisms were many and varied, and even produced riots in the capital Juba when it was rumoured that surplus Egyptian farmers were to be moved south.

Worse was to follow when oil was discovered in 1978 around Bentiu. At first it seemed that all Sudan's problems were over and there was loose talk of Sudan joining the newly enriched states of OPEC. However, from the outset it inflamed political feeling in the region. The first blow was struck when the government announced that instead of refining oil at Bentiu in the south it would be piped north to a new refinery at Kosti for 'technical' reasons. To make matters worse, that plan was cancelled to be replaced by the proposed building of a pipeline direct to Port Sudan for the export of crude oil so that Sudan's worsening economic predicament of the early 1980s could be more swiftly countered by selling unrefined oil for hard currency. In an effort to achieve these objectives Nimeiri became ever more manipulative especially on the question of redivision; he even proposed a new region for the oil field to be known as Unity Region. Few things did more to promote disunity.

The political and economic tension within the south contributed to continuing social problems in the heterogeneous region. Peace initially brought new posts throughout the region for which there was intense competition. But in time there were charges that many of those in government service (and there were few other employers) were increasingly corrupt, while the lack of similar opportunities for later generations of school and university graduates fuelled resentment. Many who sought work drifted north, where hot money from oil-rich Arab states (intent allegedly on making Sudan the breadbasket of the Arab world) was creating something of a bonanza. But by the late 1970s it was clear that much of the money had been absorbed in Sudan's endless sands (and the vaults of Swiss banks) and as the bottom dropped out Sudan's economy, some southerners drifted back south, rapidly finding that there was little to which to return. Security, always difficult in the south, began to decline and from as early as 1980 there were reports of armed bands operating in remote areas, especially in the Upper Nile and Bahr al-Ghazal. It was not yet civil war, but it boded ill.

Second civil war
Perhaps the first ominous sign was when armed bands in eastern Upper Nile began to identify themselves collectively as Anya-nya II, clearly implying something more political than mere banditry. However the major step in the reopening of civil war came with the army mutinies of 1983. At the heart of the mutineers lay the 6000 ex-Anya-nya who had been taken into the army in 1972 but never fully integrated. When they were stationed around the south beside northern troops, relations had given rise to moments of insecurity; but when in May 1983 there was an order for whole companies to be moved north there was resistance. One of those who had just arrived in Bor was John Garang de Mabior, an ex-Anya-nya officer with a doctorate in economics. Threatened by northern forces, Garang led the ex-Anya-nya men into the bush towards the Ethiopian border where in time they were joined not only by men of other garrisons but by former policemen, prison officers and game wardens, and later by many others.

Once in the bush Garang and his men linked up with Anya-nya II, but relations deteriorated (partly over ethnic tensions) and the existing Anya-nya II declined, eventually being turned by the government to fight on its side. Garang's men took the name Sudan People's

Liberation Army (SPLA) and soon formed a formidable force. In this the SPLA was helped by the international situation. In the 'new cold war' of the early 1980s the Horn of Africa had become an area of regional rivalry for the superpowers, with the Soviet Union backing Ethiopia, South Yemen and Libya (aligned from 1981 in the Aden Treaty), while the USA supported Egypt, Sudan, Somalia and Kenya. As a result the SPLA was able to receive Libyan-supplied Soviet arms and training from the many Cuban instructors in Ethiopia, and soon proved adept with the equipment in the field. Ethiopia also supplied logistical support, money, a radio that was heard across Sudan, and an international outlet. While the USA and Egypt were disturbed by the policies of Nimeiri that had contributed to war in the south once more, they had built up the army and thus contributed indirectly to the escalation of violence by giving Nimeiri a significant military option.

There was also a more local dimension to the international politics of the area. Sudan had for years permitted, and sometimes encouraged, the activities of first Eritrean and later Tigrean guerrillas across her border; in addition to which various Arab countries and later the USA also backed the activities of different groups. In consequence Ethiopia was very ready to assist the SPLA in southern Sudan, even without the broader international rivalries of the area.

As a result the war itself intensified, going far beyond the scale and range of the first conflict. Estimates in the late 1980s put the SPLA forces as high as 40,000 men; and the Sudan army was also expanded, as the latter too sought international help, most successfully from Iraq. In addition to those who joined the main belligerents, both sides armed informal militias, often resuscitating local ethnic conflicts as a result. This was particularly apparent in northern Bahr al-Ghazal when raids by Arab militias did much damage among their neighbouring Dinka.

Few areas of the south were unaffected by the war and the devastation it brought was immense. Many in the countryside were forced to flee for the greater security of the few towns that soon swelled with refugees, causing hardship from lack of accommodation, health facilities and food. As many as 2 million of the 6 million southerners may have fled, many to northern towns as well as to African neighbours; and in 1989 it is estimated that 250,000 died from famine in spite of the efforts of the United Nations' Operation Lifeline. Militarily the war was fought right across the south, and by the late 1980s the SPLA was gaining the upper hand. Most of the countryside was in its hands, and the towns were also falling, leaving the government controlling only a handful of centres throughout the whole region. While the SPLA did make some attempt to establish a new administration, it was not noted for its effort or success on this front; and much of the south was left with nothing.

Ideologically the SPLA was different to the Anya-nya of the first war as well. Then the call had ranged from federalism to secessionism and had settled for regional autonomy. The SPLA called for the national reconstruction of Sudan. The main problem, it argued, lay in Khartoum with Sudan's elite. Economically and culturally it was exploitative and repressive, with the rise of the Muslim Brotherhood (later the National Islamic Front, NIF) and the imposition of Islamic law as the final indicator. It was this that had to be reversed, not only by the action of the southerners, but solidarity from similarly exploited regions in the east and west, and commitment by radical elements among Sudan's intelligentsia.[6] In practice regional solidarity was slow to develop while the war produced a hostile reaction among the urban north as well as some sympathizers. Nevertheless, whatever the prescription, the war did promote the feeling on all sides that there was something seriously wrong with Sudan politically and economically.

That feeling was reflected in the political instability in Khartoum which intensified during the 1980s. The long period of stability under Nimeiri (more in appearance than reality) was ended in 1985 partly because the *intifada* (uprising) of that year received some of its inspiration from the war in the south (just as had happened in 1964). The outlines of subsequent events also reflected the earlier episodes. A confused transitional period was followed by a return to liberal democracy, in which a new prime minister, this time Sadiq al-Mahdi, sought unavailingly to take a tough military line. His failure, and the predictable instability of successive coalition governments, gave way once more to a military coup of middle-rank officers in June 1989. Whereas Nimeiri 20 years before had been associated with the left, the new men under Brigadier Omer al-Bashir, turned for backing to the right, in the form of the NIF and especially its manipulative leader Hassan al-Turabi.

The military successors of the SPLA and the political instability in the north did little to facilitate successful negotiation of the kind that had occurred in 1971–2. Belatedly but unsuccessfully Nimeiri had tried to buy Garang off with an offer to make him effective regional commissioner. The first real chance came following Nimeiri's downfall in 1985. The Alliance, a grouping of professionals, generally of leftish complexion, had been prominent in the *intifada* and duly made the running in contacts with the SPLA. A major conference took place at Koka dam in Ethiopia and the two sides went a long way towards agreement. However, the ruling Transitional Military Council, in which senior army officers were dominant, was reluctant to seize the opportunity, preferring to delay decisions for the elected government that took power in 1986. Sadiq al-Mahdi had to seek peace, but he was autocratic and unimaginative, and although he too went to Koka dam to meet Garang in 1987, it was an acrimonious confrontation and achieved nothing, with both men reverting to the military option.

However, Sadiq came under renewed pressure as the political and economic situation continued to deteriorate. The first breakthrough appeared to come in December 1988 when with Egyptian pressure, the Unionist Party negotiated an agreement with the SPLA which included the freezing of Islamic law. Then early in 1989 there was an ultimatum from the army to the prime minister that he had to find an alternative to the path of war. Alarmed, Sadiq appeared to be taking steps and there are those who believe that the Muslim Brotherhood-backed coup of 30 June 1989 was designed to forestall an agreement with the SPLA. Subsequently there were further peace efforts, especially involving former US President Jimmy Carter in December 1989 (his second major effort in the Horn), but the gap between the new regime and the SPLA appeared as wide as that with its predecessor.

After the coup of 1989 and the failed peace talks which followed it, the new regime took stock. There were those in the NIF who felt that the non-Muslim south could be allowed to separate (though this was still not the SPLA's aim). However any such thoughts were swiftly dispelled by those who saw in the south an opportunity for Islamic proselytism which could in time be extended elsewhere in East Africa. The route to this goal lay through confrontation with the SPLA and by mid-1992 three developments had assisted the new regime.

The first event was the downfall of the regime of Mengistu Haile-Mariam in Ethiopia early in 1991. This led to the rapid retreat of the SPLA from Addis Ababa, and then the forcing of hundreds of thousands of refugees from southern Sudan sheltering in western

Ethiopia back into the devastation and warfare from which they had originally fled. This hurried exodus was propelled by attacks from groups in the new ruling Ethiopian People's Revolutionary Democratic Front (EPRDF), for the Tigreans in particular had benefited from the support of successive Sudanese governments, and there were even reports that Sudanese army trucks and troops were among the first into Addis Ababa, hoping to capture SPLA leaders.[7] This ejection from Ethiopia left the SPLA more dependent on its other access routes via Kenya and Uganda, and while generally sympathetic to its cause, both would like to see peace in Sudan (since conflict has brought spill-over problems to both in the past) and both have come under broader international pressure to encourage the SPLA towards peace. (Of lesser importance, though not irrelevant, has also been the victory of Idris Deby in Chad. He was permitted to build up for his successful attack on Hussein Habre in 1990 in Darfur in western Sudan with the help of Libya, and, like the EPRDF in Ethiopia, expelled the SPLA from Chad.) The Sudan government was thus feeling boosted on the regional front, as its London mouthpiece proclaimed 'these countries (in north-east Africa) are at peace with themselves and with their neighbours and grateful to Sudan for it.'[8]

The second development that appeared to favour the government was the split in the SPLA that took place in August 1991. The division emerged among a faction based at Nasir in Upper Nile led by Lam Akol and Riak Machur. The breakaway group accused Garang of being autocratic, and also of forcibly conscripting children into his army. His undemocratic character was said to be reflected in his holding of 45 political prisoners since 1985. A second charge was that SPLA policies needed revision. In particular the aim of provoking a countrywide revolt against Khartoum had proved over ambitious, and they should now pursue a policy of secession for the south instead. (Paradoxically it was claimed that the Nasir group was aided by Khartoum, and it did sign an agreement early in 1992.) Outsiders suggested that the split in the SPLA also reflected ethnic tensions, especially between the Nuer and Shilluk of Upper Nile and the Dinka, the largest ethnic group in the south. On the ground the split led to bitter fighting between the two wings, now known as the SPLA Mainstream (Garang) and SPLA United (Machur), which was served only to benefit the government.

The third advantage for the government came in its international relations. Inheriting a large foreign debt, and suspicion over its

Islamic fundamentalist character, Sudan soon seemed isolated. Libya offered support, but could be capricious, while other Arab neighbours and the West increasingly regarded Sudan as an international pariah, especially when it sided with Iraq in the Gulf War of 1990–91. But this isolation was partially broken in 1991 with the flowering of relations with Iran. Radical elements in Tehran saw an opportunity to use Sudan to promote Islamic fundamentalism, and this led to Iran's supply of arms and hardened Shi'ite fighters with experience in Lebanon and Afghanistan, as well as funding for major purchases of new equipment from China.

The three favourable developments permitted the Sudan army and the newly formed popular militias to stage their biggest offensive of the war and recapture several towns in Equatoria. This stung the SPLA into tightening its own siege of Juba in the summer of 1992, and then launching an attack that penetrated the city before government troops forced a withdrawal and exacted retribution on the populace.

But, in addition to Islamic fundamentalism, there was another relevant new dimension in international politics. Gone was the second cold war, and in its place there came recognition by the West in particular of the need to work for regional peace in areas where the cold war had contributed to conflict in the past. The Horn of Africa as a whole was one such area, and the USA emerged as a major backer of attempted settlements in the region. This involved both official and unofficial American initiatives, but it proved relatively unsuccessful in the case of Sudan. Nigeria was also involved, since it too was a Muslim–Christian country, and after considerable effort did get representatives of the Sudan government and the two factions of the SPLA to Abuja in June 1992. Although a diplomatic communiqué resulted, it was clear that important differences of outlook between Khartoum and the SPLA persisted; nevertheless, the Nigerians were determined to persist and further talks at Abuja took place in 1993, but with no greater success.

Efforts were made again in 1994 by both Sudan's African neighbours and the USA to promote peace talks, but the only achievement was a fragile agreement of the two main wings of the SPLA. Significantly, the agreement involved the acceptance by Garang of Machur's wing's call for 'self-determination' for the south, a call widely regarded as a fig-leaf for secession.

Conclusion

At the time of writing the tide of war has turned once more from the negotiating table to the battlefield with government troops undertaking yet another 'final offensive'. Weakened though the two main wings of the SPLA have been, and tenuous though relations are between them, it is no guarantee of government success. It places great strain on an already bankrupt and internationally isolated regime to continue to wage war; even if successful in battle, it also leaves open the possibility of continuing guerrilla operations in the south, especially with certain African neighbours that would feel threatened by an outright government victory. Victory for the SPLA, in the line of the EPLF in Eritrea or the EPRDF in Ethiopia, looks even more unlikely. If that was ever to be seriously contemplated, it was the era of Mengistu in the late 1980s, when instead the SPLA after brief incursions into northern territory appeared to wait upon the old formula of war in the south triggering a favourable change of regime in Khartoum. Certainly war did play such a role in 1964, 1969, 1985 and 1989. A further change of regime, especially if the current offensive fails, is a possibility, but it is no guarantee of peace: only in 1969 did change lead to an eventual peace process.

That process, however, failed to find a formula for long-term stability in Sudan, as much because of the evolving character of national politics as regional developments in the south. If Sudan is to remain one state, it will need to find a political formula for the whole country and not just for the south. Yet division, though now higher on the agenda with the SPLA's call for self-determination, is no ready-made solution. The border of north and south is a very grey question that would be hotly disputed, especially with an undeveloped oil field at its heart, while the travails of the SPLA of the last three years indicate the political obstacles to stable government within the south. Without a solution conflict will continue. It has already devastated much of the limited development that had taken place in the region, killed hundreds of thousands, and displaced millions. Southern Sudan has known little peace from whoever ruled in the north since the mid-19th century when the 'modern' world intruded once more on the region; but probably nothing was as devastating as the last decade of war has been. With such a history it remains a possibility that conflict is as likely to continue as is any form of peace to transpire.

Notes

1 William Y. Adams, 'North and South in Sudanese History', *Second International Sudan Studies Conference Papers* (University of Durham, 1991), pp. 17–24.
2 R. Gray, *A History of the Southern Sudan, 1839–1889* (Oxford University Press, 1961).
3 Father Saturnino Lahure, quoted in John Markakis, *National and Class Conflict in the Horn of Africa* (Cambridge University Press, 1987), p. 155.
4 J. Garang, *The Dilemma of the Southern Intellectual: Is It Justified?* (Ministry of Southern Affairs, Khartoum, 1971).
5 Nimeiri is depicted as a 'machiavellian' figure in R. Jackson and C. Rosberg, *Personal Rule in Black Africa* (California University Press, Los Angeles, 1982).
6 The fullest pictures of SPLA thinking are in Mansour Khalid (ed.), *John Garang Speaks* (KPI, London, 1987); and A. Ahmed and G. Sarbo (eds), *Management of the Crisis in the Sudan* (Centre for Development Studies, Bergen, 1989).
7 *Sudan Democratic Gazette*, July 1991.
8 *Sudan News*, 2 July 1991.

References

Abel Alier, *Southern Sudan: Too Many Agreements Dishonoured* (Ithaca, London, 1990).

Africa Watch, *Denying "the Honour of Living": Sudan, a Human Rights Disaster* (London, 1990).

H. Assefa, *Mediation of Civil Wars: Approaches and Strategies in the Sudan Conflict* (Westview, Boulder, 1987).

P. Bechtold, *Politics in Sudan* (Praeger, New York, 1976).

M. O. Beshir, *The Southern Sudan: Background to Conflict* (Hurst, London, 1968).

M. O. Beshir, *The Southern Sudan: From Conflict to Peace* (Hurst, London, 1975).

R. O. Collins, *Shadows in the Grass* (Yale University Press, New Haven, 1983).

M. W. Daley and Ahmed Alawad Sikainga (eds), *Civil War in the Sudan* (British Academic Press, London, 1993).

L. M. Passmore Sanderson and G.N. Sanderson, *Education, Religion and Politics in Southern Sudan, 1889–1964* (Ithaca, London, 1981).

Panos Institute, *War Wounds* (London, 1988).

Peace in Sudan Group, *War in Sudan* (London, 1990).

P. Woodward, *Sudan 1898–1989: The Unstable State* (Lynne Rienner, Boulder/Lester Crook, London, 1990).

D. Johnson, 'North-south Issues', in P. Woodward (ed.), *Sudan after Nimeiri* (SOAS and Routledge, London, 1991).

6· THE CONFLICT IN THE WESTERN SAHARA

George Joffe

On 6 September 1991, a United Nations-sponsored ceasefire came into effect in the disputed territory of the Western Sahara, thereby ending a state of war which had been in existence since early November 1975.[1] Shortly afterwards, a 100-member advance guard of what was eventually to be a 2275-member UN force,[2] known by the acronym MINURSO (United Nations Mission for the Referendum in Western Sahara), moved into place to police the ceasefire throughout the 252,120 square kilometre region.[3] The ceasefire ushered in a UN peace plan which had been accepted by both the Moroccan government and the Western Saharan national liberation movement, the Polisario Front,[4] in mid-1990 and approved by the UN Security Council in Resolution 658/1990. The detailed plan, designed to ensure the organization of a referendum for self-determination among the Western Saharan population, was finally approved on 29 April 1991 and a $200 million budget for its operation was accepted by the UN Security Council on 17 May 1991 as Resolution 690/1991.

The plan involved a heavy reduction of the 160,000-strong Moroccan armed forces (the Forces Armées Royales, FAR) in the disputed territory to 65,000 men under MINURSO surveillance, the confinement of the remaining forces to designated areas, the establishment of Saharan People's Liberation Army (SPLA) camps in pre-arranged localities. There was then to be an exchange of prisoners and, later, a return of Saharan refugees from among the 165,000 persons resident in refugee camps controlled by the Polisario Front around the Algerian border town of Tindouf. Proper voting lists were to be prepared with the agreement of both sides and, after a short electoral campaign, the referendum was to take place in January 1992.[5]

In fact, no referendum had been held by January 1992 and, although the 374-member advance guard for the MINURSO force was in place, little progress had been made on the rest of the UN peace plan. There had been objections from Morocco to the plan before the ceasefire was actually introduced and, once it was in place, other problems surfaced. The MINURSO units were unable to deploy all their forces and had difficulty supplying those who were deployed. Although Morocco released over 200 Sahrawi prisoners, as required by the plan, its armed forces extended their control over the 20 per cent of the Western Sahara which had not been within their defence lines before. This unilateral military action stimulated furious protests from the Polisario Front, since it involved breaches of the ceasefire agreement. MINURSO observers agreed that this was the case, but, by then, there was little that could be done to reverse the situation.

Further difficulties surfaced over the actual voting lists to be used for the referendum process. According to the UN plan, these were to be based on the lists of those recorded in 1974 in the Spanish census of the region, after review by 38 tribal elders – half appointed by Morocco and half by the Polisario Front – in Geneva in June 1990. Problems arose, first because of accusations of attempts by the Polisario Front to falsify the lists in its favour[6] and then because Morocco insisted, in August 1991 just before the ceasefire was due to come into effect, that an additional 120,000 names of persons it claimed originated from the region should be included in the voting lists. At the same time, a further 38,000 Moroccans were hurriedly moved into the Western Sahara, apparently in order to create a demographic 'fact' that would be difficult to eradicate at a later date, whatever the outcome of the referendum would be.[7]

These problems coincided with the end of UN Secretary-General Xavier Perez de Cuellar's tenure of office and, almost as his last official task, the secretary-general compiled a report for the UN Security Council over the difficulties that had arisen. He proposed that the criteria for those eligible to vote should be enlarged to include those who had been intermittently resident in the Western Sahara for a period of 12 consecutive years before December 1974 or continuously resident there for the previous six years, whether or not they were included in the census, or to those whose fathers were born in the region.[8] This would have added, it was estimated, a further 30,000 to 40,000 persons to the lists and would have greatly weighted them in Morocco's favour.

Despite French and American support, the UN Security Council, in a highly unusual move, decided to ask the incoming UN Secretary-General, Dr Boutros Boutros Ghali, to prepare a new report by the end of February 1992.[9] The acceptance of the original report was delayed until the end of 1991, when it was finally adopted over Chinese and Cuban objections, largely because the outgoing secretary-general refused to alter it in any way. Boutros Ghali, in turn, called on Morocco and the Polisario Front to compromise on a solution within three months. Otherwise, he claimed, the whole UN peace-keeping operation would be seriously compromised.[10]

UN difficulties with the referendum plan had actually begun earlier, when computer disks, handed over by the Polisario Front, mysteriously made their way into Moroccan hands. Furthermore, in December 1991, the then UN special envoy to the Western Sahara, Johannes Manz, resigned, to be replaced by a former Pakistani foreign minister, Yaqub Khan, whose appointment was met with considerable suspicion by the Polisario Front. In addition, complaints, both from the Polisario Front and UN observers in the field, of Moroccan violations of the ceasefire began to mount up, while MINURSO members also complained about Moroccan restrictiveness and interference with the group's functions.

By May 1992, despite preliminary discussions in New York under Yaqub Khan, little progress had been made in establishing the compromise sought by the UN secretary-general. As a result, a new three-month extension was granted, accompanied by hints that if the two sides could not come to some agreement, the UN Security Council, which authorized the original MINURSO deployment, would have to find some other type of solution. Morocco, however, was no longer prepared to wait and, on 4 September 1992, included the Western Saharan populations in a long-anticipated referendum on constitutional change in Morocco. The Moroccan government also promised that the Western Sahara would participate in municipal and legislative elections, due in mid-October and in November respectively.

These developments were viewed with considerable dismay in New York, for they meant that, in legal terms at least, Morocco had effectively annexed the Western Sahara. These anxieties paralleled the anger that was growing inside MINURSO towards Moroccan obstructiveness, which had prevented free movement and the appropriate supply of essential stores, and at the apparent indifference of the UN bureaucracy over what was happening. It would probably have been truer to say that there were increasing anxieties in New York that this initiative, legally the most ambitious of UN peace-keeping projects to date,[11] was close to failure and that there appeared to be little that the UN could do to avoid this conclusion. The Polisario Front, meanwhile, has made it clear that it will renew hostilities should the UN peace plan break down.

Algeria, despite its internal problems and its constant advice to the Front to make peace with Morocco, also publicly made it clear in August that it would not stand idly by if hostilities did recur. Nonetheless, it is unlikely that this would precipitate full-scale war between the two North African neighbours, if even relations did cool in the wake of renewed fighting. Algerian leaders have in private repeatedly warned the Front of Algerian neutrality in such circum-stances, while Algeria's domestic problems have relegated the issue of the Western Sahara to the sidelines of Algerian political life. In addition, Morocco has successfully pursued a policy of encouraging desertions from the Front's ranks, which has considerably weakened its military coherence. It is now extremely difficult to see any outcome other than Morocco's formal *de facto* annexation of the region, an annexation which eventually will come to be recognized *de jure*.

These developments are worth following in some detail because they highlight the intractability of the Western Sahara conflict to conventional forms of resolution. The Polisario Front, which has depended on Algerian support for the past 16 years, cannot relinquish its demands for a referendum, even though the Algerian authorities have cooled their support for the Front as their relations with Morocco have improved since diplomatic links were reestablished in May 1988. Morocco, on the other hand, will not relinquish the Western Saharan territory it claims as part of its national territory and which it has occupied since late 1975. Indeed, the Moroccan monarchy probably would not survive any compromise on this issue, given the widespread convictions in Morocco itself that the Western Sahara really is part of Morocco's pre-colonial political heritage. The explanation of these irridentist attitudes is buried in the history of how the conflict actually arose.

Background to the conflict

There is little doubt that the conflict over the Western Sahara is a direct result of the lengthy decolonization process in Africa. Morocco achieved independence in 1956, with decisions, first by France and then by Spain, to relinquish control of their protectorates to the indigenous authorities. These comprised the Moroccan sultanate which, under Mohamed V, had closely collaborated with the Moroccan independence movement, Istiqlal – founded in 1944 – and the various institutions of state control created by the colonial powers but under the authority of the sultanate. These included the armed forces, now renamed the FAR, and the various security and police services. The newly independent Moroccan state also had to contend with the military arm of the independence movement, the *jaysh at-tahrir* (army of liberation), which operated autonomously from Istiqlal. As far as the sultanate was concerned, the *jaysh at-tahrir* was contaminated by radical elements which were not necessarily prepared to collaborate with it in the future.

The new state still had, furthermore, a series of border problems to resolve. Although Spain had abandoned its protectorates of northern Morocco in 1956 and Tarfaya in 1958, it retained control of the Atlantic coastal enclave of Sidi Ifni until 1969 and still retains control of its *presidios* of Ceuta and Melilla on Morocco's Mediterranean coast, which were acquired in the 15th and 16th centuries respectively. Morocco also claimed vast tracts of the Sahara; from the Atlas mountains southwards as far as Timbuktoo and the Niger Bend and from the oasis complexes of Gourara, Touat and the Tidikelt westwards to the Saharan Atlantic coast. The Moroccan government argued that the eastern section of these areas had come under Moroccan control as a result of the Sa'adi dynasty's expansion eastwards in 1526.[12] These territories had then been illegally transferred by French administrative fiat to Algeria between 1912 and 1956.[13] Shortly thereafter, the region southwards to Timbuktoo fell under Sa'adi control as the result of the invasion of Sudan, but was eventually integrated into l'Afrique Occidentale Française, a development which was roundly rejected by the Moroccan nationalist movement.[14] Indeed, until 1969, Morocco refused to recognize

Mauritania as an independent state because of this historical tradition.[15]

The Spanish presence in the Western Sahara

Precisely the same arguments were directed towards Spain's continued presence in the Western Sahara which had formally been proclaimed as a Spanish colony in 1885.[16] The initial occupation there, however, had been confined to the coastal settlement of Villa Cisneros, and Spanish expansion into the interior was not undertaken until 1934, although the actual borders had been set by three Franco–Spanish conventions in 1900, 1904 and 1912.[17] Complete development of the region now claimed by Morocco, however, had really only been undertaken after World War II.

The catalyst for this was the revived Spanish interest in the region's economic potential. The Western Sahara had been transformed from a colonial possession into a Spanish province in 1958, just as such interest began to grow.[18] The result was a growth in employment and educational opportunities for the indigenous population and the consequence of this, in turn, was a sudden and large-scale sedentarization of the Sahrawi population around the new urban centres of El-Aiyun, Bou Craa and Smara, as well as at the earlier Spanish settlements of Villa Cisneros and La Guera. This sedentarization, in turn, had a profound effect on Sahrawi social attitudes and undermined the traditional tribal structure of Sahrawi society. These effects were buttressed by new employment and educational opportunities for the sedentarized population.

At the end of the 1960s, the Spanish authorities provided for a degree of Sahrawi political integration by creating an appointive tribal assembly, the Djemaa, which acted as a consultative body to the executive authorities. It was this process of increased integration into the social and political systems created by Spain that initiated a growing sense of a specifically Saharan identity in place of the earlier traditional tribal loyalties.[19] This, in turn, combined with growing Sahrawi awareness that the Spanish Sahara was now the last European colony on the African continent to generate a nascent Saharan nationalism specifically concerned with independence.

Moroccan links with the region

This development within the Western Sahara, which was predicated on Spanish interest in phosphates, iron ore, oil deposits and marine fishing reserves, coincided with the articulation of Moroccan claims on the Spanish colony. The background to the claims was based in history, specifically in the pattern of interaction between the tribal populations of the Western Sahara (the Tekna, the Reguibat, the Ouled Dlim, the Ouled Tidrarin and the Arosien[20]) and the traditional Moroccan sultanate. By the latter part of the 19th century Moroccan political interests in the Western Sahara revived, in large part because of the sultanate's anxieties over growing European interest, both British and Spanish, in the region. Furthermore, from the Western Sahara itself the sultanate could count on support from the influential Ma al-Aynin family based at Smara and exerting effective control over the Saquiat al-Hamra. This continued through the reigns of Mawlay Hassan I, Mawlay Abd al-Aziz and Mawlay Abd al-Hafidh, with the family increasingly depending on the sultanate for military supplies to resist European advance. By 1912, when the sultan was forced to sign the Treaty of Fes, thus bringing the French Protectorate into being, the Ma al-Aynin family members decided that they would, instead, usurp the sultanate itself, thereby indicating the degree to which they saw the fortunes of the Moroccan sultanate as being part of their own future. The attempt was short-lived but indicated the degree to which there were political and social connections between the two regions.

The nationalist claim

The Protectorate period, of course, profoundly impeded the continuation of such links. The simple creation of administrative boundaries, as the Sahara was distributed among different European administrations, ensured that this would be the result. Nonetheless, they were to become of acute importance to the nationalist movement, once it reformed in 1944, after repeated attempts to repress it during the 1930s. The first sign of this new irridentism was revealed by the veteran Moroccan nationalist, Allal al-Fassi, in a speech on 27 March 1956, and a map indicating the full extent of Istiqlal's claims appeared shortly afterwards in the party's newspaper, *al-Alam*.[21] The claim was espoused officially by Morocco in late 1957 and the sultan, Mohamed V, gave it his personal approval in a speech at the Saharan outpost of M'Hamid in the valley of the Wad Draa on 25 February 1958.

In part, this official approval of Istiqlal's claims on the Western Sahara reflected official relief that the attention of the turbulent *jaysh at-tahrir*, created shortly before independence in northern Morocco to fight for liberation, had been diverted southwards to support nomadic resistance to the Spanish presence in the Western Sahara.[22] Violent opposition to Spain had erupted among the northern nomadic populations in 1956, in emulation of Morocco's success in forcing France to grant independence and involved the Reguibat and the Tekna. It soon provoked a military response from Spain and France which was still in control of the neighbouring territories of the Algerian Sahara and Mauritania.

Eventually, a combined Franco–Spanish operation – the operation of the French possessions of the Algerian Sahara and of Mauritania were also threatened by the nomads and their *jaysh at-tahrir* supporters – code-named 'Operation Ouragan' swept these indigenous forces out of the Western Sahara and into southern Morocco in early 1958. Although members of the *jaysh at-tahrir* were eventually absorbed into the FAR, the defeated nomads had to reestablish themselves in southern Morocco. There they have remained, to become a bone of contention in the process of establishing who should be entitled to vote in the UN-sponsored referendum 34 years later. Their descendants, after all, are those whom Morocco argued should be included in the lists in addition to those originally registered under the Spanish census of the Western Sahara population in 1974.

Moves towards conflict

'Operation Ouragan' effectively ended direct Moroccan interest in the Sahara issue for the next decade and a half. Although Morocco's claim was not abandoned – and pressure was regularly applied on Spain at the United Nations over decolonization of the Western Sahara – in bilateral relations with Spain the issue was not emphasized, particularly once King Hassan II came to power in 1961 and decided to encourage good relations with Spain. At the same time, Morocco continued to seek support inside North Africa for its claim, even if it was not prepared to confront Spain. During negotiations with Algeria's president, Houari Boumedienne, over the Algerian–Moroccan border in 1971–2, for example, the Algerian leader is believed to have acquiesced in a Moroccan and Mauritanian decision to divide the Western Sahara between them, once Spain had withdrawn.[23] Morocco, nonetheless, publicly continued to support the UN principle of self-determination largely because its two partners in this secret understanding insisted on its remaining secret. Nor did the Moroccan government apply pressure on Spain to speed its departure from the disputed territory.

Two different sets of events now interacted to precipitate the final crisis. One of these reflected Moroccan domestic policy, while the other revealed the growth of Sahrawi nationalism and its consequences on Spain's position in the Western Sahara. There was, in addition, the intensifying international pressure on Spain to end its colonial occupation of the Western Sahara – by then almost the last colony left on the African continent.

In the early 1970s the stability of the Moroccan monarchy was increasingly called into question. This unrest erupted in an army-backed coup attempt, when military cadets stormed the king's summer palace at Skhirat, just outside Rabat on the king's birthday on 10 July 1971. Although the attempt failed and those involved were savagely punished, a further attempt to overthrow the monarchy occurred in August 1972 when King Hassan's personal aircraft was attacked by Moroccan fighter aircraft from their base at Kenitra. The conspirators on this occasion were linked to the defence minister and *éminence grise* of the regime, General Oufkir, who committed suicide immediately after the failure of the *attentat* against King Hassan.[24] Although both events could be explained away by simple reference to discontent within the elite structures of the regime, they both reflected far wider issues, as was soon to be made clear. Less than a year later, in March 1973, there was a spate of urban terrorism and an attempted rural rebellion in the Tineghir–Goulmima region of the southern High Atlas mountains.

Although the latter set of incidents were attributed by the government to left-wing dissidents supported by Algeria and linked to Morocco's major left-wing political party, the Union Nationale des Forces Populaires, the royal palace appreciated that the incidents, like the two earlier coup attempts were symptomatic of a deeper social malaise. The fact was that popular support for the monarchy had ebbed seriously during the 12 years since Hassan had come to the throne. There was also widespread social discontent because of worsening economic conditions and the political situation seemed to have reached a stalemate because the political parties were apparently unable to cooperate within the limits on democracy set by the palace. It was against this background that, in mid-1974, King Hassan resolved to bring the Western Saharan issue back to the diplomatic foreground, as a means of trying to rebuild a national consensus in support of his regime.

Quite apart from these domestic considerations, however, there was also a concomitant objective diplomatic reality to which Morocco had to respond. Pressure in the UN had finally convinced the Franquist regime that it could no longer try to hold on to its Western Saharan colony under the fiction that it was now an integral part of Spain without some degree of popular legitimation. As a result, in August 1974 it decided to hold a referendum for self-determination, as required by the UN, in which the Sahrawi population would be offered the choice between continued integration in Spain, with internal regional autonomy, or complete independence.

The Spanish decision had been encouraged by changes inside the Western Sahara itself. After the failure of the Reguibat rebellion in 1958, Sahrawi society had undergone a radical change as a result of the new opportunities for employment and education mentioned above. By the late 1960s, these changes had produced a new nationalist leadership, educated in Morocco and Spain, which began to agitate for independence by building a popular support base for itself within the Western Sahara. Towards the end of 1967 a formal movement called the Harakat at-Tahrir ala-l Saquiat al-Hamra wa-l Wad ad-Dahab (Liberation Organization for the Saquiat al-Hamra and the Wad al-Dahab), was formed by a Reguibi, Mohamed Sidi Ibrahim Bassiri. Although the movement was suppressed after demonstrations in al-Ayyoun in 1970 and its founder disappeared, the stage was now set for the emergence of a more radical national liberation movement, the Polisario Front (Frente Popular para la Liberación de Saguia el-Hamra y Rio de Oro: the Popular Front for the Liberation of the Saquiat al-Hamra and the Rio de Oro).

The Polisario Front was created by a small group of Sahrawi students at Mohamed V University in Rabat under the leadership of Mustapha Sayed El-Ouali between 1971 and 1973. They had originally tried to work though the leftist political spectrum in Morocco but finally decided that they should dedicate their efforts to creating a viable national liberation movement within the Western Sahara itself. By May 1972, after arrests of Sahrawi militants in Tan-Tan, it became clear that the Moroccan authorities were intensely suspicious of the Front and would not tolerate its activities on their territory. As a result, El-Ouali reformed the movement and, at a secret meeting in the Western Sahara close to the Mauritanian mining centre of Zouerate on 10 May 1973, the Polisario Front was formally proclaimed by a small nucleus of ten militants. The movement, which rapidly acquired popular support, began a hit-and-run guerrilla campaign against the Spanish administration and army in the Western Sahara.

The new liberation movement enjoyed a degree of protection in Mauritania, where it was allowed to base itself – although the authorities did not espouse its objective of independence, since they, like Morocco, claimed the Western Sahara as part of Mauritania's post-colonial inheritance. Material support was provided by Libya, and Tripoli became the initial publicity and diplomatic base for the Front. Its activities in the Western Sahara soon began to produce results, with Spain offering internal autonomy in early 1974 to its compliant local assembly, the Djemaa. At the same time, the Spanish authorities tried to create an alternative nationalist movement, the Partido de la Unión Nacional Saharaui (PUNS) – just as Morocco had tried, somewhat earlier, to create the Mouvement de Résistance 'les Hommes Bleus' (MOREHOB). Both movements soon vanished into oblivion in the face of the widespread support within the Western Sahara for the Polisario Front.[25] By late 1974 it had become clear to Spain that it would have to offer the option of independence to the colony because of the success of the Front.

In the face of the new Moroccan diplomatic offensive to 'recover' the region as part of pre-colonial Morocco, Spain argued that there had been no superior political control by another power over the region before it colonized the Western Sahara. Morocco, therefore, had no pre-emptive rights that would obviate the application of the principles of decolonization laid down by the United Nations Charter and UN General Assembly Resolution 1514 (XV) of 1960. These Spain proposed to test in a referendum of self-determination by the Sahrawi-s for either full independence or continued links with Spain. Morocco rejected the Spanish argument and, in the face of Spanish intransigence, suggested at the United Nations that the issue of the decolonization of the Western Sahara should be examined by the International Court of Justice at The Hague, in order to determine whether or not Morocco's claims of pre-colonial sovereignty over the region were justified. As a result, the Court was instructed, on 17 December 1974, under a United Nations General Assembly resolution passed four days earlier, to provide an advisory opinion on two related questions: first, was Western Sahara (Rio de Oro and Sakiet El Hamra) at the time of colonization by Spain a territory belonging to no-one (*terra nullius*)?; if the answer to this were to be in the negative, the second would be to ask what were the legal ties between this territory and the Kingdom of Morocco and the Mauritanian entity?[26]

The conflict itself

As part of the process of countering Spanish proposals for decolonization and eventually, of persuading the United Nations to transfer the issue to the International Court of Justice, Morocco had ensured Mauritanian support by a secret understanding in October 1974 that the Western Sahara should eventually be divided between the two countries. Algeria, meanwhile, had become very worried by the implications of a successful Moroccan recovery of the territory, not least because of the geopolitical implications, but also because of the advantages that an independent Sahara would have for Algiers. Large iron ore deposits at Gara Djebilet, close to Tindouf, remained unexploited because of the difficulty of moving ore to Algeria's smelting plants at Annaba, on the Mediterranean coast. An agreement with Morocco for land transfer to a Moroccan port and onward maritime transport to Annaba had reached a stalemate because of the failure of the two countries to ratify their 1972 border treaty (it was finally ratified only in 1989). The Western Sahara offered another convenient route for the transport of the ore. Algeria would also have benefited from access to Western Saharan phosphate and fishing resources. Algerian President Houari Boumedienne's most acute concern, however, was what it saw as a deliberate Moroccan attempt to circumvent the normal process of decolonization to its own national and geopolitical advantage. As a result, from early 1975, Algeria began to provide assistance to the Polisario Front.[27]

Other countries also began to note the growing crisis in north-west Africa. Morocco was successful in eliciting support from the Arab world, particularly from the conservative monarchies of the Gulf, although Arab radicals, such as Libya and Algeria, opposed its ambitions over the Sahara. Arab motives were mixed: on the one hand, Arab moderates and conservatives were anxious to support a state with similar political assumptions; on the other, there was a general sentiment that the Arab world should avoid political fragmentation, particularly of any new states thus created might align themselves with other radical regimes. In Europe and the USA, there was a common concern to support a government which was seen as a staunch pro-Western ally, although popular opinion, particularly in Spain, was often sympathetic to the Sahrawi case. Washington and Paris, however, were determined to ensure the stability of the Moroccan monarchy and realized that this now depended on its success over the Western Sahara issue.

The crisis finally came to a head in early November 1975, after the International Court of Justice delivered its opinion on 16 October: rather than resolving the issue, this paved the way for conflict. It decided, unanimously, that the Western Sahara had not been *terra nullius* and that by 14 votes to 2 and by 15 votes to 1 there had been legal ties between it and Morocco and Mauritania respectively. However, these ties, according to paragraph 162 of the opinion, did not amount to territorial sovereignty and that, therefore, there was no reason not to apply the principles of self-determination to the decolonization process in the Western Sahara.[28] The Moroccan government seized on the first part of the judgement as justifying its claim and, immediately after the judgement was published, began to organize a massive popular demonstration to take over the Western Sahara. Eventually, up to 524,000 Moroccans volunteered to join the 'Green March', as the operation was code-named, and the Moroccan government, by an impressive feat of logistics, massed 350,000 of them on the borders of the Western Sahara, close to Tarfaya, by the end of the month.[29]

The Spanish authorities were now in a serious quandary over what policy to adopt. On the one hand, Morocco was clearly determined to take over the territory by force: units of the 61,000-strong FAR had already entered the Western Sahara and taken over outlying Spanish posts which had been abandoned after clashes with guerrilla units of the Polisario Front. On the other hand, they were in no doubt over the popularity of the Polisario Front, having witnessed the mass demonstrations in its support during a UN mission in the territory in early May 1975, an attempt to sample popular opinion. The United Nations also had few doubts; indeed, the report of its mission, published the day before the International Court of Justice rendered its opinion on the dispute, had concluded that the majority of the population within the Spanish Sahara was manifestly in favour of independence.[30] However, the situation for the Spanish government was rendered extremely difficult by the fact that the crisis coincided with the onset of Generalissimo Franco's final illness and the consequent succession crisis. Thus, although Spain could have resisted a Moroccan attempt to invade the Western Sahara – despite the international condemnation that would have followed firing on unarmed demonstrators – Spanish domestic politics made this an impossible scenario.

As a result, even before the start of the Green March, the Spanish authorities secretly negotiated an agreement with Morocco and Mauritania in which sole administrative responsibility was ceded to a tripartite temporary administration; responsibility would be shared with Morocco and Mauritania until the end of February 1976, when Spain would finally withdraw. The 'Madrid Accord', as this agreement became known, was notable for one feature, however; although Spain withdrew its administration from the Western Sahara, it did not cede sovereignty over the region to its two partners. There was thus, in theory at least, the possibility that Spain could eventually come to an arrangement with the Polisario Front as its sovereign successor or, at the very least, continue to press for a proper referendum for self-determination in international fora. The Accord represented a pragmatic response by Spain to an increasingly fraught situation at a time when its own domestic stability would not have permitted resolute resistance to Morocco's determination to 'recover' its 'lost territories'.

The Polisario Front, now openly backed by Algeria, was not prepared to make such an accommodation, however. It first organized the evacuation of up to 40,000 Sahrawi-s to three camps established to the south of Tindouf on Algerian territory just over the Western Saharan–Algerian borders.[31] Then, with Algerian backing, it began a determined guerrilla campaign against Moroccan and Mauritanian forces in the Sahara. The Front proclaimed the Saharan Arab Democratic Republic (SADR) on 26 February 1976 – the same day as the tripartite administration in the Western Sahara set up by the Madrid Accord came to an end. The SADR was to act as the diplomatic and administrative arm of the Front, which continued to embody Sahrawi aspirations for national liberation.

The Front's strategy soon became clear; Moroccan forces were kept under a constant threat by a guerrilla campaign, while the major military effort by the Front was directed against the much weaker Mauritanian forces in the southern Wadi ad-Dahab region. By 1978 Mauritania was ready to abandon the struggle, after the Wild Daddah regime had been overthrown by an armed forces coup. However, despite a truce declared by the Polisario Front the Mauritanian government was unable to sign a formal peace because of Moroccan pressure. Eventually, after a brief renewal of hostilities and Algerian mediation, the new government signed a formal peace agreement – the Algiers Agreement – whereby Mauritania renounced all territorial claims on the Western Sahara. Although Moroccan troops stationed in Mauritania were withdrawn, however, they were redeployed in the regions of the Western Sahara originally under Mauritanian control.[32]

Morocco, meanwhile had, become engaged in an ever more costly conflict. Its armed forces were expanded, with 80,000 stationed in the Sahara by 1980 and over 100,000 stationed there by the mid-1980s.[33] Re-equipment of the armed forces between 1987 and 1992 was set at $1 billion. The cost of the conflict also escalated to between $2 million and $5 million a day, with up to 40 per cent of the budget being devoted to defence-related expenditure and the conflict directly costing the equivalent of 14 per cent of national expenditure by 1984.[34] By 1990 it was estimated that the annual cost of the conflict had been around $300 million.[35] Much of the direct impact of these costs had been mitigated by aid from the Arab states of the Gulf, which was estimated to be of the order of $400 million in the mid-1980s. Nonetheless, Morocco's concomitant economic crisis – it had to reschedule its $11 billion foreign debt in 1983 and engage in an IMF-supervised economic restructuring programme which did not end until 1993 with foreign debt by then around $23 billion – made the war extremely difficult to sustain.

These economic burdens were worsened by the actual progress of the conflict. Until 1980 the guerrilla tactics of the Saharan Popular Liberation Army (SPLA), the Polisario Front's military wing, forced the FAR out of its outlying positions and back to the core of Smara, Bou Craa, El-Ayyoun and Villa Cisneros, now renamed Dakhla. Bou Craa and Smara were actually attacked and the all-important 60 km-long phosphate conveyor belt system which took the ore to El-Ayyoun for export was severely damaged. Eventually the Moroccan army developed a system of static defences which gradually enabled it to regain control of 80 per cent of the Western Sahara. These consisted of a series of six sand walls constructed between 1980 and 1987, together with sophisticated warning devices and the pre-positioning of garrisons along their length. Although the SPLA was able to breach the wall system, it was not able to penetrate in depth because of the relative closeness of Moroccan forces. As a result, SPLA offensive military action became more and more concentrated on supplementing the Polisario Front's diplomatic activities.

Indeed, as the SPLA's freedom of military action declined, the SADR gained ever greater recognition. By 1990, 71 states had recognized the SADR as the Sahrawi government-in-exile. In addition, from 1983 onwards, the Polisario Front attended meetings of the Organization of African Unity (OAU) as its 51st member – a development that caused Morocco to boycott formal OAU meetings for the next seven years. Indeed, in 1984 Morocco formally withdrew its membership of the OAU over the issue. The OAU had already endorsed the call for a referendum for self-determination in the territory from 1979 onwards.[36]

This diplomatic success was mitigated, however, by a change in government in Algeria at the end of 1978, when Houari Boumedienne died unexpectedly. After 1980, his successor, Chadli ben Jedid, made it clear that Algeria now expected the Polisario Front to attempt to achieve its objectives through diplomatic channels, rather than by success on the battlefield. This limitation on the Front's freedom of action was increased by the fact that Libya had, since the start of the 1980s, begun to rein in on aid to the SADR. The Libyan change of heart based on Colonel Qadhafi's growing dislike of what he saw as the impending 'Balkanization' of North Africa if the SADR did wrest control of the Western Sahara from Morocco. It was intensified by Libya's growing isolation inside North Africa, particularly from Algeria, which culminated in 1984 in a short-lived federal agreement with Morocco – the Arab-African Union.

Morocco also benefited from Western assumptions about its strategic significance in north-west Africa and the Arab world. Its three most important allies in the developed world – France, Spain and the USA – all concurred in the view that, whatever the outcome of the Western Saharan conflict, the stability of the Moroccan monarchy must not be jeopardized. As a result, France, which had provided direct military support to Mauritania before 1979, ostensibly to protect French nationals working there, particularly in the iron mines at Zouerate, but in reality to aid the Mauritanian government's weak armed forces, continued to be Morocco's major arms supplier. After the collapse of the Shah's regime in Iran in 1979, the Carter administration removed restrictions it had placed on arms sales to Morocco. After 1981, the Reagan administration actively encouraged military aid to Morocco. Spain, for its part, turned away from the sympathetic approach towards the Polisario Front which had characterized the years immediately after the death of Generalissimo Franco,[37] seeing Morocco as a strategic and favoured commercial partner. Even the EEC – despite frequent protests in the European Parliament, where sympathy for the Polisario Front was strong – attempted to adjust to the reality of Moroccan occupation of the Western Sahara. Although European states and the USA still formally encouraged a referendum among the Sahrawi-s for self-determination, in practice they increasingly accepted the *de facto* Moroccan annexation of the region.

Morocco, in its turn, devoted considerable funds to establishing its presence in the Sahara. Military and administrative personnel were lured there by high salaries and special privileges. Official development funds of around $100 million were invested in expanding existing towns and developing the region's limited resources. Two loan issues on the private capital market in Morocco were also raised and heavily over-subscribed.[38] One, in March 1985, raised $45 million. Migrants from Morocco itself swelled the population which rose from its 1974 figure of around 74,000, according to the Spanish census carried out in that year, to 162,000 according to the Moroccan census of 1981. El-Ayyoun itself, now renamed Layyoun, expanded to a population of 90,000.[39] Ambitious plans were proposed to exploit the region's tourist potential once the conflict was ended, and foreign companies, including Club Méditerranée, moved into the nascent industry.

By 1987 Morocco felt sufficiently confident of its position in the Western Sahara to be prepared to consider a mediated solution to the conflict. A UN mission visited the region in December and November 1987 to see whether a peace plan could be organized. During 1988 relations inside North Africa improved, with Morocco and Algeria renewing diplomatic relations, which had been broken off in May 1976. At the same time the five North African heads of state attempted to find an acceptable solution to the dispute and, in the aftermath of the meeting, King Hassan accepted the idea of a referendum. The idea gathered momentum in February 1976 with the creation of a regional confederation, the Union Maghreb Arabe (UMA), and as a result of UN mediation which led eventually to direct contacts between the Polisario Front and Morocco. Fighting in the Western Sahara died down, although sporadic outbursts still occurred. This was largely because Algeria, by now in the throes of a serious economic crisis resulting from the collapse of oil prices in 1986 and savage countrywide riots in October 1988, was anxious to avoid any further disruption of the North African scene.

In 1990 these moves towards a UN-sponsored peace plan intensified. The Polisario Front had declared a unilateral truce in November 1988 as a gesture of goodwill and, no doubt, as a result of Algerian pressure. Although it was broken several times thereafter, these moves towards reconciliation followed on from calls for direct contacts between Morocco and the Polisario Front as part of an eventual sponsored peace process, first from the UN in 1985 and thereafter from the OAU and North African states. Although there had been infrequent secret contacts between them, it was only in 1989 that formal contacts were made. Morocco, meanwhile, had begun a policy of reconciliation by encouraging desertions from the Polisario Front, which eventually involved one of the founder members, Omar Hadrami. Nonetheless, the bulk of the movement held firm, insisting on the long-sought referendum for self-determination. It is difficult to avoid the conclusion, however, that Morocco has been able to create conditions favouring a solution of the conflict along the lines it seeks and that the referendum is, as King Hassan has made clear, merely a device to legitimize Morocco's annexation of the Western Sahara.

The justification

It is undeniable, however, that this dispute has not simply been the result of the cynical imposition of the Moroccan government's will on a small, relatively defenseless Sahara community. There is little doubt that the vast majority of Moroccans have actively supported Morocco's claims to the Western Sahara. There is equally little doubt that the vast majority of Sahrawi-s have, equally fervently, demanded self-determination and independence. This contradiction in attitudes bears examining because it throws considerable light on why Morocco has been successful in pursuing its claim to the Western Sahara, despite the obvious economic, social and political costs.

The Sahrawi case is simple. The population of the Western Sahara has demonstrated by its resistance, first to Spanish and then to Moroccan occupation, that it is a 'people', in the words of the United Nations Charter.[40] The term 'people' here corresponds to the definition of a 'nation' or national community: a distinct ethnic group which is a homogeneous community, not only culturally homogeneous but culturally distinct from any other community.[41] In such a circumstance, the United Nations Charter endows such a group with the rights of self-determination over its form of government and state structure, a right which is reinforced by UN General Assembly Resolution 1514 (XV) of December 1960 which amplifies the details of Article 73 of the United Nations Charter. The result is that the process of decolonization involves an act of self-determination by the Sahrawi-s as a former colonial people. This should then result in the selection of one of three options: independence, integration into an existing state or association with an existing state.[42] This is, after all, precisely what the Polisario Front has been demanding since 1975 and what Algeria argued before the International Court of Justice in its intervention in the Western Sahara case in 1974–5.[43] Of course, since 1973, the Polisario Front has also constructed a historical pedigree for Sahrawi nationalism stretching back to the Almoravids in the 11th century. In many respects, this national history has, as is the case with all nationalist histories, the quality of myth for, even if it is historically accurate, its purpose is not the dispassionate analysis of historical events but the justification of the claim to national identity.[44]

The Moroccan case is more complex. Formally, at least, it too depends on the United Nations Charter and UN General Assembly Resolution 1514 (XV) of December 1960. Paragraph 6 of the resolution provides that referenda for self-determination must not disrupt the territorial unity of any state that existed as such before the colonial period began. Indeed, Moroccan sensitivity on this point – which reflects anxiety over large sections of Algeria annexed from Moroccan control by French administrative measures as well as the question of Western Sahara – prevented it from subscribing to the 1964 OAU Cairo Declaration which established the inviolability of colonial frontiers in Africa.[45] In Moroccan eyes, therefore, the Western Sahara was part of its pre-colonial state territory and thus cannot be alienated by a referendum for self-determination that includes independence as one of its possible objectives. It was on this basis, after all, that King Hassan objected to Spanish proposals for a referendum in 1974 and it was also on this basis that he agreed to a referendum supervised by the United Nations which, as far as Morocco was concerned, would merely confirm Morocco's recovery of its territory.

This conclusion, however, flies in the face of the decision of the International Court of Justice, when it rendered its advisory opinion in October 1975. The Court, after all, decided that, although there were legal ties between the Western Sahara and Morocco at the time of Spain's declaration of its colonial claim in 1885, these did not amount to ties of territorial sovereignty. Morocco, however, claimed that the opinion supported its contention, a claim that was backed up with mass support inside Morocco which has been sustained ever since.[46] The key to this apparent conundrum lies in the way in which the Moroccan claim was originally formulated and to the original nature of the Moroccan state.

The pre-colonial Moroccan state can legitimately claim historical continuity reaching back to the foundation of Fes in the early 9th century under Idriss II. However, that state bore little resemblance to the concept of the modern nation-state that developed in Europe after the Augsburg Compromise in 1555 and the French Revolution 234 years later. Instead of being based on the concept of state sovereignty over a specific territory, legitimized by the consent of a national community which inhabited the state, the pre-colonial Moroccan state was typified by its legitimization through Islamic constitutional precept and expressed through communal sovereignty. The ruler of the state, the sultan, who was also 'commander of the faithful' and thus embodied both temporal and spiritual power, could rule by communal consent only if he maintained a proper temporal order for the correct practice of Islam. Conversely, the extent of his power was not merely expressed through his coercive and fiscal power but also by the readiness of individual communities to recognize his authority.[47]

It was for this reason that Morocco claimed sovereign rights before the International Court of Justice, arguing, *inter alia*, that the role of the Ma al-Ainin family and the general recognition of the sultan's status in Friday prayers throughout the region indicated that Moroccan sovereignty was accepted in pre-colonial times by the local Sahrawi population. The argument went further, however, for by sovereignty Morocco meant *territorial* sovereignty and it was this element that the Court refused to accept in its opinion. Yet, Morocco was bound to argue such a case, once its independent and sovereign existence as a pre-colonial state was accepted.

The reason for this lies in the nature of the colonial experience in Morocco – and elsewhere in Africa and Asia. The modern and independent Moroccan state derives its legitimacy both from its historical past and from its reformulation during the colonial period as a state which seeks legitimacy in a world of nation-states as a nation-state, as required by the United Nations Charter. Yet, as we have seen, pre-colonial legitimacy did not arise from the concept of a Moroccan 'nation'. This concept arises directly from the nature of the struggle for independence, when the independence movement, Istiqlal, in formulating its demand to present to France for independ-ence, necessarily used a European-style political vocabulary – even though, at the same time, it addressed its indigenous power-base in more traditionalist and Islamic constitutional terms. The result was that the newly independent Moroccan state in 1956 no longer conceived of itself simply as an Islamic state re-created but as a state with a territorial definition. Inevitably, therefore, it articulated its arguments over its pre-colonial existence and extent in terms that reflected its colonial experience – and claims over sovereignty had, perforce, to be expressed in terms of territorial sovereignty.

Against this background, it is hardly surprising that the Moroccan government should have sought so hard to justify its claim to territorial sovereignty, and that the Polisario Front should have struggled even more strongly to resist it. Nor is it surprising that King Hassan's government should have found such a strong and favourable public response for its claim to the Western Sahara; nor, indeed, that that public support should have been sustained during the past 17 years. Nor, finally, is it surprising that Morocco cannot compromise on its basic sovereignty claim, if the Alawite monarchy wishes to survive. Once sovereignty is granted, then Morocco may well prove to be flexible over the final constitution to be adopted for the Western Sahara – from full integration to decentralization along the pattern of the German *Länder* system, for example. Sovereignty, however, is the ultimate prize both for the Polisario Front and for Morocco. Whether it is to be obtained without further conflict depends on the degree to which the United Nations and Algeria can bring themselves to acquiesce in Morocco's victory.

Notes

1 Seddon D., 'Briefing: Western Sahara Tug-of-War', *Review of African Political Economy*, 52 (November 1991), p. 112.
2 Staff Report to the Committee on Foreign Relations of the United States Senate, *The Western Sahara: The Referendum Process in Danger*, US

Government Printing Office (1992), p. 15. By January 1992 there were 374 MINURSO personnel in position, including 198 military observers.

3 For general information over the Western Sahara, see Thompson V. and Adloff R., *The Western Saharans*, Croom Helm (London, 1980) or Anon, 'The Western Sahara', in Mostyn T. and Hourani A. (eds), *The Cambridge Encyclopaedia of the Middle East and North Africa*, CUP (Cambridge, 1988), pp. 451–3.

4 The Polisario Front is the political wing of the Sahrawi government-in-exile, the Saharan Arab Democratic Republic, whose military wing is the Saharan Popular Liberation Army.

5 Seddon D., op. cit., p. 110.

6 *Financial Times*, 6.11.1991.

7 See Seddon, op. cit., pp. 110–13.

8 *Le Monde*, 18.11.1991.

9 *The Guardian*, 6.1.1992.

10 *Le Monde*, 4.3.1992.

11 Chopra J., 'The Absence of War and Peace in the Western Sahara', *Testimony before the Committee on Foreign Relations of the United States Senate; Sub-Committee on African Affairs: Hearing on 'UN Peacekeeping in Africa: the Western Sahara and Somalia'*, 1 October 1992, pp. 30–32.

12 Abun Nasr J., *A History of the Maghrib in the Islamic Period*, CUP (Cambridge, 1987), pp. 214–17.

13 Joffe E. G. H., 'Frontiers in North Africa', in Blake G. and Schofield R., *Boundaries and State Territory in the Middle East and North Africa*, Menas Press (Wisbech, 1987), pp. 40–43.

14 See Maazouzi M., *L'Algerie et les etapes successives de l'amputation du territoire Marocain*, Dar El-Kitab (Casablanca, 1976).

15 Thompson V. and Adloff R., op. cit., pp. 52–3.

16 The original declaration is given in Brownlie I., *African Boundaries: A Legal and Diplomatic Encyclopaedia*, RIIA (London, 1979), pp. 438.

17 Hodges T. (1982), 'Introduction', *Historical Dictionary of Western Sahara*, Scarecrow Press (London), p. 6.

18 An insight to the impoverished status of the Western Saharan colony until then is given by Tony Hodges, 'The Western Sahara File', *Third World Quarterly*, 6, 1 (January 1984), p. 81.

19 Hodges T. (1983), *Western Sahara: Roots of a Desert War*, Laurence Hill & Co. (Westport, CT), p. 151.

20 See Hodges (1984), op. cit., p. 78; Hodges (1982), op. cit., 'Tribes'; and Hart D. M. (1962), 'The Social Structure of the Rgibat Bedouins of the Western Sahara', *Middle East Journal*, 16, 4 (Autumn 1962) for details of tribal structures in the region. The classic study is Caro Baroja J. (1955), *Estudios Saharianos*, Consejo Superior de Investigaciones Científicas, Instituto de Estudios Africanos (Madrid).

21 Fessard de Foucault B. (1975), 'La question du Sahara espagnol', *Revue française d'études politiques africaines*, 10 (November 1975), p. 78.

22 Large elements of the *jaysh at-tahrir* were incorporated into the new Moroccan armed forces under the Crown Prince, Mawlay Hassan. However, many partisan leaders, particularly in southern Morocco,

resented the compromises that the newly independent government had made, including allowing French troops to remain in the country. They sought a new field for operations outside the control of the new Moroccan authorities – the Western Sahara was the obvious target (Hodges (1983), op. cit. pp. 72–7). The parallel with the situation under Mawlay Hassan I is difficult to avoid!

23 Hodges (1983), op. cit., pp. 116–17.
24 There is some doubt over whether he actually committed suicide, see Perrault G., *Notre ami, le Roi*, Gallimard (Paris, 1990), pp. 163–73.
25 By far the best description of the development of the Polisario Front is given in Hodges, op. cit. (1983), pp. 149–72.
26 International Court of Justice (ICJ), *Western Sahara Case: Advisory Opinion of 16 October 1975* (The Hague), p. 14.
27 Hodges, op. cit. (1984), p. 96.
28 ICJ, op. cit., pp. 60–1.
29 Hodges, op. cit. (1983), p. 211.
30 Report of the United Nations Visiting Mission to Spanish Sahara 1975, *General Assembly Official Records*, 30th Session, Supplement 23, UN Document A/10023/Rev.1, p. 66.
31 These camps have been vastly expanded in recent years and now house up to 170,000 persons – although not all of them may really have originated from the Western Sahara. They are totally dependent on UN and Algerian humanitarian aid.
32 Seddon D., "Morocco and the Western Sahara", *Review of African Political Economy*, 38 (1987), p. 27.
33 Nonetheless, dissension within the armed forces appears to have continued and the Moroccan commander in the Sahara, General Dlimi, died in a mysterious road accident in Marrakesh in January 1983. Some sources claimed that was the result of an unsuccessful coup attempt. (Seddon, op. cit. (1987), p. 42).
34 Ibid., pp. 28–9.
35 Richards A. and Waterbury J., *A Political Economy of the Middle East: State, Class and Economic Development*, Westview Press (Boulder, 1990), pp. 210.
36 Seddon, op. cit. (1987), p. 32.
37 The Polisario Front representative in Madrid was expelled in September 1985, after the SPLA attacked a Spanish trawler off the Western Saharan coast and killed two Spanish fishermen. Seddon, op. cit. (1987), p. 35.
38 Joffe E. G. H., 'The Political Economy of Privatisation in Morocco', *Morocco*, 1 (1991), p. 63.
39 Centre d'Etudes et des Recherches Démographiques, Situation démographique régionale au Maroc: Analyses comparatives, Ministère du Plan (Rabat, 1988), pp. 248–57.
40 See the preamble to the Charter: 'We the peoples of the United Nations . . .' and Article 1.2, in which one of the purposes of the United Nations is stated as being 'to develop friendly relations among nations based on respect for the principle of equal rights and self-determination of peoples'.

41 Smith A. D., *Nationalism in the Twentieth Century*, Martin Robertson (Oxford, 1979), pp. 2–4.

42 Joffe E. G. H., 'Self-determination and *uti possidetis*: the Western Sahara and the "Lost Provinces" ', in Beschorner N., Gould St. J. and McLachlan K. S. (eds), *Sovereignty, Territoriality and International Boundaries in South Asia, South West Asia and the Mediterranean Basin*, Geopolitics and International Boundaries Research Centre, School of Oriental and African Studies (London, 1991), p. 22.

43 Mohamed Bedjaoui, ICJ, *Western Sahara Case*, Vol. 4, p. 497, and Vol. V, pp. 319 and 502, 1975.

44 Joffe E. G. H., 'The International Court of Justice and the Western Sahara Dispute', in Lawless R. and Monahan L. (eds), *War and Refugees: the Western Sahara conflict*, Pinter (London, 1987), p. 23.

45 Joffe, op. cit. (1991), pp. 22–3.

46 Open opposition to the government's claim to the Western Sahara has been very small, being confined to one faction of the clandestine leftist Front Progressiste – Ilal Aman. Undoubtedly, the severity of the government's reaction to such opposition will have discouraged many other potential protesters. Yet, the vast majority of observers concur that there is still massive support for the government's claim, even if, after 17 years of conflict, there are some who wonder whether the sacrifices that have been made are really justified.

47 These concepts are discussed in detail in Joffe, op. cit. (1978), pp. 16–30.

7· REBELLION IN LIBERIA AND SIERRA LEONE: A CRISIS OF YOUTH?

Paul Richards

The linked West African crises of civil war in Liberia and insurgency in Sierra Leone share a number of features with the better-documented conflicts in Somalia, Mozambique, Angola and southern Sudan: notably, the weakness of the state and traditional sources of authority within civil society, the emergence of warlords as key political actors, and the deployment of large numbers of juvenile conscripts in the fighting. Three of these low-intensity African conflicts (van Creveld 1992) might be considered, primarily, marginal products of the Cold War and its aftermath (Somalia, a state with no pre-colonial roots, ruled by a clique kept in power by US–Soviet rivalry in the Indian Ocean; Angola and Mozambique, theatres of Cold War conflict, with the added complication of South African involvement). The fourth example – conflict in Sudan – is generally seen in terms of a struggle between competing cultures and religious ideologies. Liberia and Sierra Leone, however, were largely untouched by Cold War politics and South African intrigue, and are part of a region of Africa noted historically for cultural syncretism and accommodation among world religions. Conflict in Liberia and Sierra Leone requires to be considered from a more exclusively African perspective (Young 1990; Wilson 1992).[1]

Perhaps it is because of the need for a focus on local political culture in their interpretation that the events described below attracted relatively little international press analysis.[2] British newspapers at times printed pictures arising out of the Liberian civil war without any accompanying story. The Independent (date; Saturday Review section) produced a full-page colour photograph of Nigerian peace-keeping troops negotiating a temporary ceasefire, armed with toys and sweets to entice the pre-teenage rebels. Other press images have included pictures of a hooded guerrilla looting a large white teddy bear from a Monrovia shop, a woman rebel fighter in elegant head tie, gold earrings and necklace, cradling an AK-47 with spare ammunition clips carefully taped in place ready for battle, and boy soldiers from various Liberian factions stripped for Kung Fu combat or dressed in horror comic masks or women's dresses. It is as if picture editors were unable to resist images that were otherwise bizarre beyond explanation to a European audience.

It would be a mistake, however, to regard warfare in Liberia and Sierra Leone as no more than an obscure post-colonial African 'tribal' conflict. The absence of religious conflict or a background of superpower rivalry directs attention to a mix of factors linking wilderness, minerals and youth with quite broad future implications for Africa as a whole, and for international policies towards Africa. In both countries conflict was triggered by small groups of rebels aiming, under the influence of Libyan revolutionary populism, to overthrow entrenched and corrupt regimes. The two conflicts quickly escaped control by their prime instigators. Continuation then depended to a large extent on two sets of factors: first, a struggle (influenced by Senegambian, Guinean, French, Ivoirian, Lebanese and local business rivalries) to control a range of valuable wilderness resources (mainly diamonds, gold, other minerals and tropical timber); and second, the fate of a youth constituency, recruited to the rebel cause following the near-collapse of two state systems upon which it had earlier depended for education and employment.

Realignment of trade and command over mineral and forest resources dominate accounts of the Liberian struggle, though sometimes 'displaced' as ethnic rivalry. Anthropologists have long argued that 'ethnicity' is a key resource for the organization of trading diasporas in West Africa, so it should be no surprise that competition to control trading network opportunities frequently presents itself as 'ethnic conflict'. But since control of diamonds and forest resources are without doubt factors in the politics of rebellion in Sierra Leone it is of some interest to discover the rather muted role of ethnicity in this second struggle. Closer comparative examination of the Sierra Leonean and Liberian data suggests the potential if neglected importance of the political culture of youth as a key to understanding the spread of endemic low-intensity warfare in both countries.

As notes of economic opportunity in a recessionary landscape, the wilderness economies of interior Liberia and eastern Sierra Leone, dominated by tropical timber and diamonds, and threaded through by networks of clandestine trade, provide employment and hope for significant numbers of potentially dissident, part-educated, rural youths modernized by exposure to international media, and alienated from the state by the collapse of educational and formal-sector employment opportunities. Young people in the region treat media violence (e.g. Kung Fu films, CNN footage of the Gulf War) as a drama in which they read significant messages about their under-utilized and unrecognized powers of inventiveness and daring (Richards 1994, cf. Morgan 1994). These films are inspiration for a youth political culture required to address the paradoxes of peripheral modernity, physical hardships associated with exploitation of forest resources, and the violence of diamond mining. Rambo is a hero figure not far removed from the violent, amoral, forest-going trickster of Mende tradition, Musa Wo (cf. Cosentino 1989).

Local interpretations of media violence serve as a prop to dreams of youth empowerment; rebel strategists sought to play upon this enthusiasm – early in the Liberian civil war a relief worker in Gbarnga, Liberia, reported on the BBC Africa Service that five video parlours ran films of violence 24 hours a day for young rebel recruits – and to transform these dreams into reality with weapons and supplies of confidence-boosting drugs. 'Crack' cocaine, it has been alleged, helped turn children playing with guns into fearsome warriors, with bizarre and terrifying results. Teenage and pre-teenage rebels took part in massacres attired as if acting out scenes in a Rambo or Bruce Lee film. Subsequently, these underage combatants found out that they had been ensnared in violence from which there was no turning back, cut off by a burden of atrocities from the civil communities to which formerly they had been attached.[3]

Rebel commanders in Liberia and Sierra Leone seemingly retained little control over the tiger they had chosen to ride. Other parties found they could just as easily play the youth card, and rival factions and movements proliferated, using very similar recruitment and mobilization procedures. There was then little sense or safety for these youngsters in turning back, even when their leaders sought compromise or were driven from the scene. In some cases, orthodox soldiers and local village communities came to regard these teenage and pre-teenage warrior recruits as only dubiously human. In some cases they were hunted down and killed as a standing threat to the very idea of society; locally, I heard the view expressed from time to time that these young warriors would indelibly retain the marks of their rebel initiation in the forest into an alien social order (that they had been drugged with rebel 'medicine' for which there was no antidote). In such circumstances, bands of armed youngsters perhaps concluded that their best hope was to continue to live off their wits and the land, under commanders of their own choice, and to offer their service to any interested business backer of aspiring political faction with an eye for trouble. The long-protracted peace negotiations in Liberia and the continuation of fighting in Sierra Leone is probably best explained not by the intransigence of rebel leaders but the internal incoherence of their movements. Two projects to capture and reform the state having been shelved, 'business as usual' has probably already returned to the diamond districts and tropical rain forests of Sierra Leone and Liberia, but now adjusted to a greatly increased norm of youth violence.

Two rebellions: background and basis for comparison

National Patriotic Front of Liberia

A small group of about 100 to 150 commandos (mainly Liberians, but assisted by Burkinabes and Sierra Leoneans, trained, according to some accounts, in guerrilla camps in Benghazi and Burkina Faso) infiltrated Nimba County in north-east Liberia from Côte d'Ivoire on 24 December 1989, to launch a military campaign against the government of Samuel Doe. This was the nucleus of the National Patriotic Front of Liberia (NPFL). A comparable group, the Revolutionary United Front (RUF), this time led by Sierra Leoneans who had earlier fought with the NPFL, assisted by Burkinabe mercenaries and NPFL military personnel, crossed the eastern border of Sierra Leone from territory controlled by the NPFL on 23 March 1991. Once launched on their offensives in remote regions, on the periphery of states weakened by ethnic rivalry (in the case of Liberia) and by economic mismanagement (in the case of Sierra Leone), these two dissident groups sought to establish a mass base by recruiting large numbers of local youths under the flag of ethnic allegiance.

The NPFL transition from a small insurrection to local mass movement was greatly assisted by Doe's reaction to the first news of rebel activity in Nimba County. Doe assumed the NPFL incursion was a resumption of the attempted coup in 1985 by Nimba County elements in the Armed Forces of Liberia (AFL). This coup attempt had been led by Doe's erstwhile army commander, the late Thomas Quiwonkpa, a Gio from Nimba County. Government troops directed violence against civilian communities in Nimba County without discrimination or restraint; entire villages were burnt and their populations massacred. Youngsters who escaped quickly rallied to the NPFL. Thereafter, the NPFL represented itself, internationally, as the champion of the Mano and Gio (Dan) peoples of Nimba County threatened by Doe's undoubted ethnocidal brutality.

Although the NPFL sought to support the Nimba County people against Doe it cannot be considered an 'ethnic' movement in origin. The original guerrilla contingent was ethnically mixed, trained in Libya, and shaped by Libyan revolutionary ideals. Commandos from Burkina Faso and some Sierra Leonean dissidents who were later to regroup under the banner of the RUF, fought alongside political exiles from Doe, and former AFL soldiers driven from Liberia by the purge of Quiwonkpa supporters.

NPFL leader Charles Taylor claims mixed Americo-Liberian and Gola (some say Vai) descent. Unlike Quiwonkpa, Taylor is a highly educated man, trained as an economist in the USA. He was once director of the government procurement agency under Doe, but fled to the USA in 1983 to avoid being tried for embezzlement.[4] He was later arrested by the American authorities, and escaped jail while awaiting extradition to Liberia. He lived in exile in Ghana, but was twice briefly incarcerated by the Ghanaian authorities. This he blamed on machinations by other exiles associated with the Liberian People's Party, and allegedly is the root of his subsequent antipathy to Amos Sawyer as interim president of Liberia. According to Tarr (1993), Taylor approached the embassy of Burkina Faso in 1987 for assistance to overthrow Doe, where his request was received by the Burkinabe ambassador to Ghana, Mme Mamouna Qattara, a client of Captain Blaise Compaore. At the time Ghanaian leader Jerry Rawlings was attempting to mediate a quarrel between Burkinabe leader Thomas Sankara and his deputy Compaore. Compaore, visiting Accra, requested Taylor be released into his custody, a step Rawlings found preferable to handling over Taylor to Doe or the American authorities. Not long afterwards Compaore mounted a successful coup against Sankara (with the help, it is rumoured, of

Liberian dissidents already trained in Libya) and subsequently introduced Taylor to the Libyans (Tarr 1993).

A skill demagogue, with a talent for media presentation, Taylor claimed leadership of the NPFL on grounds of a commitment to democracy.[5] The extent of his popular support is hard to assess. It would be hazardous to project the potential democratic appeal of any factional leader in a war in which all parties have routinely deployed, or tolerated the use of, terror against civilian populations (Ruiz 1992).

The Revolutionary United Front
The RUF incursion into Sierra Leone was modelled on the NPFL incursion into Nimba County. A two-pronged attack from NPFL-controlled territory in Liberia was launched at the end of March 1991. It was aimed at potentially dissident populations in inaccessible border regions in Pujehun and Kailahun Districts.

Rebel misinformation prompted the All People's Congress (APC) government of President Momoh to believe that this was an uprising of the Mende people. Eyewitnesses say villagers were ordered at gunpoint to wave palm fronds (the symbol of the Mende-dominated Sierra Leone People's Party [SLPP] proscribed in 1977 when a one-party constitution was introduced) and shout in favour of multi-party democracy. In the main these appeals to ethnic solidarity appear to have been treated by local populations with scepticism (the Momoh government had just authorized a resumption of multi-party democ-racy, and the real SLPP was in the process of being revived); the intent of the rebels would seem to have been to provoke from Momoh the same kind of intemperate overreaction against local civilian populations that had served to recruit youth to the NPFL cause in Liberia. This did not happen. The APC paramilitary forces (the only potential opposition to the rebels at the time, since the regular army had long been kept short of arms and ammunition for fear of an anti-APC coup) retreated in the fact of an intense campaign of rumours mounted by the rebels.

Local populations, defenceless against rebel advance, bore the brunt of terroristic violence. Young people were forced to join the rebels at gunpoint, or were shot for running away. There were bizarre public executions of local merchants, minor government functionaries and recalcitrant chiefs, in which at times local youthful conscripts were forced to take part (Wilson 1992). These executions seemed to owe something to methods used earlier by Renamo in Mozambique.

But lacking an APC response equivalent to Doe's barbaric misadventure in Nimba County, terroristic violence targeted against local (and often respected) government functionaries proved counter-productive, serving severely to undermine the RUF's credentials to political reform. Victims were local people, and the government functionaries picked out for intimidation and execution were often far from being the hated 'fat cats' that RUF strategists perhaps had in mind. Even if not always highly regarded for their work, extension agents and dispensary attendants struggling to survive, without regular salary payments for months on end, were more likely to be seen as victims of APC incompetence than agents of APC oppression. All this implies considerable miscalculation, or lack of familiarity with current conditions 'on the ground' on the part of the RUF.

The leader of the RUF, Foday Sankoh, is a former corporal in the Sierra Leonean army imprisoned for alleged involvement in an attempted coup against Siaka Stevens in 1969. Sankoh's animus against the government of President Momoh is said by some to stem from brutal treatment received in prison. Others speak of his determination to settle accounts for being made the stooge for a rebellion against Stevens in which other more senior figures in the army escaped blame. He is thought to be from Makeni in North Sierra Leone, but some believe him to be a Loko.[6] After his release Sankoh ran photographic studios in Bo, the capital of the diamond areas of central Sierra Leone, and Segbwema, a town in the central part of Kailahun District close to the Liberian border. This gave him considerable knowledge of the diamond-rich terrain and a wide range of local contacts. The fact that he was well known in the region may not have been altogether to his advantage, since few of his former contacts rated him a credible equivalent of Charles Taylor. The persistent popular view in central and eastern Sierra Leone was that he was no more than Taylor's agent. The RUF's greatest problem was to establish that it was more than a diversionary 'front' for the Taylor faction in Liberia.

The guerrillas directing military operations for the RUF appear to have comprised two distinct groups. The first (and perhaps larger) element was made up of NPFL fighters 'on loan' from Taylor and a contingent of Burkinabe mercenaries (Sierra Leonean military sources reckoned 'at least 50' in the Pujehun sector alone). The second element – less 'visible' in eyewitness accounts of the incursion, and perhaps depleted by defections once the counter-productive impact of rebel terror against local communities became apparent – comprised Sierra Leoneans with a background either as student dissidents exiled for their opposition in 1977 to the late president Siaka Stevens or as fugitives from the rough justice of the Sierra Leonean diamond fields. Some of these Sierra Leoneans were judged by their accents to have been long resident in Liberia. Other Sierra Leoneans may have been recruited overseas; credit cards and identification abandoned after the rebels were driven out of Pujehun in August 1991 indicated a middle-class background in the USA for at least one rebel commander.

As with the NPFL, there is no evidence that ethnic loyalty was a factor in recruitment; all parts of Sierra Leone seem to have been represented in the RUF. Again, training appears to have been provided by the Libyans in Benghazi, and perhaps also by the Burkinabes (the existence of any such facility in Burkina Faso is hotly denied by President Compaore). It is alleged that Sankoh, and the other Sierra Leoneans, fought alongside Taylor's troops in the NPFL incursion into Liberia, in return for promises of assistance from Taylor when the time was ripe for the RUF bid to invade Sierra Leone.

Systematic comparison of the fortunes of the NPFL and RUF is an attractive analytic proposition. Here are two rebellions, constructed along similar lines, sharing personnel, and operating in broadly similar cultural and social environments, but with sharply divergent fortunes in terms of their local reception. Beneath the accretions of subsequent events, notably NPFL's rapid reincarnation as an 'ethnic uprising', it is possible to gain some sense of the shared background of the two movements. Ethnic tension is then seen as an *opportunity for*, rather than as a *cause of*, rebellion in Liberia and Sierra Leone. The roots of the present violence (I argue) more plausibly lie in attempts to capitalize upon youth alienation beyond the retrenched margins of two African states blighted by recession and political mismanagement

The NPFL campaign in Liberia

The seeds of the NPFL rebellion were laid in the coup of 12 April 1980 that brought Samuel Doe to power. This coup was widely seen as the revenge of the rural Liberians against the long-entrenched rule of an Americo-Liberian elite opposed to the interests of the indigenous peoples of the interior. In some accounts, the Doe regime, resulting from the coup, was in large part an alliance between some of the least advantaged, and least educated, ethnic groups in rural Liberia – the Mano, the Gio and the Krahn. There was apparently later a falling-out between two factions – the Gio–Mano group from Nimba County and Doe's own Krahn group, who it was alleged had the lion's share of the spoils of office. One of the original coup makers, Corporal (later General) Thomas Quiwonkpa – a Gio associate of Doe in the 1980 coup – was dismissed as army commander in 1983. On 12 November 1985, one month after an election, widely judged to have been heavily rigged, Doe survived a coup attempt and executed Quiwonkpa as its instigator. Various accounts circulate of shocking treatment meted out to Quiwonkpa's mutilated body. According to Kieh (1989) some 4000 Quiwonkpa supporters (mainly Mano and Gio) were massacred by vengeful members of the AFL. A number of Mano and Gio soldiers in the AFL fled the country, to re-enter the country four years later as part of the NPFL incursionary force.

With good reason, then, Doe feared that Nimba County might be the source of further coup attempts. It appears that one Nimba-based group, aiming to avenge the events just described, planned to make an assassination attempt on the president while he was *en route* to Krahn country. This home visit, to celebrate his birthday, was a crucial opportunity for the plotters, because Doe paid meticulous attention to his security and rarely travelled out of town. The plans are said to have been discovered by two Mandingo traders. Seized by the plotters, the traders sued for their lives, but later broke a promise of silence and warned the president of his danger. The Mandingo merchant community was close to Doe and assisted the president in a number of his business ventures. Locally, the story of the exposure of the assassination plan is cited to account for NPFL ethnocide against the Liberian Mandingo. But there are good reasons (developed in more detail below) for concluding that NPFL anti-Mandingo sentiment has deeper and less circumstantial roots, related to the struggle to control the clandestine economies of the region. This point has become obscured by the general level of ethnic violence in Liberia, and becomes clearer only from systematic comparison of NPFL and RUF strategies in the field.

Some Liberians think that Doe led a charmed life because he was protected by strong magic, some of it supplied by Mandingo sorcerers in return for business favours. His relative longevity as president, despite his evident brutality, may owe more, however, to shrewd security advice from the Israelis. The Americo-Liberians see the history of their return to Africa in terms of a black Zionism, and the Tolbert regime broke ranks with the rest of the OAU by restoring diplomatic ties with Israel after the 1973 war (Gershoni 1989). Despite a flirtation with Libya (Amoo 1993), Doe confirmed this policy, and the Israelis were keen, it has been suggested, to see Doe survive (Kieh 1989). Israeli interest in Liberia (and now Sierra Leone – the National Provisional Reformation Council (NPRC) government recognized Israel immediately after the coup overthrowing President Momoh in April 1992) may also owe as much to their involvement in world diamond trade, and a concern to monitor, and perhaps divert, earnings from Sierra Leone diamonds that currently move through Lebanese business channels into Beirut. Apparently, some of this wealth has been used in the past to fund warring factions (both pro- and anti-Israeli) in the Lebanese civil war.

As noted above, the NPFL incursion was launched from Côte d'Ivoire with the assistance of commandos from Burkina Faso; Tarr (1993) suggests there may have been 700 Burkinabes in all. Charles Taylor's connections with Compaore have already been noted. Liberians explain the tacit support of President Houphouet-Boigny of Côte d'Ivoire in the following way. A step-daughter of the Ivoirian president was married to A. B. Tolbert, the son of President William Tolbert of Liberia. As members of the Tolbert cabinet were being executed by Doe, in public and before the world's media, in Monrovia, Houphouet-Boigny appealed for his son-in-law to be spared. Doe agreed, but later reneged on his promises. The younger Tolbert was seized from the French embassy, where he had sought refuge, and killed. Houphouet-Boigny was thus from the outset hostile to the Doe regime, and this explains his quiet tolerance of the NPFL as it prepared for the invasion of Nimba. However, it is unlikely that personal factors alone are sufficient to account for Ivoirian and Burkinabe support for the NPFL. Economic interests (the impact of the collapse of commodity prices on the Ivoirian economy), ideological factors (continued commitment, in the Burkinabe case to the elements of the youth revolutionary political programme that inspired Thomas Sankara) and Libyan foreign policy in sub-Saharan Africa must also be given due weight. French and Ivoirian-based Lebanese commercial interests have been important in supplying the NPFL (and perhaps the RUF also) with credit and access to equipment, in return for business concessions in minerals and tropical forest products (Tarr 1993).

After the brutal reaction of the AFL to the first news of the NPFL incursion, local volunteers rallied to the rebel cause with little apparent hesitation; some were pre-teenage orphans. In subsequent months the NPFL consolidated its initial gains, trained its new recruits, and began to advance against Doe's forces through the Liberian interior towards Monrovia. By June 1990 NPFL fighters were within striking distance of the capital, and Liberia had become 'a slaughterhouse' (Tarr 1993). Even in times of peace the capital is home to more than a third of the population of Liberia, a number now swollen by large numbers of refugees from in the interior. On 1 July the NPFL launched a two-pronged offensive, cutting power and water supplies and all road connections to the city (Amoo 1993). In effect a prisoner in his own executive mansion Doe seems to have contemplated, but then rejected, resignation in early July. Liberia lacked a functional government, but the remnants of the AFL around Doe were still sufficiently well-armed to exact a high price of the NPFL were to try and take Monrovia directly. Taylor hesitated. Doe loyalists meanwhile continued to exact revenge on their resumed ethnic enemies from among the Mano and Gio communities in Monrovia, including one particularly appalling massacre of a large congregation at worship in church.

Faced with prospects of anarchy, and further massive suffering by unarmed civilians unable to flee fighting likely soon to engulf the capital, the Economic Community of West Africa (ECOWAS), with international encouragement, sought to establish a mediation process. At the first meeting of the ECOWAS Standing Mediation Committee in Banjul (6–7 August 1990), the call was issued for a national conference of all political parties in Liberia with a view to establishing an interim government. The mediation committee also resolved to establish a multinational peace-keeping force (ECOMOG, the ECOWAS Monitoring Group) to facilitate the encampment and disarmament of the warring parties. Although the NPFL had itself, in June, called for an all-party peace conference Taylor rejected the invitation to attend the First All Liberia Conference in Banjul, December 1990, apparently feeling so close to victory that the NPFL could now risk 'going it alone'. Six political parties and ten interest groups taking part in the peace conference proposed an Interim Government of National Unity (IGNU), but the NPFL refused an invitation to join (Tarr 1993).

Taylor was also opposed to the peace-keeping force ECOMOG. His troops fired on the first ECOMOG contingents to land in Monrovia 24–25 August 1990, but was unable to prevent their deployment (Tarr 1993). Meanwhile, Doe continued to cling to the threadbare trappings of power in a presidential mansion fortified against military and mystical dangers. To the end he seems to have retained some idea of doing a deal with a now divided opposition. This apparently explains why he ventured to ECOMOG head-quarters on 10 September 1990 to take part in a meeting between Doe loyalists and a splinter group known as the Independent National Patriotic Front of Liberia (INPFL). This armed faction (the first of eight now contesting the civil war in Liberia) had been formed by Prince Yormi Johnson, a choleric and unstable former army officer, who broke with Taylor in February 1990 after being accused of executing his own men.[7] The meeting turned into a shoot-out, with 60 of Doe's men killed, while ECOMOG troops looked on. A severely wounded president was dragged off to Johnson's head-quarters on the outskirts of Monrovia, where he was tortured to death by Johnson's men in front of video cameras. Copies of the tape circulated very widely in Liberia and other West African countries (Davidson 1992) to the great political disadvantage of the NPFL leader as a potential presidential successor to Doe. Taylor had set himself up as the only man capable of ridding the country of the monster Doe, and in rejecting participation in IGNU vowed to attend the June OAU summit as president of Liberia. The circumstances of Doe's capture and death seriously damaged ECOMOG's reputation as a peace-keeping force (Amoo 1993).

An attempt to end the stalemate by a second peace conference of all parties to the civil war in March–April 1991 in Monrovia confirmed the Banjul arrangements for an interim government, headed by Dr Amos Sawyer, but was again undermined by the withdrawal of the NPFL. The interim government had indefinite tenure until elections could be arranged under the provisions of the Liberian constitution (Tarr 1993). Dependent on ECOMOG protec-tion, its writ has never run far (in effect, it administered only the greater Monrovia area). Taylor's opposition to IGNU reflects a legacy of personal animosity between himself and IGNU members such as H. Boima Fahnbulleh, but more importantly because by this stage in the civil war the NPFL was in control of 80–90 per cent of the national territory of Liberia (an entity, unrecognized by the international community, termed 'Greater Liberia' in NPFL parlance).

A further sequence of attempts to bring the armed factions together, and to build a peace process involving the NPFL, then took place under the chairmanship of Houphouet-Boigny in Yamassoukro. The fourth of these accords, agreed in November 1991, provided for the encampment and disarming of the various military factions under ECOMOG supervision, pending general elections. In March 1993 Yamassoukro IV was endorsed by the UN as the only agreed basis for a comprehensive peace settlement in Liberia. It had the defect, however, of not making a full allowance for various factions that had emerged from the carnage of the earliest phases of the war. The most important of the newer factions was ULIMO (the United Liberian Movement for Democracy), an alliance formed in Sierra Leone among Krahn and Mandingo refugees from NPFL ethnocide. Fighting alongside the Sierra Leone army against RUF rebels in 1991, ULIMO crossed back into Liberia in 1992 and made significant gains at the expense of the NPFL.

But even before the serious complication of ULIMO became apparent Yamassoukro IV was undermined by Taylor's refusal to abide by the basic terms of the agreement. ECOMOG forces, deployed in NPFL territory in 1992 to supervise the encampment process and monitor the flow of arms and fighters across international borders, were subsequently attacked and forcibly disarmed by Taylor's troops. In one incident at Vahun soldiers from a detachment of Senegalese troops in ECOMOG were killed in a shoot-out with NPFL fighters, and the Senegalese contingent to the peace-keeping force was withdrawn. This in effect strengthened Nigerian dominance of ECOMOG, a factor seized upon by Taylor to increase justification for dragging his feet over the Yamassoukro Accords. The basic NPFL claim that Nigeria lacked neutrality in the Liberian civil war seemed to stem from alleged close pre-war ties between Doe and senior figures in the Nigerian military government. Later, the focus of Taylor's concern was alleged military collaboration between the peace-keeping forces and ULIMO.

If some commentators stressed the significance of close personal ties between Nigerian head of state Ibrahim Babangida and other West African leaders (such as President Momoh in Sierra Leone) opposed to Taylor, others felt the Nigerian position to be governed more by regional rivalries involving the Libyans, the French and Côte d'Ivoire. Nigerian bias against the NPFL might also be explained by fears that the youthful dissidence tapped by the NPFL rebellion would remain a potent strategic threat to other countries in the West African region, including Nigeria itself, if the NPFL rebellion succeeds.

An uneasy peace prevailed in Liberia from March 1991 to October 1992. During this time the NPFL consolidated its administration based on the small provincial town of Gbarnga in north-central Liberia, exported timber and minerals through the ports of Buchanan and Greenville, and stockpiled arms. This war *materiel* was destined for a second all-out attempt to capture Monrovia. This campaign (Operation Octopus) was launched on 15 October 1992, and brought the NPFL into open and decisive confrontation with the ECOMOG forces. Resisting the advance of Taylor's troops ECOMOG then went on the offensive against the NPFL early in 1993, with the tacit backing of the international community.[8] ECOMOG operations included the bombing of the ports of Buchanan and Greenville, to disrupt NPFL export routes and weapons supply lines. The journalist Karl Maier (1993) reported that one of the effects of the bombing was to consolidate Taylor's support in the areas controlled by the NPFL.

According to Tarr (1993), the Libyans decided in 1991 that the NPFL revolution was largely a sham, but renewed their support for the Operation Octopus venture. After the failure of the NPFL attempt to take Monrovia by storm, a further series of negotiations among the warring factions was begun in Geneva on 11 July 1993, with Taylor having dropped the precondition that he should head any interim administration before elections. This led to the adoption of a new framework for the peace process in Cotonou, against a background of endemic warlord violence, with an NPFL leadership less in control of this violence than at any time since the civil war began. Fighting erupted once again in a number of areas in early 1994, this time involving the NPFL and armed breakaway groups.

The RUF campaign in Sierra Leone

By early 1991 the civil war in Liberia had reached stalemate. The military focus then shifted, in March 1991, to eastern and southern Sierra Leone.

The RUF attacked eastern Sierra Leone from NPFL territory in Liberia at two points – Koindu at the extreme northern end of Kalaihun District, and the Mano river bridge in Pujehun district on the road from Monrovia in the south. The northern group progressed as far as Daru in southern Kailahun District, where it was held by Sierra Leone government forces substantially reinforced by Guinean soldiers fighting under the terms of the Guinea–Sierra Leone defence pact. In the southern sector stealthy progress was made over a period of several months in the general direction of Freetown across Pujehun District as far as Sumbuya. The main targets of the first phase of the RUF campaign was to build support for the movement in remote areas close to the border, where it was anticipated that disillusion with the APC government was at a maximum, and to capture Bo and Kenema. These two provincial headquarters towns between them control much of the diamond business of eastern and central Sierra Leone.

The initial fighting was in the hands of a small, partly mercenary commando force, while an army of conscripted Mende youths was raised and trained *en route*. A number of rural primary school buildings in captured areas were pressed into use as training camps for this purpose. Many youngsters ran away to avoid conscription. Only among the diamond-digging populations on the border itself (where young people typically maintain an unofficial dual nationality) was it possible to detect signs of significant voluntary adhesion. Elsewhere, considerable application of terror (see below) seems to have been necessary.

Had Bo or Kenema been taken during this early phase of fighting the first cohorts of the youth army were to have been unveiled as 'evidence' of a popular uprising by the Mende people against a corrupt APC government. The crucial step of forming this 'indigenous' force, however, dictated a slow rate of progress by rebel commanders. In the interval a campaign of rumour and misinformation was deployed to spread alarm and despondency, and these affected the resolve of the APC government.

In Bo, the campaign of misinformation about rebel progress rather backfired, by having its greatest impact on the expatriate relief and development community, who fled the town on two occasions, on false rumours that rebel attack was imminent. The first of these evacuations – by a convoy of relief vehicles in the middle of the night – spread panic in rural areas along the route. The second occasion descended into farce, with the management of one development project, safely ensconced in Freetown, instructing its workers by radio to harvest the ripening avocado pears in the project compound, lock the office, and bring all the vehicles to the capital for safety, whereupon the drivers were given their bus fares to return to Bo to await their fate. After an envisaged attack (26 April 1991) failed to materialize the citizens of Bo awoke to the ludicrous side of what was happening, but also to the realization that they were alone in the world, and needing to look to their own defences.[9]

The presence of mercenary forces at first misled the APC government and neutral observers alike into thinking that the RUF was a thinly disguised proxy for the NPFL intent on diversionary operations to weaken Sierra Leonean commitment to ECOMOG (whose main rear bases were in Freetown). Only later was it apparent that the RUF was a distinct movement of dissident Sierra Leoneans. This led the APC government into an initial miscalculation with fateful consequences.

President Momoh and his principal advisers seemed to have taken seriously the idea that the RUF was an uprising by Mende dissidents from Kailahun District.[10] That such a misunderstanding might occur, in a government in which non-Mendes were the dominant voices in cabinet, seems to have been a deliberate calculation on the part of rebel strategists.[11] Communications between Freetown and parts of the country under rebel attack were abysmal or non-existent, and the rebels themselves started deliberate rumours greatly exaggerating their rate of progress. Uncorroborated reports broadcast on the BBC Africa Service (a major news medium in provincial Sierra Leone, where the national radio station is often inaudible) heightened the confusion. At one point in April 1991 it appears that a panicky State House, haunted by its own fears of a Mende uprising, contemplated a strategic withdrawal of troops and police from Mende districts, and the *de facto* partition of the country along ethnic lines. This was by no means as tactically disastrous as the ethnic violence unleashed by Doe's troops in Nimba County. Nevertheless it deeply alienated the Mende communities by then bearing the brunt of the RUF terror campaign. It also seems to have been a factor that shaped decisively the political perceptions of the young officers from the war front who overthrew the APC regime in April 1992.

By this time, however, information about the true character of the rebel movement was beginning to come together from the accounts of people escaping from districts already overrun. Many young people evaded enforced enrolment by fleeing into the forest where they survived for weeks or months as best they could, before using their superior knowledge of byways in the bush to reach Bo or Kenema. Escape seems to have been particularly common in the southern war zone where Liberians and Burkinabes may have substantially out-numbered the Sierra Leonean element in the initial RUF force, and where military progress appears to have been hampered by the logistics of looting. Conscripted youngsters spent much of their time headloading stolen property for the mercenaries, whose bonuses were reputedly very small ($5000 each to take Bo and Kenema) and may not in the event have been paid in full (it is said that this led to a subsequent dispute between Sankoh and Taylor). This did little for the campaign to win hearts and minds, or to convince local opinion that the RUF was serious in its proclaimed ambition to restore the country to multi-party democracy. Those who lived through the rebel invasion point, in particular, to the politically counter-productive impact of the contingent of Burkinabe commandos (rumoured to have been paid for by a loan from Taylor) fighting as part of the RUF. Survivors allege that they were responsible for some of the worst acts of brutality, but also for a number of political absurdities in the earliest phases of the campaign worthy of a comic opera. The democratic and patriotic credentials of the RUF were, apparently, read out *in French* to the one group of bemused Mende villagers by a Burkinabe commander whose guerrilla curriculum had omitted the study of any more appropriate local languages. Having delivered himself of a pantomime version of the international agenda for 'good governance' in Africa to the bafflement of the assembled village notables he was carried away in pomp – headloaded down a bush path in a looted car by a gang of 16 local teenage conscripts.

While the military progress of the RUF in Sierra Leone bears no comparison with the NPFL's rapid sweep through Liberia, its political success was even less marked. Little attempt was made to organize civil administration in overrun towns and villages. In fact, it seems doubtful whether the RUF at times even had a single military command structure. Escaping civilians reported settlements controlled by an isolated rebel commander surrounded by a guard of local teenage conscripts. Civilians were in some cases moved out of their settlements and rehoused in temporary clearings in the forest, reverting to a pattern, known from ecological evidence, to have prevailed under 19th-century warlord control in the forested bound-ary wildernesses of eastern Sierra Leone and western Liberia.

In general, the RUF appears to have overestimated the political comparisons with Liberia. The APC government was unpopular, but it was a mistake to think that President Momoh was in any way comparable to the violent and barbarous President Doe. Rural Sierra Leoneans were materially poorer than equivalent Liberians before the war, but had regular contact with school teachers, junior government functionaries, pastors and Muslim clerics capable of interpreting national and international political trends. As Clapham (1976) has shown, Liberia and Sierra Leone are only superficially similar in the extent to which they are dominated by their capital cities. The Liberian state was in reality always much more highly centralized, whereas Sierra Leonean politics was (and is) much more broadly based, in regional terms. Sierra Leone has more provincial towns of note than Liberia. And even under one-party politics MPs and ministers were often genuine popular local choices. In short, the periphery had much greater influence over events at the centre than in Liberia. Above all, rural Sierra Leoneans had already had more than a year in which to discover the true misery of war from the regular recitation of horror stories from the many Liberian refugees to whom they had offered shelter. These are all significant factors in explaining the failure of the RUF to elicit the kind of local political support earlier enjoyed by the NPFL in Liberia.

The invasion was turned during the second half of 1991, when government forces, assisted by Liberian irregulars, counter-attacked and drove the southern rebel group out of Pujehun and back down the road from Joru towards the Mano river bridge. The Liberian irregulars, re-formed as ULIMO, then took control of the southern border region (later carrying the fight to the NPFL in Grand Cape Mount County, Liberia). The main RUF contingent in the north, after consolidating its initial gains in Kailahun District, was unable, apart from sporadic raids, to make any progress beyond Daru, the strategic crossing-point of the Moa river, firmly defended by the Guinean contingent.

On 27 April 1992, with the conflict in Kailahun at a stalemate, young Sierra Leone army officers, in Freetown to protest poor conditions at the war front, ended 24 years of APC rule in a near-bloodless coup. The new NPRC government comprised both civilians and young military officers, several with direct experience of battle-front conditions or from communities ravaged by the fighting. The new government directly espoused political objectives close to those claimed by the RUF. Many Sierra Leoneans and outside observers thought (perhaps naively) that NPRC reforms, and a commitment to a timetable for return to the democratic process, would lead to a rapid cessation of hostilities. Although some field commanders appear to have favoured negotiations, the RUF in fact soldiered on. The NPRC government made the ending of the war by military means its prime objective.

The continuation of hostilities at this point is consistent with the view that the RUF had collapsed into factions, some mainly or solely concerned to control mineral wealth from the clandestine economies of the Liberia–Sierra Leone border region. Unable to capture Kenema, the northern group shifted its attention, after the NPRC coup, to the diamond-rich district of Kono.[12] Forays in August and September 1992 were followed by the capture of Koidu, the key centre in the local diamond economy. Koidu changed hands several times before the RUF was pushed back during the first half of 1993 towards its strongholds east of the Moa river, in southern Kailahun (especially towns and villages around Pendembu and along the northern border of the Gola Forest). On the Liberian side of the border ULIMO activity threatened to cut off the RUF from its NPFL allies and cross-border weapons supply routes.[13] There was some suggestion that RUF leaders found it difficult to withdraw from the fray as a result of financial obligations to Taylor and the NPFL incurred during the initial invasion.[14]

It is noteworthy that alien guerrilla element in this renewed phase of fighting was subdued or absent and the youthful Sierra Leonean conscripts to the RUF much more prominent (local press reports of an engagement near Bunumbu in March 1993 claimed the involvement of over one thousand RUF combatants). The zeal with which these young fighters continued to fight surprised some observers, and has been put down to the ready availability of confidence-boosting drugs. Equally possibly, however, armed banditry in a diamond-rich and inaccessible forest landscape makes for a perfectly viable economic way of life not greatly different from modes of existence in the more remote diamond field operations before the rebellion. The youth army forged by the RUF may now be beyond the control of its one-time leadership.

NPFL and RUF: an interpretative comparison

The NPFL initiated the Liberian conflict by invading Nimba County, hoping to build support to overthrow Samuel Doe. Imitating NPFL methods of waging low-intensity conflict in the Kailahun and Pujehun Districts of eastern Sierra Leone, the RUF similarly hoped to build a rebellion that would overthrow the APC government of President

Joseph Momoh. Both NPFL and RUF were prepared to use terroristic methods against local populations, and to exploit existing ethnic and inter-generational tensions. Important motivating factors include personal ambition (especially Charles Taylor's unshakeable determination to be President of Liberia), Libyan-inspired student-based revolutionary idealism, and business intrigue to secure control of rich mineral and timber resources in the zone of conflict (the western segment of the Upper Guinean Forest formation). However, the specific methods used by the rebels and the relative success of these methods can be fully understood only by taking fuller account of the socio-political context. The analysis below seeks to suggest that there was nothing accidental about the way in which the NPFL and RUF went about their work, but that they waged war according to a strategy built on deep knowledge of local political culture. The tragedy of Liberia and Sierra Leone, however, is that this kind of cheap, low-intensity warfare, based on the manipulation of features of local political culture, is a game that other similarly endowed parties can readily play. The entry costs are low and the learning curve is short. With the splintering of the two main rebel movements, and the organization of several more recent movements with rival ambitions, warfare has become endemic in the region. Chronic low-level conflict shading off into gangsterism and banditry will be difficult to eradicate within the forests and diamond fields of Liberia and Sierra Leone while the basic societal tensions remain unresolved. It is the purpose of the following sections to describe the sources of some of these tensions and the way in which factional violence in Liberia and Sierra Leone has fed upon them.

Anti-trader sentiment
Commentators on the Liberian civil war refer to ethnicity as a factor, often without distinguishing two kinds of ethnic animus: first, factional rivalries among clientelist groups in the army and other state organizations (e.g. tension between the Krahn clients of Doe and the Gio and Mano clients of Quiwonkpa); and second, rivalries based on competition between trading networks or between merchants and local political interest (e.g. historical tension between local land owners and the Mandingo trading diaspora).

Tensions of this second kind seem to have been exacerbated, perhaps intentionally, by the NPFL in its bid to establish a power-base in Nimba County. Such tensions led to the killing of many

Mandingo traders and in turn help account for the rise of ULIMO as a defensive alliance between the Liberian-domiciled Mandingo (led by Alhaji Kromah) and Krahn refugees (including ex-soldiers from the AFL). The evidence that violence against rural traders was not confined to Nimba County but was also a deliberate objective of the RUF campaign in Sierra Leone suggests a shared strategic concern, perhaps reflecting Libyan anti-mercantile influence.[15]For the NPFL and RUF the exploitation of anti-trader animus served the twin purposes of terrorizing and driving out the local representatives of the Guinean migrant trading diaspora and building popular local support for the rebel movement through cancellation of onerous debts owed to local traders (most of whom are the *de facto* money lenders of the rural economy throughout Liberia and Sierra Leone). The policy appears to have been relatively more successful in Liberia than in Sierra Leone. To understand why this was so, account has to be taken of the different degrees of social incorporation of Mandingo traders in different parts of the West African forest zone from Casamance to Côte d'Ivoire, but more especially in the central portion either side of the Liberia–Sierra Leone border.

The Mandingo homeland is the basin of the Upper Niger. Here the Mandingo are one of most prominent ethnic groups in the Republic of Guinea (rivalled in political influence only by the Fula). But for several hundred years a Mandingo diaspora has been threading its way through the forests of Sierra Leone and Liberia, looking to establish and control trading opportunities with both the coast and the savannas to the north. The Mandingo are generally credited (along with the Fula) with bringing Islam to the people of the forests of Liberia and Sierra Leone, but often in a syncretic form, with considerable emphasis on magic. Unlike the Fula, who tend to be temporary residents with a long-term commitment to return to their homeland in Guinean Futa Jallon, members of the Mandingo trading diaspora have attempted to settle where they find the best business opportunities, buying diamonds, gold and agricultural produce, lending money to villagers and running small village shops.[16]

Historically, forest communities have taken a range of attitudes to Mandingo mercantile networks. Broadly speaking, Mandingo traders are more integrated within local society at the western end of the Upper Guinean forest block (eastern Sierra Leone) than towards its centre (north-east Liberia). According to Blanchard (1973) the Mano – one of the main groups rallying to the support of the NPFL after its initial incursion into Liberia – long resisted the settlement of Mandingo traders in their midst. 'Mandingos were never allowed to settle in Mano towns, establish regular markets, grow crops locally, join the secret society or take part in town affairs . . . Their patterns of behavior were judged socially unacceptable', but the Mandingo traded magic to control and direct lightning and 'sold predictions on the outcome of war' (Blanchard 1973, p. 111). In Kailahun District in Sierra Leone, by contrast, Mandingo merchants and warriors successfully established themselves in Mende communities in the 19th century, married locally, and are now well integrated within local settlements and political institutions. It would seem that by and large the problems of finding an accommodation between the values of Mandingo mercantilism and local agrarian egalitarianism have been overcome.[17]

East-West variation in local acceptance of the Mandingo perhaps reflects the fact that the opening up of the forest to commerce is historically much more recent in parts of Liberia than in eastern Sierra Leone. But also germane to the argument is that much of Sierra Leone has long been thoroughly 'mandingized' (transformed by Manding cultural values), even areas outside the specific reach of Mandingo trading networks (see Linares 1992 for discussion of the relative degrees of 'mandingization' of the Diola groups in Senegal: the more recent phase of rebellion in Casamance has points of similarity to the situation in Liberia). Manding cultural values reach the limit of their geographical range in Côte d'Ivoire and Burkina Faso. In these two countries politics are shaped to a significant degree by Akan cultural and social values, and Manding influence appears at times to be perceived as a cultural threat, especially when backed by mercantile power. The historical acceptance of communities originating in the Manding world of the Upper Niger seems to be based on the condition that they settle as 'traders without trade' (Launey 1982). Anti-Mandingo sentiment, and the assertion of peasant populism within the confines of chiefly rule, are more characteristic of traditional political culture in communities drawing historical inspiration from the Ashanti and Voltaic worlds. This might be a factor in Ivoirian and Burkinabe support for the NPFL. Whether Libyan support for the NPFL and RUF also reflects a perceived concern for the potential power of Mandingo mercantilism in the West African sub-region is not known. The Libyan leadership, however, has until recently used the country's oil revenues to underwrite a strong in-country anti-mercantile populism. Classic sentiments of concern to release 'the poor' from the grip of a usurious merchant class are one of the ingredients in the 'Green Book' ideology that inspired some student radicals in Sierra Leone from about 1975.[18]

But while anti-Mandingo sentiment is a significant factor in the Liberian civil war and Sierra Leonean rebellion, it may be important to distinguish between grass-roots sentiment directed against historical communities of Mandingo traders in Nimba and elsewhere in Liberia and the efforts of the NPFL, RUF and their commercial supporters to bend such sentiment to the dispossession of a rather different stratum of Mandingo trading interests in the sub-region – namely, large-scale traders from the Senegal and Upper Niger basins. These traders are a modern, international, business elite, equally at home in Paris or New York and in Conakry or Dakar. Some are of Senegalese extraction. Others are of Guinean, or indeed, Sierra Leonean origin, and maintain their links with the historical 'Mandingo' trading communities of the Upper Guinean forest formation. Sierra Leoneans sometimes signal the difference between this regional business elite and ordinary rural Mandingo traders by referring to the former as 'Maranka' ('Moroccans').

Allegedly, Maranka interests control an important share of the unofficial diamond trade from Sierra Leone. Although firm evidence is in short supply, it is estimated that diamonds account for about a third of all Sierra Leone's GDP, and that the greater part of this trade passes through the hands of around 25 officially recognized diamond dealers (mainly Lebanese) and about 17 major unofficial dealers (several of whom would be classed as Maranka). The unofficial dealers are presumed to handle the greater part of the 30–40 per cent of Sierra Leone's diamond wealth that is smuggled each year, much of it (pre-war) through Monrovia. Powerful Maranka-Mandingo businessmen had a similar grip on clandestine business opportunities in interior Liberia. Supposedly, much of this wealth found its way through networks linking Monrovia, Conakry and Dakar to Europe and the Middle East.

If the NPFL came to fan the flames of anti-Mandingo sentiment in the Liberian interior much is obscured by Doe's barbaric excesses in Nimba County. The evidence of anti-trader 'populism' is much stronger in Sierra Leone, where public execution of Mandingos, ostensibly to 'liberate' farmers from the oppressive grip of village merchants, seems to have undermined rather than increased support for the RUF. Two main reasons may be advanced. First, many Mende villagers are themselves traders, and were not easily fooled by the populist economics of the rebels. A public demonstration by the RUF in Gaura Chiefdom of the rising cost of rice under the 24 years of APC rule, followed by the promise that under RUF rule all rice would be distributed free, seems to have been met with due scepticism by all but the most incorrigible village optimist. Second, Mandingo traders, as long-term residents of the forest borderlands of eastern Sierra Leone, are often intermarried with their Mende host families. A Mandingo trader interviewed in Malen Chiefdom owed his life to prompt intervention by a Mende chief, who ransomed him from the local RUF commander for a substantial sum. His feet had been smashed meanwhile by 'the boys' (the local euphemism for RUF hoodlums), leaving him a cripple.

Some RUF commanders may have realized quite early on that anti-merchant populist rhetoric, backed by terroristic violence against Mandingo traders, was not bearing its expected fruit in terms of popular support. They sought to diversify their attack by including a second 'enemy', the Fula. In some accounts this was in revenge for a Fula trader who fired on the RUF when its fighters first crossed from Liberia. Fula traders, however, were a poor target since they are less likely than the Mandingo to reside in Mende villages; many Fula produce traders base themselves in urban centres such as Bo and Kenema, and travel through the rural areas to buy produce only when commodities such as kola and coffee are in season. They have fewer local marriage links. For these reasons they were able quickly to absent themselves at the first sign of trouble. The RUF could condemn their 'economic crimes', but lacked a ready target to hand.

Youth mobilization

Libya offered refuge to dissident students from Sierra Leone and Liberia over a number of years, and the revolutionary message of Gaddafi's 'Green Book' has percolated quite widely among youth groups in the two countries for some years now. There seems little doubt that both NPFL and RUF commanders entered Liberia and Sierra Leone intending to appeal to prior 'revolutionary' awareness of local youthful dissidents. But they also appear to have had well-considered techniques for enforced mobilization should this message be lacking in spontaneous appeal. These techniques of coercion were more clearly in evidence in Sierra Leone, where the RUF's initial 'ethnic' call to arms was a very limited success, dictating a switch of effort towards mobilization of border-zone diamond-digging youth; this was based on the perhaps correct calculation that this alienated group could be more readily detached from existing structures of state and civil society than other target groups in the countryside of eastern Sierra Leone.

A principal tactical issue for both movements, but more especially the RUF, in stirring up rebellion is how to detach youth from local civil society. By their scorched earth actions in Nimba County, Doe's ill-disciplined troops handed the requisite tactical advantage to the NPFL on a plate. The RUF had to work harder. Three elements can be discerned in the initial RUF campaign in 1991. First, the police and other civilian representatives of government were put to flight by a well-orchestrated campaign of rumours (based on the circulation of letters to villagers predicting when an attack would commence, and the consequences of resistance). Second, villagers were terrorized by violence against chiefs, traders and minor civil servants, the main repositories of power in a local clientelist political system. Third, youths were conscripted and encamped for military training, local primary school buildings being pressed into service as camp head-quarters. According to eyewitness accounts, laggard recruits were sometimes forced at gunpoint to take part in atrocities against family members or community leaders. Villagers report being required to witness the terrifying spectacle of public beheadings in which the victim's neck was cut, working from back to front with a blunt blade. The purpose of these atrocities seems to have been to bring about an irrevocable break between conscripts and their communities. Subsequently, youth conscripts could not escape for fear of reprisals.

A similar logic explains why conscripts and recruits were branded with tattoos to identify them as members of NPFL and RUF. Recipients would then know, or were told, that these marks were a warrant for harsh treatment, and perhaps summary execution, if ever they were to fall into the hands of opposing forces. Sierra Leonean journalists witnessing military operations in Kono report their shock and amazement at hearing young rebels, freshly captured in the fighting and high on drugs, openly taunting their captors to shoot them summarily.

Amnesty International (1992) reports summary military executions of young rebels when the RUF suffered its first reverses in 1991. It has also been alleged that on occasion outraged villagers took the law into their own hands, lynching youngsters known or thought to have been involved in atrocities. It is conceivable that RUF strategists counted on such reactions to discredit the government of Sierra Leone with the international community. This was not an issue for the NPFL in Liberia where Doe's murderous troops discredited themselves without provocation. Amnesty International's report (1992) in the war in Sierra Leone disproportionately focussed its criticisms on atrocities committed by government troops. Queried on this point, Amnesty argued that any imbalance in its treatment of the issue was a consequence of the fact that the organization is able adequately to protest human rights abuses only to legally recognized governments.[19]

The RUF project to recruit or conscript disaffected youth seems to have been a considerable success. In Kailahun District this in part reflected geographical factors (the area controlled by the RUF is directly connected to NPFL territory by numerous smuggling tracks through the forest). But success here also reflects social conditions in these inaccessible and ethnically heterogeneous forested boundary wildernesses (Davies and Richards 1991; Richards 1995). The populations of young diamond diggers on the border are especially ambiguous in their national loyalties, and their activities are often clandestine, taking place in unlicensed forest workings far from any official scrutiny. Young people here are typically inured to a life of hardship and violent disputation. They often belong to families divided by the border, and before the war routinely maintained both Sierra Leonean and Liberian identity, finding supplies and entertainment at times easier to organize in Monrovia than in Kenema. Some joined the rebels without much persuasion. In eyewitness accounts from the area adjacent to the main rebel stronghold on the northern edge of the Gola forest the resulting squads of youthful RUF warriors – alternating between bouts of bush warfare in carefully laid ambushes on lonely forest tracks and periods of hectic diamond mining – seem hardly distinguishable from the gangs of youngsters found before the war throughout the remote Sierra Leone–Liberia border country, fighting for their economic survival in remote forest diamond workings under arduous and often violent conditions. Under the RUF they may have experienced conditions not dissimilar to those they were used to before the fighting began. Before the war an unknown number of border-zone forest diamond crews worked for

Liberian-based backers. Diamond prices in, and regularity of supplies from, NPFL territory, may have been better than those received from Sierra Leone before the outbreak of hostilities.[20]

Before the coup that brought the NPRC to power in Sierra Leone the RUF looked a beaten movement. Its effective resumption of hostilities in late 1992 has been explained in a number of ways; as a last desperate attempt to secure a negotiating position, as a threat to the stability of ECOMOG during Taylor's October 1992 campaign to take Monrovia, even as a counter-coup organized by elements within the deposed APC government. What is striking, however, is that even when the main thrust of the attack on Kono had been blunted there were still reports of apparently local and spontaneous activities by isolated bands of youthful rebels. Government troops made considerable progress against RUF bases in Kailahun District in late 1993, but there were renewed rebel attacks in early 1994 on Tongo Field, villages close to Koribondo (Bo District), and around Faama (Nomo Chiefdom) close to the Liberian border (all in diamond-mining areas). The NPFL leadership appeared hard put to control similar random outbreaks of fighting in Liberia. The NPFL claimed that the horrifying massacre of refugees at Harbel in April 1993 was faked by its opponents to bring it into disrepute; perhaps more likely it was freelance killing by a splinter group attempting to build an independent power-base through terror tactics of the kind first deployed by the NPFL.

These terroristic outrages seem at times to be quite without military strategic objective. The leader of a small group of rebels (a force of no more than ten) that briefly took control of Pujehun on 17 June 1992 could not give a coherent account of his motives even to those who (before the war) knew him well. Seemingly, terroristic violence is seen to be such a powerful way of making political capital that it has now become a regular medium of empowerment for young activists traumatized by several years of unremitting conflict. This suggests that the further evolution of patterns of violence in the region may follow the dictates of a symbolic logic not easily quelled by military means alone.

Youth politics and clandestine economy in the forests of Liberia and Sierra Leone: a new 'target migration'?
Libyan-inspired youth politics, the attempt to wrest control of profitable mineral and forest resources from the Mandingo, and the

military support of Burkinabe commandos seem to be common and well-attested features of both the NPFL and RUF rebellions. By themselves, the first two factors are fairly readily understood against the background of the history and economic development of Liberia and Sierra Leone, though it is at times harder to see why they have come together in this particular instance. The third factor – the involvement of Burkina Faso in the internal affairs of two Anglophone countries with few historical ties to the Voltaic region of West Africa – is inherently more puzzling. If the entire package seems at first glance distinctly improbable, closer examination suggests a way of connecting these three elements.

Although eyewitness accounts agree concerning the role played by Burkinabe commandos in Sierra Leone it is not clear whether these commandos were mercenaries in the strict sense, or had some degree of tacit political support from the authorities in Burkina Faso. President Compaore strongly denies that NPFL and RUF guerrillas trained at a military camp in Burkina Faso. In September 1992 the US government, for the first time, claimed to have definite proof of Burkinabe support for the NPFL, and the US ambassador to Ouagadougou was recalled for consultations.

President Compaore's Libyan connections and support for Taylor have been mentioned above. What is not clear is why it is in the political interest of the Burkinabe leader to offer political support to the NPFL and RUF.

President Compaore can be seen in some ways as a 'broker' between the volatile youth politics of the Sankara period in Burkina Faso and the much more conservative politics of the ruling elite in Côte d'Ivoire. As a landlocked, Francophone state with massive problems arising from pressure of population on a low and depleted resource base (and a consequent intense crisis of unfulfilled youth expectations) Burkina Faso has to tread a fine line between the interests and expectations of its economically more powerful southern neighbour and the unspent revolutionary zeal of its own frustrated youth. One interpretation of the coup that brought Compaore to power is that it resulted from differing perceptions among the Burkinabe leadership about how to balance the Libyan-influenced aspirations of revolutionary youth and the older-established political ties that bound Burkina Faso to the much more conservative political elite of Côte d'Ivoire.[21] Burkina Faso is highly dependent on the Côte d'Ivoire economy, not least for employment of migrant labour and transport access to the sea. The Compaore coup (quietly welcomed, it is said, if not supported, in French diplomatic circles) may have helped redress the balance in favour of the established political and economic links with Côte d'Ivoire.

Tarr (1993) cites reports in the French press alleging the involvement of French, French-based and Ivoirian-based business interests in supporting the NPFL. Success for the NPFL would seem certain to strengthen Liberian business with Abidjan and weaken flows of wealth through Guinea. Any such re-routing of trade and business opportunities would obviously be advantageous to entrepreneurs with business interest in Côte d'Ivoire. Abidjan is still the main focus for French-orientated trade in the region. Despite the opening-up of the Guinean economy after the death of Sekou Toure, anti-French feeling in Guinea remains strong. The possibility arises that President Compaore, caught in a difficult balancing act between his own Libyan-inspired radicals, and Ivoirian and French business interests important to the future of the impoverished Burkinabe economy, might have found it quite convenient to broker an alliance that serves conveniently to deflect unspent revolutionary zeal towards two third-party countries about which he perhaps cares little, while at the same time retaining credibility with influential parties closer to home (especially in view of Houphouet-Boigny's well-known hostility to Doe).

As a venture in appeasing domestic radical youth sentiment Burkinabe involvement in the RUF invasion of the mineral-rich forested borderlands of eastern Sierra Leone might be considered to strike some interesting resonances, at the level of political symbolism, with longer-established and more peaceful migrations of Burkinabe youth to acquire wealth in the forests of southern Ghana and Côte d'Ivoire. Labour migration to the cocoa farms of Côte d'Ivoire and Ghana used to be cited in the literature as the classic case of 'target migration' – work undertaken for a limited period with a specific cash objective in mind (classically the purchase of a radio or bicycle). Since Liberia and Sierra Leone are the 'forest backwoods' of a savanna realm (the Manding world of the Upper Niger basin) that lies outside the historical range of Voltaic peoples, intrigue in the internal affairs of these two countries, in the name of youth progress, comes with much lower political costs attached than would any similar involvement in the affairs of the states immediately to the south. But such support or sympathy would at the same time chime with the historical experience of many Burkinabes that involvement in shaping the fate of the forest spells wealth.

Of course, the numbers of Burkinabes involved in the fighting in Sierra Leone and Liberia were relatively small (an estimate of 700 Burkinabes involved in the NPFL, according to Tarr 1993). However, they seem to have had a disproportionate impact in spreading terror. Survivors stress that it was the lack of any local language, knowledge, contacts or sympathies that made these Burkinabe commandos such effective instigators of terroristic violence. The Sierra Leonean rebels may at times have found it hard to follow their lead, and some are reported to have abandoned the rebel movement when they saw its impact on their defenceless country-folk.[22] As in any war the greater the social distance between warrior and victim the easier it becomes to kill for an idea. In this case the idea seems to have reduced in the end to a new and more violent form of target migration, with looted stereo sets, motorbikes and cars substituting for the radios and bicycles of earlier times. Perhaps this is why, as Tarr (1993) reports, the Libyans eventually concluded that Taylor's revolution was fake. There is some irony (though little comfort) in the fact that Burkinabe preoccupation with the logistics of looting almost certainly lost the RUF its initial military advantage, and perhaps sealed the fate of the rebellion.

Conclusion

The linked rebel movements in Liberia and Sierra Leone, competing for the mineral- and forest-resource-rich interior economies of 'Greater Liberia' and eastern Sierra Leone, sought to mould two sets of local social circumstances to their own ends with different degrees of success. First, they sought to undermine the power of immigrant trading diasporas in Liberia and Sierra Leone by stirring up local anti-merchant animosities. Second they recruited (or captured) significant numbers of youthful labourers from forested mineral-rich backwoods, and formed them into dissident forces capable of radical destabilization of local civil society. These young (and often underage) warriors deployed a distinctive apparatus of post-modern terror, including Renamo-style ritualized violence influenced by global media images.

The NPFL, having played upon historical-ethnic antipathy to a Mandingo merchant diaspora in the Liberian interior, came to embody the aspirations of a considerable constituency of rural

Liberians. Whether military confrontation with ECOMOG early in 1993 pushed it in the direction of terminal fragmentation is hard to judge. The RUF, much less successful in raising the spectre of populist anti-merchant factionalism among economically sophisticated forest communities of eastern and southern Sierra Leone, failed to establish any real political roots in interior eastern Sierra Leone, though gaining support to some extent from existing local and cross-border factionalism. Its youth army may now have broken up into freelance militias, some of whom have resumed business as consortia or armed diamond miners. Unless these militias can be convinced they have some kind of future in Sierra Leone under a new youth-orientated regime (Opala 1993), endemic low-intensity warfare, shading off into recurrent diamond-field banditry, may yet to prove a stubborn obstacle to that country's further political and economic progress.

Every student of African politics knows about ethnic factionalism. Indeed, it is regularly pressed into use as a blanket explanation for distant conflicts otherwise too difficult to document and comprehend. The youth factor has had much less attention in debates about conflict in Africa, yet it may take over from ethnicity as a consideration of more general future importance in a continent with such a high proportion of young people potentially alienated from wider civil society by failures of educational systems and employment opportunities. The antidote to the further spread in Africa of violence based on the enrolment of disaffected youth will require particular attention to be given to those factors likely to engender the confidence of the younger generation in the structures of state and civil society. The recent experience of Liberia and Sierra Leone suggests that fashionable concern with forest conservation and human rights will mean nothing unless the international community is prepared to renew its enthusiasm for those old and unfashionable concerns, education and employment.

Notes

1 It would be appropriate here to acknowledge the very many helpful comments I have received on earlier drafts of this essay from Liberian and Sierra Leonean colleagues; I have presumed that at this delicate stage in the history of their countries they might not wish to be named publicly, but I thank them warmly nevertheless. I would also like to thank Louis Brenner, Christopher Fyfe, Steven Riley and Tom Young for providing me with material and for helpful comments on the draft, and Mary Moran

and Joseph Opala for providing me with pre-print versions of their important essays on aspects of youth culture and violence in Liberia and Sierra Leone. I have also gained (I hope) from an exchange of views with Lord Eric Avebury, Chairman of the (UK) Parliamentary Human Rights Group, even though we hold rather different points of view on many of the issues under discussion.

2 Military action in eastern and southern Sierra beginning in March 1991 received especially scanty coverage; even *The Guardian*, normally reasonably well-informed on Africa, omitted to mention Sierra Leone in its 1992 end-of-year global review of the world's theatres of war. So far, scholarly coverage of the two conflicts has also been very limited in scope. Recently, however, a number of useful factual surveys have appeared (e.g. for Liberia, Amoo 1993 and Tarr 1993; for Sierra Leone, Musa and Musa 1993). For two recent and interesting papers by anthropologists trying to grapple with youth cultural dimensions of the two conflicts see Moran (1994) and Opala (1993).

3 It is estimated that 150,000 people have been killed and 750,000 people displaced as refugees during the first three years of the Liberian civil war. I know of no comparable figures for Sierra Leone, though the numbers will be much smaller in both cases. Numbers say nothing, however, about the trauma suffered by populations compelled to witness or take part in appalling and intentional acts of brutality. One of the worst of these shocking events was a massacre (5 June 1993) of about 500 refugees (men, women and children) at the rubber plantation at Harbel outside Monrovia. According to eyewitnesses, this was the work of a handful of teenage combatants who in a night of killing deployed ever more bizarre ways of despatching their victims. The first was described as a five-year-old boy whose head was sawn off with a blunt blade while his parents were forced to look on and applaud.

4 An economist by training, and former president of the Association of Liberians in the USA, Taylor 'somehow found himself in Monrovia at the time of the 1980 coup' (Amoo 1993). Back in the USA after his break with Doe he escaped from a county jail after a US court ruled that he could be extradited to Liberia on corruption charges. As Amoo observes, this was common sense rather than evidence of criminality, since Taylor was more likely to have met an untimely end than stand a fair trial under the Doe regime. The agreement of the US authorities to extradite in such circumstances is perhaps surprising.

5 An example would be the Channel 4 (UK) television news item on Liberia in December 1992. During the course of an interview with Taylor, the NPFL leader appeared to claim that he had already won an electoral mandate (perhaps 'as good as won' was intended?). One of a very small number of television news broadcasts in UK about the Liberian civil war, this substantial item was ostensibly about the partisanship of the Nigerian-led peace-keeping forces, but was itself a distinctly unbalanced account, since it included two extracts from an interview with Taylor without seeking any comment from the internationally recognized interim government. NPFL and RUF have both displayed a certain competence

in dealing with a less-than-vigilant international community, both through their skill in handling modern media, and a mollifying commitment to the post-Cold War international diplomatic rhetoric of multi-partyism, free trade and anti-totalitarianism. Lacking sophisticated lobbyists, such as the pro-Renamo Mozambique Institute in London – this is a low-cost war – the results are at times amusingly absurd. Charles Taylor, advocating the NPFL case to British television viewers in the interview cited above, stated his implacable opposition to President Babangida in Nigeria and Chairman Strasser in Sierra Leone on the grounds that they had seized power by military means, precisely as his own troops were attempting to storm Monrovia by force! Embarrassed by similar contradictions, RUF leader Foday Sankoh was heard to argue on the BBC Africa Service that his ambition was not to usurp the presidency but to reach Freetown and have himself appointed electoral commissioner in order to supervise multi-party elections. The primary purpose of blather of this sort seemed to be to buy time free from scrutiny by Western governments and human rights organizations in order for the two rebel groups to reconstruct themselves as endemic ethnic uprisings.

6 By an ethnographic quirk of history, Loko – a language close to Mende – is identical with the language spoken by the Gbande people of north-west Liberia, and this may have some bearing on support for the RUF from within Liberia.

7 Some Liberians believe that the CIA helped arm Johnson, having mistaken him for another (more politically credible) figure already killed in the fighting.

8 The ECOMOG strategy won the support of the USA, and the UN approved an arms and trade embargo on the Liberian warring factions. The willingness of the Bush administration to make a military intervention in Somalia but not in Liberia (despite the US historical connection) struck many observers as distinctly odd (not to say hypocritical), and was a point of concern to humanitarian campaigning groups in the USA (Ruiz 1992). The cynical explanation is that it would not look good on television (the Liberian forests are too reminiscent of Vietnam, perhaps?). French government attitudes to the Liberian civil war were also ambiguous, with some tacit sympathy (and perhaps support) for the NPFL reflecting personal closeness between Houphouet-Boigny and President Mitterrand and the Ivoirian president's concern to see Doe ousted.

9 The sentiments of the popular song by the Kabba Brothers issued shortly after the NPRC coup: *WOl dOn lEf na wi han* (The world is left in our hands). I would like to take the chance, here, to pay tribute to that irrepressible sense of humour among Sierra Leoneans, even as disaster stares them in the face, that makes their country such a life-enhancing place in which to work. One villager, who himself only narrowly survived the rebel invasion, told me about a group of soldiers who had bought magic bullet-proof war jackets from a local Mandingo magician. When not all their company returned from a night-time fight with the rebels the survivors sought out the magician, threw him his jacket, cocked their

rifles, stood him up against the wall and proposed testing the efficiency of his product there and then. When a bystander asked why they had not thought of such an experiment *before* they had paid for the jackets, the soldiers, too, saw the funny side and spared the man's life.

10 This was a viewpoint dismissed out of hand by some Mende young men with whom I happened to listen to an early message from Foday Sankoh broadcast on the BBC Africa Service (an appeal to the international media to meet him in a press conference). This could not be a Mende 'call-to-arms' since Sankoh spoke with a 'northern accent'. Some thought 'he must be from Makeni'. He was identified by other listeners as 'the short man' who once ran a photographic studio outside the Public Works Department compound in Bo. The listeners then drifted away to resume their interrupted football training.

11 The 'Up-Mende' of Kailahun had been particularly badly bruised by political events during the Siaka Stevens era (especially at the time of the 1977 election), and were thought (perhaps rightly) to be a major potential source of anti-APC sentiment within the country. It says much for the political discipline of the Mende people that they were not easily fooled by rebel misinformation, even when it appeared that their government was about to abandon them to their fate. But it is also right to note to the credit of the APC government, where a vein of restraint and decency at times moderated its venality and inefficiency, that President Momoh was not tempted into the kind of violent overreaction unleashed by Doe's troops on the civilians of Nimba County.

12 There is some evidence that the campaign for Kono was a long-planned objective of the RUF, not a last-minute switch. Refugees from one town in southern Kono report that in 1991 they helped a young man settle who claimed to be displaced by the first phase of fighting; only after the arrival of the RUF in 1992 did he reveal himself as a spy with a carefully compiled list of members of the town citizens' defence group. Unless he was a well-prepared opportunist this would suggest long-term planning on the part of the RUF. In the event the invasion of Kono may not have been an altogether fruitful move in political terms, since beforehand the military action was limited to the remoter parts of Mende country. While confined to the backwoods of Kailahun and Pujehun the war seemed remote to many influential Sierra Leoneans from Freetown and the Northern Province. The Kono diamond fields are especially hetero-geneous from an ethnic point of view, and the capture of the Koidu created refugees among all sections of the community, including the economically powerful Lebanese.

13 There was also renewed hostility in the southern sector after the NPRC take-over. Seemingly, the RUF garrison at Sulima fell to government troops after bombardment during the rainy season of 1992, but a more or less isolated rebel group at or around Fanima on the eastern side of the Moa was active throughout 1993. It has been suggested that this group made effective common cause with some of the dissident survivors of the local *ndogboyosoi* movement of the mid-1980s, this accounting for its obduracy, even though cut off from reinforcements from NPFL territory.

Ndogboyosoi was a rural rebellion stemming from conflict between the late APC Vice-President, Francis Minna (executed for his alleged involvement in a coup plot in 1987) and a local political rival in Pujehun District. Having re-armed itself from a successful raid on an ammunition store, the Fanima group was allegedly responsible for briefly successful attacks on Pujehun town in 1993 (twice) and 1994.

14 It has been alleged that Taylor himself invested in the RUF rebellion, and that relations between Sankoh and Taylor have at times been strained by the apparent misdirection of funds intended to pay Liberian and Burkinabe mercenaries.

15 Another viewpoint would be to regard the evidence of ethnocide against Mandingo traders as the outcome of an established local hostility that the NPFL was unable, or unwilling, to control, rather than the consequence of NPFL 'populist' ideology. However, there is clear evidence in eyewitness accounts of the invasion of Sierra Leone that anti-trader 'populism' was an explicit element in the revolutionary programme of the RUF. The Guinean Mandingo and Fula resident in Bo, when a rumoured RUF attack was imminent, were quite clear in their own minds about the RUF's ethnocidal intentions; several thousand fled to Guinea amid scenes of great panic on the night of 25–6 April 1991.

16 'Being Mandingo', however, is a cultural orientation. Not all Mandingo actually originate in the Mandingo Heartland of the Upper Niger basin. In some respects, the label refers simply to any trader who is *locally settled*. The Francophone literature Mandingo designates this broader sense of the term by using the Mandingo word for trader (*Dyula*).

17 Relative to the situation in rural Liberia, that is. In the context of a detailed analysis of local political rivalries generated by the 1986 general election, and its aftermath (an alleged coup plot in 1987), Ferme (1992) shows that the Mandingo-versus-indigene axis can still be a very powerful plane of polarization in Mende rural politics. It is worth noting, however, that in the case she describes the Paramount Chief of the Mende chiefdom in question was Mandingo. This emphasizes the distinction I wish to draw – namely, that on the Sierra Leone side of the Sierra Leone–Liberia border Mandingo elements tend now to be firmly embedded within local hierarchies of political power, and have long ceased to be regarded as a stranger element within local society.

18 The Libyan-inspired 'Gardener's Club' was an important factor in student radicalism at Fourah Bay College in 1977 (so-called because it met in the Botanical Garden). In turn it inspired the 'Future Shock' group formed by student radicals at Njala (the other constituent college of the University of Sierra Leone). Influential in student politics over a decade or more, this second group produces the newsletter *Front-line Push Magazine* and continues to debate radical alternatives for Sierra Leonean society. Although intensely opposed to the corruption apparent throughout the country under APC rule, this magazine has also been equally critical of the cynical abuse of the rural poor of which the RUF has been guilty. It offered qualified and cautious approval of reforms introduced by the NPRC.

19 Correspondence with the author, 1992. Clearly this is an area of tactical weakness in the defence of human rights in Africa that has a direct bearing on the later intransigent attitude of the NPRC government in Sierra Leone.

20 In Pandebu, on the Liberian border, east of Gola forest, young men seeking supplies before the war had the option of walking eight hours through the forest to the nearest road point in Sierra Leone, to wait for one (unreliable) vehicle a day to take them on the four- or five-hour journey to Kenema, or walking three hours to a point in Liberia where a taxi would take them to Monrovia the same day.

21 I was with a group of Sierra Leonean students on the day Sankara's death was announced, and can testify to the impact of this charismatic youth leader on the thinking of young people more widely in West Africa.

22 Stories circulate about one woman fighter in Bunumbu, who is said to have returned to Gbarnga in the early weeks of the RUF incursion to resign her command and voice her disgust to Sankoh and Taylor at the unrestrained looting of, and violence against, local populations.

References

Amnesty International, 1992. *The Extrajudicial Execution of Suspected Rebels and Collaborators*, London: International Secretariat of Amnesty International, Index AFR 51/02/92.

Amoo, S. G. 1993. 'ECOWAS in Liberia: The Challenges and Prospects for African Peacekeeping', unpublished paper, Conference of the Defence Intelligence College, Alconbury, Cambridge, UK, 6–7 May 1993.

Blanchard, D. 1973. *The Impact of External Domination on the Liberian Mano Economy: An Analysis of Weber's Hypothesis of Rationalism*, PhD thesis, University of Indiana, Bloomington.

Block, R. 1992. 'EC's Timber Imports Fuel Liberia Civil War', *Independent on Sunday*, 22 November 1992.

Clapham, C. 1976. *Liberia and Sierra Leone: An Essay in Comparative Politics*, Cambridge: Cambridge University Press.

Cosentino, D. 1989. 'Midnight Charters: Musa Wo and the Mende Myths of Chaos', in W. Arens and I. Karp, eds, *The Creativity of Power*, Washington: Smithsonian Institution Press.

Creveld, M. van, 1992. *On Future War*. London: Brassey.

Davies, A. G. and Richards, P. 1991. *Rain Forest in Mende Life: Resources and Subsistence Strategies in Rural Communities around the Gola North Forest Reserve (Sierra Leone)*, report to the UK Overseas Development Administration: Department of Anthropology, University College London.

Ferme, M. C. 1992. *"Hammocks belong to men, stools to women": Constructing and Contesting Gender Domains in a Mende Village (Sierra Leone, West Africa)*, PhD dissertation, University of Chicago.

Gershoni, Y. 1989. 'Liberia and Israel', *Liberian Studies Journal*, 14(1), pp. 34–50.

Kieh, G. K. 1989. 'An Analysis of Israeli Re-penetration of Liberia', *Liberian Studies Journal*, 14(2), pp. 117–29.

Kleinman, A. and Kleinman, J. 1991. 'Suffering and its Professional Transformation: Towards an Ethnography of Interpersonal Experience', *Culture, Medicine and Psychiatry*, 15(3), pp. 275–301.

Launey, R. 1982. *Traders without Trade: Responses to Change in Two Dyula Communities*, Cambridge: Cambridge University Press.

Linares, O. 1992. *Power, Prayer and Production: The Jola of Casamance, Senegal*, Cambridge: Cambridge University Press.

Maier, K. 1993. 'Liberians Flee "peace-keeping" offensive', *The Independent*, 25 March 1993, p. 13.

Moran, Mary 1994. 'Warriors or Soldiers: Masculinity and Ritual Transvestism in the Liberian Civil War', in Constance R. Sutton, ed., *Feminism, Nationalism and Militarism*, Arlington, VA: American Anthropological Association/Association for Feminist Anthropology.

Musa, S. and Musa, J. Lansana 1993. *The Invasion of Sierra Leone: A Chronicle of Events of a Nation under Siege*, Sierra Leone Institute for Policy Studies, Washington, DC.

Opala, J. A. 1993. 'Ecstatic Renovation: Street Art Celebrating Sierra Leone's 1992 Revolution', typescript, 1 April 1993.

Richards, P. 1994. 'Videos and Violence on the Periphery: Rambo and War in the Forests of the Sierra Leone–Liberia Border', *IDS Bulletin*, special issue on media and information in development, ed. Susanna Davies (in preparation).

Richards, P. 1995. *Fighting for the Rain Forest: Resources and Political Culture on the Liberia–Sierra Leone Border* (in preparation).

Ruiz, Hiram A. 1992. *Uprooted Liberians: Casualties of a Brutal War*, US Committee for Refugees, 1025 Vermont Ave., NW Suite 920, Washington, DC.

Tarr, S. Byron 1993. 'The ECOMOG Initiative in Liberia: A Liberian Perspective', *Issue: a Journal of Opinion*, 21(1–2), pp. 74–83.

Wilson, K. B. 1992. 'Cults of Violence and Counter-violence in Mozambique', *Journal of Southern African Studies*, 18(3), pp. 527–82.

Young, T. 1990. 'The MNR/RENAMO: External and Internal Dynamics', *African Affairs*, 89 (357), pp. 491–509.

8· THE ENDING OF THE COLD WAR IN AFRICA

Peter Lyon

Africa appears, if at all, among the marginalia of most contemporary grand strategists and writers in warfare and military matters generally. Apart from the phenomenon of the *coup d'état*, African examples are seldom prominent in the taxonomies or glossaries of the current compendiasts of conflict. Whether this is a well-grounded, negative general judgement inspired by due consideration and knowledge and deliberate rejection or merely the adventitious result of ignorance and prejudice is difficult to determine, though the second often seems much more likely than the first.

The end of the Cold War and the dissolution of the USSR and of Yugoslavia offer ambiguous portents, or analogies, or omens, for contemporary Africa. The end of the Cold War suggests scenarios for the immediate future where the prospect of general or world war has greatly diminished; the superpower rivalry within Africa[1] will not be renewed, at least not in the foreseeable future, and certainly not in the terms that were evident in the 1970s and 1980s. The dissolutions of the USSR and of Yugoslavia do, however, serve as dire reminders that the world political map certainly has not jelled permanently into place, that the break-up of federations, of unions – and the success of secessionists – is not everywhere doomed.

Even so, the way of the would-be secessionist is hard. The would-be secessionist more often ends up in gaol or on the gallows than in parliament and/or in a presidential palace. Were these not the verities, the instructive lessons, of the 1950s, 1960s and 1970s,[2] validated by the experiences and failures of Katanga (later Shaba province) in the former Belgian Congo (now Zaire) or of Biafra in

Nigeria? What, however, of the 1990s, during which there has already been the dissolution of the Soviet Union and of Yugoslavia, and perhaps now of Somalia? Will tidal waves of domino-like secessions (to mix the metaphors) henceforth engulf Africa radically to redraw the overall political and territorial map, which has been in general terms remarkably stable since those Olympian acts of partitioning and cavalier apportionments of territory were performed by European statesmen in Berlin in 1884–5, by men who usually did not themselves ever even visit Africa? And yet violence in contemporary Africa certainly is not confined to would-be secessionists. Coup-makers, actual or putative, communalism, tribalism, religious funda-mentalism, economic dissonances and sheer misery, as well as relative deprivations, can each and all contribute to the seething stew of conflict within contemporary Africa. Verily there is here surely another complex of '*plus ça change*. . .'. And what of external, that is to say extra-continental, stirrings, boostings, or ingredients, in the conflict cocktails of Africa? What is their provenance, their current and likely future and significance? This chapter is particularly focussed on these last two questions – though, inevitably, it touches on many others too.

Africa in geopolitics[3]

Africa, the second largest of the continents, has an area (including those off-shore islands conventionally included as part of the continent) of approximately 11,700,000 square miles (30,300,000 square kilometres). The continent stretches for about the same distance north and south of the Equator, about 5000 miles (8000 kilometres), but two-thirds of its land mass lies north of the Equator and nearly four-fifths is within the tropics. The east–west extent is 4600 miles (7400 kilometres).

Apart from the North African littoral, always part of the Mediter-ranean world, and some of its coastal fringes, Africa generally remained 'the dark, unknown continent' for most of the outside world until the late 18th century. Undoubtedly the physical environment presented outsiders with many obstacles and challenges. There are no deep bays or gulfs penetrating far inland and comparatively few rocky headlands affording shelter to adjoining bays. Shorelines are often surf-bound, and sometimes backed by large, though shallow, lagoons, frequently with mangrove clumps in them. Large rivers are rather few and, apart from the Congo, end in deltas or are blocked by sand-bars.

Rapids and falls fairly near to the coast discouraged penetration upstream, and navigation on most African waterways is restricted by the variable thalwegs and by the other great seasonal fluctuations of volume. These various difficulties would not have proved insuperable had the resources of the continent been sufficiently attractive to encourage outsiders to overcome them; but they certainly acted as discouragements even when they did not actually prevent European penetration. Apart from the iniquitous slave trade (practised by Arab slavers as well as Europeans), it was only in the 19th century that missionary activities and then the quest for gold and diamonds led to large-scale penetration and then to territorial annexation. Even in the late 20th century the realities of limitations imposed on development by physical conditions should be recognized. Several large-scale projects carried out since World War II have been vitiated largely because inadequate attention has been given to the obdurate facts of terrain, climate, water supply and soils.

European interventions contributed to the present-day shaping of the African continent in two main ways. In the first place, they defined its boundaries, producing precise linear configurations and most of the basic units of its present-day political cartography. The African states system of today was embryonically outlined by the time of the Treaties of Berlin of 1884–5, in the days of the so-called European 'Scramble for Africa'. Second, the Europeans sucked Africa decisively, if untidily, into a series of involvements with the wider world. This meant not only the North African littoral and the Maghreb, which had always been part of the Mediterranean world, but many other parts of the continent, including not least southern Africa (especially South Africa, with the development of its gold and diamond industries), became sucked into the world economy. Many of Africa's resources, especially its mineral resources, became regarded, as they are today, as significant parts of world markets. With these involvements, these external linkages, also came some-times involvement in extra-African quarrels and conflicts.[4]

The age inaugurated by the aeroplane transformed man's use of Africa's *écume*. It is often in the least developed parts of the earth that air communication is most prized. Most sizeable African countries nowadays maintain their most valuable internal mail, passenger and express services to principal centres by air. They also link up with what are, for them, main centres in other African countries in international flights. The full map of contemporary international flights within Africa, however, is still remarkably sparse by comparison with Europe and North America and depends considerably on schedules maintained by extra-African airlines and carriers, or by African airlines twinned with extra-African air companies. Indeed, regular airlines which skirt or traverse the whole of Africa have, since the 1960s, for the first time placed the whole continent in close juxtaposition, giving a degree of literal meaning to the previously merely poetical expression or cartographical convention that the whole continent of Africa is one unity. Even today, by comparison with North America and Europe, Africa has far fewer air routes which are regularly flown, although landing fields and supplies are becoming, if very unevenly, more numerous for those who wish to charter planes.

Talk of pan-continentalism, and especially of pan-Africanism, began in the late 19th and early 20th centuries, though the record of actual accomplishment was exiguous.[5] In this regard G.K. Chesterton's observation on one of the more grandiose of Cecil Rhodes' injunctions, 'to think in continents', was pertinent. 'It is just as easy to think in continents as to think in cobblestones', Chesterton said. 'The difficulty comes when we seek to learn the substance of either of them.'

It was, however, only from the late 1950s and early 1960s, as decolonization proceeded apace, that Africa began to participate actively in the world's states system. In 1950 there were only four independent states in Africa (Egypt, Ethiopia, Liberia and South Africa); by 1963–4, when the Organization of African Unity was launched, there were just over twenty, and by 1990 there were fifty. Since the late 1950s Africa has inescapably been drawn into world politics, is deeply affected by and often has to submit to the rhythms of changing relations between the extra-African major powers. One expert commentator[6] has argued that the Angolan crisis of 1975 assumed for Africa the significance that Dien Bien Phû had for South East Asia in the mid-1950s, as did the Suez crisis for the Middle East at approximately the same time. He concludes that the multi-lateralization of Africa's international relations is probably an irreversible fact, though the further claim that the influence of the superpowers on the continent in 1990 is considerably greater than in 1960 appears wry in the later 1990s and serves as a reminder that unilinear change is not an ineluctable law of human nature or of human history.

Africa in contemporary geopolitics

Much of Africa today is afflicted by chronic drought, desertification, famine, by many natural and man-made disasters. These dire situations demonstrate time and again the vastness of human suffering, and calls for the moral reach and acute sympathy of a Fydor Dostoyevsky to encompass their depth and range. The major catastrophes are beyond the capacities of the countries concerned, or even the whole continent, to handle. Thus there is increasing talk nowadays of the need to invest the United Nations with the authority and resources to cope internationally with major disasters and conflicts; the record of the recent past, however, points to the inherent difficulties and limitations of such instrumentalities.[7]

Although the UN Secretary-General Boutros Boutros-Ghali (an Egyptian national, incidentally) has called for a standing UN 'peace enforcement unit' to be made up of 1000-man, well-armed contingents from member states, and to be deployed under the authorization of the Security Council, so far this proposal has met with a deafening silence, especially from the USA, the one remaining superpower but notably loath to relinquish its self-appointed role as world policeman to the UN, or to pay up its outstanding dues. UN peace-keeping activities thus remain *ad hoc* and highly specific operations.

In 1992 there were twelve UN peace-keeping operations in being, three of them in Africa with another six in the Mediterranean or Middle East (Cyprus, Croatia and Bosnia, South Lebanon, Jerusalem, Golan Heights and Iraq/Kuwait). The three African UN operations were:

- in Angola, where a verification mission (Unavem II) was set up in 1988 to monitor the withdrawal of Cuban troops. It consists of 350 officers, 90 police and 400 election observers for the autumn 1992 plebiscite; the cost is estimated to be $110 million.
- in the Western Sahara, with a referendum mission (MINURSO) which was set up in 1991 with a strength of 375 to prepare and supervise a referendum on the political future of this territory and people. Moroccan and Polisario Front disagreements hitherto have held up arrangements on who should be allowed to vote. This operation is estimated to cost about $60 million a year.
- in Somalia (UNOSOM), where the UN mission was being deployed in 1992 to help deliver food to the 4.5 million Somalis

facing imminent starvation due to drought and civil war. The 3000 military personnel are intended to protect convoys and to try to negotiate ceasefires between warring clans. This operation is expected to cost more than $100 million.

Arms transfers

The world's major arms market in the last 20 years has been dominated by a relatively small number of stable and long-term relationships, both on the supplier and the recipient side. According to Stockholm World Watch Reports (SIPRI),[8] only three African countries figured among the world's leading importers of major weapons in the years 1984–8; Egypt was fourth (after Iraq, India and Saudi Arabia), Angola was seventh and Libya was tenth. In the years 1979–83 Libya was the only major African recipient of Soviet arms; in 1984–8 both Angola and Libya were. In the years 1979–83 Egypt was a major recipient from the USA, France, China and the UK; and Libya was also a recipient from France, and Nigeria from the (then) Federal Republic of Germany. In the years 1984–8 both Angola and Libya from Africa received major supplies from the Soviet Union; Egypt was recipient from the USA and from China, and Nigeria from the UK. Angola and Libya (together with India, Iraq and Syria) accounted for over 75 per cent of Soviet arms exports in the years 1984–8, but since the late 1980s these Soviet shipments to Africa have virtually ceased. For Angola, the Soviet supplies seemed closely related to the activities of Cuban troops there, and these troops were withdrawn subsequent to the UN-sponsored agreement signed by Angola, Cuba and South Africa in Geneva on 15 November 1988. MiG-23 aircraft in Angola were flown by Cuban pilots and surface to air missiles (SAMs) were manned by GDR personnel – activities which ceased in Africa as domestic difficulties mounted in the homelands of these mercenaries.

At the time of writing, the impact of the dissolution of the Soviet Union on the arms trade of Africa is ambiguous and pointing in contradictory directions. On the one hand, the desire of Russian leaders to get hard currency has impelled them to sell off many weapons at bargain-basement prices; but most African states still lack the hard currency to make such purchases. Furthermore, the poor performance of Soviet-designed and -produced weapons held in Iraq's armoury during the Gulf War has diminished the attractiveness of Soviet or Russian as compared with weaponry produced in North

America or Western Europe. Diplomatic détentes between neighbours can also reduce the quest for foreign arms. Thus, according to Reuter reports from Harare on 20 August 1992, Zimbabwe cancelled a $400 million (£209 million) order for Russian MiG-29 fighters because of a lessening of tension between it and South Africa.[9]

The technology of warfare does not stand still, and, although African states and economies are not in the forefront of the world's innovators in the production and export of weapons, they do have access to the world's markets for arms. For the foreseeable future African governments (or their major challengers) bent on acquiring sophisticated weapons are likely to seek them from extra-continental sources rather than to manufacture them themselves.

All in all, the prevailing patterns of relationships strongly suggest that the distribution of major conventional weapons is principally determined not by economic or market forces but by political and strategic evaluations. The indications in the mid-1990s are, however, that military expenditure, major arms acquisitions and militarization are on the decline in Africa.

The nuclear dimension

Recent evidence indicates that Africa is still only involved in continuing controversies about nuclear weapons. For Africans, it is the two quasi-pariah regimes of Israel and South Africa and their nuclear capabilities which are their principal concerns.

The Nuclear Non-Proliferation Treaty (NPT) was signed on 1 July 1968 and came into effect on 5 March 1970. Its text is short and consists of five main elements:

- a commitment by nuclear-weapon states not to transfer nuclear weapons to any other state;
- a commitment by non-nuclear-weapon state signatories not to seek to acquire nuclear weapons;
- the mandatory acceptance by all non-nuclear-weapon states of the safeguards system of the International Atomic Energy Agency (IAEA) – this accounts for the peaceful use of all nuclear materials within their state and all nuclear exports;
- a general commitment that all parties to the treaty should be allowed to exploit fully the peaceful uses of nuclear energy;
- a commitment by the nuclear-weapons states to negotiate, in good faith, the 'cessation of the nuclear arms race'.

The treaty also calls for a review conference every five years, and states that 25 years after it has entered into effect, i.e. in 1995, a conference shall be convened to decide whether the treaty shall continue in force indefinitely, or shall be extended for an additional fixed period or periods.[10]

The fourth review conference of the NPT met in Geneva between 20 August and 15 September 1990, conducted a lively debate on a wide agenda, but was unable to produce a final agreed document. Of the 140 signatories of the NPT, 84 chose to be represented at this fourth review conference. Tanzania and Zimbabwe were represented by observers for the first time but South Africa was absent. Israel, also, had observer status. Egypt and Nigeria from Africa played an active part, the former stressing the need to strengthen the existing commitment by all the nuclear-weapon-possessing states to aid any non-nuclear-weapon state threatened or attacked with nuclear weapons, the latter proposing that a conference should be convened to negotiate a standard agreement on 'negative security assurances' between the nuclear-weapon states and the NPT non-nuclear-weapon states. Many participants, the Africans not least, expressed their concern about the nuclear-weapon capabilities of Israel and South Africa, and urged them to sign the treaty, accept IAEA safeguards on all nuclear materials within their states, and support the creation of nuclear-weapon-free zones in their region.

The NPT review conference of 1990 was followed within six months by the Gulf War over Kuwait, with its demonstration of the efficiency of America's precision weapons (and the relative in-efficiency or uncompetitiveness of Iraq's major armoury of weapons, mostly of Soviet origin). This war helped to focus attention on the importance of the NPT regime, and the nature of the post-Cold War world. Zambia and Tanzania, which had long resisted pressure to join the NPT because of its discriminatory features and concern about South Africa, announced their accession in 1991. In June that year the Foreign Minister of South Africa said that his country had decided to become a party and thus to submit all nuclear materials to full-scope safeguards. By September 1991 the safeguards agreement had already been concluded and brought into force. South Africa handed over an inventory of its nuclear materials and facilities, and by the end of the year Agency staff were verifying its authenticity. The South African decision makes the spread of nuclear weapons unlikely in this region of the world and opens the possibility of creating an African nuclear-weapon-free zone. Of the remaining front-line states, Angola and Namibia indicated their intention to accede to the NPT, and Zimbabwe acceded in June 1991. Despite continuing, if slow, proliferation globally and no marked recent general agreement within the NPT, the shadow of a nuclear Armageddon does appear to be diminishing rather than lengthening over Africa at present.

Africa's patrons depart

'Time was when African states could rely on a post-colonial superpower patronage to build their infrastructure, or at least subsidise their elites. One superpower has collapsed and the other is devoting its energies to propping it up. Africa must look to the once vilified multinational companies and even to South Africa for sponsorship, and it will be painful.'

The Times, editorial, 24 January 1992

Under the same title as this chapter's subsection *The Times* editorial ruminated on the fact that the West, the North, the OECD world (these terms are only loose and general, and proximate synonyms), has lately come to accept and assert, in the words of Britain's Minister for Overseas Development, Lynda Chalker, that 'poverty neither excuses nor justifies tyranny, torture or corruption', though the continent still displays not only too much poverty but a lot of its alleged progeny – of tension and conflict – too. The political practices of African dictators can, however, no longer be plausibly dismissed mostly as a legacy of colonialism. The age of decolonization has passed into one of post-colonialism – even apartheid is being superseded, though for what remains to be seen. Blame increasingly is being placed on leaders who spend more of their national income on guns than on cassava, and less perhaps on those outsiders who patronized them with their support and aid. African leaders have some autonomy and responsibilities as well as being involved in the affairs of the wider world, the global village.

All over Africa today the existing state structures (and their often only nominal national unities) are being severely stretched and strained. This needs to be taken fully into account by those who propose new and large federations or confederations, continental markets or other nostrums of conflict management and amelioration. For surely it is unwise to believe that those who cannot comfortably manage problems at a national or parochial level will do better at higher levels with larger units.

Africans used to remark wearily that 'when two elephants fight it is the grass that suffers'. In the early 1990s the grass on many African savannas was beginning to grow upright again; and most of the fighting that continues is of low intensity. A verdict pronounced by editorial writers for *The Economist* (21 December 1991 – 3 January 1992) is as applicable to Africa as it is to the current international scene generally:

> War shows no sign of going out of fashion. If it cannot be banished, peacemakers can only work to keep it local and to control the spread of the nastier weapons, from mustard gas to nuclear bombs. Notwithstanding some worries, those efforts are proving reasonably successful. Should they fail, however, the post-cold-war world of the early 1990s may come, in retrospect, to look like a golden age of peace.

Meanwhile, it is generally true to say that the greatest direct threats that most African countries face presently and for the foreseeable future come from within their own borders – threats of coups, of secession, of tribalism, of violence formented by and expressed in terms of ethnic and religious identities.[11] While it would be wrong to discount entirely the disruptive factors originating outside particular countries, or even from outside the continent of Africa altogether, these are not the main ingredients fomenting or festering within the contemporary cauldron of Africa.

For outside powers even contemplating Africa in military terms in the 1990s, this continent poses logistical labyrinths, strategic swamplands and many fierce, localized but combustible quarrels. As long as such a state of affairs prevails, then non-intervention is likely to be avowed and preferred to military intervention. It would be naive, however, to assume that all state policies are based on careful and accurate assessments of the costs and benefits of intended activities or that military force is now forsworn as a weapon in the armoury of chancelleries. Precisely because overt military activities by outside powers are unlikely in Africa in the immediate future, if and when they do occasionally occur then they are likely to be both important and controversial as well as escalatory. A classical Chinese curse thus applies to the Africa of today and tomorrow: Africans do live in 'interesting times'.

Notes

1 See Zaki Laidi, *The Superpowers and Africa: The Constraints of a Rivalry 1960–1990*, translated from the French by Patricia Baudoin (London: University of Chicago Press, 1990). This is a study of sub-Saharan Africa; North Africa is excluded.

2 See Peter Lyon, 'New States and International Order', in *The Bases of International Order*, ed. Alan James (London: Oxford University Press, 1973). See also J. D. Hargreaves, *Decolonization in Africa* (London: Longman, 1988).

3 I know of no comprehensive and systematic up-to-date treatment. But for some elements, see Derwent Whittlesey, 'Africa, an Exploitable Continent', in *The Earth and the State* (New York: Henry Holt & Co., 1939), pp. 304–94, and R. J. Harrison Church, 'The Impact of the Outer World on Africa', in *The Changing World: Studies in Political Geography*, ed. W. Gordon East and A. E. Moodie (London: Harrap & Co., 1956), pp. 723–39.

4. But Africa claims only four perfunctory references, and seven pages altogether, in Quincy Wright's otherwise magisterial and encyclopaedic *A Study of War* (second edition, with a commentary on war since 1942; London: University of Chicago Press, 1965). For data subsequent to 1965, see the annual publications of the International Institute for Strategic Studies (IISS), London, and of the Stockholm Institute for Peace Research (SIPRI).

5 See, further, Peter Lyon, 'The Pan-Continental Movements of Asia and Africa, 1947–58', in *Australian Outlook*, June 1959, pp. 100–111, and *Neutralism* (Leicester University Press, 1963), pp. 109, 145–7; and Colin Legum, *Pan-Africanism* (Pall Mall Press, 1964).

6 See Laidi, op. cit.

7 See, for example, Alan James, *The Politics of Peacekeeping* (London: Chatto and Windus for the IISS, 1970); and for a brief summary of the twelve UN peace-keeping operations in being in 1992, see *Independent on Sunday*, 6 September 1992.

8 For a perspective view, see SIPRI, *The Arms Trade with the Third World* (Stockholm: Almquist and Wiksell, 1971), and for data in subsequent years, see IISS and SIPRI annual surveys, especially the latter's year-book, *World Armaments and Disarmament*.

9 See *Financial Times*, 20 August 1992.

10 See John Simpson, 'The 1990 Review Conference of the Nuclear Non-Proliferation Treaty: Pointer to the Future or Diplomatic Accident?', *The Round Table*, 318, April 1991, pp. 139–54.

11 See, further, B. Bozeman, *Conflict in Africa: Concepts and Realities* (Princeton University Press, 1976), and for a searching review of this book by a professional anthropologist, a specialist on Somalia, see I. M. Lewis, 'Culture and Conflict in Africa', *Journal of International Studies*, 6 (2), Autumn 1977, pp. 175–81, which says, *inter alia*, that this is 'a tendentiously ethnocentric enterprise, informed by highly legalistic western assumptions which bear little relation to the realities of power anywhere'.

9. ANGOLA: ENDING THE COLD WAR IN SOUTHERN AFRICA

Kathryn O'Neill and Barry Munslow

In December 1988 a significant milestone was achieved in the retreat from Cold War politics. The USA presided over the official signing of a peace agreement paving the way for South African, Cuban and Soviet military disengagement from Angola and the independence of Namibia, marking the beginning of the end of the internationalization of the war in Angola. On 21 March 1990 Namibia finally became independent under government by the South West African People's Organization (SWAPO), following elections deemed to have been 'free and fair' by the United Nations, ending the final chapter in the saga of African decolonization.

Across the border to the north, the government of the Movimento Popular de Libertação de Angola (MPLA) and the Union for the Total Independence of Angola (UNITA) finally signed a ceasefire agreement in Lisbon in May 1991, just six days after the last contingent of Cuban troops was flown out of Luanda. The Portuguese-mediated negotiations, under the watchful eye of American and Soviet observers, succeeded at a time when the military situation had once again reached a stalemate. Government troops had made significant military gains into UNITA strongholds in the south-east of the country in early 1990, but UNITA was able to respond effectively and step up its operations in the north, regularly attacking water and electricity supplies to the capital. The Cuban and Soviet withdrawal from Angola marked the demise of socialist bloc influence in the region. The USA replaced South Africa as the principal supporter of the UNITA opposition forces to the MPLA government. Angola's rich natural resource base and strategic location meant that the country commanded some attention from the Bush administration, while Africa in general was barely registering on the foreign-policy agenda of Washington.

This chapter examines changes in the foreign policies of the two superpowers of the 1980s and the effects of their global rapprochement on the conflicts in Angola and Namibia, for this is where the Cold War confrontation in the region has been most intense. We begin by outlining the dramatic military confrontations of 1987–8 in southern Angola, focussing on the crucial battle for Cuito Cuanavale which marked a decisive shift in the regional balance of power, after which the South African government decided to pursue a negotiated end to the conflict in Angola and accept free elections to determine the future of Namibia. The Cold War confrontation by proxy peaked when there were direct clashes between Cuban and South African troops in June 1988. This threatened to embroil the superpowers yet further, just at the time when they were hoping to cooperate in defusing regional centres of conflict starting with a negotiated deal on Afghanistan.

Events on the battlefield

The impetus for a negotiated settlement to the regional conflict emerged from a recognition by all the parties concerned that a purely military solution was no longer feasible. Such a decision was reached, however, only after a major escalation of the military confrontation.

Fighting between South African and UNITA forces on the one side and Angolan government troops supported by the Cubans and Soviets on the other, came to a head in early 1988, centring on the garrison town of Cuito Cuanavale in Kuano Kubango province.[1] On the outcome of this battle much would be determined.

The final showdown began in August 1987 when the Angolan government army FAPLA (Armed Forces for the Liberation of Angola) embarked on an offensive against the town of Mavinga, held by UNITA since 1981. This was repelled by the SADF (South African Defence Force), who intervened in a cross-border operation from Namibia to save UNITA from defeat, as they had done in a similar protective operation in 1985. However, Pretoria's strategic aim on this occasion was more ambitious, namely to take the government stronghold of Cuito Cuanavale to the north by March 1988 in a counter-offensive, thus enabling UNITA to launch even deeper attacks into Angolan territory protected by South African air support. The strategic aim was to create a sufficient zone of security in the centre-south of the country such that a provisional government could be installed at the UNITA headquarters in Jamba. It was hoped that this would strengthen the hand of the rebels to enable them to become a party to any negotiations. In response Cuban reinforcements arrived in the form of the 50th Division, led by General Ochoa Sanchez, the architect of the victory against the SADF in the Angolan war of 1975–6, bringing the total number of Cuban troops stationed in the country up to 40,000 according to official figures.

In mid-to-late January 1988 there were sustained clashes between Angolan and South African forces about 80 kilometres east of Cuito Cuanavale. FAPLA seemed dangerously close to losing the town, with the South Africans cutting off the vital Cuito River bridge and attacking supply convoys.[2] Despite the heavy shelling they were unable to knock out the air base at Cuito altogether. Although the runway was too vulnerable to be operational, Angolan forces were still able to use their mobile radars and helicopters for counter-attack, with the back-up of MiG-23s flying in from Menongue.[3] The Cuito airfield was an important strategic target for the South Africans, being the base from which the Angolan Air Force launched its attacks on the UNITA-held town of Mavinga in September 1987.

Reports of South African fatalities first began filtering through in November, when more than twenty deaths were announced by Pretoria, along with the first public admission of the military intervention. By February the Angolans claimed to have destroyed a total of 40 South African aircraft with Pretoria admitting a loss of 25.[4] However the loss of two Cheetahs (an upgraded version of the Mirage), was particularly serious, as only 12 were thought to be operational.[5] The Mirage cannot openly be bought on international markets due to the effectiveness of the United Nations arms embargo, making them difficult and costly to replace. South Africa has comparatively limited access to anti-aircraft missiles and radar systems using the latest technology, and Angola's sophisticated Soviet-supplied radar defence system along with MiG-21 and MiG-23 fighter planes proved vastly superior to the ageing Mirage jets. The loss of air superiority increased the stakes for the South African forces. Military chiefs decided that a massive land assault on Cuito was not advisable as casualties would reach unacceptable levels. Instead they opted for a drawn-out artillery battle, attacking with long-range G-5 and G-6 howitzers, helicopters, Valkiri multiple rocket launchers, over 400 armoured car and tank units, backed up by heavy air support and at least three battalions of infantry (an estimated 6000 men), along with 4000 UNITA rebels. The SAAF (South African Air Force) kept up its attacks, bombing the town of Xangongo in Cunene province, and purporting to hit SWAPO bases at Lubango and Ngiva (the capitals of Huila and Cunene provinces respectively) with eight Mirage and five Impala fighter planes. However, Lubango was probably a target not because of any SWAPO base but because it was FAPLA's main southern air base and command centre.

In late March the battle at Cuito was still raging. UNITA went ahead as planned and declared a provisional government at Jamba on 24 March, with Jeremias Chitunda nominated Prime Minister. The SADF announced further casualties but prepared for yet another assault on the town. FAPLA units were reinforced by a convoy of 500 vehicles sent from Menongue, and in spite of sustained shelling they still maintained control of the town and the new temporary bridge.[6]

South Africa's loss of vital air superiority, with a consequent increase in the domestically politically sensitive 'white body count', prompted Pretoria to reassess its entire Angola/Namibia strategy. While the South Africans were not decisively defeated at Cuito, they faced political costs of continuing the fighting that were much too high. For only the second time in the Angolan conflict, the myth of South African invincibility on the battlefield had received a body blow, providing a significant boost to the morale of the Angolan government forces. The first occasion was back in 1975 when South Africa invaded Angola to install a UNITA/FNLA government (the FNLA, National Front for the Liberation of Angola, had been supported by the USA since the early 1960s), but were turned back by Cuba's Stalin organ rocket launchers at the gates of the capital, brought in to reinforce the MPLA troops.

The South Africans were caught out by a change in FAPLA/Cuban tactics, with the deployment of Cuban reinforcements in the south-western area of Angola close to the Namibian border. The aim of the new offensive was undoubtedly to neutralize the southern front – a virtual no-go area for the Angolan military because of the South African presence since the early 1980s – in a political manoeuvre designed to strengthen Angola's position in the first round of meetings held in London in May 1988 between the Angolan, South African, Cuban and US governments.

On 27 June, a Cuban-led air and ground attack on the Ruacana hydro-electricity scheme at Calueque, close to the Namibian border, took the South Africans completely by surprise. The attack, involving 12 MiG-23 fighter planes, led to direct clashes between Cuban and SADF troops, resulting in serious losses. The SADF acknowledged 12 whites killed, but according to Luanda there were more than twice as many fatalities.[7] The attack confirmed the shift in the balance of regional military power away from South Africa.

Operating more than 300 kilometres from the Namibian frontier and over 400 from their nearest main base, the SADF had become logistically overextended. As a result of the new Cuban/Angolan tactical moves, an estimated 4000 SADF troops involved in the fighting around Cuito Cuanavale had risked becoming bogged down in the Angolan rainy season, having their route cut off back into northern Namibia. Only then did the military strategist in Pretoria turn to the politicians to negotiate a ceasefire and secure a safe withdrawal of SADF forces from southern Angola, following almost a year of intense fighting.

A formal ceasefire was announced on 8 August 1988, after a meeting of senior military representatives from South Africa, Angola and Cuba on the island of Sal, Cape Verde, in July, and the SADF pull-out of Angola was completed by 1 September.

Retreat from Cold War politics

The rapidly changing arena of international politics has had a major bearing on events in Angola and Namibia, both politically and militarily. The new era of 'constructive cooperation' between the superpowers, aimed at defusing global and regional centres of conflict, coupled with the escalating political and economic cost of Pretoria's military occupation of Namibia and destabilization of Angola, became key factors in facilitating a negotiated settlement of the conflict. US and Soviet stakes in the Angolan conflict dramatically increased from 1985, but the ensuing military deadlock prompted both superpowers to agree to seek a negotiated settlement to the war, each putting pressure on their respective allies in the process. Chester Crocker, US Assistant Secretary of State for African Affairs throughout most of the 1980s and the mediator of the negotiations, termed this change a 'convergence of interests' between the USA and the USSR, with each round of talks preceded by a meeting between Crocker and leading Soviet officials.[8] After the signing of the accords at the end of 1988, Crocker praised his Soviet counterpart, Deputy Foreign Minister Anatoly Adamishin, for his 'close, practical and effective co-operation' in creating 'a case study of superpower co-operation in the solution of regional problems'.[9]

The initiative for improved relations between the USA and the USSR came largely from the latter, in response to domestic political and dire economic circumstances. Given increasing problems at home and within the Eastern bloc, the Soviet Union was seeking to reduce its Third World commitments, in the knowledge that it could no longer afford to underwrite peripheral socialist economies which had proved even more fallible than their original Soviet model, nor support liberation movements across the globe.

Soviet policy

Since the mid-1980s, a growing diversity of thought has been encouraged within the former Soviet Union on the analysis of Third World states and the foreign policy to be adopted towards them, and this is reflected in changing attitudes towards southern Africa. Different approaches have been dominant at particular times. The coming to power of a wave of revolutionary Third World regimes in the 1970s encouraged those who believed Western imperialism to be on the defensive. At this time the viewpoints of what David Albright terms the 'revolutionary democratic' school was in the ascendancy, seeing the Third World on an inexorable march towards socialism.[10] 'Social-oriented states' were encouraged to build up long-term structural relationships with the Soviet Union which included the provision of military support. Increasing Soviet involvement and influence on the periphery was regarded as being in no way incompatible with the move towards a strategy of global détente.

Since Gorbachev came to power in the mid-1980s, there has been a marked reduction in this confrontational stance. As early as March 1986, he indicated that the Soviet Union was trying to help find political solutions to the Angolan conflict as part of a wider policy decision by the ruling Communist Party to seek negotiated solutions to all regional conflicts. From the late 1980s a school of thought gaining influence inside the Soviet Union recognized that the Third World would have to pass through a capitalist phase of development. It was critical of efforts at socialist transition on the periphery to date and wary of the heavy financial cost of supporting such regimes at the expense of engineering critically necessary domestic economic re-structuring. The desire to reduce confrontation with the West in the Third World occurred at a time when the USA was reasserting its power on the global periphery, thereby increasing the cost of confrontation. As a reflection of this Soviet change of emphasis, it is significant that ideologues in the Central Committee's International Department were replaced by career diplomats more amenable to the search for negotiated solutions to conflicts.

A learning curve is apparent in the Soviets' dealings with 'socialist oriented' underdeveloped states. With the Soviet Union now counting the cost of its own strategy of heavy industrialization and the socialization of agriculture, all but the most blinkered are now agreed that such development strategies applied on the periphery have proved disastrous.[11] The fundamental economic weakness of the Soviet economy precluded any alternative to integration with the global market economy for 'socialist-oriented' regimes on the periphery, in addition rapidly undermining the extent to which they would be supported militarily through the various friendship and cooperation treaties. Weaknesses in the economic capacity of revolutionary states was accompanied by a weakness of political organization among the ruling vanguard parties, which singularly failed to resolve internal, regionally based political dissent.

Moscow's foothold in southern Africa was secured in the 1970s, in the aftermath of the Watergate scandal and the US defeat in the Vietnam War, which limited the political will of the US government to become heavily involved in another Third World conflict, even clandestinely through the CIA.[12] Soviet and Cuban support to the MPLA proved decisive in the internal struggle for power in 1974–6 against UNITA and the FNLA – who were backed by South Africa and the USA – in the conflict over who would replace the departing Portuguese colonial power.

Soviet policy towards Angola since the decisive entry of Cuban troops in 1975 provided the MPLA with large-scale military and to some extent political support, but not the economic assistance to match. Ironically, revenues from American oil companies operating in Angola have paid for Soviet and Cuban military equipment and personnel, and the USA, despite withholding diplomatic recognition of the MPLA, remains Angola's main trading partner, buying two-thirds of its oil.

1985–6 saw a dramatic rise in South African military expenditure, the Soviets supplied an extra $2 billion of military aid to the MPLA, including more MiG-23 fighter planes.[13] These increasingly sophisticated supplies were crucial in helping FAPLA begin to break South Africa's domination of the skies, eventually enabling the Angolans to inflict serious losses on SADF ground troops backing UNITA operations. South Africa claimed that Soviet officers were directly involved in the FAPLA offensive on Mavinga in August 1985, as a way of drawing the USA further into the conflict, and this was one of the main factors prompting the subsequent decision to provide aid to UNITA, as the USA was unwilling to see a change in the internal balance of forces in the MPLA's favour.[14]

Soviet involvement continued in the preparation of the offensive of August 1987 on Mavinga, with the whole operation coming under the direction of General Konstantin Shaganovich. Soviet military aid increased by a further $1 billion, bringing the estimated total over the previous decade to $4 billion.[15] But as in 1985 South African military intervention yet again saved UNITA from defeat, and obliged a retreat by Angolan government forces.

Neil MacFarlane has reviewed changing Soviet attitudes towards southern Africa, charting the growing interest in negotiated reform rather than confrontation as the route for engineering change in the sub-continent.[16] Their heavy involvement in the region taught the Soviets that inflicting a total military defeat on the South African and UNITA forces was not possible, and they also witnessed a continuing economic and political deterioration in the country. Yet 'Moscow was unwilling to walk away from the Angolan conflict. To do so would have severely damaged Soviet prestige and would have eliminated the principal position affording the Soviet Union a role in the politics of southern Africa.[17] Hence Moscow determined to pursue a political settlement, and in mid-1987, following their urgings, the Angolans accepted the linkage between the independence of Namibia and Cuban troop withdrawal from Angola. This was insisted upon by the USA and for long had been a stumbling-block to negotiations. By 1988 the Soviet Union began to put pressure on the MPLA to reach a compromise agreement with UNITA. In August, Adamishin urged the Angolan government to 'start a dialogue' with the rebels.[18] However, military pressure had also to be placed on South Africa to deliver them to the negotiating table, hence the escalation of fighting in 1987–8. Writing in 1989, MacFarlane concludes his assessment:

> The record of the past three years shows continued Soviet commitment to do what is possible short of direct intervention to prevent disastrous defeat for the MPLA and to improve prospects for a settlement that would stabilise the situation in Angola, preserve a role in government for Moscow's local ally, and maintain Soviet prestige... In sum, Moscow appears amenable to cooperative ventures in regional conflict settlement but not to exclusion from the region.[19]

It is a measure of how quickly the whole international scene has been changing that the very idea of maintaining a significant role for the Soviet Union in southern Africa appears far-fetched in the 1990s, given the decisive rejection of communism world-wide and an increasing introspective concern with growing internal political and economic turmoil inside the Soviet Union. US influence in southern Africa has strengthened. However, under President Bush there appears to be far less of a pro-active US policy in southern Africa than there was under Reagan, and the USA itself is facing considerable economic strains.

A further significant and related shift in Soviet policy occurred towards South Africa. Instead of encouraging ANC military confrontation, Moscow now preferred a political settlement.[20] This change in attitude was cemented when the Soviets continued contacts with Pretoria following the Namibia/Angola settlement.

In southern Africa then, two shibboleths of Soviet policy were finally overturned. One was that the key to change in South Africa lay through the route of armed struggle and the other was the viability of a centralized state-planned socialist economy. Senior experts of the Institute for African Studies at the USSR Academy of Science affirmed in October 1989 that the southern African conflict required a political and not a military solution and that the USSR would not undermine the industrialized countries' historic trade links with the region. Furthermore, it was emphasized that economic underdevelopment did not provide the prerequisites for socialism and that existing centralized planning had been far too rigid and unrealistic.[21]

The political landscapes of Eastern Europe and southern Africa remain in a state of flux. Political and economic changes in the Soviet Union have had momentous effects on Angola, Mozambique, Namibia and South Africa. In 1989 the Frente de Libertação de Moçambique (FRELIMO) renounced its role as a vanguard Marxist-Leninist party, moved towards negotiations with the rebel forces of the Mozambique National Resistance (MNR, usually known as Renamo) and became the 'model' structural adjustment reformer. The MPLA followed with the decision at its congress in December 1990 to adopt a multi-party system and moved, albeit haltingly, towards market-oriented economic policies, after finally obtaining membership of the International Monetary Fund (IMF) and World Bank. The South African Communist Party began a much belated rethink of its *Weltanschauung*. The SWAPO government in Namibia was careful not to rock the boat of the conditionalities of the all-important aid givers.

US policy

With Ronald Reagan's assumption of the US Presidency in 1980 a [handwritten: 1981] new Cold War era ensued, fought out in the main in Third World locations.[22] A policy of 'Constructive Engagement' was developed for southern Africa in which the goal was to encourage change in South Africa through dialogue rather than economic pressure and to work with South Africa as a regional ally to combat Soviet and Cuban influence. Hence the USA created a linkage issue between the withdrawal of Cuban troops from Angola and negotiations for Namibian independence. The USA was happy to give the green light for South Africa to confront the Angolan government and its Soviet allies. In turn, the Soviets indicated firmly that they did not intend deserting their allies, setting the stage for an escalating confrontation in the 1980s, which, as it turned out, could not be conclusively resolved militarily.

The urgency for a negotiated solution of the war in Angola on the part of the USA stemmed from the desire to have something to show for its eight-year policy of 'constructive engagement'. This was partly in order to justify a continuation of this approach as the best way to bring about a negotiated end to apartheid in South Africa.

The decision to provide $15 million of covert military aid to UNITA was taken by the Reagan administration in 1986 in the context of its perception of the East–West confrontation and a desire to counter increasing Soviet involvement in the southern African region. Considerably larger sums than this were being channelled to UNITA through a variety of sources including from arms sales to Iran, as revealed by the Oliver North 'Irangate' scandal.[23] Following Savimbi's visit to Washington in January 1986, Reagan hailed the UNITA leader as a 'freedom fighter' combating 'Soviet expansionism' in Angola, and as such he qualified for military aid. In February 1986, after the South African had intervened to save UNITA from defeat in a FAPLA offensive in August 1985, Crocker stated that the USA would not stand idly by and see UNITA 'overrun by Soviet-backed armed aggressive elements'.[24]

The decision to provide UNITA with military assistance was made possible by the repeal of the Clark Amendment in July 1985. This legislation had been passed in 1976, putting an indefinite ban on military aid to any of the warring factions in Angola without prior Congressional approval.

The rationale behind the move to supply UNITA was to 'nudge the Luanda government towards a negotiated settlement of the Namibian independence issue and of its own civil war'.[25] Clearly, some senior US officials believe the objective was achieved. As Reagan's National Security Adviser, Lieutenant-General Powell stated: 'It was only after the US began military aid to the UNITA freedom fighters in 1986 that the Angolan regime started to take seriously the idea of a negotiated settlement.'[26]

However, the decision to supply UNITA initially made a negotiated settlement seem more unlikely, as the MPLA broke off talks with

Washington in protest. Crocker and senior State Department officials disagreed with other elements of the US administration over the issue of funding UNITA, and were reluctant for such a measure to be taken, as it would undermine US claims to the status of a 'neutral mediator' in any negotiations. The decision, strongly backed by President Reagan, was probably taken to counter-balance the pressure exerted on Pretoria by Congress through new sanctions legislation. Reagan was opposed to sanctions as an instrument of pressure on South Africa, but recognizing the support for sanctions, he tried to pre-empt calls for tough economic measures against Pretoria by issuing an Executive Order in September 1985 outlining limited action. This failed to stem the mounting pressure for sanctions within Congress, which overrode the presidential veto to pass the Comprehensive Anti-Apartheid Act in October 1986.[27]

At the height of the debate over sanctions against the regime in Pretoria and aid to UNITA, Savimbi's costly and impressive public relations campaign through the US company Black, Manafort, Stone and Kelly to improve his movement's image was highly successful.[28] On his visit to Washington, he met with President Reagan and the Secretaries of State and Defence. At the same time, he consolidated his support from right-wing members of Senate prominent in the campaign to push Chevron (Gulf) Oil out of Angola. The strength of this campaign was enough to prompt Chester Crocker to urge the company to reconsider its role in Angola. During the struggle for independence in 1975, Gulf Oil was the MPLA's main financial backer, and has since enabled the MPLA to pay for Soviet and Cuban military aid.

The decision to aid UNITA enabled the USA to placate Pretoria while also satisfying right-wing Americans who were anxious to see the US defend its interests in the face of rising Soviet involvement.

The 'effective and appropriate' support promised for UNITA was rumoured to include Stinger anti-aircraft missiles, delivered via Zaire's Matadi port and the air base at Kamina. However, the extent to which these missiles have been used is disputed, as the evidence is contradictory. There are numerous references citing delivery of Stingers to UNITA by the CIA, and Savimbi said he was 'in possession of the best missiles as far as the air is concerned',[29] but independent sources confirming their use remain scarce. One possibility is that the USA supplied the weapons under the proviso that Washington must first authorize their use.[30] This would seem a plausible explanation. Washington could keep the pressure on the MPLA to negotiate, while at the same time placating Pretoria and conservatives at home with the knowledge that the USA would not allow UNITA to be defeated militarily. If Washington had sanctioned the use of Stingers in the battle for Cuito Cuanavale, which was a South African rather than a UNITA affair, then the outcome could have been different. The crucial point is that the USA was apparently prepared to see South Africa lose its air superiority, thus further putting pressure on the regime to move towards a negotiated settlement.[31]

Discussions between the USA and Angola reopened on April 1987 and in July Angola's President dos Santos publicly called for negotiations to end the conflict. South Africa responded positively to the idea in October and the formal negotiations between South Africa, Cuba, Angola and the USA opened in May 1988 at the height of the battle for Cuito Cuanavale. A breakthrough came the following month when Angola accepted the principle of a Cuban troop withdrawal without insisting on an end to US support for UNITA. Such a decision could be used to reassure South Africa that the UNITA card would remain to keep pressure on the Angolan government after the loss of Namibia as a launch pad for further South African military support to UNITA. The setback on the battlefield proved a trump card in bringing South Africa to reach a negotiated solution and in August Pretoria announced its troop withdrawal from Angola.

During the negotiations between the four parties involved, much rested on the outcome of the US presidential election in November 1988. Its relevance to an overall settlement on Angola and Namibia can be seen by the speed with which the negotiations were concluded once the outcome was known. There was some pressure on Crocker in the run-up to the election to show that progress had been made in the talks. The election was held on 8 November, and a settlement was reached at the end of talks held in Geneva on 10–15 November. The Angolan government had been stalling in the hope of a victory for the democrat candidate Michael Dukakis, who had promised not to fund Savimbi's rebels. When the MPLA realized that, under Bush, US aid to UNITA would continue, it decided to settle for an end to South African support for the rebels as the best compromise it could obtain. The agreements signed in New York in December 1988 secured Namibia's independence process, the phased withdrawal of Cuban troops from Angola over a 27-month period and an end to South African assistance to UNITA, but not of American aid to the rebels. The USA, in a letter from President-elect George Bush dated 6 January 1989, ensured Savimbi of continued military and diplomatic support.[32] But at the same time there were indications that it was preparing the ground for diplomatic recognition of the MPLA, something which successive administrations have refused to give. As a prelude to this, the State Department announced it was considering reclassifying the MPLA as a 'radical nationalist movement' rather than 'communist'.[33] However, the Bush administration did not move any further in this direction.

To a certain extent, the US had already achieved its objectives with regard to Angola – namely the total withdrawal of Cuban forces, and the MPLA turning its back on Marxist policies. President dos Santos admitted that some of the country's economic problems were due to excessive socialist planning. However, despite this warming in relations, the USA remained the only country to vote against Angola's membership of the IMF in 1989.[34]

Why the negotiations succeeded

Global developments towards ending the Cold War helped set an agenda for resolving regional conflicts. The low-intensity warfare that had brought revolutionary regimes to power on the periphery in the 1970s was ironically employed to undermine the viability of those regimes through the use of 'contra' style forces. While South Africa's policy of regional destabilization, carried out under its rubric of total strategy, provided a convenient ally to the global US policy of rolling back 'communism' throughout most of the 1980s, it could not be allowed to go too far and challenge overall US hegemony in the region. Reasserting US hegemony required curbing the influence of the military within the South African decision-making process, exercised through the powerful State Security Council and wresting the key instruments of South Africa's regional foreign policy, UNITA in Angola and Renamo in Mozambique, away from South Africa's control. The aim was to delink UNITA from South African influence using Namibia as a launch pad and switch the operations to Zaire under US control.

Washington was prepared to reassert its influence and power over Pretoria to achieve its objectives. Anxious to score a success within the policy of 'constructive engagement', the US did not intervene to prevent the South Africans being defeated militarily at Cuito Cuanavale. They were able to take advantage of the struggle over decision-making inside South Africa between the military and the Department of Foreign Affairs, with a greater likelihood of reaching a settlement if the latter retained the initiative towards Angola.

Some elements of the regime in Pretoria clearly resented the US role in the whole process. The military were annoyed by Chester

Crocker's announcement of a diplomatic breakthrough in late January 1988, gaining Angola's and Cuba's acceptance of the principle of a total Cuban withdrawal, just when the SADF was planning to play their trump card at Cuito Cuanavale. Defence Minister General Magnus Malan later insisted to parliament that a solution to the conflict would be an African one, not one 'imposed by the superpowers'.[35]

The USA could bring all parties to the negotiating table by judicious use of the carrot and the stick. Dangling as a carrot was the possibility that the West would help to renegotiate South Africa's massive debt with the war in Angola, which cost an estimated 4 billion rand a year by mid-1988 and placed an onerous burden on the economy.[36] The stick was South Africa's weakness in military technology on the battlefield, largely as a result of the international arms embargo, which tamed Pretoria's generals. The carrot for Angola was similarly a growing need both to reschedule its debt, only possible via IMF membership, and seek peace as a prerequisite to revive its shattered economy. While the South African military stick waving over Angola was removed, the USA would keep up the pressure on the Luanda government by continuing to fund UNITA via Zaire.

The negotiations offered all the parties something for which to claim credit. The Soviet Union could reduce its financial and military commitments to the region, help its MPLA ally remain in government at least for a few more years, and contribute to reducing East–West tension. Cuba could withdraw, claiming credit in securing Namibia's independence and inflicting a blow to South African regional dominance. Pretoria could claim credit for removing the Cubans from the region and reduce the heavy burden of defence expenditure, thereby releasing funds for long overdue internal reforms, particularly in black education. The USA not only helped 'roll back' communism but also reasserted its regional hegemonic power over both the Soviets and South Africa.

With the Cold War in southern Africa drawing to a close, the prospects for reaching an eventual settlement of the domestic conflict in Angola appeared brighter than ever before. US Secretary of State, James Baker, and Soviet Foreign Minister, Eduard Shevardnadze, took advantage of their presence at the Namibian independence celebrations to try to reach a joint strategy on the Angolan civil conflict. Mr Shevardnadze predicted then that a peace settlement was possible by July 1991, following the completion of the Cuban troop withdrawal.[37] The terms of the peace agreement signed by the Angolan government and UNITA provided for a ceasefire, after which all lethal military aid from the United States of America and the Soviet Union would stop. Britain and France would assist in forming a national army in a process to be completed before elections in September 1992.

The Cold War conflict phase had come to an end, but the peace settlement signed between the MPLA and UNITA at Bicesse in May 1991 was to prove fragile in the extreme. When the National Assembly election results were announced in October 1992 with MPLA the clear winner in the legislative elections, and Jose Eduardo dos Santos well ahead of Jonas Savimbi (UNITA) in the Presidential elections, Savimbi resumed the war. The United Nations declared the results to be generally free and fair, but the international community lacked the will to intervene to restore peace. The US in particular, owing to the change in administration following domestic elections in the autumn of 1992, failed to take a strong line with their longtime ally Savimbi.

Angola then descended into the bloodiest period of its history. We have analysed the reasons for this in detail elsewhere.[38] In essence, troop demobilisation and the creation of a new national army plus a stronger international commitment (both in terms of mandate and resources) were the essential but unfulfilled prerequisites for a successful completion of the peace process. The Cold War may have long since ended but conflict in this part of Africa was still continuing. Not until the end of 1994 was a new peace agreement signed between the two parties. Some doubts remained over whether the latest agreement would hold.

Notes

1 For detailed coverage of this conflict see C. Pycroft and B. Munslow (eds), *Southern Africa: Annual Review 1987/88, Volume 2. Regional Review*, London: Hans Zell Publishers, 1990, chapter 21.
2 *Africa Confidential*, 5.2.1988.
3 *Observer*, 31.1.1988.
4 *ANGOP*, no. 91, 22.2.1988.
5 J. Marcum, 'Africa: A Continent Adrift', in *Foreign Affairs*, 68 (1), 1989, p. 166.
6 *Financial Times*, 15.3.1988.
7 *Africa Confidential*, 15.7.1988.
8 *Financial Times*, 16.11.1988.
9 *Financial Times*, 15.12.1988.
10 D. E. Albright, 'The USSR and the Third World in the 1980s', *Problems of Communism*, 38 (2–3), 1989, pp. 50–70.
11 For an early critique of such failures see B. Munslow (ed.), *Africa: Problems in the Transition to Socialism*, London: Zed Books, 1986.
12 See the account by the former chief of the CIA Angola Task Force, John Stockwell, *In Search of Enemies*, New York: Norton, 1978.
13 *Africa Contemporary Record*, 1985–6, p. A33.

14 Mavinga is a town of key strategic importance to both FAPLA and UNITA. It is located between Jamba, the UNITA headquarters, and Cuito Cuanavale, FAPLA's main forward position and airfield from which the offensives of 1985 and 1987 were launched.
15 *Africa Contemporary Record*, 1986–7, p. A25.
16 Neil MacFarlane, 'The Soviet Union and Southern African Security', *Problems of Communism*, 38 (2–3), 1989, pp. 71–89.
17 Ibid., p. 85.
18 Economist Intelligence Unit, *Country Report, Angola*, no. 3, 1988.
19 MacFarlane, op. cit., p. 89.
20 *The Independent*, 16.3.1989.
21 Conference on *Problems of Socialist Orientation and Democracy*, Institute for African and International Affairs, Feldkirchen-Westerham, Bavaria, 20–22 October 1989.
22 F. Halliday, *Cold War, Third World*, London: Century Hutchinson, 1989.
23 See P. Nesbitt, 'Terminators, Crusaders and Gladiators: (Private and Public) Western Support for Renamo and Unita', *Review of African Political Economy*, 43, 1988, pp. 111–124.
24 *Africa Contemporary Record*, 1985–6, p. A71.
25 Ibid., p. A22.
26 P. Nesbitt, op. cit., p. 23.
27 *Africa Contemporary Record*, 1986–7, p. A255.
28 For details of this publicity campaign see P. Nesbitt, op. cit.
29 *Herald Tribune*, 23.2.1987; *Financial Times*, 15.3.1988; *The Guardian*, 14.11.1988; *The Guardian*, 21.11.1988.
30 *Africa Confidential*, 24 June 1987.
31 For a discussion of South Africa's vulnerability in battlefield military technology during the Angolan confrontation see T. Ohlson, 'The Cuito Cuanavale Syndrome: Revealing SADF Vulnerabilities', in G. Moss and I. Obery (eds), *South Africa Contemporary Analysis*, London: Hans Zell Publishers, 1980, pp. 181–90.
32 *Herald Tribune*, 13.11.1989.
33 *Natal Mercury*, 28.11.1988.
34 *Financial Times*, 26.6.1989.
35 *The Independent*, 17.5.1988.
36 R. Davies, 'South African Regional Policy before and after Cuito Cuanavale', in G. Moss and I. Obery (eds), op. cit., p. 173.
37 *The Guardian*, 20.3.1990.
38. B. Munslow, 'Sustainable development and the peace process in Southern Africa: the experience of Mozambique and Angola', in K. Cole (ed), *Sustainable Development for a Democratic South Africa*, London: Earthscan, 1994.

10· NAMIBIA: FROM BLOOD AND IRON TO RECONCILIATION

Reginald Herbold Green

One Namibia, One Nation
– National Motto

Namibia is a large, desert-locked land on three frontiers. To the south the Namqua, to the east the Kalahari and to the west the Namib wall it off from easy access. Only on the north is there a less forbidding barrier – the Kunene River and a savanna plain and there the historic cultural/political cluster was transriparian (and therefore after colonization divided by a frontier).[1] And that frontier too was far from even the southern entry point of colonialism into Angola – Lobito Bay – so that the Portuguese did not establish administration down to the Kunene until after 1900. That explains the late entry of Europeans – whether explorers, traders, missionaries, invaders or settlers – and why it remained (in European eyes) a blank space which could be seized by Imperial Germany and then allocated to it by the Congress of Berlin.

Until its colonization as German South West Africa, Namibia did not appear to be a very promising piece of real estate – especially as the UK had annexed its only deep water port (Walvis Bay) to keep it out of any other maritime power's hands.[2] German settlement was moderately unsuccessful – a pre-refrigeration cattle economy far from the coast had distinct economic limitations; ostriches proved ephemeral, though karakul sheep (Persian lamb) proved a modest success. However, the Germans found that the old African copper workings at Tsumeb were on a substantial ore body and – more dramatically – accidentally discovered the coastal diamond deposits, thus establishing the foundations of the mineral-centred economy which still characterizes Namibia in terms of output and exports though not of employment.

To exploit Tsumeb – and to defend the colony from its people – the basic west–east and north–south rail net was built together with a poor, silting but large port at Swakopmund and a deep-water but narrow channel one at Luderitz. Like other German colonies South West Africa was a doubtful proposition for settlers, mildly to significantly profitable for traders and miners but an economic loss to the German state. Indeed, until the 1950s Namibia did not pay its colonial masters – German or South African (under a League of Mandate read as a road to annexation). The substantial expansion of base-metal mining dates to the 1950s as does a reasonably viable cattle and karakul sector and the build-up of fishing. Diamond mining was initially taken over by de Beers to avoid competition and virtually (once totally) closed when markets were weak. Only after World War II was Oranjemund expanded into a major producer and, even then, with the wide swings in output characteristic of a market-balancing mine. Uranium oxide production dates back only to the end of the 1970s.

Before the 1950s the key concerns were strategic and to show the flag; any economic hopes were rather ill-articulated. Then, as later, white farmers were seen as crucial to security and were paid for staying on the land for that reason.

The Namibia into which the Germans pushed – and whose occupation South Africa completed – was a large, relatively empty land. Perhaps 500,000 people lived there (versus 1,750,000 at independence about a century later), concentrated in the arable/mixed farming lands of the north which were never occupied by Germany and were more formally made a labour reserve by South Africa on foundations built to serve German mines and railway construction. In the rest of the country a series of small states coexisted and federated; as their economy was based on cattle, wars were waged, largely for grazing space. Larger state formation might have been beginning but was cut off by colonization.[3]

It would be wrong to describe pre-colonial Namibia as being characterized by tribal ethnic conflict. Europe during the medieval and state formation period was at least as prone to war and boundary changes. Trade, including specialization of labour in copper mining and smelting, crossed state and cultural group boundaries; peaceful contact was common and some of the federated units, for example the Windhoek Kingdom, included factions from several cultural groups (and were opposed by other factions of the same groups).

The conquest
The German conquest began with information collection from explorers, missionaries and traders and moved on to 'peaceful' land acquisition through exceedingly dubious treaties – often with persons who had no standing to make them. It was extended by enforcement of the treaties and sanctions against groups who 'violated' them. The armed conflicts were carried out on a piecemeal basis which avoided pitting the limit German and black auxiliary forces against all or most Namibian groups at the same time.

That approach broke down soon after the turn of the century. In 1904 the Herero people rose against German land and cattle theft and their own reduction to serfdom. With part of the German forces pinned down to guard against further attacks by forces from Ovambo kingdoms after an initial assault on the border fort at Namutoni, the Herero forces nearly threw the Germans out. Reinforcements from Europe turned the tide and after the decisive Battle of Waterberg (Hamakari) the Germans drove the Herero into the Kalahari to die of thirst or trek to Botswana. Well over half the Herero nation perished.

The Herero had sought a coordinated attack by the Nama but the message was intercepted and the Nama rose after the destruction of the Herero army. They too were defeated and about half died in concentration camps. The two wars broke armed resistance by the Herero and Nama and 'cleared' land and/or 'acquired' cattle to bolster German settlement. It also led to an exceedingly racist and repressive rule (even by German colonial standards) until 1914. In 1914 the South African army captured German South West Africa with some black support, promising to reverse the sins of German colonialism.

In fact while the League of Nations awarded the Crown of Great Britain a Class C Mandate to be exercised by the Crown's Ministers in South Africa, in order to ensure the welfare and development of the people, South Africa acted on quite different lines. It consolidated the German land theft and reserve system and pursued a policy of expanding control including the northern area never actually occupied by Germany. The last armed conflicts extended to the 1930s but none was on a scale to threaten South African rule. The initial armed resistance had been broken; during the long years of Namibia's economic stagnation the combination of settler farms, mines and towns with black labour reserve areas providing unskilled labour, begun under the Germans, was reinforced and used for recruitment to the South African mines, as well as to Namibia's mines and ranches.

The road to the liberation war

Namibians were never reconciled to alien rule both because it had been so brutally imposed and because it continued to be so harsh. For them the German 'blood and iron' slogan applied to the South Africans as well – African blood shed by European iron. However, until the mid-1960s, armed conflict was seen as impossible. The resistance turned on specific cases of land theft, labour abuse and community relocation to townships as a means to end mixed black and white urban areas or clean out 'black spots' in white ones. These met with resistance – either *ad hoc* or via trade unions – which was consistently broken with an iron fist.

Less noticed at the time was a shift in church positions. Namibia was – and is – a very Christian country. Its largest churches were Lutheran from the German period, followed by the establishment of Roman Catholic, Anglican and African Methodist Episcopal (AME) institutions; only the white branch of NGK (one of the Dutch Reformed churches in South Africa) was significantly Afrikaner. To assert the churches were not racist or at least paternalistic until World War II would be inaccurate, but they never had the crusading racial supremacy core of the old NGK. And in the 1950s and 1960s the black Lutheran churches became independent under black Namibian leadership – as the AME had always been. The Anglican church under three expatriate bishops, crusading first for justice, later for national self-determination, became outspokenly political even before the Lutherans, while the transition in the Catholic church was slower. Further, church schools and hospitals were both better regarded by Namibians than state ones and increasingly seen by the South African regime as subversive. The schools taught syllabuses (in English) which, whatever their limitations, were far removed from Bantu education while the medical network – perhaps because it was basically serving black Namibians and many of its senior staff were European not South African – stood in sharp contrast to the tightly segregated state system. From the 1960s on, the South Africans sought to take over or to close down the church schools and to a lesser extent the church hospitals as subversive.

After 1945 modern opposition to colonial rule began to form. It was for two decades focussed on achieving UN action to enforce, transfer or revoke the mandate (the last finally done by the General Assembly in 1967 and endorsed by the International Court of Justice in 1971) and on peaceful organization and petitioning domestically. At first the traditional Herero leader Hosea Kutako took the lead and was supported by his council and some other traditional leaders. However, from 1960 political parties emerged, notably the South West African National Unity (SWANU), supported predominantly by urban intellectual Herero, and the South West African People's Organization (SWAPO), (largely led by the Ovambo with membership drawn from workers and school teachers).

The parties pursued the two-track strategy of mobilization and petition domestically and quests for international intervention externally until the mid-1960s. By then SWAPO had become the dominant party. In the face of South African repression and the combined sloth and ineffectiveness of international action, it added a third route – armed struggle – with the first battle in 1966.

SWAPO versus the apartheid system

SWAPO went to war to end the apartheid system and perceived independence from South Africa as integral to that goal. It acted in a context in which the structures South Africa had put in place to operate apartheid profitably had become the means to its undermining and to SWAPO's rise.

Land theft had turned over half of the usable land to white ranchers and, very secondarily, to farms. It had crowded most Namibians into reserves which increasingly became stagnant ponds of growing poverty and of ever more numerous bubbles of discontent rising to the surface.

From 1962 South Africa attempted to create first a constellation of Bantustans under a white central government and then a quasi-federal system with all key power (including revenue) in the hands of the 'whitestan' and a central government it expected to control by communal veto, subsidies and the greater education and experience of the white political leaders. The exercise became ever more frenetic – and surrealistic – until the late 1980s, when South Africa turned to trying to create a domestic Namibian blocking force to ensure a compliant – but eventually independent – Namibia.

These initiatives were – with three exceptions – monumentally unsuccessful. In both the densely populated north and in the south the Bantustan–homeland–state authorities were unpopular and demonstrably both corrupt and inefficient. Elections were either so rigged as to be palpable frauds, ending with negligible turnout or – in the case of the Damara – anti-South African majorities.

The Herero traditional leadership after Chief Kutako's death was seduced and did not carry many Herero with it. A breakaway separatist faction from SWAPO gave a base in the isolated Caprivi Strip. The community of mixed ancestry known as Rehoboth or 'Baster' (the name they use), who had been transplanted from South Africa as a political pawn, began to fear that equality would wipe out their dominance over their black workers and switched from ardent nationalism to supporting South Africa (and a pathetically facetious unilateral declaration of independence from Namibia in 1990 which the state declined to notice until it died unseen, unheard and little mourned). But the three exceptions amounted to at most a tenth of the black population.

Attempts to create viable coalitions of credible racially defined parties also foundered. In 1980 South Africa expected a Smithorewa* victory in Lusaka and had a chairman of South West Africa's proto-government ready to fly there as the first stage to a managed election towards an equally managed independence. The actual results in Zimbabwe caused a more critical look at the strength of the non-white parties, and at the difficulties of rigging an externally observed election credibly; by the late 1980s South Africa was considering a non-racial party designed to secure a blocking role in the constitutional drafting and adoption process and after independence.

Shifts in attitude to colonial Namibia
Before the economic expansion of 1945–70, colonial Namibia was preserved by 'contract labour': fixed-terms contracts were for single males and regulated to prevent choice of employer. Labour was cheap and (since firing meant sending the individuals concerned back to the north and destitution for their families) relatively malleable. But the system created a national working class and a national consciousness

---

* A combination of Ian Smith and Bishop Muzorewa

as well as more mobility than was desirable from a security point of view.[5] Because most contract labourers were Ovambo, the national consciousness and militancy was strongest, earliest among them both at contract work and on their home areas. 'Contract' became the symbol of all that was oppressive in the colonial regime. 'Breaking contract' meant mobilizing – or later taking up arms – against the system.

The single male dormitory compound became – as the manager of the de Beers diamond mines put it – the best recruiting ground for SWAPO he could imagine. In 1970–71 the rising objection to 'contract' welled over into a national strike. While broken, or ended with a deceptive settlement which gave little, the heritage of the strike in terms of national contacts and militancy greatly strengthened SWAPO and the perception that only independence could bring basic change.

In the late 1980s trade unions again became active – following South African union law reform – and played roles both in improving wages and conditions and, more important, forming a civil society infrastructure for the liberation effort.

Apartheid, even (or perhaps especially) with puppet dependent homelands and political spear-carrier roles at territorial level, became ever more unpopular. Its evolution towards Bantu education in Afrikaans was bitterly resisted and led (perhaps ironically) to mass support for English as 'the language of liberation'. Until its rapid relaxation after the mid-1980s, it also alienated otherwise apolitical middle-class and rich black Namibians by constricting every aspect of their lives. Even afterwards it characterized most black–white relations, whether official, private or in the workplace.

The church's position shifted steadily over the period. From uneasy acceptance of authority it moved to firmer petitioning through endorsement of independence and then to affirming that it was for each individual to decide whether violence against an unjust occupation regime was justified. By providing chaplains to SWAPO but, in general, not to the South African armed forces, the churches arguably made clear their leaders' own individual views. The churches had joined the unions as a civil society infrastructure for the liberation movement. The South African reaction of taking over schools and hospitals, destroying the Anglican St Mary's Odibo complex (seen as a seed-bed for SWAPO leadership) and the Lutheran Omipa Press, as well as allowing troops to desecrate churches did not deter the churches – it did arouse intense anger among previously apolitical Namibians.

The international context also began to shift. In 1967 the United Nations, fed up with South African stonewalling and refusals to cooperate, revoked the Mandate and in 1971 secured an opinion from the International Court of Justice endorsing its right to do so. While its *de jure* substitute administration – the UN Council for Namibia – was very far from having any *de facto* power in Namibia, it did focus attention on and mobilize support for the educational and forward planning side of the liberation struggle. The international status of Namibia apparently did deter South Africa to a degree – while harassed, SWAPO's Namibian wing was never banned, and neither was the newspaper supporting it. Thus it was able to maintain a domestic organization and communication presence.

And in southern Africa the independence of Angola in 1975 opened access to the main body of Namibia to SWAPO's People's Liberation Army of Namibia (PLAN). Since Angola had become independent under an MPLA government, despite South African armed intervention on behalf of UNITA (backed by financial, training, logistical and equipment aid which never ceased and after 1981 grew sharply), it was more than ready to answer South Africa's aggressive stance by providing bases and support for PLAN.

The independence of Zimbabwe in 1980 had a major impact psychologically – albeit not directly militarily. It made Namibia the 'last colony' in southern Africa, gave renewed reason to believe that long, hard struggles could be won and showed that internationally supervised elections were virtually unriggable. For South Africa those were very unwelcome implications, for SWAPO highly reinforcing and reassuring ones.

SWAPO's strategy

SWAPO's strategy was not solely military, nor did the organization ever express a preference for winning by fighting its way to the Orange River as opposed to negotiation. The strategy had four girders:[6]

1. domestic political mobilization via internal SWAPO groups with close links to churches and unions and, less consistently, with certain much smaller Namibian nationalist parties;

2. external political mobilization to win international diplomatic support and finance both for PLAN and for the combination of civil governance (and food), thus providing for about 75,000 refugees as well as its broader education and pre-independence planning operations;
3. the operation of its civil governance and capacity building programmes, probably ultimately totalling over $50 million a year (largely from Western European and international agency sources, balancing approximately equal Middle and Eastern European support of PLAN);
4. armed struggle aimed at destabilizing the occupation regime and at imposing on South Africa the burden of potential loss of life within fiscal and white military forces as a means of forcing serious negotiations or – at worst – of building up to a long, slow military victory.

In all of these SWAPO was broadly successful. Its presence in Namibia remained widespread, while also maintaining a low profile. The combination of effective civil governance (even if only in the refugee settlements which it – and not the United Nations High Commission for Refugees – ran) and pre-planning/education for independence, together with an army that South Africa was clearly failing to crush, led to SWAPO being taken seriously as a substantial force and as an almost inevitable government (or partner in government) to be. The education and health services for its refugee settlement became among the best in Sub-Saharan Africa – far better than the South African occupation regime provided. The war did first destabilize the northern ranching economy, then sucked in a South African operation against PLAN (and its Angolan hosts) that eventually cost about $1000 million a year, and finally built up a white military death toll in Namibia (including accident and illness deaths) comparable to that of the USA in Vietnam given the relative USA and white South African populations.

**War without victory, negotiation without resolution:
1966–88**
The war in Namibia was a long and escalating one that eventually involved something like 20,000 PLAN troops and 100,000 South African and South West African military personnel, including special,

paramilitary police and other auxiliary units. It was a war of attrition whose aim to undermine the opponent's will and resources to continue was more central than final military victory. The latter was never SWAPO's central objective and by the end of the 1970s probably had ceased to be South Africa's, at least in terms of operations in Namibia.

Therefore, the war was necessarily paralleled by negotiations. SWAPO's basic aims were Namibian independence under a SWAPO-led government without restrictive covenants maintaining South African hegemony and white privilege. South Africa's shifted from installation of a Bantustan coalition government to a mixed government including (and emasculating) SWAPO and towards a highly restricted independence bound by covenants, retention of the Port of Walvis Bay and an ever-present brandished threat of destabilization. Clearly these two positions were in basic conflict, with neither side willing to give substantial ground unless forced to do so by the course of the war or by third parties.

South Africa's war and negotiating strategies were confused by the issue of what its basic objectives in Angola were. After the failure to install a friendly government in 1975, these were nominally to protect its occupation of Namibia by destabilizing Angola; this would be achieved through UNITA acting as a proxy force continuously and South African forces invading repeatedly. However, there was at least a secondary thought of going further and installing a coalition or UNITA regime which would not merely provide a buffer for occupied Namibia, but also oil supplies and a manufactured goods market for South Africa. That goal evidently precluded genuine independence for Namibia – indeed, if achieved, made it unnecessary.

Third-party non-African involvement was dominated by Cold War considerations or spin-offs. Western powers increasingly viewed Namibian independence as both inevitable and desirable. All pre- ferred a moderate government, albeit their perceptions of SWAPO varied fairly widely. The USA – as well as being less hostile to South Africa, especially between 1981 and 1988 – was obsessed with the idea that Cuba was a great power and so placed its support for Namibian independence in pawn in order to get Cuban forces (and preferably the MPLA government) out of Angola. African involve- ment – especially that of the front-line states (Tanzania, Zambia, Botswana plus Angola, Mozambique and Zimbabwe on independ- ence) and Nigeria – was totally pro-SWAPO. Except for Angolan, and to a much lesser extent Zambian, provision of bases and cooperation with PLAN (and pre-1975 military training in Tanzania), its importance was partly psychological and partly that Western states saw total intransigence on Namibia as, to varying degrees, inconsistent with satisfactory diplomatic or economic relations with the African states.

PLAN and the escalation of the liberation war
PLAN's initial military actions were small and in the Caprivi Strip – accessible from Zambia but isolated from the rest of Namibia. Their scale rose gradually in the late 1960s as did infiltration westwards in the north and south to the central ranching and mining area around Grootfontein. By the end of the 1960s, South Africa viewed these as a significant nuisance, a perception which deepened as PLAN developed new routes via southern Angola to the main body of northern Namibia.

With the independence of Angola and the failure of the initial South African invasion in 1975, PLAN's logistical and base position was greatly strengthened. From then on PLAN effectively could not be destroyed militarily without either occupying most of Angola, installing a new government, or buying the MPLA government's connivance which South Africa, rather surprisingly, never seriously tried. Repeated South African raids and invasions, paralleled by building up UNITA, had a terrible cost for Angola but only slowed PLAN's advance to having a semi-permanent presence in most of northern Namibia and forcing South Africa to extend the 'operational' war zone almost as far south as the suburbs of Windhoek.

Repression in Namibia and a brutal, massively staffed military occupation regime in the north caused severe hardship for most Namibians and death to a significant number of them. It neither broke PLAN nor reduced its support. The northern European ranching zone was crippled and business confidence demolished but the economy and administration still functioned. The growing war bill and the loss of 2000 to 3000 white lives in action, of wounds, from sickness and through accident between 1964 and 1988 were increasingly heavy burdens on South Africa. Equally, however, PLAN was in no position to consolidate and expand a major territorial base in the north and push down to Windhoek, if only because of South African air supremacy. The war had reached a stalemate with both sides able to inflict damage but not to win, both able to continue for an extended period of time, both convinced that time was on their side.

The limits on negotiations

SWAPO always wanted a negotiated independence – indeed it had gone to war to force serious negotiations.[7] South Africa refused to negotiate directly, first preferring to attempt to build up anti-SWAPO coalitions in Namibia and – when that showed very limited results and international pressure increased – via Western (and ultimately Angolan) mediators. However, until 1988 South Africa was unwilling to accept the possibility of a genuinely independent Namibia. This was because it feared the domestic psychological and political spin-offs at home and hoped to continue reaping the economic rewards of colonial rule (minus the more than offsetting military costs); it also had somewhat ill-defined ambitions to secure a cooperative regime in Luanda and probably genuinely feared an advance of Cuban and ANC forces to its Orange River frontier with Namibia. To a substantial extent its leadership had come to believe their own myths of 'total onslaught', 'communist threat' and 'SWAPO terrorism' and to be trapped within them.[8]

No amount of SWAPO reasonableness could dent that position. This was especially true because no-one knew better than the South Africans how to gut a constitution of its entrenched clauses by semi-legal means once a majority government existed in an independent state; they assumed SWAPO in power would behave as they had done. SWAPO's rhetoric was vaguely socialist, strongly nationalist, pro bills of rights, independent trade unions and redistribution (especially of land) but relatively pragmatic (or unclear) on specific policies. This did little to convince South Africa it could live with them and aroused rather mixed reactions in the West. Its concentration on pre-planning and educating for a Namibian state was generally seen as impressive – but ominously so by South Africa.

International negotiations turned on the attitudes and objectives of the major Western powers who were consistently hesitant to take strong positions against South Africa but became more and more negatively disposed towards its domestic repression, regional aggression and Namibian occupation policies. Because Namibia was – with the Mandate revocation of 1967 and the ICJ opinion of 1971 – inescapably an international issue, they felt forced to attempt to broker independence.

After supporting hortatory, and vetoing compulsive, Security Council Resolutions between 1970 and 1976, the USA, UK and France together with the German Federal Republic and Canada in 1977 created a Contact Group to attempt to achieve a UN-supervised independence process acceptable to both South Africa and SWAPO. This process continued – marked by a plethora of resolutions and meetings – between 1977 and 1988 with little progress on specific details. However, it did lead to a growing entrenchment of the position that UN-supervised free and fair elections were central to any acceptable independence process and would require a powerful UN civil and military presence to supervise and to protect.

In general SWAPO agreed to compromises; South Africa stalled or raised complex new objections; the western powers had little sense of urgency and were hampered with the USA's obsession over Cuba and its somewhat odd perceptions of the Angolan government as hard-line, expansionist Marxist-Leninists (one neither the rest of the Contact Group nor US big business shared). Until the Zimbabwe elections, South Africa was at least contemplating running a rigged election with UN observers to give it credibility. The Zimbabwe result put paid to that dream and the inauguration of President Reagan gave hope for more US support if South Africa were to play up the themes of the 'evil empire', 'total onslaught' or anxiety about Cuba.

In the course of the talks – which except for an abortive meeting in 1981 never brought South Africa and SWAPO face to face to negotiate – SWAPO considerably strengthened its image with the German and British governments. The Germans reached a meeting of minds on the place of German settlers (accepted by their representatives), while SWAPO's championship of the English language and openly stated desire to return to the Commonwealth (from which it had been removed by South Africa's resignation in 1960) sounded well in official British ears. The UK in any case was attuned by its decolonization experience to negotiated independence settlements, not war *à outrance*. But as of 1988 the war and the negotiations had both reached stalemate. Neither SWAPO, South Africa nor the Contact Group could afford to pull out, but nor could any of them see an acceptable resolution.

The war and the talks interacted in that South Africa launched incursions into Angola and terror raids on refugee camps as well as stepping up internal repression at key points in negotiations. SWAPO interpreted this as a strategy of provocation designed to cause it to break off talks and, therefore, declined to do so.[9] South Africa – perhaps counter-productively – insisted (at least a dozen times) that it had broken the back of PLAN and at the same time loudly warned of 'terrorist threats' and up to 2500 PLAN forces in northern Namibia, which did little for its credibility but, probably, much to convince outsiders that the war would not go away.

To transition: Cuito Cuanavale and after
The deadlock ended in 1988, with a major South African retreat and a settlement broadly acceptable to the Contact Group and to Angola and only moderately less so to SWAPO.[10] What had happened on the war, international actor and consequently on the negotiation fronts?

South Africa's adventurist forward strike commando policy had ended in grief in southern Angola. Cuito Cuanavale had become the hinge of fate opening the door to Namibian independence. A major South African invasion, partly to protect its UNITA clients but perhaps also seen as pushing on to install them in Luanda now that they again enjoyed substantial US backing, achieved its initial objectives in late 1987 but got bogged down near the small town of Cuito Cuanavale in 1988. Unwilling to risk massive, undeniable white casualties, South Africa put in its front-line air force and long-range artillery on an unprecedented, whirlwind scale.

First, the Angolan air force gained the upper hand and, after heavy losses, South Africa was forced to pull out its planes, losing attack support and defensive air cover. Second, the artillery became an isolated pawn, unable either to force Angolan capitulation or to retreat. Third, a mixed Angolan–PLAN force rolled up the South African positions west of Cuito Cuanavale and swept to the Namibian border. South Africa faced the loss of the best of its artillery park, massive casualties in a forced retreat of its expeditionary force and the grim prospect of seeking to defend northern Namibia when PLAN, not it, had air cover. That type of defeat it knew could not be sustained domestically; it had to negotiate its way out of the box that appeared ever more like a coffin.

Taken together with the already heavy fiscal and death-toll costs, the need to negotiate a peace with Angola led South Africa to abandon its strategic aim of holding Namibia. 'Who lost Namibia' was still a cry it feared to face in white South African elections, but it hoped via the UN-supervised electoral process to achieve a coalition government, including its friends; it also hoped to use the Walvis Bay transport vice plus the threat of destabilization to enforce the absence of non-Namibian forces and the presence of continued economic linkages on terms favourable to South Africa.

Angola, with a rising war bill and a collapsed oil price, was amenable to any settlement which removed South African forces, ended massive South African support for UNITA and – in its view – provided a UN-supervised route to genuine Namibian independence. It was encouraged in this stance by the USSR which wished to improve relations with the USA and to reduce its external commitments. The USA saw a settlement as achieving two goals: getting the Cubans out of Angola and removing the Namibian issue from the international agenda by installing a UN-supervised electoral process. It was not, however, willing either to recognize the government of Angola or to halt support to UNITA.

SWAPO was not directly involved in the negotiations between South Africa, Angola, the USA and the USSR in 1988 – apparently the price for excluding UNITA. While it welcomed their broad lines, it also felt that not enough UN powers had been provided to ensure against electoral fraud and that too many elements in the UN package remained dangerously vague. In particular, the UN role in supervising the electoral register and the vote count, the provision of UN-monitored base camps in Namibia for PLAN forces in the territory on the effective date and the question of legislative and executive authority in the period between the election of a Constitutional Assembly and Independence gave them cause for concern.

As 1988 opened there was a rapid shift from deadlock to an agreed South African withdrawal from Angola and acceptance by all parties that the United Nations Technical Assistance Group (UNTAG) should go in under the general proposals which had been on the table for at least five years. This was not a result either from negotiation on details, a negotiated breakthrough on areas of disagreement or a change of heart by any party. It was the result of major changes in the military and external alliance contexts leading each party to recalculate its balance of gains and losses.

Angola indisputably was a winner. It cleared its territory of South African forces, lessened support for UNITA and – in its view – achieved an independence process from which SWAPO was sure to emerge as the governing party of Namibia. At the same time it increased its ability to talk with the USA – albeit not winning an end to US support of UNITA.

The USSR improved relations with the USA – by 1988 an overriding foreign-policy goal – and reduced long-distance commitments which were incalculable as to duration or cost. It too believed it had won in terms of the agreed course regarding Namibia.

The USA achieved four aims. First, it secured Cuban withdrawal from Angola. Second, it ended being in an exposed position as the main obstacle to forcing South Africa to leave Namibia. Third, it kept a free hand to support UNITA and to defer recognition of the government of Angola. Fourth, it acted in open cooperation with the USSR both improving relations with it and safeguarding itself from third-party criticism if something went badly wrong.

South Africa was a loser. It had *de facto* been forced to abandon its forward policy of destabilizing Angola and, perhaps, installing a friendly regime there. However, significant South African military and business voices had already challenged that strategy and President Botha may well have wished to resile from it. More seriously, it had lost in its long struggle to keep Namibia South African or convert it into a Bantustan. That loss could be limited – by seeking to ensure SWAPO had no majority (or at least not the two-thirds majority necessary to adopt a constitution unilaterally) and by using economic leverage and military threats to keep Namibia in line after independence. It could be disguised – if the limitation of loss strategy worked – by saying that the 'red tide' had been halted and that South Africa's international position had been strengthened. But the reality of the loss could hardly be denied.

The front-lines states – who were on the fringes of the negotiations – believed the results of the negotiations were clear gain. Angola was freed of the South African war and – even with US backing – UNITA could not win without massive South African support. The open defeat of the forward strategy in Angola would, it was hoped, reduce pressure on Mozambique and Zimbabwe. The UN process with a reasonably strong UNTAG would surely lead to a SWAPO electoral victory.

Ironically, the least satisfied party may well have been SWAPO. It could not decline to accept terms which Angola and the Frontline States accepted and it had no doubt South Africa had been forced to give ground. However, it had three reservations. First, it had in fact not been a party to the final negotiations on the activation of the UN plan and the composition of UNTAG; this seemed to it to continue the history of outsiders making decisions about Namibia over the heads of Namibians – as at the Congress of Berlin. Second, it did not trust South Africa's willingness to carry through what it had agreed – even in respect to Angola – and feared abortion of the UN–UNTAG process by South Africa with its dirty tricks departments making it appear to be SWAPO's fault (e.g. by dressing South African special forces in PLAN uniforms to create incidents). Third, it did not like the large areas of ambiguity in the old UN plan, none of which had been clarified in late 1988.[11]

In retrospect it is easy to say in the mid-1990s that suspicion of South Africa was overblown. This is, however, to assume that President de Klerk's journey towards peace in South Africa is simply a continuation of President Botha's. That is fairly clearly not correct (Botha after all called for a 'No' vote in the white referendum of 1992, reaffirming the government's mandate to negotiate a new constitution). Further, as late as early 1990 the course that President de Klerk would follow was far from predictable – perhaps most of all to himself. Dirty tricks up to independence and the threat of both economic and military destabilization after independence were not unreasonable expectations.

Transition to reconciliation

The transition to elections and independence jointly supervised by UNTAG and the South African administration began with problems. South Africa distrusted UNTAG and the UN Special Representative – and the feeling was reciprocated. SWAPO believed South Africa intended to abort the electoral process or to manipulate it. Further, it doubted UN toughness in facing down South Africa over contested procedural issues. Neither South Africa nor SWAPO was convinced that UNTAG and/or the UN Special Representative would or could be a fully impartial and tough referee.

The process of transition nearly ended in its first days. The initial UN plan called for confining PLAN forces in Namibia to bases in Namibia. South Africa had never admitted that such forces existed – despite constant statements that there were hundreds or thousands of PLAN 'terrorists' in northern Namibia – apparently on the grounds that they did not have permanent, visible military encampments. The 1988 Agreements provided that SWAPO forces in Angola should be moved out of southern Angola. SWAPO repeatedly told the UN it would have forces reporting to UNTAG on day one. From mid-1988

SWAPO and, more explicitly, South African assertions of PLAN troops in Namibia ranged from 500 to 2500. On day one between 1500 and 2000 PLAN troops sought to report to UNTAG. No UNTAG officers were in northern Namibia to report to. Instead, South African forces – out of base in violation of the agreement – began to massacre the PLAN troops. The UN accepted South Africa's claim that all of the PLAN forces had just crossed the border (some may well have done so); it also condoned the South African breach of the agreement, negotiated with South Africa and the Contact Group but not with SWAPO and – while obtaining a ceasefire by South Africa – forced the re-expatriation of all survivors to Angola. At that point SWAPO's faith in UN impartiality or steadfastness sank to near zero and the Special Representative was called South Africa's 'Deputy Administrator General'.[12]

That, however, proved to be the low point. Once deployed, UNTAG did keep the South African troops in base, monitor police and prevent open coercion. The Special Representative forced changes in the initial registration and counting procedures adumbrated by the AG. Slowly, SWAPO's confidence in the UN recovered.

Election goals and independence
South Africa's election strategy was plain. It poured money into several parties (not all with their knowledge), engaged in disinformation peddling against SWAPO and in espionage against all parties and counted on white farmers and small town employers coercing their employees to vote, if not for the Democratic Turnhalle Alliance (DTA) (South Africa's chosen instrument) then at least not for SWAPO. What precisely it hoped to achieve is unclear – at the least to deny SWAPO a two-thirds majority, probably to deny it an overall majority and conceivably to have an assembly majority favourable to South Africa. In the event it achieved only the first.

SWAPO's goal was to achieve a two-thirds majority and its fallback position a simple majority. It suffered from poor access to voters on white farms, in some small towns and in the Herero 'homeland'. Further, it faced a series of pointed questions concerning persons detained (or in some cases alleged to have been detained) and tortured at the time of a South African spy scare and a split (led by the present DTA leader). Perhaps unwisely, it refused to admit that the duration of the detentions and treatments of the detainees had been wrong, much less to sanction any of those directly responsible. This did quite clearly cost it votes.

In the event SWAPO had over 55 per cent of the votes and the DTA over 30 per cent. SWAPO had its simple majority in the Assembly but the DTA plus a small white settler party had a blocking third. The stage appeared set for protracted deadlock (and continued South African rule, possibly beyond the original UNTAG term). In the event the Constitution was agreed rapidly and unanimously.

This unexpected result had four causes:

- First, given the clear SWAPO majority, the other parties viewed a SWAPO-formed government as inevitable and were disposed to reach compromises;
- Second, no party – not even the DTA – felt any loyalty to South Africa which had treated Namibia as a colony and its white settlers as colonial subjects to be informed rather than consulted and, in the end, had abandoned them when it suited South African interests;
- Third, both SWAPO and other parties were well aware of the clear contrast between peaceful final transition and reconciliation in Zimbabwe and the more fraught ones in Angola and Mozambique and all wanted Namibia to follow the Zimbabwe route;
- Fourth, SWAPO wanted no delay to independence (and to its forming a government) and was ready to agree to massive entrenchment of social, political and property rights in the Constitution (as, in fairness, it had proposed in some of its own earlier pre-constitution papers).

The result was speedy adoption of a Constitution[12] embodying virtually all generally recognized rights in provisions which cannot be amended even by a unanimous vote of parliament or in a national referendum. In general it is an admirable document. Such doubts as there are relate to whether too many specific provisions which apply to basically procedural issues are entrenched in a way which makes it too inflexible and whether some provisions (perhaps to bridge gaps that could be resolved quickly) are too vague, for example those on regional government and the second house of the national assembly and also on affirmative action.

From the adoption of the Constitution at the end of 1989 to independence on 20 March 1990, events flowed smoothly. This may well have been due in part to the initial phase of President de Klerk's path towards reconciliation based on ending apartheid and establishing some form of majority rule. Independence came on a wave of optimism and goodwill as well as (virtually unheard of just before independence) a building boom.

Since independence

Since independence euphoria has inevitably evaporated but reconciliation moves ahead.[13] South Africa – at least at state and armed forces level – has not sought to destabilize. Rather it has agreed that the Orange River frontier runs on the middle line (not the north bank as previously asserted) and agreed a joint 'transitional' management of the Walvis Bay enclave in full knowledge that this can only mean a transition to Namibian sovereignty. Nor has South Africa asserted any off-shore fishing rights. Rather it scrambled its plans to assist in Namibia's arrest of Spanish trawlers, flagrantly violating Namibia's exclusive economic zone when they fled into waters off-shore from the Walvis Bay enclave. It is over these two years that de Klerk's changes in South African state policy were crucial in creating a context favourable to peaceful reconciliation in Namibia likely to continue even more so under President Mandela.

On its side, Namibia has been gradualist and pragmatic in reducing economic links with South Africa. It has given two years' notice of its intent to establish an independent currency and tariff system. While some imports have been diverted away from South Africa, these have been to lower cost sources and can be seen as purely pragmatic business deals. Some fishing licences have been awarded to vessels landing their catch at Walvis Bay.

In office SWAPO has pursued a prudent – indeed cautious – economic policy. Compared with South Africa or its administration of Namibia, the independent state's fiscal and monetary policies have been models of rectitude. Conflicts with private enterprises have been relatively few and none has been nationalized.

Namibia has a free and variegated press (even if no impartial newspaper). The state radio and television are much more balanced and much less overtly a government mouthpiece than under South African rule – probably no more so than in some Western European countries. A disagreement between SWAPO (both as a party and as the governing party) and the trade unions ended pacifically with the latter successfully establishing their full autonomy. The National

Assembly is a reasonably harmonious body and while debate can be sharp no efforts are made either to filibuster or to ram through legislation without debate.

The land question was kept on the back burner until 1991, when a national consultative conference (including white farmers) was held. Its recommendations – even though clearly endorsing transfers to black farmers and ranchers – are seen by most (including most white farmers) as pragmatic, gradualist reform. There has been no massive exodus of white settlers and a majority have taken Namibian citizenship.

To assert that the process of reconciliation has been costless or is certain to continue would be distinctly over-optimistic and dangerous in obscuring issues needing to be faced. However, that kind of facile short-sightedness does not appear to characterize Namibia any more than does febrile alarm.

First reconciliation with South Africa has been seen to require paying of the 'debt' (to South African financial institutions) illegally issued by the occupation regime after the revocation of the Mandate. Similarly, winning a reputation for fiscal prudence both domestically and internationally has limited expansion of social services and human investment in terms of both quantity and quality. The same considerations – combined with poor global mineral markets and a desire to induce new investment in replacement mines and in petroleum exploration – have led to very slow moves to renegotiate mining regimes – including with Rossing Uranium, whose licences and investments all post-date the revocation and are legally void *ab initio*.

Domestic reconciliation has slowed progress in at least three major areas – labour law, affirmative action (which is constitutionally mandated but in very vague terms) and the land question. Here the government is on a tightrope between the very different perceptions of white farmer and employer and black farmer (or would-be farmer) and trade unions. On affirmative action there is a potential conflict with personal equality of rights clause of the Constitution – both are entrenched, unamendable clauses. However, as with mining legislation, licences and tax regimes, progress on labour law has speeded up; so has consideration of options regarding land and affirmative action.

The fiscal burden of reconciliation has been high. Civil servants in practice cannot be fired simply because their functions have vanished or they are not competent to perform them. As a result, 15,000 to 25,000 public officials (a majority, but not all of them high-salaried white personnel), whose sole ability was to administer apartheid and repress resistance to it, remain on the payroll. This is not merely a serious fiscal drag; it hampers employment of qualified black Namibians whose services are needed.

A final problem on the governmental side is <u>policing</u>. The crime rate has risen, to the intense disquiet of black as much as of white Namibians. Part of this is the normal aftermath of a war. But part relates to a police profile which has been lowered – sometimes to near invisibility – on standard, properly defined law enforcement. The hold-over personnel, especially white officers, are well aware of their historic image and have retreated into doing as little as possible in order to avoid conflict.

Finally, it would be wilful blindness to ignore that <u>racism</u> is alive and well (doing ill) in the attitudes and actions of many (mostly white) Namibians at a personal level and in workplace relations. At top level most management (not all) are committed to reshaping relations in the workplace but the same does not apply to lower management and foreman levels. The result is both poor labour relations and great difficulty in raising labour productivity or achieving union–management cooperation, even when both top managers and union leaders are committed to and have creative ideas about improving this situation.

More positively, all of these tensions are known and openly discussed in Namibia. That may be the strongest evidence that they can be contained. After three decades of disorder and war all factions of the Namibian people are committed to retaining the more peaceful, less fraught period entered into in 1989–90 and aware that doing so requires finding and acting on syntheses or compromises of interests.

The most massive problem is reducing both racial inequality in economic results and the incidence of absolute poverty. These are both necessary for the continued viability of reconciliation and themselves depend on it.[14] The stark contrast during the 1980s of Zimbabwe with Angola and Mozambique and of Botswana with occupied Namibia underlines the second point and, perhaps less self-evidently, the first. Growth will not by itself cure either inequality or absolute poverty, but without fairly rapid growth the resources to do so will not be available. This is especially true because redistribution by cuts in real white incomes has distinct limits (even if not precisely knowable in advance), limits beyond which reconciliation would be jeopardized. The 2 to 3 per cent annual growth of the 1990–92 period is not enough – Zimbabwe's average annual growth of 4.5 per cent during the 1980s might just do, but only 6 per cent or better would give an adequate safety margin.[15]

That said, Namibia in terms of conflict is, to date, a continuing success story. Armed conflict has ended and – equally important – there is a dynamic move towards reducing tensions by peaceful means to ensure that it does not re-emerge. SWAPO's liberation war rallying cry 'One Namibia, One Nation' has become a motto which most white Namibians accept or even espouse and in support of which they are willing to make at least some sacrifices.

Notes

1 For fuller accounts see *National Atlas of South-West Africa*, SWAPO Namibia, Windhoek, 1983; Geographic Chapters in R. H. Green, M. L. Kiljunen and K. Kiljunen, *Namibia: The Last Colony*, Longman, 1981; 'Namibia', *Encyclopaedia Britannica*, 1983.

2 For fuller accounts of colonization see P. H. Katjavivi, *A History of Resistance in Namibia*, Currey/OAU/UNESCO, London/Addis Ababa/Paris, 1988; History and Macroeconomic Chapters, *Namibia: Perspectives for Economic Reconstruction and Development*, UN Institute for Namibia, Lusaka, 1986; B. Wood, *Namibia: 1884–1984: Readings on Namibia's History and Society*, Namibia Support Committee, London, 1988.

3 See Katjavivi, op. cit.

4 See Katjavivi, op. cit; see also *Africa Contemporary Record*, Africana, New York/London, 'Namibia', 1972/3–1989/90 [*ACR*].

5 See Macroeconomic and Employment Chapters in *Namibia: Perspectives . . .* and Green *et al.*, op. cit.

6 See P. Manning and R. H. Green, 'Namibia: Preparations for Destabilization', in D. Martin and P. Johnson, *Front Line South Africa: Destructive Engagement*, Four Walls-Eight Windows, New York, 1989; R. Green and C. Thomson, 'Political Economies in Conflict: SADCC, South Africa and Sanctions' in ibid.; see also *ACR* op. cit.

7 See UNICEF, 'Namibia', in *Children on the Front Line: The Impact of Apartheid, Destabilisation and Warfare on Children in Southern and South Africa*, New York, 1989.

8 See D. Geldenhuys, *The Diplomacy of Isolation*, Macmillan, Johannesburg, 1984.

9 See Katjavivi, op. cit.

10 See *ACR*, 1988/9–1989/90; see also K. O'Neill and B. Munslow, 'Angola: Ending the Cold War in Southern Africa', chapter 9.

11 Largely from personal discussions with and public addresses by SWAPO leaders.

12 From personal communications and public addresses by SWAPO leaders. *Constitution of the Republic of Namibia*, Government Gazette no. 2, 21 March 1990, Windhoek.

13 See D. Simon, *Independent Namibia: One Year On*, Conflict Studies no. 239, Research Institute for the Study of Conflict and Terrorism, London, 1991.

14 See J. Balch and N. Scholten, 'Namibian Reconstruction and National Reconciliation: Putting the Horse before the Cart', *Review of African Political Economy*, 49, 1991.

15 *Economic/Statistical Survey*, Ministry of Finance, Windhoek, 1990, 1991, 1992.

11· THE DYNAMICS OF CONFLICT IN UGANDA

Amii Omara-Otunnu

The impression that socio-political conflicts are endemic in Uganda is not far from the truth. The genealogy of internal conflicts can be traced to the very inception of the state. It is certainly the case that what is now Uganda was from the beginning constructed and baptized into a political entity through protracted conflicts of various descriptions, the legacy of which still haunts the country. Indeed it is accurate to characterize the history of Uganda as one whose flow and texture have been determined by conflict. Yet although it can be argued that internal socio-political conflicts have their ancestry in the colonial system, conflicts in the post-colonial period have acquired a new saliency, the logic of which is imprecise in meaning. In summary, in the recent post-colonial era, the political elites in Uganda have exhibited a high proclivity for dysfunctional use of violence with the result that the inherited colonial system now displays pervasive symptoms of political pathology.

The high incidence of socio-political conflicts in Uganda has generated a corpus of literature on the subject. The most recent are the collections of essays in *Conflict and Resolution in Uganda* (1989) edited by Rupesinghe and *Uganda Now: Between Decay and Development* (1988) edited by Hansen and Twaddle, both of which have the merit of treating the subject from the prevailing political viewpoint; however, neither of them adequately discloses the impersonal historical character nor provides conceptual clarity concerning conflicts in Uganda (see Mamdani 1989). For the most part, scholars have emphasized the following as significant factors in socio-political conflicts in Uganda: religious loyalties and ideologies (see for example Mujaju 1976; cf. Welbourn 1965; Low 1962); regional and super-power influences (Woodward 1987); and ethnic antipathies and chauvinism (Mazrui 1975; Sathyamurthy 1986; Omara-Otunnu 1987). The variables of structural socio-economic differentiations, the very character of the state and the status of ideology, all of which may be fundamental in generating socio-political conflicts in Uganda, have meanwhile been given scant attention. It is on these latter factors that this chapter focusses, in order to highlight issues which have not been given adequate scholarly treatment.

Despite the shortcomings of the current literature on conflicts in Uganda, all the analyses point to a critical consensus on one issue: that conflicts have imprinted their indelible stigma on Ugandan political morphology. The various conflicts that have been played out in the theatre of Ugandan politics have left human debris of tragic and disastrous proportions, severely compounding social relations in the country. In terms of development prospects for the country, the conflicts have seriously impaired the capacity of Uganda to deal effectively with the multi-faceted afflictions of AIDS, debt, encroaching desertification, population growth and drought. Tragically, the internal conflicts, together with the other calamities, have reduced Uganda to a country of only potential, despite being richly endowed with natural resources. In order to appreciate the nature of conflicts – which are as much an anomaly as a novel feature of Uganda, it is imperative that a searching historical analysis, which may yield theoretical hypotheses for wider general application, be carried out.

It is in this vein that I shall attempt in this chapter to delineate some of the internal and international conditions for socio-political conflicts in Uganda. I employ a historical approach because unless we can appreciate the historical forces that have generated or contributed to conflicts in the country, we cannot prescribe effective remedies to this disease that has disfigured the political landscape of Uganda. But first, let me outline that theoretical thesis of the chapter, derived from the history of Uganda.

The dynamics of conflicts in any society often depend on whether the component parts of the society perceive their interests as being in consonance with one another (see Andreski 1968, chapter 1). In Uganda, the lack of sufficient structural integration of the different parts of the country into one state and the consequent perception of divergent interests that the various constituent parts have been conscious of, have in large measure informed the dynamics of internal conflicts in the country.

The occurrences of conflict in Uganda have borne a direct relationship to the existence or absence of a viable national ideology or ethos and the degree of internal legitimacy of the authorities. When the legitimacy of those in political power has been shallow or non-existent, and there has been no dominant ideology to justify that authority, force has been used to settle political differences, with the result that internal conflicts (civil wars) have flared up. But the status of ideology and internal legitimacy has in general gained relevance in social conflicts only as a function of politico-economic power relations in Uganda, which have been intimately linked to structural integration of the state. In a nutshell, conflicts in the country have been a consequence of disturbances of socio-political equilibrium and shifts in the locus of power, together with concomitant economic benefits; there have also been shifts in society and attempts by incoming ruling groups to restructure power relations differently from that which had hitherto obtained. However, although socio-economic conditions have in large measure influenced the patterns of conflicts in the country, their tempo has generally been affected by a factor of leadership. This in turn has been conditioned by the international climate or the particular timing of conflicts.

In order to understand this historically, we must consider the processes by which present-day Uganda came into existence.

In summary, the nation-state of Uganda came into existence as a result of territorial surgery performed by European colonial powers in Eastern and Central Africa during the heyday of the new European imperialism (see Ingham 1958); and its internal character was moulded by the policies pursued by successive administrations – both colonial and post-colonial – since the beginning of the 20th century. The configuration of these two phenomena – the creation of Uganda by external forces and the pattern of policies for internal development – have had implications for domestic conflicts and their resolution in Uganda. Whereas the viability of Uganda as a state has owed much to its international personality and its validation externally, the dynamics of internal interactions and conflicts within Uganda have been influenced, if not conditioned, by economic and political policies pursued by various administrations.

By and large, the internal economic policies of Uganda's governments since about 1900 have shown a pattern of strong regional biases which have resulted in structural inequalities between different regions in the country. In addition, the socio-political policy of ethnic compartmentalization pursued especially in the colonial period, combined with economic policies, militated against territory-wide social cohesion. The impact has been that, because the different social groups do not perceive that they have the same national interests in common, social conflicts have been exhibited along ethno-regional ideological lines, in attempts either to redress historical grievances or to sustain the status quo. The significance of this for present-day politics in Uganda may be drawn out by contrast with ways in which states at other times and in other places have come into existence. Broadly speaking, there are three patterns of state formation, two of which have historically achieved viable independent states. In one, a particular social group expands by commercial and/or military means and serves as a nucleus by absorbing other groups which, over time, come to subscribe to the ideology of the dominant group. Examples include Germany with Prussia at the core (after 1850) and Italy with the House of Sicily and Piedmont forming the nucleus (after 1860). Or, to take examples in Africa, ancient Ghana with the Soninke being the dominant group (c. 1240–1500) and Bunyoro-Kitara with the Babito being the ruling class (c. 1600–1850). States formed through the process of internally generated territorial aggregation tend to be the most cohesive.

A second process for state formation results from imperial fragmentation and international crisis, in which the subjects of an imperial power, imbued with a consciousness of parochialism and grievance, join together to rid themselves of an imperial power; the ideology of liberation and justice justifies the thrust towards liberation and the actions of the leaders who accede to power once they have thrown off the imperial yoke. The United States of America (1776) and Haiti (1791–1804) are examples of this. States that come into existence through political convulsions such as these have a good chance of exhibiting longevity as long as there is consensus among the political elites in adopting revolutionary rhetoric as a dominant ideology to justify, even validate, the existence of the state.

The third pattern of state formation, however, is externally derived, and this is what happened in the case of Uganda. 'Territorial surgery' carved up administrative areas, largely on paper and not through a process which took account of conditions on the ground. This approach is not doomed to failure; it can succeed if the authorities then pursue and promote economic and social policies which can bring the people of the newly created territory together. However, in colonial Uganda, the new state was viewed as a structure to facilitate the interests of Britain. In particular, the British colonial authorities were motivated by the geostrategic consideration of controlling the Nile Valley, together with a degree of interest in exploitation of resources in the Central–East Africa region. Their agenda was not to engage in a process of state formation which would foster social cohesion; indeed social welfare and social integration ranked low in the list of colonial priorities while administrative order was at the top of the agenda. In this sense, it would be more appropriate to speak of the 'delimitation' rather than the 'formation' of the Ugandan state.

Indeed, while it is customary to speak of the process of state formation (see Kabwegyere 1974; Karugire 1980, chapter 2), in the case of Uganda the very word 'process' is also inappropriate, since both colonial and post-colonial 'states' came into existence through declaration or fiat; there was scarcely any *process* involved. The way by which Uganda came into existence renders questionable the utility of the normative concept of state formation (Seton-Watson 1977; Smith 1979). Thus, for example, on the eve of Uganda's independence in 1960, a constitutional conference was held, not in Uganda but in London, and those Ugandans who attended went there mostly as representatives of their localities and not of political parties or any other overarching countrywide grouping. The thinking behind this was described in 1959 by Governor Cohen:

> It was, moreover, a [colonial] system which looked at the problems and interests of each given area or tribe. It was not conceived in the framework of building up a state or nation; still less – and this is very natural – did it take into account the tendencies and pressures appearing in the world at large, which at a later stage were to affect tropical Africa (Cohen 1959, pp. 26–7).

At independence, in terms of structures and ideology, nothing much had changed.

When the process of state formation occurs, certain institutions and structures come into pace through which particular values are transmitted and the ideology to justify the authority in power is articulated. To some extent, this did happen in colonial Uganda, in particular through economic development and the creation of a school system. However, the very values which these fostered were externally oriented, so that the Ugandan state was defined by outside interests and events, as opposed to developing an internally validated identity which in turn could be capable of international recognition. Thus despite the high hopes brought about by political independence, the post-colonial Ugandan state was doomed to turmoil precisely because the structures, institutions and values it inherited had no sufficient internal validity. The situation was further complicated by the economic and social policies of successive governments which concentrated economic and social institutions in southern Uganda – especially in Buganda and Busoga – resulting in structural inequalities between different regions in the country. In the 1920s, for example, the thrust of the colonial administration was to refrain from actively stimulating the production of cotton or other economic crops in the northern districts of Uganda on which it was dependent for a supply of labour to be used in the producing districts of Buganda and Busoga.

For the most part the economic and social policies pursued and promoted by administrations since 1900, instead of integrating Ugandan societies, enhanced structural inequalities between different regions in the country. And because no community of interests was developed among a cross-section of Ugandans, just as in the first thirty years or so of colonial rule force was frequently used to exact compliance precisely because no viable ideology had been developed to justify the outsiders' being in power, so in the three decades that have passed since independence military means have been resorted to when the interests of rulers and ruled have diverged. Thus the treatment of Roman Catholic Buganda in 1892, Bunyoro in 1893–4 and Acholi in 1911–12 is echoed in the treatment by post-colonial regimes of Buganda in 1966 and 1981–5, Acholi in 1971–9 and 1986–91, West Nile in 1979–85, and Teso in 1986–91. The brief convergence of interests of different social groups in countries like Uganda to throw out the colonial rulers had no hope of longevity precisely because of the policies of unequal development and social compartmentalization ('divide and rule') which precluded any structural integration. This was mostly because the primary vehicles of economic and social cohesion – trade and schools – were wholly oriented to the externally generated values of the colonial authorities. The ideology of 'nationalism' united people against the colonial authorities, but once the objective of unity was no longer there, people had to live with the pre-existing structural realities of inequality and imbalance between social groups. This social disequilibrium has not only precipitated conflict but has bedevilled approaches to conflict resolution.

During the early colonial period, the military was needed to settle internal conflict. In a well-established state, military power is generally reserved for use against aliens. In the case of the early colonial states, not only did the authorities lack any internal legitimacy (such as may be derived from popular participation in politics), but they actually regarded those they ruled as alien; a unifying ideology among rulers and ruled was absent. In the later colonial period, as the indigenous people began to acquiesce to the presence of colonial authorities as a fact of life and to subscribe to the dominant ideology of the political order, the police force increasingly became the instrument of 'law and order'. In part this was due to the lapse of time and to a growing recognition by the people that military resistance was futile; it can also be partly traced to the establishment of schools and industries or wage labour and the co-option of indigenous functionaries into the colonial system.

In the post-colonial period and to date in Uganda very few concerted efforts have been pursued institutionally to establish alternative structures or internally generated ideologies which might be conducive to social and political cohesion. And it is evident that in many cases those in authority still regard their fellow citizens as aliens; for example, whereas President Obote would mobilize the police to deal with any disturbance in his native Lango district, he used the army in Luwero Triangle in Buganda. As a result of the pattern of military composition based on ethnic or linguistic affiliation, the troops deployed in Buganda were drawn from other parts of Uganda and this reinforced the approach of using the military against 'aliens'; troops were not being required to use force against ' their own' people. Obote was not alone in this approach – the pattern has been replicated in Uganda, for example, with the relentless and ruthless treatment of people from and in northern and eastern Uganda by Museveni's National Resistance Army (NRA).

The absence of a viable national ideology (or political culture) acting contingently upon the problem of structural imbalances in the country – as critical factors fuelling, if not generating, socio-political conflicts in Uganda – can be detected with exceptional clarity in the civil wars that have festered between the various 'rebel' groups and the National Resistance Army in the northern and eastern regions of the country. What the opposition groups in the north and east of the country have in common is not ethnic identity or cultural traditions, but a history of being only peripherally included in the economic structures and processes of the country. This is now exacerbated by a common alienation and suffering at the hands of the NRA troops. The most dramatic of the 'rebels' ' challenges to the government of Yoweri Museveni was the one posed by a group led by a barely literate woman known as Alice Lakwena, in 1987. In short, the conflicts in northern and eastern Uganda have flared up because the sincere sense of historical grievance of the people in those areas and their yearnings to social justice have not been effectively addressed by the NRA regime.

Thus in the context of the country's history, while individual leaders and collectively their governments do bear much of the responsibility for the tragedies and excesses of recent years, the problem is broader and deeper than any particular individual, as is painfully illustrated by the lack of improvement when one or other individual Ugandan ruler is replaced. The more fundamental problem is that the structures and institutions necessary for stable and cohesive states are not there. There is an urgent need to get beyond the point where individuals are identified with the state, and to develop a pervasive and dominant ideology which justifies the state independent of the particular individual or individuals who manage or, in many cases, use the state.

To be sure, developing structures and establishing an ideology is the more difficult, the more short-lived each 'government' is. At some point, however, the cycle must be broken. Political office should be given to individuals who have political courage and are prepared to formulate a philosophy which is acceptable to a majority and cross-section of the people in the country. This much needed internal restructuring needs to take into account international factors, such as the global economy and the necessity to find external markets for African goods. In today's international political climate, external recognition and support is both valuable and necessary, but should be secondary to broad internal popular support, without which political stability can at best be only short-lived.

One way to begin to create a community of interests within the territorial state of Uganda is to remedy the structural imbalances which successive administrations have created and/or exacerbated. This in itself is a path fraught with difficulty, because increasing the rate of investment and development in areas that have traditionally been under-served is liable to provoke the resentment of the better-established regions. It is this phenomenon which has created the pendulum swing whereby successive governments led by people from different areas have tended to undo the work of their predecessors. This approach must therefore be part of a comprehensive strategy which can be perceived to be in the interests of all, or at least the majority, of the citizenry; and most importantly, it should address the critical historical factors that have been predisposed towards internal socio-political conflicts. Such a comprehensive strategy would include the creation of an internally integrated nation-wide economy; regular elections of people's representatives to debate and decide policies; a genuine commitment to appointing personnel from all over the country to political and civil service jobs; the decentralization of power and the creation of a decentralized militia, with the possibility of ultimately abolishing the army. Currently organized neither for the protection of the state nor to fight external aggression, the army has become a parasitic bureaucracy and a repressive apparatus of the state, and there is simply no rational reason to maintain it.

This approach would not rely for its initial implementation on there necessarily being an elected government – an important qualification, given the practical reality that very few Ugandan governments of late have gained power through the ballot box – yet it would do more to realize the spirit of democracy than has many an election or formally constituted parliament, themselves merely the outward forms of democracy. In colonial Uganda, for example, the first nation-wide elections which took place less than five years before independence were outwardly impeccable but lacked any substance. For decades previously, the colonial administration had offered no accountability to the ruled and solicited almost no input from those it governed. These two fundamentals of democracy could not be magically created by simply holding elections. As former British Prime Minister Margaret Thatcher recently commented: 'It is easy to transfer the institutions of democracy from one country to another, as Britain did to much of Africa in the 1960s. But it soon becomes apparent that it is no guarantee that democracy as we know it will be practised' (British Information Service, Policy Statement 43/90, August 1990, pp. 2–3).

In political theory, a well-established state fulfils certain criteria: first, it has a defined territory; second, it has a cohesive populace; third, it exercises predominant jurisdiction over the populace and territory; and fourth, it possesses an international personality. Uganda, by and large, fulfils only the first and last of these. Elsewhere in the world, populace and authority are generally more critical, with assertion of international personality emanating from these. In a strict sense then, the concept of a Ugandan state cannot be posited simply as one of class struggles and domination; but perhaps more importantly as an instrument through which international capital pursues and protects its interests.

In Uganda, therefore, the logic of politics is inverted: international considerations tend to dictate rather than reflect such internal policies as there are; and the conflicts that arise as a result of the failure to incorporate the very people who make up the administrative state tend to overshadow and preclude attempts at meaningful internal social policies. In circumstances of prolonged or repeated civil strife, the guarantors of power are external, through the supply of financial and military resources and diplomatic support. To be in receipt of these, the political elites must speak the political language current on the international scene. Rarely do these elites couch their language in terms to which people in the villages and the shanty towns can relate; instead the key terms for political discourse – 'modernization', 'human rights', 'democracy' and so on – are concepts which are constructed externally. At a sociological level, these terms promote an orientation of values to the outside world; and so the cycle is perpetuated.

In Uganda today where civil wars are being fought, it is fair to surmise that the contestant groups in the conflict do not regard each other as part of an integrated state. This perception is a result of structural strains in society which have been brought about by governmental policies. If we are to tackle the question of internal conflict effectively and ensure viable stability and peace within Ugandan territory, we would need not only to identify the defects within the system but equally importantly to formulate solutions which would make a cross-section of the citizenry feel that they share a community of interests and values. There are two key strategies for effecting this: the first is to repudiate Article 3, Clauses 1–3 of the Organization of African Unity (OAU) Charter which gives sanction to the pattern of territorial surgery carried out by European colonial powers. In such an instance a working set of criteria based on the principle of self-determination, coupled with that of equality of rights of different nationalities, ought to be given serious consideration. The second strategy would be to restructure internal economic, political and social relations to give every group within the territorial boundaries of Uganda fair opportunities to realize their legitimate aspirations and to recognize that their own aspirations are, in the long term, most effectively achieved in concert with, rather than at the expense of, the aspirations of other similar groups. Both strategies ought to have as their objective the achievement of equitable justice in Uganda.

The Ugandan administrative territory can be regarded as a state essentially only in legalistic and diplomatic terms and not in a historical or sociological sense; as far as socio-political struggles are concerned, however, it is indeed a state in the sense that it has become the arena in which social conflicts are played out by various different groups. Such conflicts have often become Hobbesian in dimension, with the colonial 'divide and rule' replaced by African power elites' 'unite or conquer'; moreover, unlike in the colonial period, when 'law and order' was used by the authorities to facilitate economic exploitation, in the recent post-colonial era 'law and order' has been used by Ugandan elites to ensure political domination. This approach to government appears to be informed by an essentially mercantilist temper of politics in which the wielders of power have subordinated economic imperatives to political considerations. The result has been that although in Uganda the military have quite often used their awesome power to impose socio-political order on the population, the conditions thus created have generally not led to expansion of economic production. On the contrary, conditions brought about by the severity of military measures have often engendered uncertainty and impoverishment among the population due to dwindling economic activities and lack of active participation in political processes; this in turn has generally compounded and intensified conflicts.

In the historical circumstances of Uganda, where ascriptive social groups have not been sufficiently integrated into a cohesive national entity and where there is not an inclusive viable national ideology, military contests for political power and the rewards that go with it have in the post-colonial period been transformed by the protagonists into, and perceived by the population at large as, struggles between ethno-linguistic groups. But in order for the military – normally dominated by one ethno-linguistic group – to obtain the economic items they desire from society, they would first define the group to prey on. In a situation of economic structural imbalances and social disequilibria between different areas of the country, a predatory army has often harped on ethno-linguistic differences to divide 'them' from themselves. And in order for the group so defined to resist economic spoliation and to ensure its social survival at the hands of such an army, it often acquires military means to attempt to accomplish the task. Thus the cycle and efficacy of militarism have been fostered, which have fed into and perpetuated economic structural imbalances and social disequilibria.

It was in this fashion that militarism came of age during and after the military regime of Idi Amin (1971–9). The distinctive features of militarism in the country have been: devaluation of human lives; use of military methods (force) and language in social interactions; the presentation by the power elite of political problems as essentially military in nature; replacement of Western-type education and trade by military success as the criteria for upward social and political mobility; and the actual domination of civilian institutions by the military. Indeed, the most enduring legacy of Idi Amin's rule of Uganda may be militarism, which his regime nurtured and bequeathed to the socio-political system (see Omara-Otunnu 1987, chapters 8–14). The militarism during Idi Amin's rule was perhaps best captured by the grammar of power at the time: 'I can fight, therefore I must rule.' Today in Uganda, militarism has graduated that grammar into the NRA dictum: 'I fought, therefore I must rule.'

Militarism which has its shallow roots in civil–military relations and the nature of the state in colonialism has now gained sanction and social currency in Uganda, and has terminally affected socio-political processes and economic activities. It is apparent that the phenomenon began to take firm roots after the military usurpation of political power in 1971. It is indeed fair to surmise that Amin's military coup by its inherent logic set in motion forces in society whose configuration brought about militarism – and its contribution to socio–political conflict – in Uganda. These forces tended to purge organized violence of its moral ambivalence; and although they may not have made a virtue of violence, they nonetheless inscribed and offered sanction to military means as a formula in the general equation in shifting power relations and in social interactions. But it is important to emphasize that all the elements or ingredients that have gone into boosting and articulating socio-political conflicts in Uganda have occurred in the context of economic structural imbalances and social disequilibria in the country.

The seminal lesson from Ugandan history is that conflicts have reflected the nature of the administrative state and the purpose for which the territorial state was brought into existence. In general, the patterns of socio-political conflicts have mirrored the level of structural integration of Uganda and the status of internal ideology used to underpin the existence of the territorial definition. In the dynamics of conflicts in the country, the political leadership has functioned as mediating agents to balance the plethora of seemingly disparate interests which the economic structural imbalances and social disequilibria have imposed on the administrative state. Whenever the political leadership has succeeded to construct some balanced national consensus, as was the case in the period between 1961 and 1966, conflicts have been substantially ameliorated.

It was during this period of a delicate national consensus that constitutional rule flourished. The period was characterized by '[a] procedural approach to politics; a faith in legal solutions to political tensions; a relatively open society with institutionalized competition for power in the polity' (Engholm and Mazrui 1967; cf. Baldwin 1976). In this context, it should be noted that constitutional rule is possible only where and when there is some equilibrium in society; moreover, constitutionalism presupposes that society has reached some formal, if not substantive, agreement on the ground rules of politics and on the means and ends of government. In Uganda, a national political consensus (or social contract) ought to be constructed to create a conducive climate in which the more fundamental questions of economic structural imbalances and social disequilibria can be addressed, so as to establish parity of opportunity for individuals to engage meaningfully in political deliberations, the net impact of which might be to reduce occurrences of socio-political conflict.

If the national experience from 1961 to 1966 can be used to provide suggestions for the future, it is that a federal form of government based on the principle of pluralism, in which no single socio-political group would exercise hegemony over others, might be best suited to the conditions of Uganda until the country is structurally integrated into a cohesive state and has attained a socio-economic equilibrium. Such a Ugandan state would depend in large measure on internal democratic legitimacy for its viability and validation.

References

Andreski, Stanislav, *Military Organization and Society* (London: Routledge and Kegan Paul Ltd., 1968 [1954]).

Baldwin, Jr., F. N., 'Constitutional Limitations on Government in Mexico, the United States, and Uganda', in Richard P. Claude, *Comparative Human Rights* (Baltimore and London: The John Hopkins University Press, 1976).

Cohen, Sir A. B., *British Policy in Changing Africa*, Routledge and Kegan Paul, London, 1959.

Engholm, G.F. and Ali A. Mazrui, 'Violent Constitutionalism in Uganda', in *Government and Opposition*, (4), July–October 1967.

Hansen, Holger Bernt and Michael Twaddle (eds), *Uganda Now: Between Decay and Development* (London: James Currey, 1988).

Ingham, Kenneth, *The Making of Modern Uganda* (London: George Allen and Unwin Ltd., 1958).

Kabwegyere, T. B. *The Politics of State Formation: The Nature and Effects of Colonialism in Uganda* (Nairobi: East African Literature Bureau, 1974).

Karugire, S., *A Political History of Uganda* (London and Nairobi: Heinemann Publishers, 1980).

Low, D. A., *Political Parties in Uganda, 1949–62* (London: The Athlone Press, 1962).

Mamdani, Mahmood, 'How Not to Intervene in Internal Conflicts', in *Bulletin of Peace Proposals*, 20(4), 1989.

Mazrui, Ali A., *Soldiers and Kinsmen in Uganda: The Making of a Military Ethnocracy* (London: Sage Publications, 1975).

Mujaju, Akiiki B., 'The Political Crisis of Church Institutions in Uganda', in *Africa Affairs*, 75(298), January 1976.

Omara-Otunnu, Amii, *Politics and the Military in Uganda, 1895–1985* (London: Macmillan Press, 1987).

Rupesinghe, K. (ed.), *Conflict and Resolution in Uganda* (Oslo: International Peace Research Institute, 1989).

Sathyamurthy, T. V., *The Political Development of Uganda, 1900–1986* (London: Gower Publishing Company, 1986).

Seton-Watson, Hugh, *Nations and States* (Boulder, Colorado: Westview Press, 1977).

Smith, Anthony D., *Nationalism in the Twentieth Century* (Oxford: Martin Robertson, 1979).

Welbourn, F.B., *Religion and Politics in Uganda* (Nairobi: East African Publishing House, 1965).

Woodward, Peter, *Rivalry and Conflict in Northern East Africa* (London: The Centre for Security and Conflict Studies, 1987).

12· THE COLONIAL LEGACY

David Throup

It has become almost a truism that Africa has not fared well during the post-colonial era. Media reports are filled with the 'Whither Africa' debate. The continent faces a number of acute problems: low or negative economic growth rates; the world's fastest growing population with a birth rate of over 4 per cent in Kenya and Zimbabwe, so that their population doubles every 17 years; continuing marginalization in the world economy, which means that Africa has received little new foreign investment in recent years and counts for a mere 2.5 per cent of world trade; a debt burden of $270 million, greater than the continent's total economic output.[1] Several countries face widespread famine, often exacerbated by civil war, which it is estimated affected 25–7 million people in 1991; while the continent already has 5 million refugees or displaced people.[2] Political corruption is so rampant that in even a comparatively small and poor state such as Mali, former president Traore, who was overthrown in March 1991, embezzled over $2 billion, a sum greater than Mali's total external debt.[3] Several states face continuing political turmoil. In Liberia the recent settlement remains precarious, civil war rages in Sudan between the south and the fundamentalist regime in Khartoum, as well as an extremely destructive war in Angola. Elsewhere, Somalia has disintegrated into rival clans, Burundi is driven by renewed ethnic clashes, the Zairean state has nearly disintegrated, and political repression mounts in Kenya.[4] This chapter focusses particularly upon political factors which have caused or exacerbated these problems, examining the aims and social composition of nationalist movements and the development of – or failure to develop – accepted civic cultures.[5]

Africans and the colonial state

The different colonial experiences of African peoples have had a profound impact upon the post-independence performance of African governments. The colonial era determined the initial structure of post-independence political institutions, the focus of economic production, and even the strengths and limitations of nationalist and sub-nationalist movements. Colonialism created both divided and comparatively uncontested political societies. The incorporation of Africans into the international economy fundamentally changed attitudes to land ownership, which crops to grow and how to manage their cattle, soil and environment.

The colonial state in Africa

The colonial state in most parts of Africa, unlike in Asia, could not build upon sophisticated indigenous state structures. Crawford Young has pointed out that in most of Asia, where European mercantile empires were established in the 17th and 18th centuries, 'the colonial state could not superimpose itself upon existing state structures of substantial scope and institutions of social power long accustomed to the extraction of revenue from the land'.[6] Revenue, drawn from land taxation and customs duties, was much more difficult to extract in Africa and viable social and political intermediaries were much more difficult to find.[7] Only Ethiopia and Liberia managed to evade the 'Scramble' at the end of the 19th century by European colonizers. They succeeded for different reasons: Liberia from the 1840s was part of the United States of America's informal empire, a semi-autonomous state for liberated slaves; in Ethiopia, Italian colonialism clashed with indigenous Amharic expansion at Adowa in 1896.[8] Every African state experienced some form of colonial rule. Africans were forced deeper into the international capitalist economy which created different types and degrees of dependent relationships.

Colonialists needed their colonies to be financially self-sufficient. In West Africa, African production was encouraged and the population 'persuaded' by various means to grow groundnuts, cocoa, palm oil, rubber, cotton or coffee. Cocoa was one of a number of tropical exports which depended almost entirely on local African enterprise and initiative. Collection, distribution and the whole organization of the trade was in African hands from the first years of colonial rule.[9] Palm oil and rubber – two other forest region products – similarly developed under African control during the 19th century. Customs duties on these small-holder crops, and indirect and direct taxation of Africans provided the main source of revenue for colonial states in West Africa.[10]

In the areas which attracted European settlers in large numbers – particularly Kenya and the Rhodesias and, of course, South Africa – the opportunities for African cash crop production were limited or deliberately destroyed by settler political protests. Beinart and Bundy, for example, have shown how in South Africa during the 1880s and 1890s the development of a prosperous African 'peasantry', based on maize cultivation, was undermined.[11] Ranger and Mosley have told a similar story in Southern Rhodesia [Zimbabwe], although uncovering the surprising resilience of Shona peasant producers until the Depression of the 1930s; then the settler-controlled state destroyed African production to safeguard the domestic market for European farmers.[12] In South Africa no less than 93 per cent of farming land was alienated to Europeans, and in Southern Rhodesia the small settler population held half the land. In Kenya the exclusion of Africans from settling permanently in the 'White Highlands' in the Rift Valley was to become one of the major causes of Kikuyu discontent and an important factor behind the Mau Mau rebellion in 1952.[13]

Not all West Africa was a haven for peasant producers or East and Central Africa the preserve of European settlers or mining capital. In French West Africa, forced labour from Upper Volta [Burkina Faso] was despatched to plantations in the Côte d'Ivoire and the Gold Coast [Ghana], as it still is today.[14] Nyasaland [Malawi], Mozambique, Bechuanaland [Botswana] and Basutoland [Lesotho] – the archetypal 'labour reserve colonies' – by contrast, had enclaves of resilient small-holder producers.[15] Different areas in the same territory often experienced very different facts as they were drawn into the international capitalist economy. As a result, regions within the same colony, as well as different colonies, evolved economically and socially in very different ways. These differences have had lasting consequences since independence.[16]

The second major cause of increasing differentiation among Africans was education. In French and Belgian Africa, access to education was strictly controlled. Schooling was designed to produce government clerks and village school teachers and, in the Belgian colonies, a few priests.[17] Control of the education in British Africa was more relaxed. During the inter-war years, African-controlled independent schools, divorced from European supervision, began to proliferate. Africans saw education as a key to more remunerative employment. It was a social investment which enabled family members to break out of the rural small-holders' world and to gain access to wage employment in the cities. Urban wages could be invested in the small-holding, buying more land, or in the education of siblings. During the inter-war era, links between urban and rural Africans speeded up the process of rural stratification.[18]

As a result of these processes, colonial rule created new regional and ethnic hierarchies, transforming between different African peoples and within particular ethnic groups. African societies in pre-colonial times were highly hierarchical but, except in the Sahelian Emirates or inter-lacustrine East Africa and a few other places, these hierarchies were determined more by age than by wealth. The economic and social changes produced by colonialism, however, ensured that wealth and political power could increasingly be transmitted from one generation to another and used to acquire more land. Chiefly office and education were two of the keys to this new process of social differentiation.[19]

The economic disruption caused by the Depression of the 1930s and World War II marked a vital watershed to many Africans. Colonial governments increased surplus extraction to finance the colonial state in the 1930s and then to supply materials for war production and to provide dollar exports for the purchase of military equipment from the USA. Consumer goods were in short supply in Africa. As a result, the cost of living index in Lagos, Accra and Freetown rose by over 400 per cent between 1940 and 1946. The protests of the politically active, educated elite were joined after the war by rural small-holders, who resented the low prices paid for their crops by monopsonistic marketing boards and revolted against the effects on rural societies of the post-war agricultural 'betterment' campaigns of the 'second colonial occupation', and by urban workers protesting at the continuing shortage of imported consumer goods, at high rents and the failure of wages to keep pace with inflation.[20] This coalition of interests provided nationalist leaders after 1945 with a mass following in Africa's cities and rural hinterland. This coalition was sufficiently powerful to sweep aside 'de-moralized' colonial administrators in the anti-colonial post-war international climate.

The demographic legacy

Possibly the most important consequence of colonialism was its effect on population growth throughout the continent. Most of Africa until the 20th century was under-populated. Land had been freely available, while labour was scarce, unlike in early modern Europe. This demographic explosion did not begin until the 1920s. Thereafter the population began to grow almost everywhere, following the example of the Maghreb and South Africa where the expansion had begun earlier. Since independence, Africa's population has expanded at an even faster pace. In most countries, the population is rising faster than food production and nearly half the population is under the age of 15. The World Bank predicts that Nigeria's population will stabilize in the year 2015 at 459 million. If the Bank's estimates are correct, Nigeria will then be more densely populated than China or India.[21]

Urban politics

As a result of colonialism, differential access to markets and education favoured particular regions and ethnic groups. 'Tribal' or ethnic inequalities were most starkly revealed in towns where Africans from different areas met, competed for jobs and lived with one another. It was in the urban areas that ethnic identities were both most malleable and most intense, and where economic discontent in the 1940s ensured that the nationalist message was most appealing. It was through ethnic ties that new urban arrivals secured jobs and accommodation, and it was with their fellow 'tribesmen' that they socialized and spent their free hours. Ethnicity was vital to urban Africans.[22] It was in the urban environment, consequently, that ethnicity became a potent device of political recruitment and mass mobilization since it was primarily in the city that people from different regions, who spoke different languages and had different customs, really mixed. It was in towns and cities that Igbo clerks rubbed shoulders with Yoruba dockers and Hausa craftsmen, or Luo construction workers met Abaluhya 'houseboys' and Kikuyu food sellers.

Trade, education and the demands of the international capitalist economy mixed Africans in a way that had not really occurred before, forcing them to live cheek by jowl amidst people with different customs, especially different customs about religion, food and sex – three most emotive issues. Migrant labourers on European farms in settler Africa, and on African-owned plantations in West Africa, in the gold and copper mines of South Africa, Katanga and Northern Rhodesia [Zambia], and in cities throughout the continent, were drawn together and frequently into conflict with one another. One of the problems that remains to be solved is to discover precisely in what circumstances, under what pressures of social differentiation, 'modernization', or the expansion of capitalist relations of production and the development of the export economy, were Africans mobilized in competitive ethnic coalitions by members of the new African political elite – their patrons. Why was control of the state so important?[23]

The struggle for the state after independence
The answer lies in the fact that colonialism's most destructive legacy in Africa was the overmighty state. In Nigeria – arguably one of Africa's most complex economies at independence in 1960 – approximately 54 per cent of wage sector employment was provided by the state and its off-shoots, such as nationalized industries.[24] Of the 64,000 wage and salaried workers in neighbouring Niger in 1981, over 27,000 were directly employed by the government and state expenditure amounted to one quarter of gross domestic product.[25]

African politics since independence has primarily been a squabble over the distribution of scarce resources – and in Africa resources are especially scarce. African states are powerful, overmighty sources of patronage, contracts, business opportunities and employment for the Western-educated elite and, therefore, for their poorer clients. At the same time, African states are extremely weak or 'soft', lacking political legitimacy. While the struggle to control the state is of vital importance to the political and business elite, the state's services do not penetrate deep down into society. African states provide few social services to their people. Even in a comparatively 'well-run' state like Kenya, peasants and urban workers alike have to pay school fees and make supposedly voluntary self-help contributions to school building and book funds if their children are to receive a basic education; hospitals and health clinics are overcrowded or too far away to be easily reached; the electricity supply is at best irregular, and frequently non-existent. Most Africans, certainly most rural Africans who form the vast majority of the population of most countries, encounter the state and its institutions more as a predator than as a provider of services.[26]

But as Goran Hyden and many others have pointed out, rural Africans, unlike citizens of Western industrial nations, can opt out. Africa's peasants remain 'uncaptured'. They are not dependent on the state for their basic services or everyday requirements. Many Africans can withdraw from cash crop production when state marketing boards – a colonial legacy – become too demanding, extracting too high a proportion of the international commodity price to make it 'worth-while' for peasants to continue growing the crop. Rural producers, however, are free to switch their labour and land to subsistence food crops which they can consume or sell to their neighbours as Tanzania's tobacco growers did in the mid-1970s.[27] Or, if they continue to grow cash crops, they can ignore the state-controlled marketing institutions, especially if they live close to the state border, and smuggle it across the frontier to where they can receive a higher return for their endeavours. African states have a weak grip on their rural citizens.

Rural producers, who can grow their own food, are in many respects better placed than urban residents, despite the attempts of many African regimes to subsidize urban food costs by lowering producers' returns in order to ensure urban stability. Urban professionals and workers, who do not have direct access to the state, or who do not control some function within the state apparatus which others desperately need – be it merely the issuing of a trading or driving licence – cannot profit from state power. The étatist legacy of colonial rule, the centrality of the state to all attempts to accumulate wealth and the over-large and usually inefficient bureaucracy of many states are among Africa's most acute problems.

Piotr Dutkiewicz and Gavin Williams have characterized this process as the development of the 'Developmental State'.[28] Following the victory of the independence movement, 'control of political and administrative office became in turn', they suggest, 'the means for creating constituencies of state beneficiaries and clients'. Political power and administration became increasingly centralized as the autonomy of local government was reduced. Local finances, policies and even tenure of office were determined by the national bureaucracy. In Kenya, for example, the seven regional administrations, established under the *Majimbo* or federal constitution, negotiated at the second Lancaster House conference in 1962, were disbanded within a few years. Power at district level passed from locally elected officials and local Kenya African National Union (KANU) branch and sub-branch leaders to the Provincial Administration – the old District and Provincial Commissioners of colonial days – who reported directly to the Office of the President.[29] By the 1980s, even the Nairobi City Council, whose leader for most of the 1970s had been President Kenyatta's daughter Margaret, was suspended and replaced by a City Commission, appointed by the Minister of Local Government.[30] Decisions are now taken at the centre rather than in the localities. Thus, as the state acquires more and more power, taking control over the distribution of resources, and as the public sector becomes increasingly important to the economy, emasculating the fledgling private sector, competition increases to secure access or control over the state. Rival factions attempt to protect their interests by forming interlocking alliances of patrons, each with their own ethnic coalitions of clients. Meanwhile, the polity becomes increasingly divided and unstable, encouraging 'the political class to take what they can while the going is good and, if they take thought for the morrow, to invest it abroad'. Eventually, as Dutkiewicz and Williams concluded, 'fear of the consequences of exclusion from state office leads the factions which make up the political class to take advantage of all legitimate and illegitimate means at their disposal to pursue and keep power'.[31]

This is not to suggest that states do not have an important role to play in economic affairs, but that the African 'development state', a legacy of 'the second colonial occupation' in the 1940s, has been too bureaucratic and insufficiently responsive to the interests of rural producers. African political machines, as Henry Bienen realized in the mid-1970s, have more in common with old-style American machine politics than with the totalitarian, ideologically motivated, regimes of the former Soviet bloc, but the decay of democratic elections has meant that the incentive to retain close contacts with grass-roots supporters soon diminished.[32] State elites, which inherited the opportunities won by the nationalist movements of the 1950s, have been dominated by urban professionals and businessmen and are too remote from the rural poor. Policies have been devised to satisfy urban residents rather than to promote rural production and initiatives. The formation of one-party states in the decade after independence reduced the electoral influence of voters, most of whom are small-holder cultivators and village traders and artisans, making it increasingly difficult for rural complaints to permeate the bureaucratic power structure despite the importance of patron–client relationships.[33]

Ethnic sub-nationalism has been as powerful a political force in most of Africa as territorial nationalism. In many parts of the continent ethnic sub-nationalist identity – 'tribalism' – had developed before territorial identity. Indeed, based on a common culture, history, language and traditions, ethnic sub-nationalism in Africa appealed to those factors which had engendered European nationalism in the 19th century. By contrast, so-called African nationalism had few roots in local societies, in some countries being primarily an attempt by the Western-educated elite to capture control of the colonial state. Essentially an elite enterprise, in contrast to the popular appeal of ethnic sub-nationalism, territorial nationalisms were fragile constructs, liable to fragment into clientalist factions based on ethnicity, once competition for the limited resources of virtually all Africa's new states began with independence. One of the reasons for the failure of multi-party democracy in most African countries in the 1960s and for the subsequent disintegration of several countries such as Nigeria, Chad, Ethiopia and Liberia into civil war, has not simply been the intensity of ethnic rivalries but the fundamental importance of the central state institutions as a source of development funds and potential accumulation by rival elites.[34]

Larry Diamond, writing about Nigeria, has suggested that 'democracy requires moderation and constraint. It demands not only that people care about political competition, but also that they do not care too much.' The problem with democratic elections in Africa, he observed, is that 'throughout much of Africa . . . everything of value is at stake in an election, and hence candidates, communities, and parties feel compelled to win at any cost.'[35] This is not to say that kinship networks, local improvement associations, self-help groups, churches, Islamic brotherhoods and trade unions do not exert some control over the scramble for state control and patronage, providing other mechanisms of social support and resources for development, but they remain subordinate to the state. Africa's middle classes are too weak, too dependent on the state, too much members of the 'bureaucratic bourgeoisie', as Mueller argued in Tanzania, to be able to attain their ends through intermediate level institutions.[36] Without control of the state they would have no influence or private wealth. Just as Sir Robert Walpole and the great Whig oligarchs of 18th-century politics had little compunction about raiding the state's exchequer for personal resources, many African elites 'need' to do the same at this stage in the continent's political development.[37] As a result, there is a high premium for elites upon capturing and then retaining state power, despite Western political scientists and anthropologists' observations about the 'softness' of the African state! Meanwhile peasants can 'opt' into it or 'disengage'.[38]

In most parts of Africa, multi-party competition, in Western eyes an essential element of democracy and constitutional rule, failed during the 1960s. Ethnic rivalries were too intense, the state too important as a source of development funds and potential accumulation by the elite, clientelism too entrenched, and ideological and class consciousness too weak to enable the continent's fragile polities to develop an established political culture. Moreover, as President Nyerere observed in 1961, once the nationalist movement had united all Africans, 'it could hardly be expected that a united country should halt in mid-stream and voluntarily divide itself into opposing political groups just for the sake of conforming to . . . the Anglo-Saxon form of democracy'.[39] Kenyatta expressed similar views in 1974, when he warned that 'KANU is Kenya's ruling party and we will not allow the formation of another party. Let those who talk of one . . . deceive themselves.'[40]

In these circumstances, paper constitutions were ignored. Bribery spread as civilian politicians attempted to co-opt regional 'bosses', while the military seized power in a *coup d'état* in several countries to protect their own interests and to prevent the fragmentation of the state as dissident regions threatened to withdraw. Forewarned by the example of their neighbours, those countries where nationalist parties remained in power moved quickly to ban opposition parties and to establish a mechanism for reconciling conflicting demands for resources among the elite as they sought to reward their clients, establishing one-party regimes. Elsewhere the military, once established in office, had to devise similar mechanisms for controlling debate and co-opting ethnic sub-nationalist leaders and their followers. Consequently, the single party became the centrepiece of politics and administration throughout Africa, performing a similar role to the Communist Party in the Soviet Union and in Eastern

Europe. Only strict party control, within a purely nominal constitutional structure, could provide the framework to control the
centrifugal rivalries of territorial sub-nationalisms, based on ethnicity.[41]

In many countries, however, neo-patrimonialism has failed to
ensure state cohesion because resources have been too few to satisfy
the demands of different clientage networks, and ideology and class
consciousness have been too weak to enable the continent's fragile
polities to develop an established civic culture. Corruption, ethnic
conflict, the rise of Islamic fundamentalism, state repression and civil
wars are all, in part, a function not only of Africa's poverty and the
scarcity of resources, but also of the primacy of the state. The capture
of state power and state patronage is vital to the survival of patrons
and clients alike. To lose – as events in Uganda, the southern Sudan,
Ethiopia and many other countries have demonstrated – is frequently
to lose one's life and the lives of your supporters as well as to be
denied opportunities for personal and group enrichment from the
state's pork barrel.[42]

African states and economies

The primacy of the state has meant that both in those countries which
adopted 'socialist' development strategies, such as Tanzania, Guinea
and Nkrumah's Ghana, and in those which opted for a pro-capitalist
course, most notably Kenya and the Côte d'Ivoire, the state's role is
much more important than in Western Europe. Virtually all African
states have not only adopted the political authoritarianism of the
colonial state, but have also endorsed its neo-mercantilist economic
policies. The state has also played a more direct role in production.
Even the Côte d'Ivoire and Kenya, for example, have established
parastatals to produce palm oil, fruit, vegetables, rice, sugar and tea,
either in directly state-controlled plantations or through 'contract'
farming whereby local small-holders grow the crops on their land in
return for extension services, loans and guaranteed prices. Although
these 'contract' farming systems have encountered many problems,
they have performed better than parastatals, which have a poor record
for agricultural production throughout Africa. By the late 1970s, the
state-run sugar plantations had become a major drain on the Côte
d'Ivoire's resources.[43] Ghana and Tanzania sought to diversify their
industrial base by state sponsored manufacturing. State planning and
management have failed. Like their colonial predecessors, Africa's

étatist regimes have attempted to import costly high-level technology, which generates little employment and requires large amounts of foreign exchange in order to overcome the problem of 'backwardness'. Little thought seems to have been given to the technological suitability of machinery imported to promote state manufacturing.[44]

These policies further enhanced the role of the state. By Nkrumah's overthrow in 1966, the public sector in Ghana accounted for 56 per cent of wage employment, and in Tanzania 74 per cent of entrepreneurial capital formation occurred in the public sector by 1972. The Côte d'Ivoire also had a large public sector, absorbing 50 per cent of entrepreneurial capital formation in 1973, compared with Kenya's 37 per cent. Indeed, the official name for the Côte d'Ivoire's economic policy is 'state capitalism'. Although foreign investment and technology transfers have been encouraged, the government has insisted on the maximal involvement of Ivoirien managers and entrepreneurs.[45]

Stanley Trapido in his noted essay on the comparative industrialization of Germany, Russia and South Africa, emphasized the key role of the state in the extraction of surplus from these peasant societies to finance the first phase of industrialization.[46] It was hardly surprising given the Fabian ideology of British colonial administrators after 1945 and the acceptance of étatist economic management in metropolitan France that the former British and French colonies would attempt to follow state-led models of economic expansion.[47]

John Iliffe has suggested a complementary explanation for the prominent role of the state in Africa's economies, seeing the continent as *the* example of Gerschenkron's thesis of late industrialization in a world economy already dominated by well-established industrial nations. In such conditions, entrepreneurs and private capital formation are inadequate. Only the state can extract sufficient resources through taxation and provide sufficient tariff protection to promote the early stages of industrial development. It should be noted, moreover, that African capitalism emerged at precisely the same time as local traders and commercial farmers, members of the professions and of the fledgling bureaucratic bourgeoisie, captured control of the colonial state and reshaped it to promote their own interests under the banner and ideology of nationalism.[48]

Ralph Austen has provided a most useful discussion of Africa's efforts at internal transformation, identifying similarities between states of supposedly different ideological hues. He observed:

If development patterns were defined by the prominence of the state in economic affairs, all African regimes would have to be considered socialist. If the definition rested upon the capacity of public authorities to control the economy, all would be labelled capitalist. The strong position of the state in contemporary African economies is derived from the étatist colonial tradition, the weakness of indigenous entrepreneurial classes, and the shift shortly after independence, from parliamentary democracy to one-party authoritarian regimes. The economic weaknesses of these states results from their limited administrative capacity, their dependence upon external sources of capital, and the difficulty of the developmental tasks which they have taken on. The effect of this paradoxical balance has been that capitalist regimes have given less freedom to the private sector than they claim and that socialist regimes have attempted to do far more with the public sector than they are capable of.[49]

In his study of African capitalism, Iliffe identified three economic strategies for development. The socialist development policy, adopted by Nkrumah's Ghana, especially in the last five years of the Convention People's Party's (CPP) regime, and in several of the continent's poorer states in the Sahel, increased the importance of the state. In the Sahelian states, if not in cocoa-exporting Ghana, indigenous capitalist forces were too weak to provide either an obstacle or a real alternative to state-led development. Unfortunately, these states also had the smallest and least sophisticated administrative structures, ill-equipped to act as the dynamo of economic 'take-off'. The second group, identified by Iliffe, were examples of 'parasitic capitalism', ranging from the literal example of this mode – Mobutu's Zaire – where the words used to describe its elite changed 'first from "*évolues*" to "intellectuals", then to "citizens", and finally to "*acquirers*" ' – to those states such as Zambia, Liberia under True Whig rule, and the Côte d'Ivoire's self-confessed programme of 'state capitalism', where the state has sponsored the expansion of productive small-scale capitalism while taking a leading role itself.[50] Finally, Iliffe identified two cases of what he termed 'nurture capitalism' – Kenya and Nigeria – where the state has encouraged private capital formation and worked in alliance with multinational corporations and local peasant producers, rather than attempting directly to enter into manufacturing or agricultural production.[51]

The patrimonial administrative state has proved inefficient and corrupt, and has served neither the advent of socialism nor the development of capitalism in Africa. Patrimonialism has undermined the public service, sanctioning arbitrary interventions, and eroding the bureaucratic norms and decision-making processes inherited from the colonial era. Consequently, 'as in early modern Europe, the state is authoritarian and extractive, but its control is ultimately limited'. As Callaghy suggests, 'it is quasi-omnipresent, but not anywhere near omnipotent. The power of the state is not unlimited, but rather unsupervised'.[52]

Coups d'état and the role of the military

African armies have proved to be as ethnically divided as political elites. When Nigeria became independent in 1960, the army had comprised only five battalions plus two brigades of supporting units. Military professionalism had hitherto largely overridden ethnic rivalries but tensions soon emerged as the new government dominated by the Northern People's Congress (NPC) speeded up the promotion of officers from the north in an attempt to increase the proportion of northern officers from one in six at independence – a sign of the north's comparative educational backwardness. Although the north provided three quarters of the ranks, most of these came from the Middle Belt or Borno rather than the pro-NPC Hausa–Fulani heartlands. In 1958 a quota system had been introduced for new recruits to the ranks, and was extended to the officer corps after 1961. According to this arrangement, 50 per cent of recruits were to come from the north, while the east and western regions each supplied one quarter. As a result, northern officers, who had been comparatively few in number during the colonial era, began to be promoted over the heads of southern, particularly Igbo, colleagues.[53]

Early in 1965, following the political deadlock of December 1964, after the Federal General Election, a group of senior Igbo officers, most of whom were Lieutenant-Colonels, including the future Biafran leader Ojukwu, had suggested to President Azikiwe that they would be willing to stage a *coup d'état* in his favour. Ethnic political considerations, as well as purely internal military grievances such as the bottleneck in southern promotions, also motivated the junior officers, who eventually seized power on 15 January 1966. Although the coup failed, Federal Prime Minister Sir Abubakar Tafawa Balewa, Sir Ahmadu Bello, the Northern Regional Premier, and

Akintola, were all killed before Army Commander Major-General Ironsi, another Igbo, rallied loyal troops and police, and accepted President Azikiwe and the remnants of the civilian cabinet's request to assume responsibility for the government. Nigeria's First Republic disintegrated under the strains of competitive ethnic sub-nationalisms and the struggle for control over the central state and its patronage possibilities.[54]

Nigeria was not alone. In the mid-1960s, after less than a decade of independence, Africa replaced Latin America and the Middle East as the scene of military interventions in politics. Egypt had led the way in 1952 when Gamal Abdel Nasser and his cohort of Young Officers, with the support of General Neguib, had seized power; Sudan followed in November 1958, after less than three years of independence, paving the way for a series of military interventions in black Africa during the next decade.[55] Sub-Saharan Africa's first coup occurred on 13 January 1963, when President Sylvanus Olympio of Togo was assassinated on the steps of the American Embassy where he was about to claim refuge. Olympio's death sent shock waves throughout West Africa, where many suspected the hidden hand of Ghanaian intervention, ushering in an era of political instability from which the region has not yet emerged.[56]

Before 1963 had ended there had been further *coups d'état* in Congo [Brazzaville] on 15 August, where President Fulbert Youlou, a defrocked abbot, was ousted following trade-union and student-led demonstrations and replaced by a leftist Provisional Committee of Army and Gendarmerie officers under Alphonse Massamba-Debat. On 23 October the Army Chief of Staff in Dahomey [now Benin], Colonel Christophe Soglo, seized power in the first of seven *coups d'état* which took place in that country during the next nine years, two more of which (29 November and 22 December 1965) were also to be led by Soglo before he was toppled by Major Maurice Kouandete on 17 December 1967. In 1964 there was a successful coup in Zanzibar, only one month after independence, as well as army mutinies of varying severity in Tanganyika, where Julius Nyerere had to flee into hiding in a Dar-es-Salaam beach house for three days before order was restored with the help of British troops, and in Uganda and Kenya. In 1965 Mobutu seized power for the second time in Zaire, and there were two more coups in Dahomey. Few African regimes have not had to suppress an unsuccessful coup attempt or have not uncovered a serious plot to topple the government. Why have African governments proved so insecure and why has the army been so tempted to come out of its barracks and to take control of the state?[57]

African armies, like other state institutions, are controlled by this state elite which also staffs the civil service and legislative assemblies. The officer corps were active participants in the scramble for the rewards of independence, and frequently reproduce the factional and ethnic rivalries of the civilian elite. In most African countries, moreover, following the incorporation of trade unions into the corporatist councils of the state during colonial rule or the era of party-states after independence, the army has become the only effective autonomous power within the state, as events in Congo [Brazzaville] in the 1960s and Burkina Faso in the 1980s demonstrated. Indeed, in the last resort the power of civilian rulers could only be sustained with the acquiescence of the military. As Africa's newly independent regimes encountered economic difficulties, exacerbated by the Balkanization of French West and Equatorial Africa and by the adverse shift in international terms of trade in the 1960s, and as former nationalist leaders became discredited by political and economic failures, the army became a major participant in the political struggle.[58] Soldiers became involved in politics for two reasons. The army elite were themselves keen participants in the squabble for scarce resources; they wanted both to enlarge and modernize their forces. Second, the officer corps wanted to share in the process of accumulation and to secure some of the financial rewards accruing to politicians and civil servants. The rank and file of the army, however, often represented the more 'backward' regions of the newly independent state, being recruited from precisely those areas which had been least involved in the nationalist struggle. Thus in Nigeria the Tiv, who formed a large component of the ranks, supported neither of the southern parties pushing for independence nor the conservative Hausa–Fulani-dominated NPC.[59] In Kenya the Kalenjin from the Rift Valley formed a large proportion of the local battalions of the King's African Rifles. They had played a marginal role in the nationalist movement, opposing Mau Mau, and had favoured Kenya African Democratic Union (KADU), the conservative advocates of regional devolution over the more radical policies of Kenyatta and KANU which was strongest among the Kikuyu and Luo.[60] In many countries the junior officer corps was recruited from these same areas and in the first years of African independence many senior officers had been promoted from the ranks after serving many years as loyal non-commissioned officers in colonial forces. Soglo, the army commander in Dahomey [Benin], for example, who staged three *coups d'état* between 1963 and 1965, and who dominated the country's political life until his overthrow in 1967, had enlisted in the ranks in 1931, aged 22, and had been commissioned in 1941. Lamizana in Upper Volta [Burkina Faso], who seized power in January 1966, had enlisted in 1936 and received his commission 13 years later. Bokassa of the Central African Republic had joined the French army aged 18 at the outbreak of World War II and had been promoted to an officer 19 years later in 1958. Lansana in Sierra Leone, Amin in Uganda, Mobutu in Zaire and Eyadema in Togo, had all worked their way up from the bottom and had little of the educational sophistication of the political elite or civil servants.[61]

Too much should not be made of their isolation from the political elite of their countries. In Uganda, for example, Amin had worked closely with Milton Obote since 1965 and had been implicated in shady financial and political transactions with the civilian leader. Many *coups d'état* were also led by direct entry officers, who came from the same privileged background as members of the political elite, such as Gowon in Nigeria and Micombero in Burundi, who had been trained at Sandhurst and the Belgian Military Academy. Such men represented the same social forces as politicians and civil servants.[62]

Africa's armies were, and in most cases still are, comparatively small, even intimate organizations, with tightly knit officer corps. In 1967, for example, the number of African officers ranged from 17 in Togo, which was the first state of black Africa to undergo a *coup d'état*, to 1500 in Zaire and 3000 in Ethiopia. Zaire and Ethiopia, however, were untypical. Burundi, the Central African Republic, Congo [Brazzaville], Dahomey, Gabon, Gambia, Malawi, Mauritania, Niger, Rwanda, Sierra Leone, Upper Volta and Zambia, like Togo, all had officer corps of fewer than 100 men. Thus, once the politicians' legitimacy had been undermined by rising unemployment or inflation, by ethnic rivalries requiring increased repression, drawing the army and to a lesser extent the police into politics, as in western Nigeria in 1965, it was relatively easy for officers to organize to seize power.[63]

It was also, however, equally easy and just as common for officers to divide, identifying themselves with the conflicting ethnic interests or political factions. Once the fragile coalitions linking diverse local protests, which comprised the nationalist movements, began to unravel, the authority of the state could often be sustained only by force. Regional and ethnic cleavages, that were often reinforcing, had been surmounted in opposition to colonial rule but most nationalist parties were incapable of preserving this unity once competition for the state's resources began in earnest after independence. Decalo's study of the *coups d'état* in Togo, Benin, Congo, Uganda and Niger, however, has convincingly demonstrated the importance of ethnic and factional divisions within the army and between the political and military elites for precipitating intervention by the army. In the vast majority of African *coups d'état* the coup leaders have been motivated by concern about their own future and/or to stop political interference in military affairs.[64]

Once the military has intervened, the barriers against further political interventions are broken down. The first *coup d'état* destroys the attempt to inculcate the creed of political neutrality at Sandhurst or St Cyr. Even if the troops withdraw to the barracks and hand over power to a democratically elected civilian government, as in Nigeria in 1979 and Ghana in 1969 and 1979, there seems to be almost an overwhelming temptation to seize power when the economy begins to go wrong, when corruption becomes more blatant or when the political faction in power attempts to suppress its opponents. Sometimes, as in Ghana in January 1972, the army moves before the population has become totally alienated from the civilian government. Indeed, it is clear that Colonel Acheampong and his colleagues ousted Dr Busia more to advance their own careers than because they profoundly disagreed with his policies. Middle-ranking officers when Nkrumah had been deposed less than six years before, neither Acheampong nor his associates in the National Redemption Council had been favoured with administrative appointments in the military regime of 1966–9 or advanced in the army command. Aware that Busia's retrenchment policies and purging of non-Asante from the civil service was alienating many members of the Ghanaian elite, small-holders and urban workers, especially the powerful railway and dock workers at Sekondi-Takoradi, they launched a pre-emptive *coup d'état* to ensure that this time they would control affairs and access to state resources.[65]

The weaknesses of African nationalism
Some general conclusions can be drawn about the connections between the strengths of African nationalisms and the weaknesses of

Africa's post-independence political institutions and civic cultures. Nigeria between 1960 and 1966, for example, provides many insights into the processes of political disintegration in other African states, most notably in Zaire in the 1960s, Uganda and Chad in the 1970s, and Ethiopia and Somalia in the 1980s. In all these states there were essentially three major political factions, based more on rival ethnic sub-nationalist movements than on ideological divisions. In Zaire, Uganda, Chad and Somalia, as in Nigeria, temporary factional alignments owed more to political convenience than ideology. As noted above, in Nigeria the reformist National Council of Nigerian Citizens (NCNC) and Action Group, both of which drew their support from commercial farmers, traders and members of the Western-educated elite who had entered the professions, were at loggerheads, vying for the hand of the neo-traditionalists in the NPC. Zairean politics before Mobutu's second coup in October 1965 were equally uninhibited by ideological considerations, despite the Lumumbaists' protestations to the contrary. Kassavubu's Kongo-based ethnic sub-nationalist ABAKO had formed in 1950 as a Bakongo cultural society, drawing upon the foundations of the Kimbanguist movement. It was strongest around Kinshasha [Leopoldville] and was controlled by Bakongo secondary school graduates, traders and commercial farmers. Patrice Lumumba's populist Movement National Congolais, despite its attempts to live up to its name, was supported mainly by the Lingala speakers of Equatorial Province around Kisangani [Stanleyville]. Lumumba himself, however, was a Batelela, a member of a sub-group of the Mango, who lived in three of the territories' six provinces. Kassavubu and Lumumba were united, however, more by their common opposition to Moishe Tshombe's Confédération des Associations Tribales du Katanga (CONAKAT) than by any shared ideology or policies. Tshombe, a member of a junior lineage of the Lunda royal house, drew virtually all his support from the Lunda ethnic group in Katanga, and favoured secession to protect the comparatively privileged position of Katanga within the colonial political economy. Party loyalty was weak. Although the Kassavubu–Lumumba coalition held more than two thirds of seats in the National Assembly, Lumumba's first government only just managed to scrape a majority of votes at its first vote of confidence, despite distributing ministerial portfolios to a wide array of political factions and interests.[66]

Similarly in Uganda there was a split between two comparatively modernizing, pro-capitalist parties – the Democratic Party (DP) of

Benedict Kiwanuka, which appealed to Catholics, and the Protestant, northern-based Uganda People's Congress (UPC). These were locked in battle with each other for control of the new state, and with the neo-traditionalist, Buganda-based, Kabaka Yekka, which eventually entered a coalition with the UPC to cement its own Buganda power-base against the DP's challenge and the upstart Kiwanuka.[67]

Both of these governing coalitions, of course, were extremely fragile and soon fell apart once competition for state resources gained momentum after independence. In Nigeria, the army – or at least an Igbo-dominated faction of the army – moved in January 1966, to protect southern interests. By this time, Lumumba had been murdered by Tshombe in January 1961, at the behest of his former allies Kassavubu and Mobutu, and then Mobutu had overthrown Kassavubu on 23 October 1965. In Uganda, Milton Obote and his army commander Idi Amin bombarded the Kabaka's palace on 24 May 1966, forcing Sir Edward Mutesa, erstwhile Kabaka of Buganda and President of Uganda, to flee to London. In all these countries, ethnic rivalries overwhelmed the hastily cobbled together independence coalitions. Democratic structures, even the new state's supposed civic cultures, could not be sustained when the states' rival elites began to squabble over the diversion of resources.[68]

Chad has perhaps been more riven by civil war since independence than any other African state. The conflict is usually dated to October 1965, when a tax rebellion among Moubi transhumants broke out in Mangalme in the east. The revolt spread to the Borku–Ennedi–Tibesti region when French military administrators, who had stayed on after independence, were replaced by Sara administrators from the south. In pre-colonial times, the Teda and Daza factions of the Tibu in the north had controlled the trans-Saharan trade from the Muslim sultanates of Kanem-Bornu and Ouaddai, and from the great Sokoto Caliphate, in present-day northern Nigeria, to Khartoum and Mecca. Much of this trade had been in slaves, whom the Tibu captured further south among agriculturalists such as the Sara. French colonialism, however, had transformed the balance of power between the north and the south. The north, encouraged by the Sanusi brotherhood, had resisted the French conquest and found in Islamic revival a means to resist intrusion. Placed under military administration, the region had been categorized as 'Tchad inutile'. 'Tchad utile' in the south, however, was incorporated into the international economy and forced to grow cotton. Colonial development schemes, therefore, were concentrated among the Sara, who formed 40 per cent of the population and because of their access to Western education, dominated the government of François Tombalbaye at independence. The demands of the Sara-dominated state soon pushed the far north into revolt under the leadership of the Front de Libération Nationale du Tchad (FROLINAT).[69]

Although the movement's original leaders had been educated in Arab universities and trained in North Korea, they secured the support of conservative Muslim groups, opposed to the Christian regime in the south. In 1968, the Derde, the traditional leader of the Teda, fled to Libya, and his son, Goukouni Oueddai, soon emerged as an important field commander in charge of the Forces Armées du Nord (FAN). A rival Tibu leader emerged, however, from the Daza faction, Hissene Habre, who had been influenced by Maoist ideas while a student in Paris, before serving as an administrator for the Tombalbaye government until he joined the revolt in 1971. As the rebellion became increasingly serious, spreading to other Arab-speaking groups in the centre of the country, who formed half its population, Tombalbaye was overthrown in 1975 by Sara military leader Felix Malloum, who prosecuted the war with greater vigour.[70]

By this time, conflict between Oueddai, supported by the Teda, and Habre, supported by the Daza, had divided the northern revolt. Oueddai was prepared to cede the Aozou Strip, a frontier zone 100 kilometres deep, which Libya had unilaterally occupied in 1972, in accordance with an agreement between France and Fascist Italy in 1935, which had never been ratified because of the Italian invasion of Ethiopia later that year, and was prepared to negotiate with the new Malloum government in N'Djamena. Habre opposed both and broke away to form the Forces Armées Populaires with 700 supporters. Eventually, both groups were forced to participate in the Gouvernement d'Union Nationale de Transition (GUNT), brokered by the OAU in 1979, with Goukouni Oueddai as President and Habre as Minister of Defence. When the GUNT came apart in March 1980, as the two Tibu-led groups fell into open warfare, severely damaging the capital N'Djamena, Habre eventually emerged victorious with support from the Sudan and Egypt, which were determined to reduce Libyan influence, capturing the capital in June 1982. But as George Joffe has observed, 'it was clear that the Chadian situation had degenerated into an ethnic confrontation, in which ideology no longer played a role'.[71]

By this time Chad had virtually ceased to exist. Even the Central Bank had ceased to function. From March 1979 to June 1982, the south – the country's economic heart – operated as an autonomous regime, transporting cotton direct to the Central African Republic, levied its own taxes and import-export duties, and organized secondary-school examinations unlike the N'Djamena government. Colonel Kamougue and the Comité Permanent even despatched representatives to OAU summits. Road maintenance was taken over by the Coton-Tchad Company and the postal system was operated by missionary societies.[72]

Habre was able to enlist the support of the Hajeray in central Chad, led by Idriss Misikine, and the Zaghawa from the eastern frontier, under the leadership of Ibrahim Deby, forming a strong basis of support in the country's central zone, which finally defeated the remnants of the Malloum forces, whose leader Abdelkader Kamougoue fled the country in October 1982. The south and the centre had been reunified, and the possibility seemed to exist of a more securely established regime, based on the Daza, Hajeray and Zaghawa, especially when France, the USA and Iraq provided military aid to drive Oueddai into exile.

Since the death of Idriss Misikine from malaria in January 1984, however, the Hajeray have been alienated from the regime by the arrest of four senior Hajeray ministers; in June 1987 a serious revolt erupted in their Guera homeland. Even more seriously, in April 1989 three Zaghawa members of the government attempted to stage a *coup d'état*, after which Ibrahim Daby fled to Tripoli to organize a new revolt. The Sara in the south remained as discontented as ever, resentful of Daza control in N'Djamena. As Joffe has observed, 'the events of the last three years have left the Gorane [i.e. the Daza] once again the undisputed masters of military power in Chad. They have definitively reversed the post-colonial balance of power by ensuring that, as in pre-colonial times, the north once again controls the destiny of the south of Chad.'[73] The stability of the regime depended upon President Habre's ability to maintain the loyalty of his own ethnic military base and to ensure the support of other powerful patrons and their followers as state resources were distributed between Chad's ethnic groups. In 1990 this arrangement was turned upside down once more and Chad thrown into another round of murderous conflict.

The disintegration of the Doe regime in Liberia fits even more clearly the analysis of ethnic rivalry for control of the state as competing ethnic sub-nationalisms in the interior, released by the toppling of the former African–American elite identified with the True Whig regime of Presidents Tubman and Tolbert, pulled the state apart. As Christopher Clapham has observed, 'political conflict in Liberia has thus been almost solely about access to state resources, and has been of interest to little more than that section of the population which could plausibly compete for them'. Unfortunately, in Africa when the elephant and the rhinoceros fight, the grass gets trampled. Few Liberians have managed to escape the fighting which erupted between the rival ethnic elites which led to and has continued since the disintegration of Doe's regime. Perhaps the end-result of the *coup d'état* of 1980 was the replacement of a long-tested and stable distribution of resources, controlled by True Whig patrons, by a 'free-for-all in which demands increased, while the resources themselves diminished, and the acceptance [it would be too much to call it legitimacy] conferred on the political structure by longevity disappeared'.[74]

The state in Africa is the great dispenser of business opportunities and financial benefits. By controlling the state, this bureaucratic bourgeoisie can extract resources from the rural masses through direct and indirect taxation, or through the state-controlled monopoly marketing boards. It can advance the interests of particular individuals or ethnic groups or protect its privileged class position. In those states where indigenous capitalist forces were particularly weak at independence, such as Tanzania, Guinea or Mali, the state was used as a device for accumulation. But even in the Côte d'Ivoire, Cameroun and Kenya, where African commercial farmers and traders were comparatively well established, controlling the nationalist movement, the manipulation of state resources in alliance with multinational finance has proved an essential mechanism for the further promotion and profit of these indigenous capitalist forces. Since independence, the state has been the main device by which Africa's ruling classes can legitimize their accumulation.

In many countries the popular base of the nationalist movement had been narrow, consisting of only a small elite leadership and a slender popular base. Only a few countries had witnessed the creation of truly mass parties. Particularly in Francophone West Africa, the political movements that had secured independence had not been required to mobilize support among the rural and urban masses. Nationalist leaders had succeeded once they had demonstrated a reasonable degree of support and restraint. Indeed, even the two strongest political parties in the region – the PDC'I in the Côte d'Ivoire and the CPP in Ghana – had never secured the support of more than a third of those eligible to vote. The rapid pace of colonial withdrawal in many parts of West Africa had made mass nationalism unnecessary. The metropolitan powers had quickly come to terms with nationalist leaders in order to incorporate the moderates, who would not question the structure of local and international economic interests. Rapid decolonization by Britain and France, but not by Portugal which was economically too weak, also precluded the development of more radical anti-capitalist successor regimes.[75]

We have observed how the petty bourgeoisie of small traders, commercial farmers, local school teachers and clerks, led by the educated elite, were able to stitch together populist coalitions from the grievances of rural small-holders against the exactions of colonial marketing boards and the agricultural 'improvement' campaigns of the second colonial occupation; discontented urban workers and casual labourers were confronted by rampant inflation and appalling housing conditions. These coalitions, even in Ghana and the Côte d'Ivoire, where the CPP and the PDC'I could reasonably claim to be mass nationalist movements able to mobilize the people against colonial rule in both the countryside and towns, were extremely fragile political entities. Once in power nationalist leaders found it virtually impossible to fulfil the expectations which their promises and speeches had aroused. Nkrumah's often-quoted slogan – 'Seek ye first the political kingdom and all will be added unto it' – might have been a most effective device to maximize support before the transfer of power, but once independence had been secured the limitations of African states, mono-crop export producers enmeshed in the world capitalist economy, soon became all too apparent.[76]

The new Ghanaian government's popular support was undermined by adverse movements in terms of trade in cocoa in the late 1950s and early 1960s. In 1954–5, for example, farmers had produced 210,000 tons of cocoa, earning £85.5 million from exports. Ten years later, although cocoa production had more than doubled to 590,000 tons, Ghana's export earnings had actually fallen to £77 million. During the same period Nigerian cocoa production almost quadrupled from 89,000 to 310,000 tons but earnings remained static at £40 million.

Africa's states secured their independence at the beginning of a new phase in their comparative bargaining position with the industrial world of Europe and North America, just when international demand for their exports, which had been high since the middle of World War II, began to slacken.[77]

Against this economic backdrop, African governments' economic diversification plans and industrial development schemes, involving expensive hydro-electric projects and capital intensive factories, and urban-led growth, were forestalled. Those states, such as the Côte d'Ivoire and Kenya, which adjusted quickly to the change in economic climate, had comparatively developed infrastructures and secondary processing sectors, and accepted their dependent status within the international economy; they could still prosper and secure high growth rates at least until the late 1970s. But as dependency theorists pointed out, this very economic 'progress' tied them even more firmly into their subordinate role in the international economic order and fostered 'the development of underdevelopment'. Dependency theorists argued that such states would become even more dependent upon the importation of Western technology, skills and consumer goods in order to meet the expectations of their Westernized elites. Their economic growth has been restricted to secondary processing industries, such as food canning, brewing, cigarette manufacture, and more recently car assembly and battery manufacturing plants, frequently controlled by transnational capital. The heavy industrial base essential for autonomous industrial expansion has remained undeveloped. Even Kenya and the Côte d'Ivoire, it became clear in the 1980s, are on an economic treadmill and have to run even faster in order to attract yet more foreign investment to keep pace with their expanding population.[78]

The statist nature of African economies is partly a survival from the colonial era, but government intervention, as noted above, is also a product of the clientalist nature of African politics, where supporters are rewarded and potential rivals bought off by a share of the rewards from the state-controlled pork barrel. Susanne Mueller has contended that the centralized, bureaucratic nature of the African state, with its propensity to interfere in the operation of the economy, is symptomatic of the retarded nature of African capitalism. The African elite, she suggests, are not true capitalists, driven by the logic of market forces, investing in productive enterprise, but are parasites who have captured control of the state and are using ideologies such as African socialism in Tanzania and Zambia or Afro-Marxism in Angola and Ethiopia, to become ensconced as a bureaucratic ruling class, prospering on the backs of the peasantry and urban workers.[79] When things went wrong after independence, therefore, most African leaders had little political space in which to manoeuvre. The spate of declarations of one-party states in the early 1960s represented a desperate attempt to overcome the structural problems of national integration, which had been concealed during the nationalist struggle. Africa's rulers had to devise mechanisms by which alienated regions or ethnic sub-nationalist movements could be reincorporated, broadening the political foundations of the regime's popular support. All too frequently, however, this attempt to enhance the regime's stability was a pretext to destroy potential rivals and silence opposition. Danquah in Ghana and Awolowo in Nigeria disappeared into prison, discovering that opposition leaders possessed little freedom to criticize, while Busia fled the country like the Kabaka of Buganda. The search for national integration frequently justified political repression.

Nationalist movements throughout the continent had also masked class differences, concealing or momentarily transcending the conflict between the aspirations of the leadership and the hopes of the peasantry and urban workers. Ideally, of course, these class cleavages should have continued to be minimized as politicians sought support by creating clientalist coalitions based on ethnicity and patronage. These patron–client networks were the key form of political interaction and organization in many states. Many politicians were themselves 'new men', risen from the non-professional, non-aristocratic sections of society. Many were of limited means and modest education. Wolpe in his book on urban politics in the Nigerian city of Port Harcourt has described these politicians as 'men on the make', eager to convert their new political positions into social and economic gains.[80]

Civilian politicians had done well out of independence. School teachers and small town clerks had been elected to parliament, more than quintupling their salaries, securing additional car and housing allowances, and the possibility of gaining lucrative appointments to parastatal boards which enabled them to divert public funds into private accounts. Political life provided a springboard for personal enrichment and many former local activists made the most of their opportunities. Roger Tangri observed that 'political office and state power was the key by which a petty bourgeoisie could transform itself into a property owning bourgeoisie'.[81] But the struggle for state resources inevitably exacerbated political conflict as rival factions and ethnic groups competed for control, creating serious turmoil where it was unrestrained as in Nigeria or Zaire. Even within one-party regimes, the struggle to acquire and then to retain power and the spoils of office could disrupt administration and threaten national cohesion as with the withdrawal of the defeated Bemba faction from Zambia's United National Independence Party in August 1967, or in Kenya throughout the 1980s as President Arap Moi sought to entrench Kalenjin interests at the expense of the Kikuyu, whom Kenyatta had hoisted into political and economic power between 1963 and his death in 1978.[82]

Julius Nyerere in Tanzania, for one, was acutely aware of the danger of entrenching this new elite, who now controlled the party and state bureaucracy, creating an African equivalent of the Soviet bloc's 'New Class' or *nomenklatura*. The Tanzanian leader warned the people that 'many leaders of the independence struggle . . . were not against capitalism; they simply wanted its fruits, and saw independence as the means to that end'.[83] The Senegalese novelist and film producer Sembene Ousmane also denounced the new state elite, observing that 'to us, their mandate is simply a licence to profiteer'.[84] When Ousmane's judgement became widespread and nationalist coalitions began to unravel, civilian governments were endangered. Further manipulation of ethnic loyalties, ballot rigging and coercion became inadequate to silence opposition. The army became embroiled in political struggles.

One-party states, it can be argued, have been more effective at securing stability than ethnically based, multi-party, competitive systems. But a price has been paid. Donal Cruise O'Brien, describing the Union Progressiste Sénégalaise before the restoration of multi-party competition in 1977, noted how the party successfully mediated between conflicting interests and regions. 'Many who have joined the governing party,' he judged, 'have done so purely in order to enjoy the fruits of government, and are committed to no programme other than their own advancement.'[85] But if incorporation fails and conflict erupts, the military inevitably become involved.

A few countries have escaped military intervention. The disease has not really spread to Anglophone East or Central Africa. Kenya, Tanzania, Malawi, Zambia, Zimbabwe, Botswana and Swaziland have remained under civilian control since independence, although some would claim this was as much by chance as by design as all of them have experienced attempted coups – sometimes several – and rumours of imminent military intervention have been even more frequent. Nevertheless, these states – which range from avowedly socialist Tanzania and Zimbabwe to self-proclaimed capitalist Kenya and monarchical Swaziland, from democratic Botswana to Hastings Banda's repressive Malawi, from ethnically diverse to comparatively homogeneous societies – have experienced nothing like the repeated military seizures of power which have taken place in Francophone and Lusophone Africa, and in Anglophone West Africa. Ghana, for example, black Africa's first independent state, has undergone five successful *coups d'état* and the Nigerian army has also launched five successful take-overs.

Why has Anglophone East and Central Africa been so much more stable – Uganda apart? Has the stability of Kenya, Tanzania, Botswana, Zambia and the other former British territories in the region been simply a function of the comparative legitimacy of the nationalist movements in these countries? At first this may seem improbable. Political activity in Ghana and Nigeria dated back to the Depression of the 1930s. The United Gold Coast Convention had been formed in 1946 to take advantage of Sir Arthur Burns' constitutional reforms. Nkrumah's CPP swept both the local government and first elections under the liberal franchise of the Coussey Constitution to the Legislative Council in February 1951, and the CPP leader had enjoyed six years of training in power under the watchful Governor Sir Charles Arden-Clarke. In Nigeria, Azikiwe served as chief minister of the eastern region, a position which enjoyed considerable autonomy, while Obofemi Awolowo had held the same office in the west. Sir Ahmadu Bello, their counterpart in the north, had just as secure a base, bolstered by the prestige of the Sokoto Caliphate among both Hausa and Fulani. But neither Ghana nor Nigeria, despite their comparative wealth, complex infrastructure, diverse economies, and reservoir of highly trained manpower in comparison to Kenya, Tanzania or Zambia, managed to sustain civilian rule, let alone comparatively democratic political institutions for more than two decades like Botswana.[86]

Uganda, the most unstable East African state, provides a potential answer. The nationalist movement in Uganda did not have to confront large-scale European settler opposition, entrenched as in

Kenya, Zambia and especially Zimbabwe, within the colonial corridors of power. Consequently, none of the main political movements in Uganda acquired the authority of KANU, TANU, or ZANU(PF), (the African National Unions of Kenya, Tanzania and Zimbabwe). The northern-based Uganda People's Congress (UPC), the Baganda *Kabaka Yekka* and the mainly Catholic Democratic party (DP) divided the new state along its ethnic or sectional fault lines. Moreover, Obote himself lacked the prestige and authority of *Mzee* Jomo Kenyatta or *Mwalimu* Julius Nyerere which was demonstrated by their popular sobriquets – the wise old man and teacher of their fellow countrymen. But in contrast to Kenya or the territories of the former Central African Federation, Uganda's progress to independence had been comparatively smooth, ruffled only by Baganda attempts to protect the privileged position which they had enjoyed within the colonial protectorate in a new federal power-sharing and by claims at moments of crisis that Buganda might seceed if its demands were not met. After independence, however, Uganda soon fragmented along ethnic fault lines. The military intervened for the first time on the national scene in 1966, setting off the degeneration of the state's fragile political culture. By 1985, when Obote was overthrown for the second time, the Ugandan state had virtually ceased to exist, dividing into a Hobbesian struggle between rival armed camps.[87] It would seem that the protracted struggle for independence undergone in Kenya, Zambia and Zimbabwe endowed the nationalist movement with greater support than the speedier and less traumatic transfers of power in West Africa and Uganda.

Houphouet-Boigny in the Côte d'Ivoire and Senegal's Leopold Sedar Senghor have proved to be as astute and successful as Kenyatta and Nyerere. Their territories were the richest and most developed in Francophone West Africa and both leaders commanded widespread respect, as well as support, before independence not only in their own states but throughout Afrique Occidentale Française and in Paris. As leader of the Rassemblement Démocratique Africaine, Houphouet-Boigny was a powerful figure in metropolitan politics, serving in the French Cabinet in the coalition governments of the mid-1950s as Minister of Health, while Senghor was respected for his intellect and writing and for leading the nationalist movement since 1945.[88] Ahidjo in the Cameroun also managed to survive, reconciling the dissident south-west, which in the latter years of colonial rule had supported the revolt of the radical UPC opposition, and incorporating the former British-ruled region, while restraining the influence of the conservative traditionalists in the Muslim aristocracy in his own political base. Following his voluntary retirement, however, Ahidjo sought to regain the reins of power, remaining initially as chairman of the ruling party, and then attempting to overthrow his chosen successor from exile in France.[89] Mokhtar Ould Daddah remained in power in Mauritania until 1978, surviving the Sahelian drought of 1974, but was brought down by military defeats by Polisario in the Western Sahara. Since 1978, despite Mauritania's withdrawal from the Western Sahara, rival military factions have struggled for ascendancy, ushering in an era of instability. Gabon's Omar Bongo has also managed to cling to office, partly because of Gabon's oil wealth, which has enabled the president to dispense patronage widely, strengthening his alliances with local clientage leaders. Gabon's mounting economic difficulties in the late 1980s, however, have been reflected in growing criticism of the regime and mounting pressure for democratization.[90] In Guinea, Sekou Touré's repressive 26-year-old regime survived his death in 1984 by less than a week, ushering in an era of instability as rival military factions fought for control, removing political and economic power from Touré's Malinke ethnic group.[91]

The other territories of French West and Equatorial Africa were less fortunate. They were too small, too poor, too economically dependent upon a small range of agricultural or mineral exports, and too divided between different ethnic groups, to beome stable polities. At independence, for example, Niger depended entirely on road transportation. It had no railway connections to the coast, no navigable waterways, and its one international airport was an earthen landing strip. But this country of 1,188,994 square kilometres had no tarred roads and fewer than 3000 motor vehicles. Moreover, there was virtually no long-distance telephone service until the mid-1970s, communications could be maintained only by radio-telephone. The first secondary school was not built until 1931 and even in 1956, only 600 children were attending secondary schools, with only four pupils managing to pass the baccalaureate examination. Indeed, when internal self-government was introduced under the Loi-Cadre of 1956, less than 2 per cent of children were receiving primary education. Niger's literacy rate nearly 30 years after independence was still a mere 8 per cent and five out of every six Nigeriens were rural cultivators or pastoralists. Yet, despite the fact that most of these small states had few university graduates, technicians, or well-educated civil servants, they adopted centralized economic planning.[92]

Togo, Dahomey [Benin], Upper Volta [Burkina Faso] and Congo [Brazzaville] appeared inherently unstable throughout the 1960s, undergoing a series of *coups d'état* as first the military threw out the corrupt and increasingly repressive civilian administrations, and then as rival factions within the army contended for supremacy. Two coup leaders in Togo and Dahomey [Benin], however, managed to halt this cycle of political instability. Colonel Eyadema in Togo managed to remain in power from 1967 to 1991 as did Major Matthieu Kerekou in Benin from 1972 to 1991. After repressing the old political forces, based on regionally focussed ethnic sub-nationalisms, both leaders sought gradually to reduce the role of the military, establishing respectively a technocratic civilian administration and an avowedly Marxist regime under the People's Revolutionary Party of Benin, which claimed to have launched a 'people's democratic revolution'. Despite this gradual shift to a civilian order, Eyadema and Kerekou retained close relations with the army, promoting relatives and close supporters. The strength of this ethno-military base has become apparent in Togo since Eyadema was forced to resign power, following mass demonstrations in favour of greater democracy and increasing pressure from France and Togo's other creditors, stepping down to the role of a non-executive head of state. The new civilian administration has been unable to control the armed forces, which on three occasions have arrested the new prime minister, declaring their loyalty to President Eyadema.[93]

Tanzania after the 'army strike' of January 1964 has also sucessfully corralled the political ambitions of the army by politicizing both the officer corps and the ranks, turning it into a people's militia, committed to rural development work, as part of TANU's programme of *Ujamaa* socialism and national self-reliance. Despite the fact that a number of serious coup plots were discovered during the economically difficult late 1970s and early 1980s, in Tanzania, perhaps more than in any other African state, the military has been tamed and clearly subordinated to political control. Elsewhere, however, the army remains a powerful, largely autonomous force, to be antagonized by politicians at their own risk.[94]

Conclusion
Most African countries became independent at a most unpropitious time, just as international terms of trade began sharply to move

against the continent. This meant that the 'new states' had even fewer development funds and revenue to expand social-welfare provisions than nationalist leaders had anticipated. Moreover, demands upon the system increased rapidly as the continent's population grew at unprecedented rates. In retrospect, it can be seen that the colonialists got out just in time. Britain could not have sustained its authority over 100 million Nigerians. Given this demographic explosion and the adverse international economic climate, we should perhaps adjust our expectations of African states, and recognize that many – although not all – have been more successful in dealing with these problems than colonial governments would probably have been, enlisting the support, patience and loyalty of their citizens.[95]

Ethnic rivalries, however, have divided many states. Africa's nationalist movements were much weaker than they appeared to observers in the excitement of the 1950s, while the one-party state has proved less of a solution to centrifugal forces than many believed in the following decade. The *state* remains both the central arena of conflict and accumulation and is the fundamental problem in African politics. It is at the same time both 'overdeveloped ' and 'underdeveloped', too powerful as a focus of competition and as a device for extracting resources from the countryside and for crushing independent institutions, yet too weak to provide its citizens with security or services. Africa's elites have been too successful at enlisting the masses through appeals to ethnicity in order to promote their accumulation, but have failed to establish an agreed civic culture to distribute resources or to maintain the autonomy of professional bodies, churches and trade unions, which could resist or at least moderate the demands of the state.[96] As a result, leaders have all too frequently attempted to resolve their problems and differences by repression, military coups or even civil wars. Meanwhile, rural smallholders and pastoralists have survived by opting out of the state – keeping their heads by keeping their heads down.

Notes

1 The World Bank, *Sub-Saharan Africa: From Crisis to Sustainable Growth*, Washington, DC, 1989, pp. 252–61.
2 *United States' Department of State Dispatch*, 2, no. 656, 2 September 1991; M. S. Zaman, 'Silent Disasters of Africa', *World Health*, January–February 1991. See also C. G. Anthony, 'Africa's Refugee Crisis: State Building in Historical Perspective', *International Migration Review*, no. 25, pp. 574–91, (1991).

3 'Young Hands at the Helm', *Times Higher Education Supplement*, 10 November 1991, p. 1; 'Soumana Sako: Managing the Transition', *Africa Report*, 36, September–October 1991, pp. 49–51; 'Mali and Benin: Dying Dinosaurs', *The Economist*, 30 March 1991, p. 41. A commentary on the escalating political crisis in Bamako is provided in the *Foreign Broadcast Information Service, Daily Report: Sub-Saharan Africa*, 22 March 1991, pp. 25–8; 25 March 1991, pp. 21–7; 26 March 1991, pp. 24–9; and 27 March 1991, pp. 35–41.

4 D. W. Throup, 'The Construction and Destruction of the Kenyatta State', in M. G. Schatzberg (ed.), *The Political Economy of Kenya*, New York, 1987, pp. 33–74; 'Render unto Caesar the Things that Are Caesar's: The Politics of Church-State Conflict in Kenya', in M. Twaddle and H. B. Hansen, *Religion and Politics in Eastern Africa*, London, 1992; and J. D. Barkan, 'The Rise and Fall of a Governance Realm in Kenya', in G. Hyden and M. Bratton (eds), *Governance and Politics in Africa*, Boulder and London, 1992, pp. 167–92.

5 M. Bratton, 'Beyond the State: Civil Society and Associational Life in Africa', in *World Politics*, 41 (3), April 1989, pp. 407–30; and V. Azarya, 'Reordering State-Society Relations: Incorporation and Disengagement', in D. Rothchild and N. Chazan (eds), *The Precarious Balance: State and Society in Africa*, Boulder and London, 1988, pp. 3–21.

6 C. Young, 'The African Colonial State and its Political Legacy', in D. Rothchild and N. Chazan (eds), op. cit., pp. 37–41.

7 Ibid., pp. 41–52; and A. Roberts, 'The Imperial Mind', in A. Roberts (ed.), *The Cambridge History of Africa, volume 7, from 1905 to 1940*, Cambridge, 1986, pp. 49–52.

8 M. B. Akpan, 'Black Imperialism: Americo–Liberian Rule over the African Peoples of Liberia, 1841–1964', in *Canadian Journal of African Studies*, 7 (2), 1973, pp. 217–36; W. W. Schmokel, 'The United States and the Crisis of Liberia Independence, 1929–1934', *Boston University Papers on Africa*, no. 2, 1966, pp. 303–37; and J. G. Liebenow, *Liberia: The Evolution of Privilege*, Ithaca, 1969.

9 P. Hill, *The Gold Coast Cocoa Farmer*, London, 1956; P. Hill, *The Migrant Cocoa-Farmers of Southern Ghana*, Cambridge, 1963; and J. Iliffe, *The Emergence of African Capitalism*, London, 1983, pp. 24–6.

10 C. C. Wrigley, 'Aspects of Economic History', in A. Roberts (ed.), op. cit., pp. 113–21.

11 Colin Bundy, *The Rise and Fall of the South African Peasantry*, London, 1979; and W. Beinart, *The Political Economy of Pondoland, 1860–1930*, Cambridge, 1982.

12 T. O. Ranger, *Peasant Consciousness and Guerrilla War in Zimbabwe*, London, 1985, *passim*; and P. Mosley, *The Settler Economies: Studies in the Economic History of Kenya and Southern Rhodesia, 1900–1963*, Cambridge, 1983, pp. 43–85.

13 D. W. Throup, *The Economic and Social Origins of Mau Mau*, London, 1987.

14 J. Iliffe, 1983, op. cit., pp. 25–7, 81–2; and S. Amin, *Neo-colonialism in West Africa*, London, 1973, pp. 50, 139–40.

15 I. Davies, *African Trade Unions*, London, 1966, pp. 20–23; and R. Austen, *Africa in Economic History*, London, 1987, pp. 165–77.

16 J. Iliffe, *A Modern History of Tanganyika*, Cambridge, 1979, provides an interesting example.

17 R. Gray, 'Christianity', in A. Roberts (ed.), op. cit., pp. 182–90.

18 J. Iliffe, 1983, op. cit., pp. 31–2, 39, 60, 66–7; see also G. Hyden, *No Shortcuts to Progress: African Development Management in Perspective*, London, 1983, pp. 8–22.

19 J. M. Lonsdale, 'The European Scramble and Conquest in African History', in J. E. Flint (ed.), *The Cambridge History of Africa, volume 6, from 1870 to 1905*, Cambridge, 1985, pp. 684–7.

20 M. Crowder, 'The Second World War: Prelude to Decolonisation in Africa', in M. Crowder (ed.), *Cambridge History of Africa, volume 8, from c.1940 to c.1975*, Cambridge, 1984, pp. 8–51.

21 The World Bank, *Accelerated Development in Sub-Saharan Africa: An Agenda for Action*, Washington, DC, 1981, p. 176.

22 D. Goldsworthy, *Tom Mboya: The Man Kenya Wanted to Forget*, London, 1982, p. 13. T. Hodgkin, *Nationalism in Colonial Africa*, London and New York, 1957; section two remains a brilliant survey of urban African life in the immediate post-war period.

23 For Kenyatta's answer in Kenya, see D. W. Throup, 'The Construction and Destruction of the Kenyatta State', in M. G. Schatzberg (ed.), op. cit., pp. 33–46.

24 L. Diamond, *Class, Ethnicity and Democracy in Nigeria: The Failure of the First Republic*, Syracuse, 1988, pp. 30–31.

25 R. B. Charlick, *Niger: Personal Rule and Survival in the Sahel*, Boulder, 1991, p. 91.

26 G. Hyden, op. cit., pp. 194–200; and V. Azarya, 'Reordering State-Society Relations: Incorporation and Disengagement', in D. Rothchild and N. Chazan (eds), op. cit., pp. 3–21.

27 S. D. Mueller, 'Retarded Capitalism in Tanzania', in R. Miliband and J. Saville (eds), *Socialist Register 1980*, London, 1980, pp. 203–26.

28 P. Dutkiewicz and G. Williams, 'All the King's Horses and All the King's Men Couldn't Put Humpty-Dumpty Together Again', *IDS Bulletin*, 18 (3), July 1987, pp. 39–44.

29 G. Hyden, 'Basic Civil Service Characteristics', in G. Hyden, R. Jackson and J. Okumu (eds), *Development Administration: The Kenyan Experience*, Nairobi, 1970, pp. 3–22; and S. Nyagah, *The Politicization of Administration in East Africa: A Comparative Analysis of Kenya and Tanzania*, Nairobi, 1968, pp. 13–17, 20–23.

30 T. Mulusa, 'Central Government and Local Authorities', in G. Hyden, R. Jackson and J. Okumu (eds), op. cit., pp. 233–51.

31 P. Dutkiewicz and G. Williams, op. cit., p. 41.

32 H. Bienen, 'Political Parties and Political Machines in Africa', in M. F. Lofchie (ed.), *The State of the Nations: Constraints on Development in Independent Africa*, Berkeley and London, 1974, pp. 195–213. See also C. Clapham, 'Clientalism and the State' and J-F. Medard, 'The Under-developed State: Political Clientalism or Neo-Patrimonialism?', in C.

Clapham (ed.), *Private Patronage and Public Power: Political Clientalism in the Modern State*, London and New York, 1982, respectively pp. 1–35 and 162–92.

33 W. Tordoff, 'Political Parties in Zambia', in V. Randall (ed.), *Political Parties in the Third World*, London, 1988, pp. 20–21; A. R. Zolberg, *Creating Political Order: The Party-States of West Africa, passim*; and N. Kasfir, *The Shrinking Political Arena: Participation and Ethnicity in African Politics, with a Case Study of Uganda*, pp. 5–27.

34 L. Diamond, 'Introduction', in L. Diamond, J. J. Linz and S. M. Lipset, *Democracy in Developing Countries: Africa*, Boulder and London, 1988, pp. 6–12 and 20–23. See also Diamond's *Class, Ethnicity and Democracy in Nigeria: The Failure of the First Republic*, especially pp. 64–89, 139–46, 288–316; and the essays in D. Rothchild and V. A. Olorunsola, *State versus Ethnic Claims: African Policy Dilemmas*, Boulder, 1983.

35 L. Diamond, 'Nigeria: Pluralism, Statism, and the Struggle for Democracy', in L. Diamond, J. J. Linz and S. M. Lipset, op. cit., p. 69.

36 S. D. Mueller, op. cit., pp. 203–26.

37 J. H. Plumb, *Sir Robert Walpole*, 2 vols, London, 1956–60; and J. Brewer, *The Sinews of Power: War, Money, and the English State, 1688–1783*, London and Boston, 1989, *passim*.

38 G. Hyden, *Beyond Ujamaa in Tanzania: Underdevelopment and an Uncaptured Peasantry*, London, 1980, pp. 11–12, 23–5, 32–4.

39 J. Nyerere, *Freedom and Unity*, Dar-es-Salaam, 1966, pp. 195–203.

40 J. Kenyatta, quoted in the *Daily Nation*, Nairobi, 1 April 1974.

41 A. R. Zolberg, *Creating Political Order: The Party-States of West Africa*, Chicago, 1966, remains the classic account.

42 L. Diamond, 'Introduction' and 'Nigeria: Pluralism, Statism, and the Struggle for Democracy', in L. Diamond, J. J. Linz and S. M. Lipset, op. cit., pp. 1–91, provide a most useful account of struggles for the African state.

43 D. K. Fieldhouse, *Black Africa, 1945–1980: Economic Decolonization and Arrested Development*, London, 1986, p. 193; and R. Austen, *Africa in Economic History*, pp. 237–8. See also C. Young, *Ideology and Development in Africa*, New Haven and London, 1982.

44 R. Austen, op. cit., pp. 236–49.

45 Ibid., p. 238. See also D. K. Fieldhouse, op. cit., pp. 137–246, for a hostile view of state-led development.

46 S. Trapido, 'South Africa in a Comparative Study of Industrialisation', *Journal of Development Studies*, 7 (3), April 1971, pp. 309–320.

47 L. Diamond, 'Introduction', in L. Diamond, J. J. Linz and S. M. Lipset, op. cit., pp. 6–10, 22–3.

48 J. Iliffe, 1983, op. cit., pp. 64–5, 72–3.

49 R. Austen, op. cit., p. 236.

50 J. Iliffe, 1983, op. cit., pp. 77–82.

51 Ibid., pp. 82–7. See also C. Leys, 'Capital Accumulation, Class Formation and Dependency – the Significance of the Kenyan Case', *Socialist Register*, 1978, pp. 241–66; N. Swainson, *The Development of Corporate Capitalism in Kenya, 1918–77*, London, 1980, *passim*; and A.

Hoogvelt, 'Indigenization and Foreign Capital: Industrialization in Nigeria', *Review of African Political Economy*, xiv 1, January 1979, pp. 56–68.

52 T. M. Callaghy, 'The State and the Development of Capitalism in Africa: Theoretical, Historical and Comparative Reflections', in D. Rothchild and N. Chazan (eds), op. cit., p. 81.

53 The best account of the Nigerian military under the First Republic remains R. Luckham, *The Nigerian Military: A Sociological Analysis of Authority and Revolt, 1960–67*, Cambridge, 1971.

54 L. Diamond, 'Nigeria: Pluralism, Statism, and the Struggle for Democracy', in *Democracy in Developing Countries: volume 2, Africa*, Boulder and London, 1988, pp. 39–44 and 61–64.

55 J. M. Lee, *African Armies and Civil Order*, London, 1969, pp. 52–128.

56 S. Decalo, *Coups and Army Rule in Africa: Motivations and Constraints*, New Haven and London, 1990, pp. 211–14.

57 J. M. Lee, op. cit., pp. 52–128; and S. Decalo, op. cit., pp. 1–15.

58 S. Decalo, op. cit., pp. 39–43, 51–66; R. Otayek, 'Burkina Faso: Between Feeble State and Total State, the Swing Continues', in D. B. Cruise O'Brien, J. Dunn and R. Rathbone (eds), *Contemporary West African States*, pp. 18–30; and S. Andriamirado, *Il s'appelait Sankara: Chronique d'une mort violente*, Paris, 1989.

59 J. M. Lee, op. cit., p. 34.

60 Ibid,; G. Bennett and C. G. Rosberg, *The Kenyatta Election: Kenya, 1960–1961*, London, 1961, remains the classic account of divisions within the Kenyan nationalist movement.

61 J. M. Lee, op. cit., pp. 98–113.

62 Ibid., p. 102.

63 Ibid., pp. 104–7.

64 S. Decalo, op. cit., pp. 6–15. See also R. First, *The Barrell of a Gun: Power in Africa and the Coup d'Etat*, London, 1970, pp. 20–23; S. Wiking, *Military Coups in Sub-Saharan Africa: How to Justify Illegal Assumptions of Power*, Uppsala, 1983, *passim*; and A. H. M. Kirk-Greene, '*Stay By Your Radios*': Documentation for a Study of Military Government in Tropical Africa, Cambridge and Leiden, 1981.

65 N. Chazan, 'Ghana: Problems of Governance and the Emergence of Civil Society', in L. Diamond, J. J. Linz and S. M. Lipset, op. cit., pp. 106–7.

66 C. Young, *Politics in the Congo: Decolonization and Independence*, Princeton, 1965, *passim*.

67 A. Omara-Otunnu, *Politics and the Military in Uganda, 1890–1985*, London, 1987, pp. 138–81; and H. B. Hansen and M. Twaddle, *Uganda Now: Between Decay and Development*, London, 1988, *passim*.

68 This has been most clearly brought out in the Uganda case by D. A. Low, 'The Dislocated Polity', in H. B. Hansen and M. Twaddle, op. cit., pp. 36–53.

69 G. Joffe, 'Turmoil in Chad', *Current History*, 89 (546), April 1990, pp. 159–60; and R. Buijtenhuijs, 'Chad: The Narrow Escape of an African State, 1965–1987', in D. B. Cruise O'Brien, J. Dunn and R. Rathbone (eds), op. cit., pp. 49–53.

70 Ibid.; and R. Buijtenhuijs, op. cit., pp. 51–2.

71 G. Joffe, op. cit., pp. 160 [with quotation], 175–6.

72 R. Buijtenhuijs, op. cit., pp. 52–3.

73 G. Joffe, op. cit., p. 160; and R. Buijtenhuijs, op. cit., pp. 53–8.

74 C. Clapham, 'Liberia', in D. B. Cruise O'Brien, J. Dunn and R. Rathbone (eds), op. cit., pp. 99–111.

75 A. R. Zolberg, op. cit., pp. 12–27. See also R. Hodder-Williams, *An Introduction to the Politics of Tropical Africa*, London, 1984, pp. 76–88. For an interesting contemporary account see D. A. Low, 'The Colonial Demise in Africa', in *Australian Outlook*, 14 (2), 1960, pp. 257–68, reprinted as 'Africa Year 1960', in D. A. Low, *Eclipse of Empire*, Cambridge, 1991, pp. 215–25.

76 It was most clearly first recognized by Samir Amin, op. cit., especially pp. 41–75.

77 Ibid., pp. 43, 47–8; and B. R. Mitchell, *International Historical Statistics: Africa and Asia*, New York and London, 1982, pp. 201–2. See also D. K. Fieldhouse, op. cit., pp. 144–5 and 157–8.

78 R. Austen, op. cit., pp. 236–58; D. K. Fieldhouse, op. cit., pp. 163–73, 187–206; Y. A. Faure, 'Côte d'Ivoire: Analysing the Crisis', in D. B. Cruise O'Brien, J. Dunn and R. Rathbone (eds), op. cit., pp. 59–67; Economist Intelligence Unit, *Country Profile: Kenya, 1989–1990*, London, 1990; and Economist Intelligence Unit, *Country Report: Kenya, 1990*, no. 3, London, 1990.

79 S. D. Mueller, op. cit., pp. 203–26. See also Issa G. Shivji, *Class Struggles in Tanzania*, Dar-es-Salaam, 1975, *passim*.

80 H. Wolpe, *Urban Politics in Nigeria: A Study of Port Harcourt*, Berkeley, 1974, p. 118, quoted in R. Tangri, op. cit., p. 21. See also R. Rathbone, 'Businessmen in Politics: Party Struggle in Ghana, 1949–57', *Journal of Development Studies*, 9 (3), 1973, pp. 395–7, for the emergence of political activists from a 'new', i.e. lower, social class.

81 R. Tangri, op. cit., pp. 15–25.

82 *One Party States*; and D. W. Throup, 'The Construction and Destruction of the Kenyatta State', in M. G. Schatzberg (ed.), *The Political Economy of Kenya*, New York, 1987, pp. 33–74.

83 J. Nyerere, *Freedom and Socialism*, Dar-es-Salaam, 1968, p. 27.

84 This is reflected in his novels, especially *Xala*, London, 1976; and *The Last of the Empire*, London, 1983.

85 D. B. Cruise O'Brien, 'Senegal', in J. Dunn (ed.), *West African States: Failure and Promise*, pp. 173–188, Cambridge, 1978.

86 The standard accounts of the 'transfer of power' in Ghana and Nigeria are D. Austen, *Politics in Ghana, 1946–1960*, London, 1964, and J. S. Coleman, *Nigeria: Background to Nationalism*, Berkeley and Los Angeles, 1958. See also R. Sklar, *Nigerian Political Parties*, Princeton, 1963. For Nkrumah's relations with Sir Charles Arden-Clarke, see D. Rooney, *Sir Charles Arden-Clarke*, London 1982, especially pp. 126–38, and *Kwame Nkrumah: The Political Kingdom in the Third World*, London, 1988. For political developments in Botswana, see J. Parson, 'Succession, Legitimacy and Political Change in Botswana, 1956–1987', in M. Crowder, J.

Parson and N. Parsons (eds), *Succession to High Office in Botswana*, Athens, Ohio, 1990, pp. 97–142; and J. A. Wiseman, *Democracy in Black Africa: Survival and Revival*, London and New York, 1990. For a more critical appraisal, see J. D. Holm and P. P. Molutsi, 'State-Society Relations in Botswana: Beginning Liberlization', in G. Hyden and M. Bratton (eds), op. cit., pp. 77–94.

87 A. Omara-Otunnu, op. cit., pp. 138–81; and H. B. Hansen and M. Twaddle (eds), op. cit., *passim*.

88 E. Mortimer, *France and the Africans, 1944–1960*, London, 1969, *passim*.

89 J-F. Bayart, 'Cameroon', in D. B. Cruise O'Brien, J. Dunn and R. Rathbone (eds), op. cit., pp. 31–48; and M. G. Schatzberg and I. W. Zartman (eds), op. cit., pp. 1–82. See also R. A. Joseph (ed.), *Gaullist Africa: Cameroon under Ahmadu Ahidjo*, Enugu, Nigeria, 1978.

90 M. Aicardi de Saint-Paul, *Gabon: The Development of a Nation*, London and New York, 1989, pp. 23–37.

91 Guinea since 1984. See J. Dirck Stryker, 'Adjustment in West Africa: the Guinea Experience', in F. Desmond McCarthy (ed.), *Problems of Developing Countries in the 1990s, Volume II, Country Studies*, World Bank, Washington, DC, 1990, pp. 187–202, for a discussion of Guinea's response to structural adjustment.

92 R. B. Charlick, op. cit., pp. 36–7, 89–90. See also R. Buijtenhuijs, in D. B. Cruise O'Brien, J. Dunn and R. Rathbone, op. cit., p. 49; and N. V. Lateef, *Crisis in the Sahel: A Case Study in Development Cooperation*, Boulder, 1980, pp. 45–51.

93 S. Decalo, op. cit., pp. 116–31, 219–40. For military resistance to the new civilian administration, see the *Foreign Broadcast Information Service, Daily Report: Sub-Saharan Africa*, 19 November 1991, p. 14; 22 November 1991, pp. 28–9; 27 November 1991, pp. 42–5; 29 November 1991, pp. 49–57; 2 December 1991, pp. 19–29; 3 December 1991, pp. 26–9; 4 December 1991, pp. 26–9; 5 December 1991, pp. 28–9; and 6 December 1991, pp. 12–14.

94 J. M. Lee, op. cit., pp. 149–50.

95 I owe this idea to John Iliffe. For a similar idea, more concerned with the political problems of keeping the lid on Nigerian nationalists, see the observations of Governor Sir James Robertson, quoted by Prime Minister Harold Macmillan in volume 5 of his memoirs, H. Macmillan, *Pointing the Way, 1959–61*, London, 1972, pp. 118–19.

96 N. Chazan, 'The New Politics of Participation in Tropical Africa', in M. E. Doro and N. M. Stultz (eds), *Governing in Black Africa*, Africa, N.Y. 1986, pp. 55–70; and her 'Liberalization, Governance, and Political Space in Ghana', in G. Hyden and M. Bratton (eds), op. cit., pp. 130–40.

13· THE EFFECTS OF CONFLICT, I: HUMAN RIGHTS AND REFUGEES

M. Louise Pirouet

Violations of human rights are not simply the result of conflict in Africa, they are among its causes, though when conflicts occur, human rights violations usually increase and such situations generate refugees. Africa has more than its fair share of refugees, some of whom have fled as individuals from human rights violations in countries where conflict may not yet have broken out; others are involved in mass migrations either across international borders or within their own countries. The immediate cause of some mass migrations into neighbouring countries is famine, but the ultimate cause is usually civil war. This may have disrupted civilian life so seriously that farmers are unable to cultivate, or crops and livelihood have been lost when scorched earth policies have been carried out. Because of the civil war people cannot be reached by aid from their own government or are deliberately deprived of it, starvation being used as a weapon of war.[1] Armed conflict is, without doubt, the major impediment to development in many countries of Africa.

Human rights as defined by the Universal Declaration of Human Rights (1948)[2] fall into two categories: civil and political rights, which are defined in Articles 3–21 of the Universal Declaration; and economic, social and cultural rights, defined in Articles 22–8. These rights are further defined in the International Covenants on Civil and Political Rights, and Economic, Social and Cultural Rights (both 1966). A debate has been carried on in Africa as elsewhere as to which of these two sets of rights should have priority. Socialists have usually argued that economic, social and cultural rights should have priority, and that civil and political rights may have to be modified or suspended temporarily in the interests of national unity and the need for development. It is often suggested that in the poor countries of Africa the right to basic food, shelter and health services (see Article 25 of the Universal Declaration) is more important than the right to free expression (Article 19). Among African scholars who take the socialist position are Professors Osita C. Eze[3] of Nigeria and Issa G. Shivji[4] of Tanzania.

The African Charter of Human and People's Rights[5] links the two sets of rights together in its Preamble, apparently giving priority to economic, social and cultural rights, though the body of the text does not do so. The signatories of the Charter are:

> convinced that it is henceforth essential to pay a particular attention to the right of development and that civil and political rights cannot be dissociated from economic, social and cultural rights in their conception as well as universality and that the satisfaction of economic, social and cultural rights is a guarantee for the enjoyment of civil and political rights.

Kivutha Kibwana, Senior Lecturer in Law at Nairobi University, would not seem to agree with the final clauses quoted above. He writes:

> It is generally accepted that political and civil rights and economic, social and cultural rights are complementary: they go hand in hand. The right to life is endangered where the citizens cannot afford food or health care. Protection from deprivation of property is meaningless to the majority of a country's citizens if they have no property. . . Similarly, even if a high standard of living and culture has been arrived at in a country, the citizens may yearn for political and civil rights as recent events have demonstrated in South Korea and the Soviet Union.[6]

The Canadian sociologist Rhoda Howard vigorously defends the parity of the two sets of rights,[7] and in 1978 the Chairman of Amnesty International said that 'Amnesty International neither understands nor accepts the attempts sometimes made to create a conflict or a contradiction between these two sets of rights.'[8] Howard also rejects the claim made by some that human rights are a Western construct of only limited relevance to Africa.[9] This question is explored at length and very usefully in Abdullahi Ahmed An-Naim's and Francis M. Deng's *Human Rights in Africa: Cross-Cultural Perspectives*.[10] As of December 1990, 27 member states of the Organization of African Unity (OAU) had acceded to the International Covenant on Civil and Political Rights; 24 had not,[11] so to judge by this standard just over half the member states of the OAU accept the universality of civil and political rights as defined by the UN. Accession to the Covenant does not, unfortunately, mean that its provisions are honoured in practice, only that the concepts on which it is based are theoretically accepted. The right to development mentioned in the Preamble to the African Charter is one of the so-called 'third generation' rights of peoples rather than individuals formulated in the Algiers Declaration (the Universal Declaration of the Rights of Peoples 1976),[12] some parts of which underlie Articles 18–24 of the African Charter of Human and People's Rights.

There are qualitative differences between the three sets of rights. Civil and political rights are justiciable. Torture, arbitrary imprisonment or unequal pay are definable and recognizable and those who violate the rights to freedom from torture, from arbitrary arrest and detention, or who give unequal pay commit acts which can at least in theory be brought before a court and tried. In Europe the mechanisms provided by the European Commission on Human Rights and by the European Court of Human Rights frequently deal with such cases, and because most states are parties to the European Convention on Human Rights agree to abide by the Convention,[13] malpractice can be checked, and national legislation can be amended. The African Charter of the OAU also provides for such a mechanism, and some use has been made of this.[14] When we come to social, economic and cultural rights, however, it is impossible to define violations precisely or to bring to court governments who fail to grant these rights. Article 19 of the Universal Declaration grants the right to work, but not even in the developed economies of the West is it possible to enforce this. Article 24 grants the right to rest and leisure, but how is one to define a violation of this right? Article 24 is equally unenforceable: the right to an adequate standard of living is unattainable in too many poor countries. Third generation rights pose a still further problem since there is no agreed definition of what is meant by 'people'. There is an urgent need throughout the world, and not just in Africa, for the rights of minorities to be protected, but how to define these rights or protect them we do not know. The emphasis on the need for national unity in Africa has all too often led directly to repression, and the concept of pluralism and of protection for minorities needs exploring.

Article 14 of the Universal Declaration of Human Rights refers to refugees: 'Everyone has the right to seek and enjoy in other countries asylum from persecution.' The UN Convention Relating to the Status of Refugees of 1951 and its 1967 Protocol define a refugee as any person who

> owing to a well-founded fear of being persecuted for reasons of race, religion, nationality, membership of a particular social group or political opinion, is outside the country of his nationality or, owing to such fear, is unwilling or unable to avail himself of the protection of that country.

To this the OAU added:

> The term 'refugee' shall also apply to every person who, owing to external aggression, occupation, foreign domination or events seriously disturbing public order in either part or the whole of his country of origin or nationality, is compelled to leave his place of habitual residence in order to seek residence in another place outside his country of origin or nationality.[15]

This addition was one result of the Addis Ababa Conference on the Legal, Economic and Social Aspects of African Refugee Problems (1967), and gave formal recognition to what was already happening. The OAU also set up a Bureau of Placement and Education of Refugees, and in 1970 established a Coordinating Committee on Assistance to Refugees. The OAU was established in 1963 by the 32 African states which were by then independent (excluding South Africa), and concerns about apartheid in South Africa and about Portugal's refusal even to consider decolonization were high on its agenda. However, even by the time of the OAU's inauguration it was not only white intransigence in Lusophone Africa and in Rhodesia and apartheid in South Africa that were causing concern to the OAU; there was already conflict in Rwanda and Zaire, and by the time of the 1967 conference on refugees civil wars in Nigeria and Sudan were adding hugely to Africa's refugee problem, threatening continental stability and impeding development. Refugees were proving both a burden and a possible further cause of conflict.[16] We will now turn to look first at human rights in Africa and then at refugees, not forgetting the human rights of the refugees themselves once they have found asylum.

Human rights in Africa

The UN Universal Declaration of Human Rights was adopted in 1948 after World War II and towards the close of the colonial era, but the rights it defines had been foreshadowed in the American Declaration of Independence and in the French Declaration of the Rights of Man. In the years since the adoption by the UN of the Universal Declaration, understanding and awareness of human rights has grown slowly. When the Declaration came before the Assembly for acceptance, Britain expressed reservations because of Article 21 which states, 'Everyone has the right to take part in the government of his country, directly or through freely chosen representatives.'[17] Colonial powers made no effort to promulgate it in their territories although by adoption of the Declaration 'every organ of society' is pledged to do so.[18] At the time of Mau Mau in Kenya in the 1950s no-one seems to have thought of protesting about atrocities by the security forces in terms of human rights. Independence movements in Africa seldom invoked the Universal Declaration in their struggles. However, most African independence constitutions included some kind of declaration of rights, usually in the body of the constitution, sometimes in a weaker position in the Preamble. But the newly independent states also inherited emergency legislation allowing for the suspension of rights, particularly by the use of detention without trial (preventive detention). Ruth Howard notes that in British colonial territories 'Civil and political rights as the contemporary world now defines them were not practised under colonial rule' and she illustrates this in some detail; she concludes this part of her discussion, however, by noting, 'More is expected of independent governments by way of human rights than was ever expected of the British; thus the former's attacks on those rights appear much worse than the latter's outright denial of them.'[19]

The spread of human rights awareness in Africa dates only from the 1970s and is due in large part to the work of Amnesty International, which by then was beginning to develop a capacity to monitor human rights on something approaching a global scale and to get wide publicity for its findings. By then the promise of freedom which independence had ushered in had been massively broken. It is not possible to survey human rights throughout the whole continent: we will look at some case studies in order to note particular kinds of regime which have seriously violated human rights.

Throughout the 1960s and the early 1970s the people of the Portuguese colonies of Angola, Mozambique and Portuguese Guinea (Guinea Bissau) as well as South Africa and Rhodesia (Zimbabwe) continued to be deprived by colonial or minority racist governments of the right enshrined in Article 21 of the Universal Declaration to participate in government. Faced with a refusal even to consider granting them this right, the lack of which seemed to lie at the root of the denial of all other rights, liberation struggles broke out in each territory. They were least successful in South Africa because this country was the most intensively administered and the population most vigorously repressed. At the very least the apartheid regime of South Africa, as far as its non-White population was concerned, violated Articles 3, 5, 6, 7, 8, 9, 10, 11, 12, 13, 15, 17, 18, 19, 20 and 21 of the Universal Declaration, that is, almost all those articles covering civil and political rights. A lack of adequate education and health care were among the most serious violations of the economic, social and cultural rights of the non-whites. Whites who acted against apartheid also suffered violations of their human rights, particularly by the use of detention without charge or trial and sometimes by being banned. One of the first reports published by the Minority Rights Group documented the lack of rights not of a minority but of the powerless majority in Rhodesia.[20] Economic, social and cultural rights were even more seriously violated in the Portuguese territories, which were among the most backward in Africa. Yet the situation of Africans in these countries was frequently argued in economic terms only, and violations of civil and political rights glossed over by those wishing to defend the white governments. Impatience was sometimes expressed over the OAU's repeated denunciations of apartheid, and over the Commonwealth Heads of Governments' meetings being dominated by this theme, but there was plenty to complain about in human rights terms. Perhaps it was a pity that the blanket term 'apartheid' was used as a shorthand instead of the oppression being spelled out in terms of the specific internationally recognized human rights which were violated.

In South Africa as elsewhere on the continent there was a movement for the defence of human rights. As well as the African National Congress (ANC) and the Pan African Congress (PAC) there were also movements among the whites. Prominent among these was

Black Sash, the white women's movement which assisted people who found themselves victimized by South Africa's unjust laws. Then there were the individuals such as the Revd Beyers Naude, the Afrikaner minister who denounced apartheid as sin and found himself in opposition to most of his own Dutch Reformed Church; Helen Joseph, detained without trial and then banned for years for supporting the ANC; and Nadine Gordimer, also an ANC supporter who used her skills as a writer in the cause of justice and who was awarded the Nobel Prize for Literature in 1991. Her brilliant *Burger's Daughter* (1979) was a fictional memorial to Bram Fischer, the Communist lawyer allowed to die of cancer in prison because of his political allegiance and opposition to apartheid. To choose only a few names is invidious but cannot be avoided in this context.

But all too soon it became apparent that independence and enfranchisement did not guarantee respect for human rights, and African protests at apartheid were vitiated by this. African states thus played right into the hands of the white minority governments. Indeed, conflict, famine, economic collapse and oppression have encouraged some Westerners to write Africa off. But, as we shall see, there is also a rising tide of resistance to oppression. The end of the Cold War and the end of empire in Eastern Europe have played a major part in helping Africans to make their voices heard as they demand democracy and respect for basic human rights. There is a long struggle ahead, but a study of human rights in Africa must take note not only of human rights violations, but also of the growth of human rights awareness.

We will first look at two countries which suffered the oppression of 'personal dictatorships',[21] Zaire and Equatorial Guinea. Zaire is a huge country with poor communications and a multitude of ethnic groups, difficult to govern in any circumstances. It had suffered serious repression and exploitation both as the personal fief of King Leopold up to 1908, when the Belgian government was forced to intervene, and afterwards. There was no proper preparation for independence, and when it was granted in 1960, armed conflict broke out. Mobutu Sese Seko, who came to power in 1965, exploited the country for his own benefit in the Leopoldian tradition.[22] Recent developments are chillingly analysed in a Report by the (US) Lawyers' Committee for Human Rights.[23] Torture has become routine. But not even such fierce repression as Mobutu has been able to carry out has succeeded in snuffing out concepts of human rights and democracy, as evidenced by the increasingly vocal resistance to his dictatorship from 1989 onwards, and the struggle to establish a League for the Defence of Human Rights.[24]

While Zaire's violations of human rights are relatively well known, the appalling repression of the people of Equatorial Guinea (formerly Spanish Guinea) is virtually unknown. Fransisco Macias Nguema, dictatorial ruler of this tiny country from 1969 to 1979, persecuted the churches, closing most of their buildings, and ruled by terror, massacring his opponents, and driving nearly half the population into exile. He was overthrown in 1979, the same year that Idi Amin of Uganda and Jean Bedel Bokassa, 'Emperor' of the Central Africa 'Empire' were also ousted from power, 'the only African leader ever to be tried, sentenced to death, and executed for criminal acts while in office'.[25] Although one of the first actions of the new government was to release all political prisoners,[26] and a new constitution adopted in 1982 which should have led to improvements in human rights, Amnesty International's *Reports* show that violations continued. However, in September 1990, just one week after Amnesty published a report on torture in Equatorial Guinea, the president announced the establishment of a Human Rights Commission.[27] As in Zaire, we note that the demand for human rights to be respected is rising even where oppression has been most severe. It remains to be seen what this Commission will achieve.

Kenya presents a very different picture. At independence in 1963 it faced problems as great as those anywhere on the continent, and many observers foresaw trouble and had little faith in the government led by President Jomo Kenyatta. But Kenyatta was a consummate politician and won the confidence of the whites, encouraged and obtained massive overseas investment, and handled his own citizens skilfully, keeping them busy with development and self-help projects. For some years after independence Kenya was a relatively free, relatively successful capitalist country, albeit with ethnic tensions and a growing underclass. Its press was freer than most, though editors knew where the limits of free expression lay. There were rumbles of discontent and a few opponents were detained. Most ominously, the leading Luo politician, Tom Mboya, was murdered in 1968, almost certainly on government orders. Towards the end of Kenyatta's rule things slipped a little, but at his death there was a peaceful transfer of power to Daniel Arap Moi who won acclaim by freeing the 20 or so political detainees.[28]

Moi's difficulties started in 1982 when a coup attempt by some members of the air force was foiled. From this time on he became more and more afraid and increasingly resorted to detaining dissenters. Torture became routine, but the actual numbers involved were relatively small, and fewer Kenyans were forced into exile than from many other African countries, which was no comfort to those whose rights were violated. In 1988 there was a serious setback for human rights when constitutional changes were enacted placing the judiciary under presidential and party control, thereby undermining its independence; a voting system was introduced which involved, among other undemocratic innovations, casting one's vote by queueing behind the candidate of one's choice – and at this stage of the elections no-one could vote who was not a party member. There was an outcry, led by churchmen and lawyers, and those who led it were bitterly denounced.[29] In mid-1990 demonstrations in favour of multi-party democracy were put down violently and numbers of people, rather than just a few dissidents, were detained. Wild threats have been made by both politicians who support Moi and by Moi himself.[30] The Scandinavian countries have withdrawn or reduced aid, both in protest at human rights violations, and because of massive corruption. Lynda Chalker, British Minister for Overseas Development, told Moi in September 1991, however, that Kenya's human rights violations were not as bad as those of most African countries. Three months later the European Community announced that an aid package to Kenya would be withheld unless there was progress towards democracy, with the result that Moi underwent a sudden conversion to multi-partyism.[31]

At the same time there is a more sophisticated movement for human rights and democracy in Kenya than in many other African countries. The *Nairobi Law Monthly*, a popular journal dealing with legal affairs, and *Beyond*, a Christian magazine, have published good quality articles on human rights intended to educate the readers. Both have been banned; the editor of the *Nairobi Law Monthly*, Gitobu Imanyara, was detained for a year without charge of trial; the editor of *Beyond*, Bedan Mbugua, was charged with failing to make annual returns of sales to the Registrar of Books and Newspapers, and jailed for nine months, but released on bail after a fortnight and acquitted by the Appeal Court. The charge seems to have been politically motivated.[32] A group of lawyers has published a series of guides to the law including *Fundamental Rights and Freedoms in Kenya*

(1990) by Kivutha Kibwana of Nairobi University which does not hesitate to discuss the implications of the changes to the Constitution made in 1988. A national branch of the Justice and Peace Commission was set up by the Kenya Catholic Church in 1988 which has produced material to educate lay people at grass-roots level.[33] In 1990 a Commission under Professor Saitoti was set up to look into ways of making Kenya's ruling party (it is one-party state) function better. The commission was forced to listen to public complaints of all kinds, including written submissions by churchmen and lawyers, demanding multi-party democracy and the restoration of secret ballots and an independent judiciary. The changes to the constitution made in 1988 were withdrawn as a result, but dissent has not ceased because of these concessions, and it has been fiercely dealt with.[34] As Moi more and more resembles a 'personal dictator', his time seems to be running out and one fears that Kenya may yet descend into the sort of chaos which has engulfed other countries. In late 1991 the British Foreign Secretary Douglas Hurd seemed to think British investment was safe in Kenya at least for the time being.

Sudan's latest phase of repression and human rights violations arises from a different cause. Since 1989 there has been a serious decline in respect for human rights and the present repression is ideologically motivated rather than generated by a weak government whose members are determined to hang on to power or by a personal dictatorship. To what extent Sudan's first civil war (1956–73) was religious may be disputed.[35] It was resolved when a political solution was found. But the coup which brought General Omer al-Bashir to power in 1989 was driven by Islamic fundamentalism, and there seems little doubt that one reason for the putsch was a desire to sabotage negotiations which might have brought peace between North and South on terms which would have involved the freezing of Sharia Law. The National Islamic Front (NIF) was determined that a peace which set back Islamization should not be negotiated.[36] What has happened in Sudan since is closer to Middle Eastern than to sub-Saharan African developments. In some respects Sudan belongs to the Middle East rather than to Africa, but that is not true of southern Sudan, which is very different in character from the north, and this is the root of one of Sudan's major problems. The north, too, is torn apart by what is happening, for Islamic fundamentalism is far from the liberal and humane spirit of many northern Sudanese, though they seem powerless to resist it for the time being. *Sudan Update*,

Sudan Monitor and the Annual Reports of Amnesty International document the repression in alarming detail; Africa Watch's *Denying 'The Honour of Living': Sudan, A Human Rights Disaster* (March 1990) contains much material which falls outside the scope of Amnesty's tightly drawn mandate and paints a frightening picture.

We should, however, look further back into Sudan's history and its human rights record than into the present. In 1973 a State Security Act was brought in which gave an increasingly insecure President (then Ga'afer Nimeiri) the right to overrule due process of law. People with no legal training were appointed to sit in even the higher courts, and hundreds of people were detained without trial. After Nimeiri's overthrow in 1985 matters greatly improved. The judiciary regained its independence, Sudan acceded to a series of international human rights instruments (the International Covenants on Civil and Political and on Economic and Social Rights, the UN Convention against Torture, and the African Charter of Human and People's Rights[37]), and power was handed to a civilian government.[38] Before the putsch of 1989 Sudan had a burgeoning human rights movement, and a Bar Association whose fairness won international acclaim when it was granted the first grant (one is tempted to describe it as a 'posthumous' grant) of the International Human Rights Award of the American Bar Association's Section of Litigation. The Chairman of the Litigation Section said in his address that the award was intended

> to do more than just honour lawyers and judges for helping people whose rights are at risk or are being violated. In many cases, performing such deeds brings great personal risks for the judges or lawyers involved. We believe that the spotlight of international commendation will reduce the danger they face from oppressive regimes and institutions and will help them achieve their important goals. Included in recipients of this distinguished award is the Sudan Bar Association in recognition of its struggle against government oppression and on behalf of judicial independence.[39]

Whatever was happening in the north, the war against the south was pursued with a ruthless disregard for human rights. In particular, the arming of local militias to act against the rebellion in the south led to massive abuse and the reintroduction of a trade in slaves.[40]

Southerners have too seldom been considered as full human beings in Sudan. Since the putsch their situation has worsened since most are non-Muslims and their only worth as far as the NIF is concerned seems to be as converts to Islam by any means whatever. The Sudan People's Liberation Army (SPLA) of the southern region has a bad record on human rights too, and the civilian population is caught between the Sudan government army, the militias and the SPLA.[41]

In all the countries we have mentioned detention without charge or trial or imprisonment on trumped-up charges has been rife. Torture is routine in many African countries (and, indeed, in many countries throughout the world) and there is no intention to describe the procedures used – most published reports are sanitized; extrajudicial execution is all too frequently carried out, whether it be the unsolved murder of prominent opposition politicians, as in Kenya, or of hundreds of unknown people as in Equatorial Guinea; 'disappearances' are well documented for a number of countries; the press is muzzled and people are reduced to listening to overseas radio broadcast, notably the BBC World Service, in order to find out what is happening in their own countries; and even completely peaceful demonstrations are put down with unnecessary force resulting in death and injury which only serves to fuel the opposition. Heroic resistance to repression is also well documented, but these stories cannot always be told for fear of endangering relatives and associates.

Examination of the reports of such organizations as Africa Watch, Amnesty International, the Minority Rights Group or Survival International will show the extent of human rights violations. But there is rather little literature on the growth of human rights awareness. Amnesty International's *Reports* not only document violations of human rights but also show that in six African countries (Côte d'Ivoire, Ghana, Nigeria, Sierra Leone, Tanzania and Tunisia) the organization has full National Sections, and that there are groups in four more countries: independence brought huge improvements in Zimbabwe (where a decline since independence has been largely arrested) and Namibia; major improvements have taken place in South Africa even if there is still a long way to go; there is currently hope for Ethiopia and Angola and real hope for Mozambique. Small groups of human rights activists exist in a number of countries, and the Justice and Peace Commission of the Roman Catholic Church plays an important role in several more. The African Charter of Human and People's Rights is in some ways a flawed agreement

– there are too many ouster clauses – but it is nevertheless an important step forward, and it was drawn up in direct response to the human rights violations under Idi Amin of Uganda in the year of his overthrow as well as that of Macias of Equatorial Guinea and Bokassa of the Central African 'Empire'.[42] Ultimately progress towards respect for human rights must come from the African people themselves.

Refugees in Africa

Refugees have fled from all the countries mentioned above, and from many others. By far the largest number of refugees is found in Asia, but a greater proportion of Africa's population has been forced into exile than in any other continent. The greatest concentrations are currently in Malawi, Sudan and Ethiopia. These numbers have risen steadily from 1960 onwards. First there have been individuals who have fled specific threats when they have found themselves in opposition to their governments. Some of the best known of these have been ANC leaders from South Africa and other leaders of opposition movements in southern and Portuguese colonial Africa. They have also included poets and writers: Wole Soyinka, winner of the Nobel Prize for Literature, who fled Nigeria after being imprisoned for opposing the supply of arms to either side in the Nigerian Civil War;[43] the poet Dennis Brutus,[44] the novelist and poet Breyten Breytenbach[45] and the novelist Bessie Head[46] from South Africa; the poet and novelist David Rubadiri[47] from Malawi; the novelist and playwright Ngugi wa Thiong'o[48] from Kenya; the poet Okot P'Bitek[49] from Uganda, to name but some from English-speaking Africa. Some remain in exile, others have returned home when circumstances have changed. Political leaders have fled into exile whenever coups and other violent changes of government have taken place. As with the writers, some have remained in Africa, some have gone further afield. University teachers, lawyers and church leaders have also been forced into exile because they have articulated people's grievances. At one point in the mid-1970s six Anglican bishops fled Amin's Uganda and a special scheme funded by Canada helped to place Uganda's university teachers elsewhere in the African continent. Together with civil servants, teachers, and other pro-fessionals, students and businessmen, these educated and Western-ized refugees are termed urban refugees. They are far removed from their original rural backgrounds, sometimes by several generations, and do not know how to live on rural settlement schemes.[50] They are usually enterprising, and many of them have eventually done well for themselves either elsewhere in Africa or in the West where their skills have benefited their host countries. This kind of brain drain from Africa has reached serious proportions from parts of the continent. Makerere University in Uganda and its Medical School have suffered particularly badly.

Universities are politically sensitive and have seemed to pose a threat in many African states. Chancellorships are often held by heads of state in an attempt to exercise control, and senior administrators are usually political appointees, but this may simply exacerbate the trouble as any dissatisfaction then becomes political protest. A Visitation to Makerere University suggested depoliticizing these posts and appointing a well-known, apolitical figure as chancellor to help defuse such situations.[51] Secondary schools, whose pupils are often older than their European counterparts, may also be seen as potential political threats. So university students and secondary school pupils, the potential elite, may become refugees if they become disaffected or suspected of disaffection. Among the earliest student refugee flows was that of seminary students and of secondary students from southern Sudan who went on strike against severe repression and forced Islamization.[52] They fled to Uganda in the early 1960s and it was at least two years before most school students were able to continue their studies. In 1976 black South African school students fled from the Soweto riots into neighbouring countries and even, in a few cases, as far as Europe and North America.[53] In the following year Ethiopian students from what was then Haile Selassie University, Addis Ababa, fled in their hundreds from the Red Terror of Mengistu Haile-Mariam's rule.[54] We have already noticed the inauguration by the OAU of the Bureau of Placement and Education of Refugees. Two international agencies were particularly concerned with refugee education: World University Service and, until the early 1980s, the International University Exchange Fund (this was wound up after it was discovered in 1980 to have been infiltrated by a South African agent). These organizations funded students both in Africa and in overseas institutes of higher education.

The majority of African refugees are, however, rural refugees displaced from their homes by war and by war-induced famine. Although funding and food handouts come from abroad, the cost to the host countries is considerable. Refugees usually survive by finding land on which to settle and farm, but land is scarce, and this may cause friction with the local population. Aid handouts to refugees may seem to the host community to be too generous: why should they not also be given aid handouts? Refugees need medical attention and education, and either this places intolerable strains on local resources, or, if facilities are set up specifically for refugees, they are resented by the host community. Hence donor agencies now concentrate on integrated schemes which will benefit both the refugees and the host community.[55] But refugee emergencies are sometimes short-term only, and when an influx of refugees is able to return because circumstances have changed in their country of origin, such schemes are in danger of being left high and dry. And aid itself is running out. In 1980 there were some 5 million refugees in Africa: a decade later that number is little changed in spite of the return of many thousands of people to Zimbabwe, Namibia, South Africa, Angola and Ethiopia when the situation in those countries changed: new emergencies have arisen to replace those that have been resolved.

While there are refugees in almost every country in Africa, certain zones have been particularly troubled. The southern African region is one such zone, continuing conflict in Angola and Mozambique after independence from Portuguese colonial rules was fermented by South Africa's policy of regional destabilization and, in the case of Angola, interference by the USA, so that even when first Zimbabwean and then Namibian refugees were able to return home, Angola and Mozambique remained in turmoil and the numbers of refugees increased. By the end of 1991 one million Mozambiquans had fled to Malawi, and the UNHCR was so underfunded that it was unable to provide a nutritionally adequate basic diet. The other major zone was North–Eastern Africa: Sudan, Somalia, Djbouti, and Ethiopia and Eritrea. Western television viewers have been harrowed for years by films of starving refugees in the Horn of Africa fleeing from war and war-induced famine. The countries concerned are all torn apart by civil war and so unable to direct available food to those in need.[56]

Three major international conferences have been held specifically to address the African refugee crisis. The first was the Pan-African Conference on Refugees held in Arusha, Tanzania, in May 1979.[57] This was attended by most independent African states, by UN and inter-governmental organizations, by representatives of the liberation movements, and by a large number of major aid donors. It produced an impressive amount of documentation and passed a series of unexceptionable resolutions. These included calls to African states to respect the human rights both of their own citizens and of refugees.

> All African governments should make every effort to fully implement the basic instruments relating to Human Rights ... and to include the provisions of international instruments dealing with Human Rights and refugee problems in their national legislations. [Equatorial Guinea and Guinea expressed reservations.]
>
> All African governments to launch, possibly with the aid of modern communications techniques, an educational campaign to instil respect for Human Rights and tolerance of differences into all the peoples of the various nationalities in African countries whatever socio-cultural, economic or political differences may exist between them.[58]

It would be too easy to dismiss these as mere talk to impress donors. Idi Amin had just been overthrown, Bokassa and Nguema were causing grave embarrassment to their fellow African heads of state, and the OAU would, later that year, set up the machinery which eventually produced the African Charter of Human and People's Rights. There was a sense of shame abroad that Africa's problems could no longer realistically be blamed *in toto* on colonialism, even if there were also fairly high levels of that hypocrisy which characterizes politics world-wide.

Two International Conferences on Aid to Refugees in Africa (ICARA I and II) were held in Geneva in 1981 and 1984. These were pledging conferences when donor agencies at governmental and non-governmental level picked up projects and pledged funding. The projects were professionally prepared and impressively and thoughtfully presented, but ICARA I and II were qualitatively different from the Pan-African Conference. That had brought together Africans to think through issues; the ICARA conferences were Western-based and donor-directed. They broke new ground in the overall planning of refugee aid, but were not concerned with the root problems which generated refugees. Article 33 of the UN Convention on Refugees states that 'No Contracting State shall expel or return ("refouler") a refugee in any manner whatsoever to the frontiers of territories where his life or freedom would be threatened on account of his race, religion, nationality, membership of a particular social group or political opinion.' A number of African countries have been guilty of refoulement. In 1973 Kenya permitted three Ugandan politicians to be forcibly abducted to Uganda.[59] In 1982 Uganda expelled thousands of Rwandans and allowed the land on which they had been settled to be expropriated by local people.[60] In 1990 Kenya expelled a large number of Somalis, including some of its own citizens.[61] Congo Brazzaville and Burundi have harassed and returned refugees from Zaire.[62] This was one of the topics discussed by the Pan African Congress on Refugees in Africa which passed resolutions against it and sought to persuade governments to respect asylum.[63] In few countries do refugees feel completely safe: some who have fled to Europe have given as their reason for seeking asylum in the West rather than elsewhere in Africa their fear that their human rights will not be protected.

Not counted among Africa's refugees are the many thousands who have become internally displaced because of civil strife. In Sudan, for instance, a substantial proportion of the population of the south has been forced to move to the north, and many of these have been there for so long that there is no realistic hope that they will ever return home again. What is potentially the most productive region of the country is thus becoming depopulated and lost to agriculture and food production. A major reason for Africa's impoverishment is that one section after another of her population has been driven back to less than subsistence level, their previous accumulation of wealth wasted, and their land left to go back to bush. Resettlement programmes give some indication of the financial cost to a country of driving a section of its population into internal or external exile.[64]

While it is possible to discern a growing demand for human rights to be respected in Africa, progress towards the establishment of good government and so towards a reduction in the number of refugees is likely to be slow. During the early 1990s there was a sudden upsurge in the flow of refugees out of Africa (and from elsewhere) into the West. This is more likely to be the result of rising expectations of human rights observance than of a worsening human rights record in Africa. It may well indicate that since the collapse of communism and the West's successful portrayal of itself as the bastion of respect for human rights, people who would once have succumbed to hopelessness are not prepared to do so any longer. If Europe's only response to this is to turn itself into a fortress whose defences are employed against those who seek democracy and freedom, then its attempts to link aid with good governance may seem cynical indeed, and defeat their own ends. Africa for its part has to learn how to accommodate minorities and diversity.

Notes

1 See for instance Africa Watch, *Denying 'The Honour of Living': Sudan, a Human Rights Disaster*, March 1990, pp. 103–38; Africa Watch, *Evil Days, 30 Years of War and Famine in Ethiopia*, 1991.
2 Unless otherwise stated, this and other international human rights instruments can be found in Ian Brownlie, *Basic Documents on Human Rights*, Clarendon Press, Oxford, 2/1981.
3 Osita C. Eze, *Human Rights in Africa*, Macmillan Nigeria, 1984.
4 I. G. Shivji, *The Concept of Human Rights in Africa*, Codesria Book Series, London, 1989.
5 The text can be found in Eze, op. cit., pp. 240–54.
6 Kivutha Kibwana, *Fundamental Rights and Freedoms in Kenya*, in the series 'You and the Law', OUP Nairobi, 1990, p. 8.
7 Rhoda E. Howard, *Human Rights in Tropical Africa*, Rowman and Littlefield, Totowa, N.J., 1986, pp. 16–34.
8 Amnesty International, *Report 1981*, p. 1.
9 Howard, op. cit., idem.
10 Abdullahi Ahmed An-Naim and F. M. Deng, *Human Rights in Africa: Cross-Cultural Perspectives*, Brookings Institution, Washington, 1990.
11 Amnesty International, *Report 1991*, pp. 273–7.
12 Shivji, op. cit., pp. 111–15.
13 Turkey is an exception to this generalization.
14 Richard Carver, 'Called to Account: How African Governments Investigate Human Rights Violations', *African Affairs*, 89 (356), July 1990, pp. 391–415.
15 UNHCR, *Collection of International Instruments Concerning Refugees*, Geneva, 1979, p. 194.
16 See the Preamble to the OAU Convention on Refugees, UNHCR, op. cit., pp. 3–4.
17 Brownlie, op. cit., p. 22.
18 Howard, op. cit., p. 9.
19 Howard, op. cit., idem.
20 Minority Rights Group, *The African's Predicament in Rhodesia*, 1972.
21 For the term 'personal dictatorship' see Samuel Decalo, *Psychoses of Power*, Westview Press, Boulder, 1989.
22 R. Slade, *King Leopold's Congo*, Oxford, 1962; R. Anstey, *King Leopold's Legacy: The Congo under Belgian Rule 1908–1960*, London 1966.
23 [USA] Lawyers' Committee for Human Rights, *Zaire, Repression as Policy*, New York, 1990.
24 See for example Lawyers' Committee, op. cit., pp. 176–80; *The Independent*, 5 August, 4 and 30 September 1991.
25 Decalo, op. cit., p. 31. Decalo's is one of the few studies in English of Nguema's rule.
26 Amnesty International, *Report 1980*, p. 43.

27 Amnesty International, *Report 1991*, p. 87.
28 Amnesty International, *Report 1979*, pp. 22–3.
29 See, for example, David M. Gitari, *Let the Bishop Speak*, Uzima Press, Nairobi, 1988, which prints both the bishop's sermons and the press comment.
30 See for instance *The Times* [London], 11 and 18 July 1990.
31 *The Independent*, 19 August 1991; *The Observer*, 15 September 1991; *The Independent*, 5 October and 3 December 1991.
32 Amnesty International, *Report 1990*, p. 140; Urgent Actions, 6, 17 and 27 July, 1, 10, 15 and 17 August 1990; Africa Watch Reports, 5 April, 2 May and 6 July 1990.
33 *Beyond*, Nairobi, February 1988, pp. 25–7; *Nairobi Law Monthly*, no. 25, September 1990, pp. 18–19.
34 *The Observer*, 15 September 1991; *The Independent*, 14 October, 13 and 14 November 1991. On 19 November Moi began to back down, faced with the threat of the withdrawal of aid by the EC unless there was progress towards democracy.
35 Louise Pirouet, 'The Achievement of Peace in Sudan', *Journal of Eastern African Research and Development*, 6 (1), 1976, pp. 115–45.
36 Africa Watch, *Denying 'The Honour of Living': Sudan, a Human Rights Disaster*, London, 1990, pp. 18–20. The most extensive documentation on Sudan is provided by *Sudan Update*, Box CPRS, London WX1N 3XX.
37 Amnesty International, *Report 1989*, pp. 298, 300.
38 Africa Watch, op. cit., pp. 21–2.
39 *Sudan Monitor*, September 1991, p. 6.
40 Africa Watch, op. cit., pp. 65–102, 139–52.
41 Amnesty International, *Report 1991*, p. 213; Amnesty International, *Human Rights Violations in the Context of Civil War*, 1989; Minority Rights Group, *The Sudan*, Report no. 78, 1988.
42 Louise Pirouet, 'Monitoring Human Rights in Africa: A Contribution to Development?', *Critical Choices for the NGO Community*, Centre of African Studies, University of Edinburgh, 1990, p. 172.
43 *The Man Died* and *A Shuttle in the Crypt* (both 1972) are based on his prison experiences in the Nigerian Civil War.
44 Poems reflecting on his experiences in prison and in exile are found in *Stubborn Hope*, Heinemann, London, 1978, which reprints material from a selection of earlier works.
45 Breyten Breytenbach's marriage to a Vietnamese led to his prolonged exile from South Africa. In 1972 he was allowed to visit his homeland for just three months. His experiences are describes in *A Season in Paradise*, 1980. In 1975 he returned on a clandestine visit at the end of which he was arrested and sentenced to nine years in prison. *The True Confessions of an Albino Terrorist*, 1984, are based on his prison experience.
46 *When Rain Clouds Gather*, *A Question of Power*, *The Collector of Treasures* and *Serowe, Village of the Rain Wind*, 1981, were all written from exile in Botswana.
47 His poems are scattered in various anthologies. His novel *No Bride Price* was published by East African Publishing House in 1967.

48 *Detained: A Writer's Prison Diary*, Heinemann, London, 1981, recounts his prison experiences. His long list of novels is also published by Heinemann.
49 Okot P'Bitek was a fugitive from Idi Amin in Kenya in the 1970s. *Song of Lawino*, East African Publishing House, 1966, is his best-known work.
50 A. Simon-Thomas, 'Urban Refugees: Refugee Welfare in a City', seminar paper, Pan African Conference on Refugees, May 1979, Arusha, Tanzania; see also Louise Pirouet, 'Urban Refugees in Nairobi: Small Numbers, Large Problems', Conference of Africa Studies Association (UK), 1980.
51 *New Vision*, Kampala, 3 June 1991.
52 Oliver Albino, *The Sudan, a Southern Viewpoint*, OUP, 1971, pp. 4–7.
53 G. Leach, *South Africa*, 1986, Methuen, London, pp. 201–4.
54 Amnesty International, *Human Rights in Ethiopia*, November 1978; the writer's correspondence with World University Service, London, 1977–8.
55 e.g. Barbara Harrell-Bond, *Imposing Aid*, Oxford, 1986, especially chapter 8, pp. 330–66.
56 See for instance Independent Commission on International Humanitarian Issues, *Famine, a Man-Made Disaster*, Pan Books, 1985, especially chapter 8, pp. 117–24; Graham Hancock, *Ethiopia, the Challenge of Hunger*, Gollancz, 1985; Africa Watch, op. cit., especially chapter 4, pp. 103–38; Africa Watch, *Somalia, a Government at War with its Own People*, London, 1990.
57 This conference was sponsored by an impressive array of UN and other international bodies, including the World Council of Churches and the International University Exchange Fund.
58 *Report of the Pan African Conference on Refugees*, Arusha, Tanzania, 1979, Report of Committee B, p. 3.
59 In December 1973 Kenya handed over three Ugandan politicians including 'Jolly Joe' Kiwanuka, founder of the Uganda National Congress. They were reportedly all killed in Makindye Barracks. David Martin, *General Amin*, London, 1974, p. 230.
60 Jason W. Clay, *The Eviction of Banyaruanda*, Cultural Survival Inc., Cambridge, M.A., USA, August 1984.
61 Africa Watch, 'Kenya, Harrassment of Ethnic Somalis', 17 November and 6 December 1989.
62 Lawyers' Committee for Human Rights, *Zaire, Repression as Policy*, New York, 1990, pp. 119–22.
63 Pan African Conference on Refugees, Report of Committee A; paragraph 7 deals with the importance of the principle of non-refoulement.
64 Louise Pirouet, 'Refugees in and from Uganda in the Post-colonial Period', in H. Hansen and M. Twaddle, *Uganda Now: Between Decay and Development*, London, 1988, pp. 252–3.

14· THE EFFECTS OF CONFLICT, II: ECONOMIC EFFECTS

Douglas Rimmer

Thucydides, speculating in his *History of the Peloponnesian War* on the condition of the Hellenes before the population became settled and when no community could be secure against invasion by a stronger one, wrote that:

> There was no commerce, and no safe communication either by land or sea; the use they made of their land was limited to the production of necessities; they had no surplus left over for capital, and no regular system of agriculture, since they lacked the protection of fortifications and at any moment an invader might appear and take their land away from them . . . therefore [they] built no cities of any size or strength, nor acquired any important resources.[1]

In his *Leviathan*, Hobbes – incidentally, a translator of Thucydides – gave a similar economic account of that 'naturall condition' in which men would live 'without a common Power to keep them all in awe':

> In such condition, there is no place for Industry; because the fruit thereof is uncertain; and consequently no Culture of the Earth, no Navigation, nor use of the commodities that may be imported by Sea; no commodious Building; no Instruments of moving, and removing such things as require much force; no Knowledge of the face of the Earth; no account of Time; no Arts; no Letters; no Society; and which is worst of all, continuall

feare, and danger of violent death; <u>And the life of man, solitary,</u> <u>poore, nasty, brutish, and short.</u>[2]

This condition Hobbes denoted a state of war, a war of each against all, and consisting not invariably in actual fighting, but rather 'in the known disposition thereto'.

These imaginary states are not remote from the actual conditions that have obtained in many African countries in recent times. In much of the Ethiopian empire from the early 1960s, in southern Sudan between 1963 and 1972 and again from 1983, in Chad from 1965, and in Mozambique and Angola both before and after the collapse of Portuguese rule, there was no 'common Power' to hold the populace in awe, but a number of rival Powers disputing violently for supremacy. In Somalia from 1988, and in Liberia from the end of the following year, political disintegration went even further: sovereignty in those countries imploded under the pressure of warring clans and factions. Elsewhere in Africa – for example in Zaire, Nigeria, Uganda and Zimbabwe – there have been episodes, often protracted, of large-scale and violent internal conflict.

The reactions have been classical. People have fled from violence, as supposedly they did in prehistorical Hellas, but in vaster numbers than Thucydides could have envisaged. The fugitives often went to places where they could not sustain themselves, because those places were already settled, or they were denied access to resources, or because they could not wait for harvests; many starved, and more would have done so but for international relief. Cultivated plots have been abandoned, industrial enterprises frustrated, markets have decayed, external trade has shrunk. The inducements to build, and to create productive equipment, have been eroded where they have not been entirely extinguished. Physical assets made available from earlier times have not been maintained. Knowledge and education have retrogressed. Controls erected against forms of life that prey upon our species have broken down. There has been continual fear, and danger of violent death.

Militarization

Militarization and militarism have been striking features of post-colonial Africa. Military expenditures grew faster than either population or the estimates of GNP, even after the shift towards local responsibility for defence in consequence of independence had been completed; and in 1985 it seemed more than likely that this growth would continue.[3] And government by the military had become by the 1980s as much the rule as the exception in Africa. What effects have these developments had? Arguably, militarization and militarism make war more likely in some circumstances, while in others they may prevent war through giving 'the protection of fortifications'. They may occur as a consequence of war. They may follow from causes that have little or nothing to do with war. Whatever the case, armies and arms absorb resources that might have been used for other purposes.

Militarization was once seen as a force for progress in developing countries, principally on the ground that armies were 'modern' organizations, rationally managed, relatively efficient and industrious in discharge of their functions, and imbued with national aspirations. This view has ceased to be persuasive. Military expenditure has come rather to be perceived as a social burden, carried, whether voluntarily or not, to the detriment of more worthy causes. Thus the UN Economic Commission for Africa has deplored 'the military-social imbalance' whereby public expenditures on defence in the Africa of the mid-1980s were allegedly greater than those on education, and more than three times as great as those on health.[4] In the first *Human Development Report* of the UN Development Programme (UNDP), this imbalance was illustrated for each country in 1986 by the ratio of military expenditure to public expenditure on education and health combined, and by the ratio of military personnel to teachers. In Chad, Zaire, Angola and Uganda, military spending was two or three times greater than spending on education and health, and in Ethiopia and Somalia there were five times as many soldiers as teachers. For sub-Saharan Africa as a whole, the ratios were reported as 81 and 90 per cent respectively, and the ratio of military spending to GNP as 3.3 per cent. The last figure is not high by world standards. But, among individual countries, Angola was apparently spending 12 per cent of its GNP militarily in 1986, Ethiopia 8.6 per cent, Mozambique 7 per cent, Chad and Sudan each about 6 per cent. As the *Report* pointed out, those countries are among the poorest in the world, and so the least able, it might be thought, to support relatively large military establishments.[5]

The figures leave much to be desired as measurements of national commitments to the stated objects of expenditure. GNP estimates are of more than usual unreliability in Africa. Much spending on education and health is made privately, as well as publicly. Govern-

ments do not always account, through their published budgets, for all
their military expenditure; on the other hand, not all military outlays
are made for narrowly military purposes. Finally, and of most
importance, there are considerable unofficial outlays on personnel
and weapons in countries where governments are confronted by
armed oppositions. In countries of endemic warfare, the figures of
military expenditures by their governments can be only a partial
measurement of militarization.

Undoubtedly, however, there has been a rising trend in such
military spending in sub-Saharan Africa as is recorded (the UNDP
figure for 1960 is only 0.7 per cent of GNP for the region as a whole),
and this spending has become relatively large in some African
countries. What were the causes? One attempt to answer this question
used multiple regression analysis of data from 38 African countries
for the years 1978–80. With respect to the ratio of military spending
by the government to total domestic spending, it found the most
important variable to be the relative size of the budget. In other
words, governments spent more on defence the better off they were.
Next in importance was 'official use of violence against the public' by
governments controlled by the military. (Other governments were
implicitly deemed to be innocent of this practice.) With respect to the
military share of the budget, the dominant factor, not surprisingly,
was whether a country was involved in war. Also of significance was
the degree of concentration in arms supplies from abroad. In other
words, African governments strongly connected to one or other of the
superpowers tended to spend more of their budgets on military
purposes.[6]

These findings indicate that African countries in 1978–80 were
likely to have high ratios of military to total domestic spending and to
government spending if their governments enjoyed buoyant revenues,
and if they were controlled oppressively by soldiers, were engaged in
warfare and were clients of either the USA or the Soviet Union. The
findings are in the nature of a snapshot; but they might also explain
the upward trend in military spending, if the generality of African
governments by the end of the 1970s had become better off and more
military, domestically violent, insecure, and linked to external powers.

A review of the relevant literature on developing countries casts
considerable doubt, however, on the significance of military government for the share of military expenditure in either GNP or the
budget, and indeed its significance for any other major economic

outcome. Economic outcomes are attributed to structural, environmental and policy factors, of which only the last may vary among possessors of political power, and then to only a limited extent. With respect to sub-Saharan Africa, another multiple regression analysis, this time covering the period 1967–83, found no significant relationship between military rule and the relative importance of recorded military expenditures. Variations in these expenditures were chiefly explained by the importance of the threats perceived by governments to security.[7]

There are, of course, difficulties in determining which governments are military, since some of military origin have subsequently civilianized themselves, and others that are seemingly controlled by civilians may be heavily under military influence. But in Nigeria, where the government of 1986 was indubitably military, the ratio of military expenditure to GNP, according to the figures published by the UNDP, was only 1 per cent, much less than was reported for countries such as Tanzania and Senegal that would generally have been recognized as governed by civilians. In South Africa, to take the other big sub-Saharan economy, the ratio appears as 3.9 per cent. The South African government of 1986 was not military but was undoubtedly heavily influenced by the military. Yet even 3.9 per cent was apparently not high by world standards; in particular it was less than the ratios for the USA and the UK, on the governments of which military influence might well be judged to have been less.[8]

While the data are such as to make generalization hazardous, it seems possible to regard insecurity as the chief determinant of official militarization. For developing countries, the availability of military aid is also important, but usually not independently of the first factor. Also significant may be the state of government finances; soldiers and armaments are among the objects on which revenues can readily be spent, if revenues happen to be rising swiftly.

Given a constant level of external threat to a country, greater military spending might be expected to have positive economic results, by increasing security. But this relationship appears not generally to have held in Africa. More resources, both absolutely and relatively, have been used for defence, but lives and property have become much more insecure in some countries, and possibly no more secure in any. Defence, in short, has not worked. One reason is that for some countries the level of external threat has not been constant. Another is that the threats perceived by governments have been not only external threats to the populations they govern but also, or rather, threats to themselves, made by antagonists at home as well as abroad. Militarization to protect governments does not necessarily make civilian populations more secure. It has not always made the governments more secure.

The ECA and the costs of war in southern Africa

Southern Africa has been one of the two principal areas of militarization, insecurity and war in Africa. The UN Economic Commission for Africa (ECA) has published estimates of the economic losses in 1980–88 caused by the wars in this area – mostly in Angola and Mozambique but also in other countries. It refers to these losses as the costs of South African destabilization of its neighbour, or of 'frontline resistance to apartheid'.[9] The estimates are therefore of costs borne by the nine member countries of the Southern African Development Coordination Conference (Botswana, Lesotho, Malawi, Swaziland, Tanzania, Zambia and Zimbabwe in addition to Angola and Mozambique), and do not include the substantial costs borne by South Africa itself, nor those incurred by other parties to the conflicts in southern Africa, such as Cuba.

One total of the costs is reached by summing estimates of several categories of loss. Defence outlays that supposedly would not otherwise have been made are included. Among other items are the estimated losses of both actual and prospective additional production, the assistance given international refugees and internally displaced persons, and the expenses incurred through the necessary diversion of traffic to higher-cost routes. This method gives a total for the nine-year period of US $56 billion at 1988 prices. Another method is to calculate loss by comparing the actual growth of GDP over the period with the growth that might have been expected in the absence of war.[10] The result is a somewhat larger total – US $62.45 billion at 1988 prices – which is more than double the GDP estimate for the nine countries in 1988. For Angola and Mozambique the accumulated losses appear much greater – five or six times their 1988 GDPs. The 1988 GDPs were, of course, themselves affected by the conflicts that were going on.

Estimates are also given by the ECA of 'war-related' mortality in the nine countries in 1980–88. These are the deaths attributed not only directly to violence, but also to aggravation of the consequences of drought by disruptions of food supply, and to increases in the incidence of disease and malnutrition and the destruction of health facilities in the rural areas. The 'excess' deaths thus ascribed to war are estimated at 1.5 million, the total including 925,000 infants and young children. Nine hundred thousand of these deaths are believed to have occurred in Mozambique and 500,000 in Angola. There are also estimates that 1.5 million inhabitants of those countries had become refugees in neighbouring countries by 1989, while a further 6.1 million were displaced internally.

The ECA's report also includes an estimate of US $5.9 billion as the loss accumulated (at 1988 prices) in the GDP of Namibia over 1980–88, as a result of the occupation of that country by South Africa and its use as a base for military operations in Angola. This estimate is reached by assuming that the growth rate in the GDP would have been half of the 10 per cent attained in Botswana, if Namibia had been independent, instead of the slightly negative rate actually experienced. In addition, there are said to have been over the same period 90,000 'occupation-caused' deaths, including 50,000 deaths among infants and young children that would have been prevented, had Namibia been independent, by a universal system of basic health care.

Like other publications of the ECA, the report on *South African Destabilization* is politically driven. The estimates of income loss and excess mortality rest on information of such doubtful quality, and assumptions so arbitrary, as to have no standing as objective measurements.[11] They are made rather as weapons of debate and means of mobilizing opinion – as indeed the title of the report suggests. This is not to deny that the wars in Angola and Mozambique have resulted in enormous losses of life, and that the economic potential of those countries has been grievously constrained; nor that other countries, such as Malawi and Zimbabwe, have been heavily burdened from such causes as influx of refugees and loss of the cheapest transport routes for their external trade (or the costs of defending those routes). The numbers may be spurious, but what they purport to depict is real enough.

The objects of African wars
To attribute this devastation entirely to South African destabilization is, of course, to make a political point about responsibility. Unfortunately, the objects for which wars have been fought in southern Africa are less simply attributed. Other outside powers, including the USA

and Zaire on the one hand and the USSR and Cuba on the other, also intervened militarily in Angola, and contributed, intentionally or not, to the losses that have been suffered in that country.[12] In Mozambique, Zimbabwean troops deployed to defend the railways to Beira are alleged to have behaved as a violently hostile army of occupation. One destructive intervention has led to another.

In both countries, furthermore, domestic conflicts created conditions that invited or allowed the interventions by outside powers having interests of their own to advance or protect. In Angola the armed nationalist opposition to Portuguese rule was divided almost from its beginning, and, when South African forces first invaded the country in 1975, it was with the object of substituting for the Movimento Popular de Libertação de Angola (MPLA) a government in Luanda composed of the rival factions that were already fighting it, and that had already, like the MPLA itself, secured other foreign patrons. Outside intervention then sustained for 16 years a war that in its origin had been civil. In contrast, the instigation of conflict in Mozambique after 1974 can perhaps be attributed to external forces, the Resistência Nacional Moçambicana (RENAMO) having originated as a creature of Rhodesian policy, to be inherited by South Africa; while, on the other hand, the persistence of the civil war now appears to be attributable at least in part to domestic causes, arising from reactions to government policies and connected to long-lived local quarrels, ethnic differences and religion;[13] it may be doubted, therefore, that absence of outside intervention would altogether have spared Mozambique from conflict.

There has also been outside military intervention in the Horn of Africa and Chad, the other area of endemic conflict south of the Sahara, where the losses of life attributable to war may be even more appalling than in southern Africa. Powers outside Africa participated, notably the Soviet Union and Cuba in Ethiopia, but in no case has any one of them been the instigator of conflict. States of the area itself (Ethiopia, Libya, Somalia, Sudan) have also intervened in the affairs of their neighbours, but, as in southern Africa, those affairs had to be such as to encourage, even to demand, intervention:

Nomads and agriculturalists, Muslims and Christians, Arabs and Africans, clans and sub-clans all confront each other in a complex mosaic of overlapping interests and loyalties, which criss-cross state boundaries. The basic social divisions . . . create pressures on and opportunities for governments to intervene in their neighbours' conflicts, which they are seldom willing or able to resist. . . As in gang warfare, which has a similar structure, alliances are made and unmade depending on the needs of the moment.[14]

In this area, more clearly than in southern Africa, outside intervention has vastly enhanced the destruction wrought by warring factions without being itself a primary cause of conflict.

There have been wars somewhere in sub-Saharan Africa ever since colonial rule was terminated over most of the region in the early 1960s. There have been many military interventions from outside, either directly or through the arming and provisioning of one side or the other in civil conflicts. Leading cases in addition to those already mentioned include the interventions of Rhodesia in neighbouring countries, and of those neighbours in Rhodesia, in the 1970s; and of Tanzania in Uganda in 1979. The United Kingdom intervened in East Africa in 1964; so, on several occasions, did France in its former dependencies. African forces have sometimes acted, like the Cubans, as proxies for the superpowers. But they have also been deployed on the initiative of African governments, and on some occasions multinationally – as in Zaire in 1978–9, Chad in 1981–2 and Liberia from 1990. In 1984 nearly 30 instances were listed of the use of African military forces as instruments of policy in relations between independent African states;[15] and there have been many more cases since.

In general, these African wars were not directed at the redistribution of territory and population, through the aggression of one state on another. The Somali occupation of the Ogaden in 1977, which was to end disastrously in the following year, is one of very few exceptions.[16] Commonly, states intervened militarily in the affairs of other states in order to support a government against insurgency, or to support insurgents against the government. The usual purpose, in other words, was to defend or to subvert a government, to conserve or to change the location of power in the state subject to intervention. In some cases, such as the multinational interventions mentioned above, it may be argued that what was at stake was not so much the survival of a particular government as of a state. But, even in these cases, the territory and people of the state in question were not at risk of annexation by outside powers.

Wars were also not usually fought on the issue of whether states should be dismembered as an outcome of internal conflicts. The exceptions are more important here. They include the secessions of the Katanga from the Congo (Zaire) in 1960, and of 'Biafra' from Nigeria in 1967, both of which failed. In southern Sudan, claims have variously been advanced for federal status, local autonomy and full independence, but in principle if not in practice the area has remained part of a unitary Sudanese state. The Eritrean rebellion became a struggle for independence, and appeared in 1991 to have triumphed after 30 years of war; but the legitimacy of the federating of Eritrea with Ethiopia by the United Nations in 1952 had always been questionable, and the subsequent incorporation of Eritrea into the empire always highly contentious. Despite their importance, the exceptions remain exceptions. In the general case, insurgency was directed at acquiring power in an existing state, not at creating a new state.

Two factors help explain why state boundaries were so rarely contested. First, the principle of the territorial integrity of its member states had been accepted from the beginning by the Organization of African Unity (OAU), those members being acutely conscious of the artificiality of the boundaries they had inherited and of their mutual interest in declaring those boundaries to be inviolable. Second, the notion of the sacrosanct sovereign state was fortified further in Africa by membership of the United Nations and other inter-governmental associations, and was generally endorsed in the international community, and by the superpowers in particular. Attempts to redistribute territory, either among existing states or by creating new states, faced powerful, and often almost universal, international opposition, and hence were seldom made.

The general character of African wars has therefore been that of the internal power struggle, not of external aggression. Violence has commonly emerged from, or at the least been strongly associated with, domestic politics. Outside powers, both African and non-African, have intervened in these struggles and sometimes have fomented them, prosecuting quarrels of their own through proxies, and seeking to obtain strategic advantage by undermining governments. Militarization has been chiefly propelled by the insecurity of governments and the willingness of outside powers to arm either them or their opponents. By increasing and making more lethal the stock of weapons, and the numbers of people able and willing to use them, it has enhanced the destructive consequences of engaging in what, as Robert Bates has reminded us, is the most fundamental form of politics.[17]

Politics by the gun

Governments in the independent African states have characteristically sought acceptance by their citizens through the judicious distribution of patronage. Patronage could be extended as a reward for loyalty, and it could be withheld as a reminder that loyalty was due. At least in the first instance, much of this largesse has been allocated among members of the social elite, or of what has sometimes been termed the political class, selected for their personal influence over ethnic, communal and other interest groups. Opposition appeared when the system was inadvertently maladministered, or when it appeared to have become purposely and permanently biassed against some people who expected to be among its beneficiaries: '[Opposition] has inevitably been led by dissident elites: people who though qualified (at least in their own eyes) for positions of leadership, have nonetheless been excluded on ethnic, regional, ideological or even personal grounds.'[18]

Often this opposition has eventually been accommodated. But, if not, its object becomes supercession – not necessarily any reformation of government measures, but simply replacement of the governors. In the political order that has generally obtained in independent Africa, such supercession has not been peaceably attainable. Governments have been self-appointed; or have not offered themselves for re-election; or have ensured that the results of elections are what they wanted them to be. The dissidents, seeking power, and denied other means of winning it, have resorted to violence. The military coup has been a frequent manifestation. It requires, of course, that sections of the military leadership should be themselves among the 'outs', or that they identify for one reason or another with civilians who are out. Insurgency is another possibility, with implications much more dangerous. Unlike many of the military coups, it cannot be bloodless. It invites external intervention. It requires mobilization by the dissident elite, with consequences that cannot be foreseen, of social subordinates who may have grievances of their own to rectify, and objectives of their own to pursue.

Movement from the most fundamental to higher forms of politics is difficult where resolution of disagreements by force has become familiar. One military coup, as has been frequently observed, opens the door to another; and next time the strikers of the blow may not be generals, or even gentlemen. Insurgency creates conditions yet more unpropitious for political development. Conflict is difficult to eradicate when wars have been fought by guerrillas or by forces only loosely organized and fitfully commanded, when men have taken up arms for a variety of motives and distrust their allies scarcely less than their enemies, when recruitment has become impressment, and military campaigns have merged with banditry. Young men may become socialized in violence, psychologically attuned to destruction, as perhaps has happened in Mozambique.[19] Pools of weaponry may become accessible to whomever can pay.[20] Contending parties may reach political settlements, but violence has not ended if 'a child with an AK-47 can, for a day, be king'.[21] Ceasefires may be declared, but, as Hobbes recognized, the opposite of civil peace is not so much warfare as 'the known disposition thereto'.

Long-run issues

Half-a-century after World War II began, the prodigious waste of that conflict, in which some 25 million people were killed by military action or murdered in Europe and the Soviet Union alone (to say nothing of 'war-related' deaths), have been overshadowed, in most of the countries that were most directly engaged, by the effects on living standards of subsequent advances in science and technology, expansion in trade and accumulation of assets. Against all expectations, world trade after 1945 expanded faster and over a longer period than had ever been experienced before. No difficulties were found, as they had been found before the war, in finding outlets for investible funds. Partly for these reasons, Europe, which at the end of the war had been 'near death', was to show amazing resilience in recovering from the devastation it had suffered.[22] This was the case also with Japan. Indeed, it has been argued that countries defeated in the war had the good fortune to be released by their defeat, and by the occupations they consequently suffered, from the obstruction of entrenched special interests and the deadweight of outmoded institutions.[23] In those countries, and many others, the productive capacity that had been destroyed was quickly made good, and more than made good. And people everywhere, or such of them as had survived intact, benefited from the advances in applied science (antibiotics and sulphonamides, radar and jet propulsion, electronic instrumentation

and computers, petrochemicals and nuclear energy) that had been
impelled by wartime exigencies and were to continue at an accelerat-
ing rate in the years of peace.

No such positive side-effects of the African wars are apparent. The
results appear wholly negative. Societies and states have not been
strengthened by conflict. Only the killing arts have been refined.
Fanon's idea of renovating violence, that solely through the fire could
true liberation be won, can have few adherents nowadays. Violence in
Africa has begotten violence – not freedom, not dignity, not socialism,
not nationhood.

To ask whether there could nevertheless be a benign aftermath of
the conflicts in Africa may be thought premature, since warfare has
not been eradicated. But a reduction in armed conflict occurred in the
early 1990s, consequent on the independence of Namibia and the
final defeat of the imperial government in Addis Ababa; and ground
for expecting this reduction to be maintained is provided by the
disengagement of the superpowers from Africa (and the loss by one of
those entities of its status) and the moves towards political settlement
in South Africa. External intervention in the domestic quarrels of
African countries is unlikely to disappear, but it can be expected to be
much less, and the further militarization of Africa is not as probable
now as it appeared to be in 1985. Resignation by South Africa, the
Soviet Union and the USA of their roles in Africa's wars must reduce
greatly the amplitude of those conflicts – without, however, removing
their causes.

Essentially wars originate in failures to create, within the boundaries of states as presently constituted, political structures that allow
disagreements to be resolved without resort to force. The prevention
of conflict therefore requires the development of structures, and the
fixing of norms of conduct, that make compromises more readily
attainable, power contingent, and the holders of power removable by
civil procedures. In some cases, a redrawing of boundaries may also
be necessary.) The rule of law, effective checks on the state executive,
and disbarment of the military and police from politics appear to be
requirements if Africa is to become peaceful. In addition, government
must be competent in upholding the law and providing personal
security; there must for each people be a common power to keep
them all in awe.

Requirements are not the same as realizable prescriptions. Notwithstanding the enthusiasm for democratic reform in many African

countries in the early 1990s, the 'second liberation' as it was called,
doubt remained that politics in future would be conducted through
persuasion rather than patronage, that ethnic, communal and
religious hostility would disappear, that soldiers would forgo the
power of the gun. The open society has no roots in African history;
not since, nor during, nor before colonial rule. The effectiveness of
the governments in maintaining authority also remained questionable.
Clearly, property and persons cannot be safe in countries where
fighting continues, where opposing powers divide the territory, and
where modern weapons are widely available. But, even when conflicts
formally cease, there may survive a culture of insurgency, a 'known
disposition' to violence, the effects of which on trade, investment and
production will also be negative. People may be held in insecurity, as
if by a ratchet.[24]

Even if wilful violence were altogether to end, insecurity would
remain, since a feature of modern warfare has been the scattering of
land-mines, the locations of which are commonly unknown and
difficult to ascertain. The United Nations has published estimates
that nine million mines remain in Angola, one or two million in each
of Mozambique and the Western Sahara, and a million in Somalia.
These relics of war 'perpetuate a climate of terror even in places
where there might be none'.[25]

In the Hobbesian state of nature, economic activities beyond the
most basic are impossible. Many people in post-colonial Africa have
had to endure something near to this condition, if indeed they
survived at all. Where a single political authority is established, but
insecurity and the known disposition to violence persist, the more
advanced economic activities are no longer impossible, but they are
more costly than they might be. A law may be suggested: that the
nearer politics approximate their most fundamental form, the more
difficult is ascent to or maintenance of the higher forms of economic
activity.

The reason is that economic transactions require some degree of
confidence in the future, an expectation that they can be profitably
completed. For all except those most immediately accomplished, the
relevant considerations are that property will be protected, that
contracts will be enforceable, that sources of supply will continue to
be available and markets accessible; expectations, that is, of continuity
in the political conditions, laws and institutions that underlie
commercialized economic life. Political instability, insecurity or

outright conflict increase the risk that transactions will not be completed profitably, or at all. This increase in risk raises costs, for example by the need to pay higher insurance premiums, to increase provision for bad debts, to hold in reserve alternative sources of supply or markets, or privately to provide the 'protection of fortifications' for productive installations and personnel; or it causes to be revised upward the profit required in order to make a venture worth chancing. The consequence is to eliminate transactions, the anticipated returns from which cannot bear such additional costs or are insufficient when related to the heightened risk that they will disappoint. Economic activity then shifts towards purposes from which returns are more quickly and therefore more reliably obtainable. For example, accumulation of stocks (inventories) becomes more attractive relative to fixed capital formation; short-distance to long-distance trade; quick production processes (and the products thereof) to those that are protracted; defensible investments to those that are more vulnerable; consumption to saving. Time horizons shorten. Decommercialization occurs so far as subsistence becomes the preferred option. Otherwise commercialization is on a lower plane. An economic structure shaped in these ways constrains the possibilities of production further than other causes already necessitate.

A powerful additional twist in this retrogression is given through the mobility of many productive factors. Arbitrary rule, insecurity and violence may deter the entry into a country of enterprise, capital and human skills; and other resources may in consequence remain unused, or be used less productively than they might. The same causes may result in the flight abroad of productive factors. One respect in which the structural adjustment programmes followed by many African governments in and since the 1980s are judged to have failed is that inflows of foreign direct investment and commercial loans have not recovered as they were expected to do. At the same time there has been capital flight – of nearly US $30 billion from Africa (excluding South Africa) during the years 1986–90, along with a 'brain drain' of 50–60,000, according to estimates published by the United Nations.[26] There are other considerations explaining both the failure to enter and the propensity to exit, but violence and the apprehension of violence have undoubtedly played a part.

'As long,' wrote Gibbon, 'as mankind shall continue to bestow more liberal applause on their destroyers than on their benefactors, the thirst of military glory will ever be the vice of the most exalted characters.'[27] It is true that the humble business of making livings has commonly been regarded as a debased form of human activity, lacking the capacity to arouse, to inspire, to quicken the blood, as compared with combat and conquest, power and dominion. After some 30 years of war, however, accompanied by increasing deprivation and misery, the need of peace in Africa might well be judged to be overriding; and people looking humbly to make money to give more necessary guidance in social affairs than political idealists or religious zealots promising to remake men.

Businesses are exceptional among social organizations in having economic objectives as their primary purposes. Indeed, the ideal type of business is thus solely governed – more specifically, by the search for profit. Although profit-making has long been a subject of obloquy, in recent years it has become increasingly difficult to deny, in Africa as elsewhere, that the creation of more value from less usually tends to the general benefit. And although corporate businesses (more particularly in Africa, foreign businesses) are often alleged to exert self-serving political influence, the truth is that they more commonly adapt defensively to political change than instigate it, the reason being that their conduct is ruled by data different in kind from those that shape the decisions of governments, politicians and parties.

The particular animus against foreign business derives from Africa's colonial past. It was strengthened by newly fostered nationalist sentiments and by the dissemination of ideologies hostile to foreign participation in African economies and to overseas trade, on the ground the Africans are thereby robbed of their 'surplus', or kept in 'dependency' on outside capitalist interests. A Pan-African gloss has been given to these attitudes; not now any individual African state, but the whole continent, is exhorted to seek self-reliance, to avoid the dangerous contamination of strange or 'inappropriate' products and tastes, and to look inward for the possibilities of development.[28] An aftermath of the African wars would not be benign if these prescriptions were followed. More, not less, overseas trade and foreign business participation are required, if living standards are to be raised. Greater economic integration of the African states, through the removal of obstructions to trade and factor movements, is desirable, but in complementing, not substituting for, fuller participation in the world economy. In the Republic of South Africa, the importance of which in African affairs will surely grow in the coming years, the validity of this view is acknowledged by the principal parties, as also is the crucial importance of civil peace as a condition of renewing and developing overseas economic links.

The data on the basis of which businesses operate are the more reliable, and business is therefore easier to conduct, where life and property are reasonably secure, contracts enforceable, institutions stable and government policies predictable. Business, in short, is an interest entrenched in peace. This interest often becomes attachment to a status quo, and so contributes to populist hostility to business. The status quo is valued, however, only so far as its removal is believed to increase disorder, risk and uncertainty. Where reform means more honesty and efficiency in government, adherence to known rules in place of arbitrary decisions, and a greater likelihood of disagreements being resolved without resort to violence, the interest of business, whether indigenous or foreign, and indeed of all economic actors, lies in reform.

Notes

1 Thucydides, *History of the Peloponnesian War* (431–411 BC), trans. Rex Warner (Penguin Books, Harmondsworth, 1972), pp. 35–6.
2 Thomas Hobbes, *Leviathan* (1651), Part 1, chapter 13.
3 William J. Foltz and Henry S. Bienen (eds), *Arms and the African* (Yale University Press, New Haven and London, 1985), pp. 171–7.
4 UN Economic Commission for Africa, *African Alternative Framework to Structural Adjustment Programmes for Socio-Economic Recovery and Transformation* (Addis Ababa, 1989), p. 35.
5 UN Development Programme, *Human Development Report 1990* (Oxford University Press, New York and Oxford, for the UNDP, 1990), Table 18 (pp. 162–3), and pp. 76–8.
6 Edward Dommen and Alfred Maizels, 'The Military Burden in Developing Countries', *Journal of Modern African Studies* 26, 3 (1988), pp. 377–401.
7 Alexander Berg and Elliot Berg, 'The Political Economy of the Military', in George Psacharopoulos (ed.), *Essays on Poverty, Equity and Growth* (Pergamon, Elmsford, NY, 1991). The regression analysis cited in this paper was conducted by Kwabena Gyimah-Brempong.
8 *Human Development Report 1990*, Table 18, pp. 162–3. As mentioned earlier in the text, reservations are in order about the accuracy of these measurements.
9 UN Economic Commission for Africa, *South African Destabilization: The Economic Cost of Frontline Resistance to Apartheid* (New York, 1989) [ECA report].
10 To be precise, only for Angola and Mozambique – the national accounts of which might be thought to be especially useless – is this method of

computation employed. For the other seven countries, calculations were made 'on a less comprehensive basis using foreign exchange costs and production multipliers' (ECA report, p. 14).

11 The ECA report acknowledges (p. 8) that its estimates represent only orders of magnitude – a feature which, it disarmingly observes, is shared by 'almost all applied economic data at sectoral and macro level'. It adds that 'even were the estimates 25 per cent too high or too low, this would make little difference to the basic findings'. No reason is given for the choice of 25 per cent as a possible margin of error.

12 The ECA report makes a brief acknowledgement (p. 24) of support for UNITA in Angola being given by 'other governments [than the South African], including the US'. It does not mention external support of the MPLA government.

13 On the internal dynamics of the war in Mozambique, see Margaret Hall, 'The Mozambican National Resistance Movement (RENAMO): A Study in the Young, 'The MNR/RENAMO: External and Internal Dynamics', *African Affairs*, 89 (1990), pp. 491–509; Glenda Morgan, 'Violence in Mozambique: Towards an Understanding of Renamo', *Journal of Modern African Studies*, 28, 4 (1990), pp. 603–19.

14 James Mayall, 'The Hopes and Fears of Independence: Africa and the World 1960–1990', in Douglas Rimmer (ed.), *Africa 30 Years On* (James Currey and Heinemann, London and Portsmouth, NH, 1991), pp. 27–9.

15 Arnold Hughes and Roy May, 'Armies on Loan', in Simon Baynham (ed.), *Military Power and Politics in Black Africa* (Croom Helm, London, 1986).

16 Libyan designs on the Aazou Strip in Chad may also be mentioned.

17 Robert H. Bates, 'Agricultural Policy and the Study of Politics in Post-Independence Africa', in Rimmer (ed.), op. cit., p. 125.

18 Christopher Clapham, 'The African State', in Rimmer (ed.), op. cit., p. 99.

19 Young, op. cit., p. 506.

20 Of Mogadishu, it was reported in April 1991 that 'In the gun market a Chinese made AK47 or a German G3 rifle can be bought for $110. Twenty bullets cost $1.20. Bazookas, rocket-propelled grenades, machine guns, even tanks, are also available on special request. The government says it is trying to . . . buy back the guns at market rates' (Julian Ozanne, *Financial Times*, 15 April 1991).

21 Bates, op. cit., p. 126.

22 See the memorable account of that devastation in Donald Cameron Watt, *How War Came* (Heinemann, London, 1989), chapter 1. Alan Bullock (*Hitler and Stalin*, HarperCollins, London, 1991, p. 1086) cites a much higher estimate – 40 million – of 'loss of life' among the peoples of Europe and the Soviet Union in World War II.

23 Mancur Olson, *The Rise and Decline of Nations* (Yale University Press, New Haven and London, 1982).

24 Even in many relatively peaceful African countries, the authority of the law has followed a diminishing trend. Thus in Nigeria there has been no large-scale warfare since the beginning of 1970, but there have been

numerous riots, some bordering on insurrection, in which hundreds of people have been killed; while the audacity of crime is such that the police have been known to give way to superior firepower. (See *Newswatch*, August 24, 1992, pp. 9–16). Lives and property are less secure than they were 30 years ago.

25 Susan Ruel, *The Scourge of Land Mines* (UN Department of Public Information, New York, 1993).

26 *Economic Crisis in Africa: Final Review and Appraisal of the Implementation of The United Nations Programme of Action for African Economic Recovery and Development 1986–1990 (UNPAAERD): Report of the U.N. Secretary-General prepared for the session of the Ad-Hoc Committee of the Whole of the UN General Assembly, 3–13 September 1991*, paras. 214, 217.

27 Edward Gibbon, *The History of the Decline and Fall of the Roman Empire*, vol. 1 (1776), chapter 1.

28 See UN ECA, *African Alternative Framework*.

CONTRIBUTORS

Christopher Clapham is Professor of Politics and International Relations at Lancaster University. He has written extensively on the politics of Ethiopia and the Horn of Africa. His most recent book is *Transformation and Continuity in Revolutionary Ethiopia*, Cambridge University Press, 1990. He is currently writing on Africa and the international system.

Oliver Furley is an Honorary Research Fellow and former Head of Department at Coventry University. Previously he taught at Makerere University, Uganda, and he has been a visiting Professor at Duke University, North Carolina. He is the co-author with Tom Watson of *The History of Education in East Africa*, NOK Publishers, USA, 1978, and of *Uganda's Retreat from Turmoil*, Centre for Security and Conflict Studies, London 1987. He has contributed chapters and articles on East African history and politics, and has a continuing involvement with the work of International Alert on conflict resolution. He is chairman of the Midlands branch of the Royal African Society.

Reginald Herbold Green has been based at IDS (Sussex) since 1974. He first met SWAPO leaders in 1961 and was a part-time adviser to the UN Institute for Namibia and to SWAPO between 1975 and 1989. He has done research and consultancy on conflict in southern Africa and South Africa for the Government of Mozambique, UNICEF, the Economic Commission for Africa, the South African Economic Research and Training Project and the World Council of Churches. He has been in Namibia six times since the eve of independence, and is Senior Social Policy Adviser to the National Planning Commission of Mozambique.

George Joffe is Deputy Director of the Geopolitics and International Boundaries Research Centre at the School of Oriental and African Studies, University of London. He is the author of over seventy articles on the Middle East and North Africa, and the co-author of four studies of the Iran-Iraq War. He is currently writing a study of Libya, and is a consultant on matters concerned with the boundary delimitation and economic arbitration in the Middle East and North Africa.

Alexander Johnston is a Senior Lecturer in the Department of Politics at the University of Natal, Durban. Among his recent publications have been the edited volume *Constitution-making in the New South Africa*, Leicester University Press/Pinter, 1993, to which he also contributed two chapters, and journal articles on South Africa's emerging political culture, politics in KwaZulu/Natal, the South African general election of April 1994 and change in the contemporary international system. Among his present research interests are comparative ethnicity and comparative political violence.

Peter Lyon is Reader in International Relations and Academic Secretary of the Institute of Commonwealth Studies at the University of London. He has been a Visiting Professor at the Universities of California (Los Angeles), Cornell and Illinois. He has lectured, broadcast and written extensively on Commonwealth and Third World matters generally, in Britain, North America, Asia and Oceania. Among his many publications are: *Neutralism*, Leicester University Press, 1963; *Britain and Canada: Survey of a Changing Relationship* (editor), Cass: London, 1974; and the 'Commonwealth and the Third World' in *The West and the Third World* (edited by Robert O'Neill and R. J. Vincent) Macmillan, 1990; altogether he has written over a hundred articles or chapters for scholarly works and reference books.

Dr Lyon has been editor of *The Round Table: The Commonwealth Journal of International Affairs* since 1983, and is a member of the editorial boards of a number of scholarly journals. He is a life Vice-President of the Royal Commonwealth Society, a governor of the

Commonwealth Trust, and a member both of the Commonwealth Journalists' Association and of the Commonwealth Press Union.

Ali Mazrui is Director of the Institute of Global Cultural Studies and Albert Schweitzer Professor in the Humanities at the State University of New York at Binghamton, New York. He is also Albert Luthuli Professor-at-Large, University of Jos, Nigeria, and Senior Scholar and Andrew D. White Professor-at-Large Emeritus at Cornell University, Ithaca, New York. He has taught at Makerere University, Kampala, at the University of Michigan and as Visiting Scholar at many other universities. Among his books are *Nationalism and New States in Africa* with Michael Tidy, Heinemann Educational Books, 1984; *A World Federation of Cultures: An African Perspective*, Free Press, New York, 1976, and *Cultural Forces in World Politics*, James Currey and Heinemann, 1990. He gave the annual Reith Lectures in 1979 for the BBC, and his television work includes the series *The Africans: A Triple Heritage*, broadcast in 1986 and later published with the same title. Among other offices, he has been appointed to the Pan-African Advisory Council to UNICEF.

Barry Munslow is a Reader in the School of Politics and Communications Studies and a former Director of the Centre of African Studies at the University of Liverpool. He is the author and editor of a dozen books and over seventy journal articles on Africa. He has worked as a senior policy adviser to a number of African governments, particularly in recent years on sustainable development strategies. He is Visiting Professor at the International School of Social Sciences at the University of Tampere and is a frequent visitor to southern Africa. He is co-editor of *Managing Sustainable Development in South Africa*, Oxford University Press, Cape Town, South Africa.

Kathryn O'Neill is an Assistant Project Officer on the southern Africa Desk of Christian Aid. She recently spent six months planning an initiative of a group of European ecumenical aid agencies to expand their work in Angola.

Amii Omara-Otunnu is currently an Associate Professor of History and Director of the Centre for Contemporary African Studies at the University of Connecticut, Storrs. In addition to his book, *Politics and* *the Military in Uganda, 1895–1985*, London; Macmillan and New York: St Martin's Press, 1987, his articles on the role of the military in politics and the issue of democracy and democratization in Africa have been published in learned journals and scholarly books, including the *Journal of Modern African Studies*, *The Oxford Companion to Politics of the World*, the *Biographical Dictionary of African Leaders South of the Sahara*, the *Encyclopaedia of Political Parties in Africa, and African and Eastern Europe: Crisis in Transformation*. He also has a forthcoming study on the history of the Upper Nile Basin from the mid-19th to the 20th century.

Dr Omara-Otunnu's current research interest is centred on human rights and the role of law in democratic political processes.

Louise Pirouet is a former lecturer at Makerere and Nairobi Universities and Homerton College, Cambridge University. She has written on Ugandan and East African topics, including a book on *Black Evangelists*, Rex Collings, 1978; chapters in B. Hansen and M. Twaddle (eds), *Uganda Now*, 1988, and *Changing Uganda*, 1991, both published by James Currey, and journal articles. Her latest work is in the *Historical Dictionary of Uganda*, to be published by the Scarecrow Press.

Paul Richards is Professor of Anthropology at University College London and Chair of the Working Group on Technology and Agrarian Development at Wageningen Agricultural University Netherlands. Main publications are *Indigenous Agricultural Revolution*, 1985 and *Coping with Hunger*, 1968. He is currently working on a book about conflict on the Liberia–Sierra Leone border, *Fighting for the Rain Forest*. Present research interests are the social shaping of agricultural technology, advance agricultural technology and war-peace transitions in Africa, the politics of technology and African youth.

Douglas Rimmer is an Honorary Senior Research Fellow (and former Director) of the Centre of West African Studies, University of Birmingham. His publications include *Starving Poor: Ghana's Political Economy 1950–1990*, Pergamon, 1992, *The Economies of West Africa*, Weidenfeld and Nicolson, 1984, and as editor, *Action in Africa*, James Currey, 1993, *Africa 30 Years On*, James Currey, 1991, and *Rural Transformation in Tropical Africa*, Belhaven Press, 1988. He is a Vice-

Chairman of the Royal African Society and a Fellow of the Africa Institute of South Africa.

David Throup is a lecturer in the Department of Politics, University of Keele. He is the author of *The Economic and Social Origins of Mau Mau*, James Currey, 1982, and among his recent articles is 'The Changing Calculus of Political Legitimacy in Kenya', in the *Journal of the International African Institute*. He has also written a research report on the 1992 elections in Kenya, and he is currently writing a book on America's Policy towards Africa in the 1960s.

Peter Woodward teaches at the University of Reading, and was formerly at the University of Khartoum. His publications on northeast Africa include *Condominium and Sudanese Nationalism*, Rex Collings, 1979; *Sudan: The Unstable State*, Lynn Rienner, 1990; and *Nasser*, Longman, 1992. He is Editor of *African Affairs*, the journal of the Royal African Society.

INDEX

320 CONFLICT IN AFRICA